TEX⊤XƎT

Studies in comparative literature 27

Series Editors
C.C. Barfoot and Theo D'haen

Volumes published in the Proceedings of the xvth
Congress of the International Comparative Literature
Association *"Literature as Cultural Memory"*

THE CONSCIENCE OF HUMANKIND:
LITERATURE AND TRAUMATIC EXPERIENCES

EDITED BY

ELRUD IBSCH

In cooperation with DOUWE FOKKEMA
and JOACHIM VON DER THÜSEN

Volume 3 of the
Proceedings of the
xvth Congress of the
International Comparative Literature Association
"Literature as Cultural Memory"

Leiden
16-22 August 1997

Theo D'haen
General Editor

Amsterdam – Atlanta, GA
2000

Cover design: Antje Postma
ISBN 90-420-0420-7

The paper on which this book is printed meets the requirements of
'ISO 9706: 1994, Information and documentation – Paper for
documents – Requirements for performance'.

General Preface

The choice of "Literature as Cultural Memory" as the overall theme for the XVth Congress of the International Comparative Literature Association (ICLA), held in Leiden 16-22 August 1997, draws particular attention to the role literature plays as a repository of culture. In fact, this specific function of literature seems so obvious that it may well lead us to overlook the very complex questions raised. Questions such as: Which cultural phenomena precisely are being preserved in, or through, or by literature? Is literature sometimes, or often, or always a mode of praising tradition, continuity, even permanence? Is this a good thing? Is it on the contrary a reason for indicting literature (and/or the aesthetic in general)? Where is the dividing line between cultural memory and cultural heritage? Or: both literature and memory have a complicated relationship to the past, both select and edit what they register; both change and distort, in ways that are comparable as well as totally different, what they report on. If literature and memory, each in its own way, act like this, then what kind of "truth" is being preserved by their combination, by a memory that is also literature? Moreover, literature not only preserves culture, it also is itself part of culture, and even creates culture. The general congress theme allowed for the study of literature in relation to both recent and more remote sociocultural developments around the globe as well as in relation to gender and cultural studies.

The XVth ICLA Congress, attended by some 600 delegates from 52 countries around the globe, addressed the general congress theme, and the questions raised by it, in eight sections, each with parallel sessions, as well as a number of workshops and round tables. The present volumes contain the selected proceedings from these eight sections, as well as from two workshops held during the congress. Adresses by plenary speakers have been incorporated in relevant volumes.

Financial support for the Congress was provided by the Netherlands Graduate School for Literary Studies (OSL), the ICLA, the Faculty of Letters of Leiden University, Leiden University, the Research School CNWS, School of Asian, African, and Amerindian Studies at Leiden, the Royal Netherlands Academy of Arts and Sciences, the Gulbenkian

Foundation, Kooyker Booksellers in Leiden, the French Embassy to the Netherlands, the Association for Canadian Studies in the Netherlands, the Leids UniversiteitsFonds, and Brigham Young University. The Faculty of Letters of Leiden University funded the early stages of editing the proceedings. I thank them all.

I also here expressly want to thank Elly van Winden, who did the preparatory editing, and Rudi Horemans, who in his inimitable way expertly prepared all volumes of the Proceedings for the press.

During the very final stages of seeing these volumes through the press I had the good fortune to enjoy the hospitality of the Netherlands Institute for Advanced Study in the Humanities and Social Sciences, an Institute of the Royal Netherlands Academy of Arts and Sciences. I am grateful to the Rector of the Institute, and to its staff for the wonderful working environment they provided.

Theo D'haen
General Editor Proceedings ICLA '97 Leiden
General Organizer XVth ICLA Congress Leiden 1997

Introduction Générale

En faisant du thème "la littérature comme mémoire culturelle" le fil rouge de son XVe Congrès, qui s'est déroulé du 16 au 22 août 1997 à Leiden, l'Association Internationale de Littérature Comparée (AILC) a voulu attirer l'attention sur le rôle de la littérature en tant que dépositaire de la culture. En fait, cette fonction spécifique paraît souvent par trop évidente au point que nous risquons de perdre de vue les questions très complexes qu'elle fait naître. Des questions comme: Quels sont au juste les phénomènes culturels préservés dans, à travers ou par la littérature? La littérature est-elle parfois, souvent ou toujours un moyen de promouvoir la tradition, la continuité, voire la permanence? Est-ce une bonne chose? Ou serait-ce au contraire une raison pour mettre en cause la littérature (et/ou l'esthétique en général)? Où se situe la ligne de partage entre mémoire culturelle et patrimoine culturel? En d'autres mots: tant la littérature que la mémoire entretiennent des rapports compliqués avec le passé. En effet, toutes les deux, elles sélectionnent et organisent ce qu'elles enregistrent. Toutes les deux, elles modifient et déforment—de façon tantôt similaire tantôt complètement différente—ce dont elles rendent compte. Si la littérature et la mémoire, chacune de sa façon, fonctionnent de la sorte, quelle est alors la "vérité" préservée par leur combinaison, c'est-à-dire par une mémoire qui serait en même temps de la littérature? En outre, la littérature n'est pas seulement le dépositaire de la culture, elle fait elle-même partie de cette culture, voire même la crée. Le thème général du congrès établit un lien entre l'étude de la littérature et, d'une part, les développements socio-culturels récents ou passés de par le monde, et d'autre part les recherches sur les cultures ("cultural studies"), notamment l'étude de la composante culturelle des schémas masculin et féminin ("gender studies").

Le XVe Congrès de l'AILC, avec plus de 600 participants provenant de 52 pays, étudiait le thème général du congrès en 8 sections, chacune divisée en sessions parallèles, ainsi que dans des ateliers et des tables rondes. Les présents volumes contiennent les actes sélectionnés des 8 sections, et de deux ateliers. Les conférences plénières ont été incorporées dans les volumes 2, 6 et 9.

Le Congrès a reçu de l'aide financière de l'Ecole de Recherche Néerlandaise d'Études Littéraires, l'Association Internationale de Littérature Comparée, la Faculté des Sciences Humaines de l'Université de Leiden, l'Université de Leiden, l'École de Recherche CNWS, l'Institut d'Études Asiatiques, Africaines, et Amérindiennes à Leiden, l'Académie Royale des Sciences des Pays-Bas, la Fondation Gulbenkian—Commission Nationale pour les Commémorations des Découvertes Portugaises, la Librairie Kooyker à Leiden, l'Ambassade de France aux Pays-Bas, l'Association d'Études Canadiennes aux Pays-Bas, le Leids UniversiteitsFonds, et la Brigham Young University. La Faculté des Sciences Humaines de l'Université de Leiden a donné son support financier pendant les stades préliminaires de la rédaction des Actes. Merci à tous.

Je voudrais ici aussi remercier Elly van Winden, responsable du stade préliminaire de la rédaction, et spécialement Rudi Horemans, qui, de sa manière inimitable, a minutieusement préparé tous les volumes des Actes pour la presse.

J'ai eu la bonne fortune d'avoir pu passer la période de préparation finale des présents volumes au Netherlands Institute for Advanced Study in the Humanities and Social Sciences, un Institut de l'Académie Royale des Sciences des Pays-Bas. Je suis très reconnaissant au recteur de l'Institut ainsi qu'à son personnel pour tous les bon soins que j'ai reçus.

Theo D'haen
Rédacteur-en-chef des Actes de AILC '97 Leiden
Responsable général du XVe Congrès de l'AILC à Leiden

Table of Contents

Preface

Whenever literature is dealing with collective traumatic experiences, historical truth claims will interfere with the aesthetic autonomy of art. Literature finds itself in a double-bind situation. On the one hand, it will be assessed with reference to the factuality of the historical event which it tries to represent, and, on the other, it is judged on the basis of the criteria of the aesthetic function, such as formal and semantic overcoding and fictional devices that we expect when reading literature. "The limits of representation" (see the title of a book by Saul Friedlander) are constantly discussed when authors refer to the Holocaust, Gulag Archipelago, Cultural Revolution, Apartheid—to mention only the most important codified episodes in the cultural memory of the twentieth century.

Autobiographical writing, diaries, and letters, it is true, carry traces of fictionality as the subjectivity of perception never allows to cover the "objective" truth. Even documents do not record "pure" facts because selection and combination of the facts depend on the intention of the compiler and the envisaged addressees. Notwithstanding the subjective imprint of any textualization, documents, in principle, are submitted to truth claims and can be tested. Even Hayden White, who in *Metahistory* advocated the free choice of plot-structures for the historical narration, later had to admit that the factual substrate of certain events restricts the choice considerably. The history of, for example, genocide during the Nazi-regime cannot be told as a pastorale, he concedes. Rarely historians will deny that in the last analysis—notwithstanding the relativizing attempts of the narrativists—in historiography facts do matter. The question then is: would it be possible in *literary* writing to narrate genocide as a pastorale?

Literature, it is true, follows a different convention than history and one element of literary writing and reading is certainly to cope with fictionality, i.e. to create and/or process narrated events which either did not happen at all or, if they happened, have been transformed and recontextualized. The literary convention resists truth claims and writers of literature consider their work free from being judged according to the criterion of factuality. Their narratives, in many cases, are intended to contradict official historiography instead of echoing it.

Traumatic experiences, which have their firm roots in the historical reality of (groups of) human beings, are represented in both genres: in historical and in literary narrative. The literary representation, dealing with the personal processing of the collective experience, invites the reader to become emotionally involved. This empathic potential distinguishes it from historiography. But there is more. The literary representation is highly concerned with language; it is exploring its possibilities and limits, and if it reaches these limits it tries to overcome them by recourse to metaphors.

In general, the first literary reactions to traumatic historical experiences are autobiographical ones, by witnesses of the events. However, the second and third generations, the sons and daughters of the victims as well as the sons and daughters of the victimizers, tend to free themselves from this generic restriction and claim their own way of memorizing the history of their parents and grandparents. They want to explore their own limits of representation, and feel free to choose a genre, a poetic programme, a new language, be it in drama, poetry, or fiction. Whether they should write in a realistic, grotesque, ironic, or postmodernist mode depends on their own choice. Nobody will deny them the right to find their own voice, but, at the same time, nobody will deny the reader the right to answer. Different from fiction not referring to facts and events inscribed into the cultural memory as belonging to a history of suffering and intellectual disaster, the fictionalization of Shoah, Gulag Archipelago, Apartheid and other forms of oppression gives rise to controversies and highly critical reactions. Writers cannot assume that their representations will not be confronted with the factual knowledge of the events their readers have. With respect to the literature discussed in this volume the truth claim is not suspended. It is, however, not the truth of factual details or exact chronology and/or causality which is at stake but *the truth of the victims*. Critics and readers will judge a writer according to his or her responsibility with respect to the victims. Therefore, if an author chooses to deviate strongly from historical factuality and to recontextualize the historical elements in an estranging and experimental way, it matters whether he or she belongs to the group of the victims. If the latter is the case, in general, the author is allowed to take more risks.

In Section 3 of the 15th Congress of the ICLA (Leiden 1997), which was titled *The Conscience of Humankind: Literature and Traumatic Experiences*, the above mentioned problems were dealt with in the various contributions. The interaction of the ethic and the aesthetic is explicitly or implicitly discussed by the contributors in their respective analyses of representative literary texts. At the same time we learn that the alternative of denying a (literary) voice to collective traumatic experiences and remaining silent is no solution at all to the problem of what cultural memory should or could be. Literature occupies an important place within the conscience of humankind and it is worthwhile—perhaps even an obligation—for the literary scholar to give full attention to it, not in the least because of the potential of literary language to explore the limits of the representable.

Elrud Ibsch
Vrije Universiteit Amsterdam

I. Writing the Holocaust

The Cultural Uses of the Holocaust

The most controversial plays about the Holocaust are those which take it to signify something other than itself. In Israel particularly, but elsewhere as well, playwrights have "used" the Holocaust to embody a secondary discourse pertinent to their own society and their time. The three plays I discuss today are examples of such usage, in a form of cultural *construction* rather than renditions of cultural memory.

Towards the end of the Second World War, the Hungarian Jews were largely an assimilated community, with the Orthodox and the Zionists constituting only small sections within it. The Zionist Organization, which was affiliated to the Labour Zionist establishment, represented only a portion of the Hungarian Jewish community. With the advent of the Nazis in 1944 it was almost impossible to establish a concerted Jewish resistance movement and no help was forthcoming from the largely anti-Semitic Hungarian population. However, the small Jewish underground was able to rescue a limited number by means of forged documents.

Dr Rudolf Kastner, a member of the Zionist Organisation, offered his services as mediator between the Nazis and the Hungarian Jewish leadership, and began negotiations with the Gestapo in Budapest. These involved the ransoming of Hungarian Jews, for dollars, trucks, foodstuffs, soap and arms. Adolf Eichmann, in Budapest representing the upper echelons of the SS, agreed that for a payment of two million dollars Jews would not be ghettoized or sent to concentration camps. In May 1944, Joel Brand, a member of the *Vaadat ezra vehatzala* (Zionist-oriented Assistance and Rescue Committee), was granted two weeks to go from Budapest to Istanbul to seek these funds from representatives of the Jewish Agency. Meanwhile, having broken all his undertakings to the Jews, Eichmann was deporting 20,000 Hungarian Jews a day to Auschwitz, even when supplies of gas were running short.

The moment Brand moved to Syria from Istanbul he was arrested by the British and held incommunicado. The Foreign Office, and particularly Lord Moyne, the British Minister Resident in the Middle East, balked at the possibility of a large number of Jews being unleashed upon Europe and the U.K.; they feared Arab opposition to increased Jewish immigration into Palestine. There was also the real problem of supplying the Germans with merchandise essential to their war effort. While they were holding Brand, some 800,000 Hungarian Jews were murdered. Kastner was able to secure 1685 visas for a list of Jews who left Hungary on a special train, and he was thought by some to have been involved in saving a further 195,000.[1]

In 1954 Kastner was living in Israel. The centrist-left Labour Party, Mapai, was in power. Malchiel Grunewald, a Viennese refugee who had strong links with the Israeli Right and religious nationalists, accused Kastner of collaboration with the Nazis. Grunewald claimed that Kastner's failure to warn the Hungarian Jewish community, despite his knowledge of the massacre of five million European Jews, had facilitated the organization of transports to Auschwitz. It had also achieved his own rescue and that of family, friends and "prominents" aboard his train. The Israeli government sued Grunewald on Kastner's behalf on four counts of criminal libel. The judge, a supporter of the Right, found only one of these charges to be libellous, and Grunewald was let off with a nominal fine. Kastner was murdered in 1957 by people believed to have been connected with right-wing elements. He was posthumously cleared by the Israeli High Court of all charges of collaboration.[2]

---

[1] See Yehuda Bauer, "Hareka hahistori lehitrahshuyot" [The historical background to the events], n.d.

[2] The Court found that Halevi had based his conclusions on a lack of recognition of the conditions that the Jews in general and those serving on the Relief Committee in particular had suffered during the occupation of Hungary.

The controversy about Kastner endures in Israel to the present day. Its underlying source was Kastner's affiliation to the Labour Zionist-Jewish Agency establishment that had favoured negotiation, while his accusers, the right-wing Revisionists, prized Jewish rescue through underground activities.[3] Grunewald's counsel, also a supporter of the Israeli Right, later Begin's Minister of Justice, accused the then Prime Minister Ben-Gurion of direct complicity in the extermination of the Jews in Europe.[4] The trial became an excuse for renewed party political confrontation by Mapai and Herut, the Revisionist opposition. This bitter conflict between the two factions had its antecedents in the political struggles of the pre-Israel Zionist movement.[5] In fact, the trial became a trial of Mapai and early Zionism. Judge Tamir did not deny the assumption that its political aspects interested him more than the legal quarrel.

This is the background to my three plays, all of which are documentaries. Each of the playwrights appended to his playtext a bibliography attesting to its historical accuracy. However, each playwright "read" the documents—often the same ones—differently. We must therefore question the relationship of the plays to their historical sources, particularly in light of the controversy regarding the "traditional privileges of history over story."[6] This paper does not deal with the crisis of Holocaust representation or—except very briefly—the relationship between history and fiction.

According to Herbert Lindenberger, "...historical plays are at least as much a comment on the playwright's own times as on the periods about which they are ostensibly written"[7] He adds that the more history plays concern themselves with politics and power, they enjoy a closer relationship with reality than other works. When the events portrayed in a play are derived from documented sources and are recent enough for living memory, it is classifiable as a documentary rather than a history play. To the extent that documentary drama purports to be drawn from docu-

3   A Revisionist group, the Stern Gang, assassinated Lord Moyne in 1944.

4   Tom Segev, *The Seventh Million* [Hebrew], Keter and Domino, 1991, p. 251. According to Yehuda Bauer, the 1977 swing in favour of the rightist Likud Party in Israel was in some degree due to the Kastner affair. *Jews for Sale? Nazi-Jewish Negotiations 1933-1945*, Yale, 1994, p.3.

5   Eli Ered, letter to *The Guardian*, 19-1-1987

6   Jesus Benito, "*The Charneysville Incident*: the narrator as historian." In Susan Onega (ed.), *Telling Histories*, Costerus New Series, 1996, p. 190

7   Herbert Lindenberger, *Historical Drama*, University of Chicago Press, 1975, p. 5.

ments, the audience more easily accepts its closeness to reality.

Yet despite its pretensions to direct closeness to reality, the documentary play, like any form of drama, offers a very selective view of events. It is cut and shaped into an artistic structure. According to Peter Weiss, the selectivity involved in documentary drama is far more likely to be subjective than objective, leading to the problem of untrustworthy documentaries. Documentary can never be fully authentic, Weiss continues, "since to meet the limits of the stage, the material must be pruned, an inevitably subjective process." Above all, documentary theatre "takes sides." Weiss concludes: "The playwright chooses his subject for this kind of treatment because he wants to invite a partisan judgment."[8] *All* documentaries are therefore untrustworthy. Naomi Jacobs writes:

> The close interaction of historical characters with fictional ones, and the tight way in which historical events are interwoven with imaginary ones finally produce in the reader an "anxiety of critical reception"...[9]

However, an audience which knows that real personages are being represented on the stage is generally willing not only to grant a large measure of credence to the events it sees, but it also more easily allows itself to be persuaded by the author. The contemporary reality which the play attempts to express therefore becomes less an historical than an *ideological* reality.

Now, the plays themselves, not in chronological order. First, *Kastner* by Motti Lerner.[10] Counteracting the well-documented evidence against Kastner, Lerner attempts to redress the balance and presents Kastner as a courageous and moral individual—albeit flawed—driven by the plight of the Hungarian Jews to shed his honour and pursue the sinister negotiations with Eichmann and his lieutenants. In his preface to the playtext Lerner indicated his departures from his historical sources. His play is loosely constructed as a trial, with each short scene presenting its

---

[8]   Styan, J.L., *Modern Drama in Theory and Practice 3*. Cambridge and New York: Cambridge University Press, 1991, p. 182-183.

[9]   Naomi Jacobs, *The Character of Truth. Historical Figures in Contemporary Fiction*. Carbondale and Edwardsville: Southern Illinois University Press, 1990, p. 74.

[10]   Israel, 1985. Published in Hebrew by Or Am, 1985.

witnesses and evidence, and the audience constituting the jury. Structurally, documentary plays often tend to take the form of actual or symbolic trials in which the audience is expected to judge. Issues become polarised, reality is reduced to bare essentials and details irrelevant to the play's central arguments are ignored. Above all, a trial play directs the audience towards some conclusion determined by the author from the start.

Lerner's *Kastner* opens with the indictment spoken by Kastner's adversary, Grunewald, and ends with Kastner's own defence. However, Lerner does not attempt to answer the historical question: did Kastner deal in Jewish blood in self-serving negotiations with the Nazis, or was he a hero who rescued as many Jews as possible? While Lerner's text leaves this question unresolved he attempts to defend rather than condemn Kastner's actions. He grapples with the problem, posed by Bauer, of whether Kastner was justified in negotiating with the Nazis.[11] Lerner stated in an interview that his intention was to portray Kastner as a person who placed life above national honour.[12] This precept, illustrated by Kastner's actions in the play, is more pertinent to modern Israel than to the conditions of Kastner's own time.

Lerner's Kastner is convinced that any physical resistance to the Nazis means certain suicide in the conditions of the time. He is an enigmatic figure who risks his life by defying Eichmann; he alienates his family and members of the Jewish leadership. In one scene he refuses a train visa for the leader of the Orthodox Jewish community in Budapest (Phillip von Freudiger, who later damagingly testified at the trial). It was incidents such as this that earned for Kastner his sobriquet of collaborator, and selective rescuer.

Ultimately Lerner's objectivity gives way to exculpation, confirmed by Kastner's speech at the end of the play, which reads like the defence's summation.

[11]   Bauer, p. 3.

[12]   *Davar*, 12-07-1985.

> Your honour, the only ghetto in all of Europe whose
> inhabitants remained alive was the Budapest ghetto and
> this was despite the absence of activities which you might
> call "heroism". The ghetto was saved thanks to the connec-
> tions I made with Hermann Kromey and with Kurt Becher
> of the S S... Because of these connections the prosecution
> called me "the Nazis' greatest merchant".

At the end of the play we remain none the wiser about Kastner the man
or the character, although we learn a great deal about the real Kastner's
activities.

Lerner's play asked crucial questions, one concerning the curious
inadequacy of the *yishuv* (pre-Israel Jewish Palestinian Settlement) in the
matter of assisting the European Jews. Another concerns those Jews
whom the activist Revisionists judged as having gone passively "like lambs
to the slaughter". In repudiating this persistent accusation, Lerner's play
proposes the rescue of Jewish honour through some, or any, form of
action, even the distasteful bartering of Jewish lives for cash and supplies.
This is the play's point: speaking to modern Israel, Lerner defends his
rendition of Kastner's character by emphasising its lack of mythological
or archetypal heroic attributes, and by proposing virtue in resistance other
than by force of arms. In his final speech in the play Kastner refers to
"activities which you might call 'heroism' ". Lerner's comment in an
interview helps to clarify this point:

> We have grown up on the myth of Massada, the myth of
> heroism and suicide hcroes ... Kastner is a hero who
> remains alive at any cost. He does not appear to be a hero
> in our eyes. He was a go-between, he was "protected",
> haughty, a briber, a negotiator, buying and selling, a man
> who never held a gun in his life ... not appropriate for an
> heroic myth ... We can't continue to nourish "suicide
> heroes". Perhaps this was essential in Jewish mythology on
> the way to [the establishment of] the State, but to go on
> clinging to that mythology is suicide. Look where it's
> leading us. Kastner believed in negotiation because to him
> human life was the highest principle.[13]

---

[13]   *Davar* (Israel), 12-07-1985

Lerner suggests that Kastner's form of resistance makes him an acceptable "hero" for the Israeli public. His Kastner therefore serves as a political metaphor and a warning to modern Israel that negotiation may ultimately serve far better than the exercise of force. The play also questions Israel's attitude to diaspora Jewry, validating the diaspora Jew as active rather than powerless and acquiescent.

The second play is *Perdition* by Jim Allen.[14] The trial-plays of the 1960s served as expressions of certain political tensions of the time. So it was with Allen's play, albeit twenty years later. It was to have been produced in London by the Royal Court Theatre Upstairs. However, it caused an unprecedented controversy in Britain. After representations from official Jewish bodies, historians, other prominent figures, and a deluge of public argument, the theatre cancelled its performances. Despite his characters being fictional, the long bibliography Allen appended to the play implies its documentary status. Historical figures are referred to in the play, but Zionism, not Kastner, is on trial.

Perdition, which is an anti-*fascist* polemic, like *Kastner*, exemplifies the method of manipulation within the documentary genre. Allen distorts both fact and interpretation in order to draw conclusions about the entire Zionist movement and the character of the State of Israel. His selection of events from the historiography of wartime Europe is consonant with his rejection of Zionism. According to Peter Weiss, "Although facts were the proper basis of a documentary play, such a play was likely to be written as a form of protest, so that the imaginative contribution of the individual artist lay in the choice and arrangement of the play's ideas"[15] and, in Allen's case, of the historical facts. He sought to realise the real aim of documentary theatre which, according to C. D. Innes, is "to produce political action, if only in the form of discussion rather than aesthetic appreciation..."[16] Only one viewpoint was allowed to triumph in Allen's play: anti-Zionism and anti-Israelism, based primarily on self-proclaimed anti-Zionist sources. The play includes a barely veiled hint of Holocaust revisionism despite its dedication, which reads: "To the Jews of Hungary who were murdered by the Nazis at Auschwitz." According to one of the

14   London and Atlantic Highlands: Ithaca Press, 1987.

15   Styan, p. 182.

16   Robert Skloot, *The Theatre of the Holocaust*, University of Wisconsin Press, 1992, p.111.

play's leading characters the Zionist leaders in Hungary became "the Zionist knife in the Nazi fist", and Hungarian Jews "were murdered not just by the force of German arms but by the calculated treachery of their own Jewish leaders."

Set in the 1980s, with the *dramatis personae* all fictional, the play recapitulates familiar facts. Ruth Kaplan has written a pamphlet accusing Dr Miklos Yaron of collaboration with the Nazis in the extermination of Hungarian Jewry. Yaron is, of course, a barely disguised portrait of Kastner. Kaplan charges, in addition, that he remained silent in the face of the deportations so that he could have his train. The real Kastner is condemned as having been the prime mover in this arrangement. Allen bases much of his trial's "testimony" on Eichmann's *Confessions*, published in 1960, and used in evidence at his trial in 1962. The central indictment of the play is spoken by Kaplan's counsel, Scott:

> Our contention is that before the Final Solution the Nazis wanted the Jews out of Europe and the Zionist leaders were only too happy to oblige - providing they went to Palestine. Thus, in form, if not in essence, the interests of Nazism and Zionism coincided. Once the extermination programme began, it then became a salvaging operation: the salvation of the best "biological material", the "prominents", the pioneers and the Zionist youth who would help to build the Jewish homeland in Palestine.

This is the premise upon which the play is based. The accusation is not so much against "Yaron" and "Kastner" as collaborators as against the Zionists, of whom both men are representatives (as was the real Kastner), for sacrificing European Jewry. The play claims that Zionism and Nazism were compatible ideologies with shared objectives.

It is with interpretations such as these that the degree of documentary veracity becomes most pertinent. To which Zionist leaders does Allen refer? He makes no distinction between the Zionist Right and Left. There are other uncorroborated statements: "most of the Zionist leaders", "the Zionists became Hitler's favourite Jews," "a majority of Jewish leaders acted as filing clerks in the extermination process" and so on. However, the truth or otherwise of these statements, however inflammatory they are, is less relevant here than the method by which the artist transforms documents into art and art into propaganda. In this case Allen does so by his "choice and arrangement" of facts. He makes the argument opposing his main thesis so feeble as to be negligible, and the character presenting it, Yaron, weak, unconvincing and prejudged by the play as guilty. Yaron's counsel is incompetent while Ruth Kaplan's is powerful, confident, eloquent and persuasive.

The hostile responses to the play came from historians rather than literary scholars. They did not dispute the validity of issues posed by the Kastner case, one of which was certainly the "lambs to the slaughter" argument, but they disputed the uses made of it by Jim Allen and British left-wing anti-Semitism. The only novelist to join the fray, Frederic Raphael, sagely made the distinction between imagination and distortion, and between art and journalism, suggesting an answer to the question of art and propaganda. Few others examined the play as a creation of the imagination. Only Lord Goodman, one of Britain's prominent cultural arbiters, asked: "Why all the fuss? it's only a play". He then subverted his question by answering "The Jews have suffered over the centuries from the dissemination of historic lies which have, alas, never been caught up or dispelled by the truth." [17]

The fundamental problem of the play is that Allen uses Zionism rather than Nazism as his exemplar of fascism, and the analogy of Israel rather than Nazi Germany in his warning about the revival of global fascism. He claimed to have conceived the play "as a small contribution to rescuing the Jews from Zionism." Like Lerner, he utilises the past and manipulates Jewish history to serve the political purposes of the present.

The third play is Heinar Kipphardt's *Joel Brand, Die Geschichte eines Geschäfts* (Joel Brand, the history of a business deal).[18] Kipphardt's purpose was different from Allen's although some of his conclusions were similar. His play faithfully follows the sources which he too lists at the end of his text. Set in short episodic scenes which move the action along something like a thriller, the play traces Brand's struggle to save Hungarian Jewry by acting as Eichmann's emissary to the Jewish Agency and Allied representatives in Istanbul. Kipphardt was born in Silesia (then East Germany) in 1922, and died in 1982 in Munich. He is best known for his documentary play *In the Matter of J. Robert Oppenheimer*, 1964, and

---

[17]   *London Evening Standard*, 23-01-1987.

[18]   Frankfurt am Main: Suhrkamp Verlag, 1965.

he followed *Joel Brand* some fifteen years later with *Brother Eichmann*, 1983, in which he makes the analogy between the Nazis and the Israelis in their treatment of the Palestinians. *Joel Brand* deals only with the minutiae of the negotiations between Brand and Eichmann, Brand and the representatives in Istanbul, and between Kastner and Eichmann.

Of the three, this play most closely follows the principles of documentary theatre. According to Lindenberger, "In theory at least, the so-called documentary dramas of the 1960s should afford the closest approximation to historical reality conceivable in drama."[19] *Joel Brand* does so, yet not without artifice: for example, the real historical characters are symmetrically paired in a kind of dance of death: Eichmann-Brand; Eichmann-Kastner; Kastner-Goldstein (a parachutist whom Kastner betrays to the Nazis); Tunney (a British official)-Brand; Brand-official Jews. "The claim implicit in Kipphardt's published notes [to *In the Matter of J. Robert Oppenheimer*] is that, while small facts are shifted around a bit, no damage is done to the essential truth of history."[20] It is, however, Kipphardt who decides the essential truth.

Eichmann's purpose, according to the play, rather than genocide for its own sake, is to draw on the wealth of world Jewry. For all the play's historical fidelity and its wholly sympathetic, even supportive, portraits of Brand and Kastner, it is not about the Holocaust, genocide, Hungary or fascism, Nazism or Zionism, but about business. It is perhaps a short step to the assumption that Kipphardt, having originated in East Germany, is preoccupied with the actual and potential evils of capitalism, but much in the play bears this out. Although Kipphardt avoids direct economic or political propaganda he had only to select and foreground known aspects of the Kastner story, to "shift facts around a bit", for his purpose to become clear. He universalises the specific as a paradigm of capitalist venality and ruthlessness. The title of the play gives his intention away: the story of a *business deal*. He stresses the characters' mendacity and greed on the one side of the deal, and their self-interested double-dealing, on the other. The Nazis' rapacity is not related to value to the Reich, but an abstraction of greed for its own sake. Kipphardt has to do little to actualise the characters of Eichmann (whom he presents as a sybarite) or Kurt Becher; yet the play projects their *venality* rather than their

---

[19]   Lindenberger, p.20.

[20]   Eric Bentlry, *The Theatre of War*. London: Eyre Methuen, 1972, p. 364.

murderousness. He therefore examines the problem of business and money by manipulating the images of historical figures to embody it.

The Jewish victims are ciphers, commodities, representing no more than the literal currency of the deal. The Jewish representatives in Istanbul are stereotypes of self-serving functionaries. They demonstrate a perhaps willful lack of understanding of the Hungarian situation. Kipphardt sees these Jews as opportunists, unwilling to antagonise the British upon whom they depend for Palestine. Fiction is threaded through minutely detailed fact: for example, even the real Brand's recorded disappointment that the "Chaim" referred to as a partner in the Istanbul negotiations was not Weitzmann but Barlasz, is included. Through many scenes these Jews parry Brand's increasingly desperate demands, calling upon legalistic and political priciples. In this way, like Allen, Kipphardt implicitly accuses the Zionists of opportunistically having sacrificed European Jews: not for the sake of saving the "best biological material" but for the achievement of the Jewish state.

Kipphardt is less interested in events than in powerful, self-serving institutions - Zionist, Nazi, Hungarian, Turkish, British. With a few deft verbal brushstrokes Kipphardt offers an intimation of their various natures; for example, the Jewish representatives agree to offer Eichmann money held in a *blocked* account, redeemable after the war! Lord Moyne makes a brief but deadly appearance. "But I ask you, Mr Brand, what will I do with 100,000 Jews? Where shall I put them?" the actual words of a member of the British Foreign Office.[21] Brand is a kind of Everyman, suffering at every turn, but living in an expressionistic rather than a tragic world.

Ultimately none of these playwrights is writing about the Hungarian Holocaust, but shaping its memory to suit his own ideological agenda formed in relation to his own political or social milieu. Lerner discusses the nature of heroism in order to counteract the established Israeli myth of the hero. This was a composite image derived from the New Jew of the *yishuv*, the sabra centric hero of 1948 and the conqueror of 1967. Through his Kastner, therefore, Lerner challenges a staple of Israeli cultural discourse. Ultimately his exposition is not about the historical Kastner at all.

---

[21] See Henry L.Feingold, *The Politics of Rescue.* New Jersey: Rutgers University Press, 1970, p. 272.

For Jim Allen the Kastner story serves only as a peg upon which to hang his radicalism, with Kastner, or Yaron, the symbol of a ruthless but unspecified Zionism that will ultimately sacrifice others, that is, the Palestinians, as it did its own. Kipphardt uses the story as a form of moral reproof, linking fascism to Western capitalism, and as a fable of the helpless innocent pitted against monsters.

Documentary drama, as we have seen, offers a selective view of history, a "high degree of manipulation" and sometimes a dangerous combination of moral didacticism and historical interpretation. However, in the case of the Kastner affair, history has already been manipulated. Even if the trial transcripts are theoretically considered to be reliable documents, the manipulation of witnesses for ideological or political ends further confuses the issue. Memoirs and interviews upon which the plays are based are therefore unreliable. Memories were distorted and people, including Brand, deliberately lied. Even the participants in the tragic tale did not know the truth in the chaos of the time. It is therefore not difficult for a creative writer to fill in the gaps. Many contemporary philosophers of history question the ability of history to reveal absolute truths, and they therefore resist what they believe is the artificial separation of history and literature. They support the post-modern blurring of the boundaries between history and fiction. Susana Onega summarises the debate:

> The contemporary creative writer becomes a historian in an attempt to fill in the gaps left by traditional totalitarian history while at the same time the philosophers of history try to achieve the same aim through the exploration of the narrative mechanisms of history-writing. Thus, the tendency to separate literature and history...may be said to have come full circle to the point where both must be united again even if as kindred narrative forms, as human constructs, that..."have no existence in and of themselves. It is we who constitute them as the object of our understanding."[22]

Our three playwrights have done just this. However: can the plays whose narrative they have so constituted be read as history? This is a dangerous formulation, particularly with regard to charged topics such as the Holocaust. Can we reject entirely the "traditional privileges of history over

---

[22] Onega, p.16.

       Literature as Cultural Memory

story?" Is it so that in order to remain faithful to what is termed the "post-modern ethos"[23] the attempt to construct an objective truth of history must be abandoned? Many theorists and philosophers of history seem to worry about history being represented as fiction. When considering the Holocaust, we have also to worry about fiction being represented as history.

Glenda Abramson
Oxford

[23]   Onega, p. 17.

Aporias of Time: A Rhetorical Figure in the Poetry of Jewish Authors after the Shoah

— I —

Literature provides us with a revealing prism through which various aspects of consciousness towards time during different periods and in different cultures can be made apparent. Human existence in time expresses itself, as Paul Ricœur has stated, in the symbolic interweavings of temporality, which can be comprehended as a language:

> If we recognize the symbolic structure of our temporal experience, we must recognize and respect the diversity of the symbolic systems which organize this experience. They are like languages. Mankind did not develop on the basis of a single language. We know of no historical era with all man having the same language. [...]. Similarly with time symbolizations—we know of no historical era when all mankind might have identically systematized temporal experience. [...]. What a given language says is not mechanically determined by its lexical and syntactical forms. It is rather that these systems constitute specific cultural codes which sometimes coincide with major linguistic groups, and sometimes cut across linguistic or cultural groups and form subgroups within themselves. (Ricœur, 1977: 18-19)

As I proclaim, a particular rhetorical figure, the aporia, appears in the poetry of three of the most important Jewish poets of this century in a dialectical relationship with a key moment of the Jewish "cultural code": a particular conception of time and history. The aporias of time in the poetic writings of Paul Celan, Rose Ausländer, Dan Pagis, and others, who for lack of sufficient time must be excluded here, are derived from the core of this consciousness, which envisions a present sense of all modes of times, the melting of past, present and future into a unity, and the primacy of the historical dimension in cultural discourse. Such conceptualizations of time and history have played a central role in the writings of Jewish authors in all periods and languages, but in the aftermath of the Shoah their pronounced accentuation is to be observed in the most ahistorical of literary forms—in poetry.

In the poetry to be presented here the aporia can be seen as a form of expression for poetic reflection about relationships between modes of time. The aporia does not refer to a concrete historical event; phonemes, words and syntactic constructions encircle a felt caesura in time: The three poets experienced the persecution and annihilation of European Jews during the Shoah as a devastating part of their lives at an early age. In their poetry they seek to contend with this caesura, which greatly formed their personal and, at the same time, their collective histories.

— II —

Paul Celan, one of the most challenging and compelling poets of the twentieth century, was born Paul (Pessach) Antschel on November 23rd, 1920 in Czernowitz. Celans intellectually vibrant and untroubled youth was abruptly halted when German troops occupied his homeland, the Bukovina. His parents were deported to Michailovka, a forced labour camp in the Ukraine, where they were soon murdered. Celan was imprisoned in a forced labour camp from 1942 until 1944. His path after the overthrow of the Nazis took him first to Bucharest, then to Vienna and on to Paris. There the poet lived, wrote and worked as translator and as a lecturer at the École Normal Supérieure until choosing to end his life in April of 1970.

Celans fifth collection of poems, *The No One's Rose*, was published in 1963. One of the most frequently cited poems of this collection, *Psalm*, begins with the lines:

> No one moulds us again out of earth and clay,
> no one conjures our dust.
> No one.
>
> Praised be your name, no one.
> For your sake
> we shall flower.
> Towards
> You.
>
> A nothing
> we were, are, shall
> remain, flowering;
> the nothing-, the
> no one's rose. (1-13)
> [...]   (Celan, 1980: 143)

From the onset the poem presents us with a problem: If we comprehend *No One* as a proper noun, then the opening lines ascribe an event to the present—*No One moulds us* (now) *again out of earth and clay*. Yet if *No One* serves as an indefinite pronoun an event is semantically negated, a negation affecting at once the present and the future: No one is moulding us now, and no one will mould us of earth and clay. The fact that *no one* clearly figures as a proper noun in the second verse and that it remains ambiguous in the third underscores the aporetical nature of the poem's first lines and of the poem as a whole. In his essay entitled *Reading* Paul de Man speaks of a similar structure in the writings of Proust:

> The disjunction between the aesthetically responsive and the rhetorically aware reading, both equally compelling, [...] functions like an oxymoron, but since it signals a logical rather than a representational incompatibility, it is in fact an aporia. It designates the irrevocable occurrence of at least two mutually exclusive readings and asserts the impossibility of a true understanding, on the level of the figuration as well as of the themes. (De Man, 1979: 72)

In *Psalm* these two levels—the figurative and the thematical—are knotted together in the temporal dimension of the poem. The two contradictory readings of *No one* are immanently related to the "we", which is made equivalent to the "Nothing" in the third verse. Just as *No one* simultaneously moulds, doesn't mould and never will mould "us" again, this "nothing-us" belongs at once to all and to none of the three modes of time: The time of the "nothing-we" is therefore to be understood as an inseparable unity encompassing the spectrum of existence: *we were, are, shall/ remain.*

An archival poem of Celan's stemming from the same period as *Psalm* states:

> [...]
> A seed is opening, you know,
> is opening, is opening
> a nightseed, in the floods, a people
> is growing, a race
> of-pain-and-of-name-: steady
> and as was always drowned
> and faithful -: the un-
> was,
> the living
> mine, the
> yours. (4-14)   (Celan, 1997: 57)

A seed opens, a people grows in the present tense. If one reads the negation "the un-" separate from the "was" from which it is in fact separated by a hyphen and a line break, then the reading might suggest a people that is not relegated to that which has passed, but is instead unpassed, a people existing in the present. Yet a different reading of the syntactic construction "the un-/was" as a semantic unit presents just as valid a meaning, although wholly incompatible with the first. In this reading a people is spoken of that never was at all. Here, just as in *Psalm*, the figurative and the semantical dimensions of the poem become entangled. The people that un-was/was is named the living in the line that follows. The poem expresses both semantically and linguistically that the past and the present of this people are not to be separated. In the poem's sense the extinguished people spoken of lives in the present. The "un-/was" people, the nothing-people, the "of-pain-and-of-name", the "nightseed" can hardly be understood as not relating to the Jewish people.

Some lines from Celans poem *Radix Matrix* may serve to further
underscore this connection:

> [...]
> Who,
> who was it, that
> lineage, the murdered, that looms
> black into the sky:
> rod and bulb -?
>
> (Root.
> Abraham's root. Jesse's root. No one's
> Root - O
> Ours.) (15-23)   (Celan, 1980: 153)

— III —

The poet Rose Ausländer was born a generation before Paul Celan
on May 11th 1901 in Czernowitz. Although her parents were not orthodox
Jews she grew up in an environment that was strongly influenced by the
eastern-european Jewish culture (Köhl, 1993:30). Her father spent his
childhood in Sadagora, a then vibrant centre of chassidic culture, but he
later distanced himself from the orthodoxy. He read Heine's *Rabbi von
Bacharach* to his daughter and greatly admired the writings of Goethe
(Ausländer, 1984: 289).[1]

As of 1943 Rose Ausländer was only able to escape deportation to
the concentration camps of Transnistria by remaining in a cellar hiding
place in Czernowitz with her mother.[2] After the factual annexation of the
Bukovina by the Red Army in 1944 Rose Ausländer left the city. In

---

[1] Source references to poems from Rose Ausländer will be designated in the following by the
Roman numeral of the volume as contained in the GW-edition and the page number.

[2] As of 1940 Rose Ausländer lived with her ailing mother, her brother Max and his wife Berta in
the Dreifaltigkeitsgasse. The street belonged to the Jewish quarter so it was made part of the
ghetto erected on October 11th, 1941. After having had her work permit revoked in March of
1943 Rose Ausländer had to reckon with deportation to Transnistrien. In: Helmut Braun, 1991:
17-18.

September of 1946 she entered the USA. She never found a lasting connection to American culture. Rose Ausländer returned to Europe where she wrote poetry in the German language until her death in 1988.

Paul Celan and Rose Ausländer met in Paris in 1957. They had known each other well in the Bukovina. Ausländer was very impressed with what she called Celans "language generating existentialism" (Ausländer, 1984a: 284-288). In the years thereafter her own poetry radically changed: broken verses frequently marked the syntax, rhyme became a near rare occurrence, rhetorical figures aimed at multiple meanings. "Time" itself appears often as a figure that can not be reduced to its apparent modes. In the poem *Gypsy* Ausländer writes:

> Gypsy
> time
> in three-fold-gown [gaun]
> she wanders
> tent to tent
> [...]   (Ausländer, 1984b: 209)

The poem *Time 1* written in 1976 begins with the lines:

> Will come the time
> is there
> passes and remains
> [...]
>
> Stars fall
> the moon
> comes and goes
> with the time
> that passes and
> remains.   (Ausländer, 1984b: 208)

Ausländer makes little use of punctuation. It is because of this that the lines can be read in dual and contradictory manners: Time will come, time is there. The simultaneity of all times is literally emphasized in the third verse of the poem: Time "passes and remains". This all in one motion.

Such a conception of time, that in spite of the division in past, present and future remains present in the now-time of the poem allows the "I" of the poem *My Breath [Mein Atem]* to extend itself into an autopoetological realm:

> In my deepdreams
> the earth weeps
> blood
> [...]
>
> The past
> has composed me
> I have
> inherited the future
> My breath is called
> now   (Ausländer, 1984c: 96)

Within the present dimension of the poem the earth weeps blood. Just as a present tense names the breath "now". "Breath", as Rose Ausländer understood it in terms of her interpretation of Baruch Spinoza's and Constantin Brunner's writings, stands for life in light of God (Beil, 1991: 338). Past in the poem therefore implies more than a mere temporal mode of that which was. Past is equated with an origin and the source of poetry. It is only by way of the past that the "I" of the poem has received its own future.

The poem *Over* reflects the notion that the now-time of life and of poetry is not conceivable without having originated in the past:

> It is over
> never
> is it over
> We are the
> immortal mohawks
> oldnew people
> [...]   (Ausländer, 1986: 56)

What is meant by this "it" that is simultaneously over and not? As in the poems previously commented upon, the aporia here is not to be mistaken for an oxymoron. For just as was the case with Paul Celans syntactic construction "the un-was" people, the contradictory lines "It is over" and "never / is it over" refer to the consciousness of time and history held by the "oldnew" Jewish people. I will return to this. But first I wish to examine an aspect of the third poet to be discussed, Dan Pagis.

— IV —

Dan Pagis was born in 1930 not far from Czernowitz in Radautz. His father left the family early in his life to establish a new home in Palestine; wife and son were to follow. This never occurred. Dan Pagis' mother died unexpectedly in 1934 and the four-year-old came to live with his maternal grandparents, who belonged to the Jewish-bourgeoisie of Radautz. When WWII broke out he too was deported to the concentration and forced labour camps in the East. In 1946 he made his way to Palestine—Eretz Israel. It was there in the Kibbutz Merchavia that he met the teacher and poet Tuvia Rübner. Young Pagis was then introduced to Ludwig Strauß and Werner Kraft. He began to write poems in Hebrew. He became a professor for medieval Hebrew poetry at the Hebrew University in Jerusalem and kept this profession until his death in 1986. It was not until 1959, thirteen years after Dan Pagis had arrived in Israel, that his first book of poems, *Sch'on hatzel, The Shadowclock* was published. The book begins with the poem *Chod hakardom, The Cut of the Axe*:

> Once we questioned the wind
> like pines before break of day,
> with eyelids heavy and hiding within
> the rings of the good years.
> But upon our trunks
> the axe blade hew knot holes
> and we saw.
> The sap dripped and solidified.   (Pagis, 1991: 9)

The fifth verse—"But upon our trunks"—marks a caesura. The two temporal modes of the poem separate: On the one hand "once", the time of the "rings of the good years", is spoken of, on the other that time that began with the blow of the axe. The poem is hardly translatable, since knot hole and the eye have the same term in Hebrew: *Aijn*. So the Hebrew original allows for the wounds themselves to see. The bloody tears shed by "our trunks" represent a very particular sap: It drips and solidifies simultaneously. At the blow of the axe a time metaphorically removed was rendered motionless. And yet time moved on.

The third cycle of the book of poems *Gilgul*, "Metamorphosis", which was published in 1970, is entitled *karon Chatum, Sealed Railcar*. This cycle begins with the *poem Eropa, me'uchar, Europe, late* (Pagis, 1991: 134):

In the sky violins fly away
and a straw hat. Pardon me,
what year do we have?
Thirtynine-and-a-half, just about,
still early, very early,
one can turn the radio off.
May I introduce; that is the wind from the sea,
the promenade comes to life, wonderfully released
it tosses bellskirts up, beats
against worried newspapers: Tango! Tango!
The city park full of music:
> I kiss your hand, madame,
> the delicate hand, white
> like the gossamer glove,
> all will still be as it was
> in dreams,
> ah, please don't be so worried, madame,
> such things never happen here,
> you will see,
> here never

The poem provides us with an indication of a historical context when it pronounces: "what year do we have? / Thirtynine-and-a-half, just about,/". The middle of 1939 was, in fact, "still" early yet as the title of the poem suggests also already "late". The unfetteredness of an ocean breeze, the tossed bellskirts still offset the troubling newspapers. But the tone of flying violins, the music from the city park, the well-known Chanson "I Kiss Your Hand, Madame" are preludes to an ellipsis: "such things never happen here, / you will see, / here never". What never happens here? The broken syntax builds towards the aporia of the last three lines. The Hebrew term "le'olam" appears in the sixteenth and eighteenth lines and provides for two equally justifiable, contradictory readings:

> it will never happen here,
> you will see,
> > here never

and the second reading

> it will never happen here,
> you will see,
> > here always

The poem's "Thirtynine-and-a-half" does not represent a period of time during the summer weeks of 1939 in Europe. The poem is written from its own time: Thirtynine-and-a-half will never occur, will never be repeated, will never be past. Each reading is to formulate the presence of a never completed "Thirtynine-and-a-half".

— V —

The aporias of time in the poems that I have spoken of do not represent a language game in the tradition of modern poetry. There is an interweaving of the Jewish grammar of remembrance with the poetic rhetoric of time. The *tertium comparationis* of these poems lies within the linguistic and rhetorical questioning of the difference between past and present. This poetry bears the pathmarks of a literary transformation of the Jewish discourse on remembrance that stretches back across millennia. The most ancient Jewish rituals and celebrations consisted of more than mere repetitions of mythical archetypes with the intention of transcending historical time. Yosef Haim Yerushalmi tells us:

> If past is to be evoked, it is not prehistorical past but historical time in which the decisive great moments of Israel's history came about. The biblical religion does not at all seek to find a way out of history, on the contrary: it is filled with history and inconceivable without it. (Yerushalmi, 1988: 21)

The weekly public readings of the Thora in the synagogues gave the collective past the cyclical quality of liturgical time without falling into a sense of determinated destiny, because the telling of the past is not a matter of evocation—it serves to make reflection of and on the present possible. Jewish liturgy never served solely to view a closed past in retrospect. It is constituted by being in the present (nichua`ch) (Barzel, 1994: 247). As the renowned historian Amos Funkenstein emphasizes:

creative reflection on past or present history, with or
without historiography in its actual sense, has not ceased at
any time. The Jewish culture was and remains determined
by an acute historical consciousness of different forms at
various times. (Funkenstein, s.a.: 11)

In questioning the boundaries between past and present, between
"private" and "collective" genealogies, the poetries of Paul Celan, Rose
Ausländer and Dan Pagis stand in this Jewish tradition. In their poems a
textual space is opened, in which the Shoah is thought not as a closed
moment of the past but as a constantly present occurrence of collective
history—a hardly describable occurrence sensed as a caesura. The aporia
of time that place us in the midst of two or more contradictory readings
are not expressions of the fundamental unreadability of literary texts as
Paul de Man suggests of the aporia that he analyses. These aporias are to
be understood as moments in which literary reflection pronounces
engagement with Jewish culture and vice versa: comparative analysis of
these poems therefore entails readings of poetry as culture and readings
of culture as text.

Amir Eshel
Hamburg

Bibliography

Ausländer, Rose. 1984. "Czernowitz, Heine und die Folgen". In: Rose Ausländer. *Gesammelte Werke in sieben Bänden: Band III*, Frankfurt am Main: Fischer Verlag.

Ausländer, Rose. 1984a. *Gesammelte Werke III*, Frankfurt am Main: Fischer Verlag. Translated by Timothy Kyle Boyd.

Ausländer, Rose. 1984b. *Gesammelte Werke IV*, Frankfurt am Main: Fischer Verlag. Translated by Timothy Kyle Boyd.

Ausländer, Rose. 1984c. *Gesammelte Werke V*, Frankfurt am Main: Fischer Verlag. Translated by Timothy Kyle Boyd.

Ausländer, Rose. 1986. *Gesammelte Werke VII*, Frankfurt am Main: Fischer Verlag. Translated by Timothy Kyle Boyd.

Barzel, Alexander. 1994. *Al miwne hajahadut. [On the Structure of Judaism]*, Tel-Aviv: Sifriat Poalim.

Beil, Claudia. 1991. *Sprache als Heimat: Jüdische Tradition und Exilerfahrung in der Lyrik von Nelly Sachs und Rose Ausländer*, München: tuduv-Verlagsgesellschaft.

Braun, Helmut. 1991. "»Es gibt noch viel zu sagen«: Zur Biographie von Rose Ausländer". In: Helmut Braun, (Ed.). *Rose Ausländer: Materialien zu Leben und Werk*. Frankfurt am Main: Fischer Verlag, 1991, p. 17–18.

Celan, Paul. 1997. *Die Gedichte aus dem Nachlass: Ed. by Bertrand Badiou, Jean-Claude Rambach and Barbara Wiedemann*, Frankfurt am Main: Suhrkamp Verlag. Translated by Timothy Kyle Boyd.

Celan, Paul. 1980. *Poems: Selected, Translated and Introduced by Michael Hamburger*, Manchester: Carcanet New Press Limited.

De Man, Paul. 1972. *Allegories of Reading*, New Haven & London: Yale University Press.

Funkenstein, Amos. s.a. *Perceptions of Jewish History*, Berkeley/Los Angeles/Oxford: University of California Press.

Köhl, Gabriele. 1993. *Die Bedeutung der Sprache in der Lyrik Rose Ausländers*, Pfaffenweiler.

Pagis, Dan. 1970. *Gilgul*. Tel-Aviv: Sifriat Makor/Massada.

Pagis, Dan. 1991. *kol haschirim [Collected Poems]*, Jerusalem: Hakibbutz Hameuchad Publishing House and the Bialik Institute. Translated by Amir Eshel and Timothy Kyle Boyd.

Ricœur, Paul. 1977. "Introduction." In: Honorat Aguessy and others (Ed.): *Time and the Philosophies*, Paris: Unesco.

Yerushalmi, Yosef Hayim. 1988. *Zachor: Erinnere Dich! Jüdische Geschichte und jüdisches Gedächtnis*, Berlin: Wagenbach.

At the Edge of Humanity: The Dismissal of Historical Truth in Piotr Rawicz's Novel *Le Sang du ciel*

Piotr Rawicz has the opprobrious distinction of being one of the least known writers in French of the Holocaust. Unlike writers (such as him) who knew first-hand the camps, those such as Charlotte Delbo, Robert Antelme or Elie Wiesel; and unlike others who were children during the war but spared deportation, or were born in the years subsequent to it, such as Georges Perec, Marcel Cohen, Sarah Kofman, or Henri Raczymow; and unlike still others who approached the Hitler time or Vichy years from an entirely sympathetic position, such as Edmond Jabès, Piotr Rawicz is rarely considered among them or any other writer for whom the troubling and insistant presence of the intended destruction of European Jewry is central. It was not until last year, when the critic and translator Anthony Rudolf published his *Engraved in Flesh* (to which I shall frequently allude here),[1] that a lengthy study of Piotr Rawicz was available. His single novel, *Le Sang du ciel*, when it appeared in 1961 through Gallimard, attracted a mixed critical response; likewise, refer-

---

[1] *Engraved in Flesh: A Study of Piotr Rawicz's Novel "Blood from the Sky"* (London: Menard, 1996). Rudolf's study is abbreviated in my text as *EF*, followed by page number cited. See also my discussion of this book in *World Literature Today* (vol. 71, no. 3, Summer 1997), pp. 560-561.

ences to it in later studies on the Holocaust are few and unsustained.[2] Just why he was and remains poorly studied by literary historians of the period is to me a mystery. It shall be one of the objectives of this short essay to attempt to tease out an answer, however tentative it might be. For the moment it is necessary to ask who was Piotr Rawicz, and what is particular about his novel that gives it enduring value in Holocaust studies?

Piotr Rawicz was born in 1919 in Lwow, then capital of East Galicia (Poland), whose Jewish population numbered thirty-five percent of the city's inhabitants (*EF*, 64-69). His mother tongue was Polish, although by the time he reached Paris in 1947 he spoke Ukrainian, Chochlis, Russian, German, and of course French, the language in which he wrote *Le Sang du ciel*; in later years, while in Paris, he studied oriental languages at the Sorbonne and elsewhere, and took degrees in Hindi and Sanskrit. In 1939 when the Nazis and Soviets signed their pact, East Galicia was occupied first by the Soviet Union and in 1941 by the Germans. Rawicz was arrested in 1942 near the Czech border and deported at about that time, as a Ukrainian (he possessed papers giving a fictitious biography and a medical certificate explaining his circumcision—both central to his novel), to Auschwitz. After a period in Auschwitz he was transferred in 1944 to Leitmeritz, near Theresienstadt, where he remained until liberation the following year (*EF*, 76-77).

Le Sang du ciel[3] emplots the occupation of an imaginary Lwow, what Anthony Rudolf calls the novel's "main geo-spiritual source" (*EF*, 64), and the terror inflicted upon its population by the occupying forces and their local collaborators, both Jews and non-Jews, events brought about, it would seem, by a *Deus otiosus* who remained chillingly indifferent to the suffering of his elected at the hands of an evil incarnate. Its protagonist is a young aristocratic Jew named Boris who, with his girlfriend Noëmi, frequently and barely escapes capture, interrogation, and torture until his eventual arrest near the novel's end. Their "pérégrinations *ad limina*" (*SC*, 24) truly deliver them to humanity's

---

[2] For the critical reception of *Le Sang du ciel*, see *EF*, pp. 101-103. See also, most recently, Sara R. Horowitz's comments in her *Voicing the Void: Muteness and Memory in Holocaust Fiction* (New York: SUNY Press, 1997), pp. 103-104.

[3] Paris: Gallimard, 1961. Abbreviated as *SC* in my text, and followed by page number cited. The novel was reprinted following Rawicz's death in 1982. An English-language translation by Peter Wiles, *Blood from the Sky* (New York: Harcourt, Brace and World, 1964), is out of print.

edge; he and his lover are reduced to wandering, "le dépaysement devint [leur] seule patrie" (*SC*, 168). The novel hinges on an absurdity, which, despite its unlikelihood, has an analogue in the life of its author. Blond-headed Boris, fluent in Ukrainian and German, defies execution by hiding behind the identity of a certain Georges (Youri) Goletz, a non-Jew whose papers he finds not long before the "Grande Action" begins. When eventually he is asked to drop his pants, his death seems certain. How to conceal the "signe d'Alliance"? The circumcision is in no way Jewish, but the result of an unfortunate medical procedure, he claims, a surgical intervention necessary for the prevention of further spreading of an infectous disease transmitted by one of the village prostitutes, "Olena, Olena la grosse" (*SC*, 262). Shortly afterwards he is irritated by a "phimosis" and consults a surgeon, who removes the inflamed foreskin. The fable does not convince Boris's captors, and so he is further examined by the prison doctor: "je ne suis pas Juif," he tells him, "mais Ukrainien. Cela—je le pense—tout le monde peut aisément s'en apercevoir; sauf les policiers que leur métier finit inévitablement par abrutir" (*SC*, 265). The doctor examines the evidence carefully, and pronounces his verdict: it is declared plausible, even probable, that the foreskin was removed during a medical not ritual procedure. Boris, as Youri Goletz, is saved.

Le Sang du ciel is recounted and even redacted (*SC*, 186) by a café owner in Paris on the boulevard Montparnasse who meets Boris, "son client," one afternoon in 1961. Boris tells him a "récit sinueux" (*SC*, 178), and gives him some notes, a kind of "journal intime" (*SC*, 124), about which the café owner remarks, "Des lettres de grandeur moyenne dont seulement certaines—et pas toujours les mêmes—prenaient des propor-tions et des formes grotesques au gré de celui qui les traçait. Mon client cherchait-il donc un moyen d'expression supplémentaire, les mots ou la manière dont il les maniait ne suffisant pas à transmettre, à fixer le 'message' qu'il considérait comme le sien?" (*SC*, 124). He admits that he is poorly prepared for the task of making sense out of the "volapük" (*SC*, 125) of notes in French and Slave and other tongues, he is hardly competent in "exégèse philologique" (*SC*, 125); nevertheless he is little by little seized by the need to save the "débris d'un récit" (*SC*, 125). What precisely is the message Boris tries to communicate?

Rawicz establishes from the book's opening pages that Boris and the imaginary Ukrainian city "d'importance moyenne" (*SC*, 14) he spends his young adulthood in are both Jewish. The novel opens in the summer of

194— (in a macabre autobiographical moment Rawicz gives the exact date, July 12th, which is his own birthdate [*EF*, 66]) during the tense days of the "Grande Action" undertaken by the invading Germans supported by locals. Tales of righteous Jews, the *tzaddikim*, come to intervene in the divine scheme are heard on the lips of locals (*SC*, 74); suicides are frequent (*SC*, 51); soap appears on the market bearing the imprint, R.I.F. ("Rein Jüdisches Fett" [*SC*, 55]); children suffer deportation (*SC*, 50); to some it is a "nouveau Moyen Âge" (*SC*, 28) while to others, such as old Hillel, master of post-Biblical history, owner of an enormous library of sources of the Talmud and a "belle collection de photos pornographiques" (*SC*, 47), it was July, yes, but "de l'an sept mille," that is, the year on the Jewish calendar which marks the end of all time.

Boris is witness to this, and to more. Perhaps the most horrifyingly sadistic scene occurs during the raids on the town. Women and children are sent into hiding, but they do not remain undetected for long. A group of soldiers led by an under-officer finds them when, mockingly, ten-year-old Yaakov "ouvrit largement la bouche et tira en direction du caporal une langue rouge, longue et large, un corridor infini tapissé d'une moquette pourpre, une langue trop réelle, terriblement réelle dans ce décor qui ne l'était pas. Telle est donc la voie qu'emprunte ce moment pour se réaliser: la langue d'un enfant, pensa Boris en entendant le caporal prononcer distinctement, lentement, une phrase presque neutre: 'Que ce garçon-là est mal élevé!'" (*SC*, 138). The café owner notes that "Boris s'abstient de décrire en détail le massacre," but continues to divulge its lurid outline: three soldiers grabbed the child while the coporal "lui découpait la langue avec une baïonnette trop grande pour cet usage." Blood flowed, "beaucoup de sang, davantage—d'après les estimations de Boris—que n'en devait contenir le corps tout entier de Yaakov." The terrified children stand petrified in silence. A girl holding Boris's arm is taken next; soldiers gouge out her eyes. One by one the children are tortured. How to describe the horror? "Ça glissait. Ça dégoulinait. Des cris stridents remplissaient la pièce comme autant de petits animaux affolés. Des bâillements, des sons vagues, des bruits monstres et bâtards. Des déchirements de sens et de peaux. Des figures géométriques, toutes les géométries qui entraient en folie comme on entre dans un bain chaud. Quelqu'un qui dit: 'La géométrie, cette preuve irréfutable que Dieu est fou, fou à lier . . .'" (*SC*, 138-139). The massacre goes on into the night. A few hours later, Boris returns to the scene with a nurse "armée d'une seringue. Plusieurs gosses mutilés souffraient encore. L'infirmière leur distribuait la mort comme les parts d'un pain d'épice fourée d'ombre" (*SC*, 139). The memory of the night returns much later to Boris; further on, when as Youri Goletz he is accorded an official status as a Ukrainian national. Cartesian precision haunts him, taunts him, but the details have lost their edge: "Oui, mais un Dieu NORMAL, un Dieu dépourvu de folie, serait-il supportable? —J'entrerai dans la démence comme on entre dans un bain chaud—il formulait et reformulait cette phrase idiote sans jamais sortir un son de sa bouche morte" (*SC*, 240).

That Boris is divided against himself is a matter of survival. He must in effect kill his Jewishness and invent a non-Jewish personality and biography out of a name, Youri Goletz. The café owner-redactor observes in his client's journals that, "Parlant de soi, Boris employait tantôt la première, tantôt la troisième personne," and he wonders, "Cette hésitation traduisait-elle un besoin obscur d'objectiver sa propre existence, besoin éprouvé couramment par ceux à qui leur existence échappe?" (*SC*, 125). Boris does not reflect so philosophically. No matter how you slice the problem of his identity, yes, it is ontological. But Boris is a practical man. When on the train journey from Lwow, funny papers in his pocket, he has a dream, a night image out of the *Inferno*, in which a voice speaks to him from a flame: "Boris, eh Boris!" (*SC*, 144) the voice cries out. He awakes "transi et effrayé: Car je ne m'appelle plus Boris" (*SC*, 144). Nor is his family name his own. All that remains is the "signe d'alliance, inscrit dans mon corps [. . .] Je m'appelle Youri Goletz. J'ai enfin acquis une profession valable: valet de ferme. Ma fausse biographie, je me la répète en pensée comme les prières élémentaires de la religion sortie de la mienne il y a vingt siècles" (*SC*, 144). Boris substitutes his self for another, he replaces his Judaism with another religion, his language for another, his country for another. He is no longer hunted but hunter, collaborator not victim. The replacement of one individual by another implies a further, more terrible substitution, which, I wish to argue, accounts for *Le Sang du ciel*'s exclusion, for all practical purposes, from the literature of the Holocaust which is charged with the task of remembering.

The novel ends with a disquieting postface which would, if taken literally, dislodge any historical perspective from its content. "Ce livre n'est pas un document historique" (*SC*, 280), we are informed:

> Si la notion de hasard (comme la plupart des notions)
> ne paraissait pas absurde à l'auteur, il dirait volontiers que
> toute référence à une époque, un territoire ou une ethnie
> déterminés est fortuite.
>
> Les événements relatés pourraient surgir en tout lieu
> et en tout temps dans l'âme de n'importe quel homme,
> planète, minéral . . . (*SC*, 280).

Some might argue that the novel's refusal of historical authenticity diffuses its capacity to represent the brutality and inhumanity of the moment; in other words, Rawicz has willingly disqualified himself from the truth. How could its narrator (in the guise of the author) deny the particular veracity of the events recounted therein? Further, from a posterior point of view, Piotr Rawicz's suicide in 1982 would seem to confirm the negation of historical specificity of his novel, or at least its author's failure to persist in memory's shadow. The fact that the novel remains largely unread today would seem to bear out Irving Howe's conclusion that while mimesis "remains the foundation" of description,[4] Rawicz often departs from the representation of reality, "abandon[ing] story and character in his straining. [. . .] We become aware," continues Howe, "of an excess of tension between the narrative (pushed into the background but, through its sheer horror, still dominant) and the virtuosity of language (too often willed and literary). Rawicz's outcroppings of expressionist rage and grief, no matter how graphic in their own right, can only seem puny when set against the events looming across the book."[5]

However, I would suggest that it is precisely in Rawicz's dismissal of historical truth and specificity that he most excitingly, if disturbingly, succeeds in witnessing the terror for future generations whom, he implores, "À défaut de souvenirs, cherchez dans votre imagination, cherchez parmi certains de vos rêves auxquels cela m'arrangerait de faire confiance" (*SC*, 68).[6] His position is revealed, not without some regret,

---

[4] Irving Howe, "Writing and the Holocaust" in *Writing and the Holocaust* Berel Lang (ed.) (New York and London: Holmes and Meier, 1988), p. 193.

[5] *Ibid.*, pp. 193-194.

[6] On the debate on the dialectic of literature or fiction and history, see, among other contributions, Berel Lang, "The Representation of Evil: Ethical Content as Literary Form," in his *Act and Idea in the Nazi Genocide* (Chicago and London: University of Chicago Press, 1990), pp. 117-161 and Lawrence L. Langer, "Fictional Facts and Factual Fictions: History in Holocaust Literature," in

early in the novel: "C'est une douleur douce qu'une ville où l'on a vécu, où sont morts les vôtres, et qui devant vos yeux se mue en Histoire" (*SC*, 14). Humanity is to the aristocrat Boris low and even despicable; the sentiment precedes the days of the Grand Action, which seems only to objectify his view: "Tout jeune," he confesses, "j'ai rencontré une image, sans jamais trouver la force de m'en débarrasser, d'en faire un récit, un poème, de la fixer. Le mal des comparaisons me rongeait. Ayant pensé pour la première fois le concept 'humanité', j'ai comme entr'aperçu un modèle de verre du cerveau humain" (*SC*, 35), in which, he describes, worms occupied two thousand cells, the one separated from the other. This image brings us to the theme of "la fraternité des abîmes" (*SC*, 206) in which Jews are forced into a "cohabitation fraternelle avec les rats" (*SC*, 25). The picture that emerges in *Le Sang du ciel* is one of terrible brutality, hatred towards Jews, and suffering without end.

And yet the ultimate message of the book seems to pass beyond the particularities of the Jewish experience of the war. Rawicz intimates throughout that there is a universal experience to be recounted. During the initial slaughter in the village, the tombstones, on which are engraved Hebrew letters, are splintered under the hammers of workers. Sacred inscriptions are destroyed, "Un *aleph* s'en allait vers la gauche, tandis qu'un *hei* sculpté sur un autre morceau de pierre retombait vers la droite" (*SC*, 53). The destruction of the Jewish cemetery is mirrored in the designification of language itself: "L'un après l'autre, les mots, tous les mots du langage humain se fanent, perdent la force de porter une signification. Et puis, ils tombent, telles des écailles mortes" (*SC*, 118). All language, the language of the Jews and of humanity, diffuses in destruction and cruelty.

One deduces a second illustration of Rawicz's universalism (a term whose Enlightenment associations would have prevented dark Rawicz, in all likelihood, from applying it to himself) in the scene of Boris's arrest by the Germans, when he sees through the window of the interrogation cell five Jews buried from their necks down, and hears "une parole humide, mi-râlée mi-chantée qui venait de loin, de plus loin que les astres" (*SC*, 156), a cry of the admission of God's singularity and unity, a gesture

his *Admitting the Holocaust: Collected Essays* (New York and Oxford: Oxford University Press, 1995), pp. 75-87. See also the essays gathered in *Probing the Limits of Representation: Nazism and the "Final Solution,"* Saul Friedländer (ed.) (Cambridge, MA and London: Harvard University Press, 1992).

performed as death nears irremediably: "Écoute *mon peuple*, Dieu est ton Seigneur, Dieu est unique. . ." (*SC*, 156) (my emphasis here and below). Has Rawicz miscited Deuteronomy 6.4, from which the phrase is derived, and which would read in French, "Écoute *Israël* . . ."? Rawicz's modification—it would be difficult to admit that he had lapsed intentionally; the "Shema Yisrael"—a pillar of Jewish liturgy and gateway to Jewish self-identification—is echoed in the final pages of the novel when Boris, now liberated from the German prison, falls into a light sleep in which he "revoyait *l'Homme* enterré jusqu'au cou, entre les détritus et les poubelles" (*SC*, 276). The five Jewish prisoners of the earlier passage become humankind itself; it is not Jews who lay buried but an abject humanity, "Leurs têtes salies, couvertes de poussière humide et de choses innommables, leurs têtes à moitié dévorées sortaient du sol telles de géants champignons" (*SC*, 156); or, if they are Jews, they clearly stand in (without echoing, so far as I can tell, Christological symbolism) for the debasement of humanity. In any case this passage does not contradict but sustains the universalism of the novel's concluding message.

Rawicz in this regard is close to Robert Antelme, who wrote in the preface to his prison memoirs, *L'Espèce humaine* (1947), that in the camps one's humanity, as a member of the species of man, was always contested: "La mise en question de la qualité d'homme provoque une revendication presque biologique d'appartenance à l'espèce humaine."[7] The questioning brought Antelme to consider the outer reaches of humanity: "Elle sert ensuite à méditer sur les limites de cette espèce, sur sa distance à la 'nature' et sa relation avec elle, sur une certaine solitude de l'espèce donc, et pour finir, surtout à concevoir une vue claire de son unité indivisible."[8] But for Piotr Rawicz the sentiment that human and not exclusively Jewish limits were constitutive of the prison experience was insufficient; Jews *were* representative of humanity, he frequently proposed in addresses given in the course of Holocaust symposia. "I do not know if I am correct," he submitted to Emil Fackenheim, "but I believe that the fate and condition of the Jewish people are the very essence of the human condition—the farthest borders of human destiny. And the fate of the 'Holocaust Jew,' the Jew of the ghetto and concentration camp, is, one

---

[7]   Robert Antelme, *L'Espèce humaine*, new and corrected edition (Paris: Gallimard, 1957/1996), p. 11.

[8]   *Ibid.*

might say, the ontological essence of that ontological essence."[9] For Rawicz, then, literature was not opposed to history, but a form of it. It is true that to many he committed the triple offense of inscribing the Jew within humanity (that is, of relativizing history), of misrepresenting some historical detail, and of mixing irony and gravity in his descriptions of Nazi horror.[10] But his objective was not solely to esthetisize the horror of the Holocaust; it was to extend its import and application to other historical situations.

Despite one's private views, however, it is impossible to deny that Piotr Rawicz's novel is, similar to so much literature of the Holocaust, a leaf in the book of Lamentations, which is for many of these books their template. It is as much a repository of cultural identity and a vehicle of its transmission as is the more orthodox Holocaust fiction and history. Since Rawicz was intimately familiar with the writings of the rabbis, it would not be inappropriate to conclude with a citation from the Mishnah, a compilation of legal prescriptions and observations dating from around 200 C.E. and which shapes the mind of Talmud. My quote is of *Pirkei Avoth* (Ethics of the Fathers) 3.2, and it is the Mishnah in which is found, to my knowledge, the only reference to Lamentations in the entire compilation. Here, the lone individual, in fixed study of the law, receives heaven's reward:

> R. Hanina the Prefect of the Priests said: Pray for the peace of the ruling power, since but for fear of it men would have swallowed up each other alive. R. Hananiah b. Teradion said: If two sit together and no words of the Law [are spoken] between them, there is the seat of the scornful, as it is written, *Nor sittest in the seat of the scornful* [Psalms

---

[9] Piotr Rawicz's response to Emil Fackenheim's *From Bergen-Belsen to Jerusalem: Contemporary Implications of the Holocaust* (Jerusalem: Institute of Contemporary Jewry, The Hebrew University of Jerusalem, 1975), p. 25. In another presentation, this during the 1974 World Jewish Congress, he observed that "On a pu dire de nous, les Juifs, que nous étions comme tout le monde mais que nous étions un peu plus que tout le monde. Il s'agirait donc, si vous voulez, d'une espèce de 'concentrat ontologique,' et aussi peut-être historique parfois. Pour nous, Juifs, il s'agirait d'une exploration perpétuelle des limites, tantôt subie et tantôt voulue." From "Solitude juive dans la création littéraire," *Solitudes d'Israël* Jean Halpérin and Georges Levitte (eds.) (Paris: Presses Universitaires de France, 1975), p. 74.

[10] For a discussion of these considerations, see the seminal essay of Terrence Des Pres, "Holocaust Laughter?," in *Writing and the Holocaust*, Berel Lang (ed.), *op. cit.*, pp. 216-233, and in particular p. 217.

1.1]. But if two sit together and words of the Law [are spoken] between them, the Divine Presence rests between them, as it is written, *Then they that feared the Lord spake one with another: and the Lord hearkened, and heard, and a book of remembrance was written before him, for them that feared the Lord, and that thought upon his name* [Malachai 3.16]. Scripture speaks here of 'two'; whence [do we learn] that if even one sits and occupies himself in the Law, the Holy One, blessed is he, appoints him a reward? Because it is written, *Let him sit alone and keep silence, because he hath laid it upon him* [Lamentations 3.28].[11]

Steven Jaron
St. Lawrence University

These remarks have benefited from the comments of Elrud Ibsch, Anthony Rudolf, and Charlotte Wardi.

---

[11]   *The Mishnah*, Herbert Danby (trans. and ed.) (Oxford: Oxford University Press, 1967), p. 450.

Esthétiques de la discrétion: Georges Perec et Robert Bober

Georges Perec (écrivain) et Robert Bober (cinéaste et écrivain), deux auteurs français contemporains, descendants de juifs polonais et ayant vécu leur enfance pendant la Deuxième Guerre Mondiale, semblent partir, dans leurs œuvres respectives, de positions pratiquement opposées concernant leur rapport à la judéité. Cette origine est vécue par Perec surtout comme une absence, voire une ignorance, et par Bober comme un lien, un lieu d'appartenance.

Les œuvres dont il sera question ici forment néanmoins un réseau où sont visibles, outre l'amitié des deux auteurs, des soucis et des procédés communs, dessinant des approches de la question autobiographique marquées par l'oblique, le détour, l'ellipse.[1] Il s'agit de textes génériquement différents les uns des autres: un roman de Bober: — *Quoi de neuf sur la guerre?* (1993); — un "catalogue de souvenirs" de Perec — *Je me souviens* (1978) — un texte autobiographique de Perec, *W ou le souvenir d'enfance* (1975) ; — un film de Bober et Perec — *Récits d'Ellis Island* (1978).[2]

Ce qui unit ces textes c'est tout d'abord le rôle essentiel qu'y joue la mémoire: le souvenir et les histoires individuelles sont constamment

---

[1]   Cf. notamment Benabou (1985), Beaumatin (1990), Lejeune (1991), Gribomont (1995).

[2]   Ces titres seront désormais désignés, respectivement, par *Quoi de neuf...*, *W...*, *Ellis Island...*

affirmés comme facteurs essentiels d'une identité par ailleurs problématique, puisqu'elle est fondée au départ, pour ces "enfants de la Shoah", sur l'anéantissement, la disparition, le vide[3]. Dans toutes ces œuvres, en effet, la question de l'identité est indissociablement liée à l'hésitation, à l'incertitude, comme le résume la formule de Perec dans *W...*, reprise par le personnage "Georges" du roman de Bober, visiblement inspiré de Georges Perec:

> Je fus comme un enfant qui joue à cache-cache et qui ne sait pas ce qu'il craint ou désire le plus: rester caché, être découvert (*W*:14; *Quoi de neuf...*:56).

En effet, ces œuvres semblent résulter d'une impossibilité initiale: le besoin d'affirmer et de construire une identité dont la base est de l'ordre de l'indicible, ce qui mène à une conscience aigue de l'importance centrale de la mémoire comme condition de survie et d'étai de cette construction[4]. La mémoire devient donc l'enjeu central de ces œuvres, comme le résume simplement Raphael, personnage de *Quoi de neuf...*:

> Demander comment on va, avec se souvenir, c'est encore ce qu'on peut faire de mieux". (p. 241)

En effet, dans ce roman qui se déroule pour la plupart entre 1945-46, ce sont les mémoires trop douloureuses de cette guerre qui vient de finir qui hantent toutes les conversations, demi-mots et silences de ce petit atelier de tailleurs, presque tous juifs. Par ailleurs, au début de *W...* de Perec, recherche autobiographique partant d'un constat de manque en ce qui concerne la mémoire, on peut lire:

> Je n'ai pas de souvenirs d'enfance: je posais cette affirmation avec assurance, avec presque une sorte de défi. L'on n'avait pas à m'interroger sur cette question. Elle n'était pas inscrite à mon programme. J'en étais dispensé: une autre histoire, la Grande, l'Histoire avec sa grande hache, avait déjà répondu à ma place: la guerre, les camps. (p.13)

---

[3] Problématique commune à bien d'autres écrivains de la même génération, comme le remarque Marcel Bénabou. (Benabou, *op.cit.*).

[4] Cf. le jeu de mots de Perec dans *W...* "Pour être besoin d'étai" (p.77).

Cette apparente "absence d'histoire" mènera le sujet, d'une part à la recherche problématique de ses souvenirs d'enfance, et d'autre part, à l'écriture d'un livre inquiétant, double, alternant des chapitres autobiographiques—la recherche de souvenirs d'enfance—et des chapitres romanesques—un récit d'aventures brusquement interrompu pour faire place à la description d'une île entièrement consacrée aux sports—W—dont la description neutre et minutieuse transpose dans les détails les plus insupportables un portrait des camps nazis[5].

Quant au volume *Je me souviens*, assumé par Perec comme une "autobiographie collective" (Perec, 1990) il s'agit d'un inventaire de souvenirs quotidiens, anodins, partageables par une même génération. Ce privilège du souvenir banal, apparemment insignifiant et platement énoncé, sans commentaire ni interprétation, est d'ailleurs une constante dans tous ces textes et il constitue un des facteurs essentiels de ces démarches concernant la mémoire et l'identité. Ainsi Georges, le personnage de Bober qui n'a pas de famille, dresse obstinément des listes de films "pour ne pas oublier":

> C'est Georges qui est à côté de moi et qui profite de l'heure
> du courrier pour refaire sa liste de films parce qu'il n'a pas
> à qui écrire, qui m'a dit qu'il faut toujours tout noter ou
> tout raconter pour s'en souvenir plus tard (p. 27).

Et le narrateur, adulte, deviendra photographe, "cherchant comment photographier non plus ce qui existait, mais ce qui avait disparu puisque c'est le manque qui donne à voir" (p. 218).

On sait par ailleurs l'importance centrale de l'"infra-ordinaire" dans le projet d'écriture de Georges Perec, dans un but d'"essayer méticuleusement de retenir quelque chose, de faire survivre quelque chose" (Perec, 1974):

> Ce qui se passe chaque jour et qui revient chaque jour, le
> banal, le quotidien, l'évident, le commun, l'ordinaire,
> l'infra-ordinaire, le bruit de fond, l'habituel, comment en
> rendre compte, comment l'interroger, comment le décrire?

---

[5]   cf. *Cahiers Georges Perec* nº2 (1988), Lejeune (*op.cit.*).

/.../ Comment parler de ces "choses communes", comment les traquer plutôt, comment les débusquer, les arracher à la gangue dans laquelle elles restent engluées, comment leur donner un sens, une langue: qu'elles parlent enfin de ce qui est, de ce que nous sommes" (Perec, 1989: 11).

La motivation centrale des deux auteurs et que nous retrouvons dans tous ces textes, se retrouve, enfin, clairement énoncée dans *Récits d'Ellis Island*. En effet, plus qu'un "reportage" sur Ellis Island—lieu de passage obligatoire et de sélection pour l'immigration américaine en provenance de l'Europe au début du siècle—ce film, sous-titré "histoires d'errance et d'espoir", rassemble les images de "ce qui reste aujourd'hui de ce lieu unique", les rares mémoires de ceux qui y sont passés, et intègre la réflexion des deux auteurs quant à leur démarche artistique, en la définissant comme partant d'un même point—l'origine juive, vécue de manière opposée par chacun d'eux.

Pour Perec, elle est signe de manque, d'absence—un "constat de carence" (Benabou, *op.cit.*):

Je ne sais pas très précisément ce que c'est qu'être juif, ce que ça me fait que d'être juif ... ce serait plutôt un silence, une absence, une question, une mise en question, un flottement, une inquiétude /.../ Quelque part je suis étranger par rapport à quelque chose de moi-même; quelque part, je suis "différent", mais non pas différent des autres, différents des "miens" (*Ellis Island,* p. 43-44).

Pour Bober, au contraire, la judéité est signe d'appartenance: "être juif pour lui (Bober)", continue Perec dans *Ellis Island*..., "c'est continuer à s'insérer dans une tradition, une langue, une culture, une communauté que ni les siècles de la diaspora ni le génocide systématique de la "solution finale" n'ont réussi à définitivement broyer" (p. 45). Ellis Island devient ainsi le lieu concret et à la fois symbolique de rencontre de ces différentes expériences par rapport aux origines. Il s'agit d'un "non-lieu", d'un "lieu de mémoire potentielle", pour ceux qui sont "conscients de ne devoir leur vie qu'à l'errance et à l'exil".

Les propos de M. Gribomont (1995), concernant *Quoi de neuf ...* pourraient ainsi être élargis à tous ces textes: "On constate que le texte fait preuve de beaucoup de discrétion, de retenue, de non-dit. Systémati-quement, l'explication, la conclusion, l'épilogue, le fin mot d'une anecdote sont escamotés dans le récit. C'est le principal, le morceau de résistance qui fait défaut, c'est l'essentiel qui est tu".

Ces textes sont en effet reliés par des stratégies communes au niveau de l'écriture et de l'approche des sujets traités, construisant par là une esthétique spécifique que l'on pourrait nommer "de la discrétion". Ainsi, les questions essentielles ne sont jamais nommées de face—mémoi-re, anéantissement, mort, vie, survie—sont obsessionnellement présentes partout, de manière biaisée, lacunaire, impliquant par là le lecteur, obligé de combler les lacunes, les non-dits des textes.

Au centre de cette esthétique de la discrétion nous retrouvons, comme le remarque Gribomont (*op.cit.*), l'ellipse, figure omniprésente dans *Quoi de neuf...*: "[ce livre] parle de la guerre en évitant soigneusement d'en parler, car si le caractère d'indicibilité de la tragédie des Juifs y est évident, jamais les causes de cette indicibilité ne sont abordées".

Or, c'est l'ellipse que nous retrouvons aussi au centre de *W...*, de Perec: dans ce livre qui alterne récit romanesque / souvenirs d'enfance, le chapitre central est remplacé par une page blanche avec trois points de suspension (...). Après cette coupure, correspondante à un chapitre autobiographique, la fiction change, et on passe sans explication aucune, de la promesse d'un récit d'aventures à la vision brutale du cauchemar des habitants de l'île de W. Dans les chapitres proprement autobiographiques, assemblage de souvenirs d'un enfant pendant la guerre, celle-ci apparaîtra à peine comme toile de fond d'un récit fait de

> souvenirs fugaces ou tenaces, futiles ou pesants, mais que rien ne rassemble. [...] Ce qui caractérise cette époque c'est avant tout son absence de repères: les souvenirs sont des morceaux de vie arrachés au vide. Nulle amarre. Rien ne les ancre, rien ne les fixe. (W, p. 93-94).

Curieusement, seul les chapitres romanesques pourront désigner, dans ce livre, de manière détournée, en la transposant à un univers sportif, la vérité de l'horreur qui est à la base de toute la recherche autobiogra-phique, mais que celle-ci n'arrive jamais à désigner/intégrer directement.

L'efficacité de cette écriture elliptique se construit à travers deux facteurs essentiels et particulièrement riches au niveau de la production du sens: la fragmentation et la démultiplication des voix. Il s'agit toujours d'assemblages de bribes d'histoires, de souvenirs, de témoignages, d'images, que les narrateurs/metteurs en scène se gardent bien de relier et d'interpréter, laissant ce travail aux destinataires des œuvres; ils se limitent à présenter les matériaux, à suggérer quelques mises en rapport, sans jamais tomber dans le piège de l'homogène, du fini, du total.

C'est ainsi qu'à la bande sonore de *Récits d'Ellis Island*, constituée par l'entrecroisement des fragments de voix/souvenirs de ceux qui sont passés par "l'île des larmes" avec la réflexion des auteurs sur leur propre démarche, correspondent des images, des fragments des lieux actuellement vides, désertés, alternant avec de vieilles photos du temps où ces lieux étaient pleins. Le tout mélange passé et présent, et intégrant les histoires individuelles dans un mouvement collectif. Ce morcellement de voix et de souvenirs, qui constitue aussi bien la liste de *Je me souviens* que la structure de *W...*, avec son alternance inexorable de fictions et souvenirs "inextricablement liés", est également à la base de *Quoi de neuf...*, où chaque chapitre est assumé par un narrateur différent qui y déploie des fragments d'histoires/souvenirs hétérogènes et toujours lacunaires, puisque c'est justement ce qui est commun, ce qui relie toutes les histoires qui n'est jamais désigné.

Robert Bober et Georges Perec apparaissent alors comme des "gardiens" de souvenirs hétérogènes qui finiront par construire leur propre identité. Ils sont à la fois oreilles attentives et voix critiques qui interrogent ces voix plurielles en quête de vérités jamais énoncées ou de réponses soigneusement tues.

Ces recherches d'identité et de mémoire ne peuvent se faire que par le langage de l'art: ainsi Raphael, le narrateur de *Quoi de neuf...* devient photographe, malgré la conscience de la difficulté "d'être dans l'événement, le vivre et en même temps le regarder, le fixer sur pellicule", et il essaye de "faire des photos fortes qui peut-être témoigneront des malheurs du monde"(p. 222-223). Un autre personnage du livre, José, découvre sa vocation d'écrivain au moment où un commissaire de police—celui qui avait fait déporter ses parents pendant la guerre—lui refuse sa demande de naturalisation:

> Il faut que je vous dise que mon identité vous êtes en train
> de me la donner...soudain j'éprouve, grâce à vous, un

immense désir: celui d'écrire. Oui, monsieur le commissaire, j'écrirai pour devenir écrivain... J'écrirai pour dire que vous n'avez pas réussi à tout anéantir puisque je suis vivant, là, devant vous, avec mon projet d'écrire. (p. 111-112).

Quant à Perec, il dira très clairement dans *W...*, que "le projet d'écrire mon histoire s'est formé presqu'en même temps que mon projet d'écrire" (p. 41) et toute sa recherche au niveau de l'écriture sera une entreprise vitale, inséparable de la recherche au niveau du souvenir: "J'écris: j'écris parce que nous avons vécu ensemble, parce que j'ai été un parmi eux, ombre au milieu de leurs ombres, corps près de leur corps; j'écris parce qu'ils ont laissé en moi leur marque indélébile et que la trace en est l'écriture: leur souvenir est mort à l'écriture; l'écriture est le souvenir de leur mort et l'affirmation de ma vie"(p. 59).

Il s'agit d'une écriture fondée sur le manque, sur le vide, qui remplit, dans le cas de Perec, la triple fonction de moteur, thème et structure textuelle (Benabou, *ibid.*): dans tous les cas il s'agit d'écrire avec le vide, l' indicible, de faire vie à partir du manque autobiographique qui constitue le sujet. Cela consistera aussi bien à rechercher de souvenirs inexistants au départ, comme dans *W...* ou *Je me souviens*, qu'à écrire un roman en se privant d'une lettre de l'alphabet, comme dans *La Disparition*. Les recherches formelles de Perec sont en effet inséparables de l'écriture autobiographique et ce lien, dans la mesure où il mène à l'intégration des expériences personnelles dans un "cadre littéraire spécifique" (Benabou, *op.cit.*), lui permet de construire une identité, entendue comme "ce qui fait qu'il est à la fois lui et identique à l'autre" (*Ellis Island*: 45) [6]

L'efficacité pragmatique des œuvres de Perec comme de celles de Bober vient ainsi, au départ, de cette maîtrise de la discrétion, d'un équilibre entre silence et parole, travaillé de manière à provoquer la mémoire, les affects et l'adhésion du lecteur / spectateur, ce qui a comme effet, selon la juste formule d'Eric Beaumatin (1990), que ces œuvres "ne permet(tent) pas qu'on les interroge sans s'interroger".

Maria Eduarda Keating
Braga

---

[6] On ressent d'ailleurs la fascination pour cette recherche "oblique" de Perec sur l'identité dans le livre de Bober, qui intègre plusieurs traits - et emprunts textuels - perequiens dans son roman.

Bibliographie

Beaumatin, E., 1990, "L'homme et l'œuvre ou comment en sortir", *Mélanges, Cahiers Georges Perec*, n° 4, Limoges, éditions du Limon.

Benabou, M., 1985, "Perec et la judéité", *Cahiers Georges Perec*, n°1, Paris, P.O.L.

Benabou, M., Pouilloux, J.-Y., ed., 1988, *W ou le souvenir d'enfance: une fiction*, Textuel, 21, Paris.

Bober, R., 1993, *Quoi de neuf sur la guerre?*, Paris, P.O.L.

Bober, R., Perec, G., 1980, *Récits d'Ellis Island*, Paris, Ed. du Sorbier.

Gribomont, M., 1995, "Quoi de neuf sur la guerre?, de Robert Bober", *La littérature des camps: la quête d'une parole juste, entre silence et bavardage*, Les Lettres Romanes (hors série).

Lejeune, Ph., 1991, *La mémoire et l'oblique*, Paris, P.O.L.

Perec, G., 1975, *W ou le souvenir d'enfance*, Paris, Denoel.

Perec, G., *Je me souviens*, Paris, Hachette.

Perec, G., 1989, *l'infra-ordinaire*, Paris, Seuil.

Perec, G., 1990, *Je suis né*, Paris, Hachette.

Théâtre de l'enfermement

Les atrocités des régimes totalitaires dans les années trente et quarante du vingtième siècle ont abondamment inspiré la littérature de plusieurs pays. Ce filon thématique est loin de s'épuiser. Parmi les ouvrages littéraires sur les camps de concentration et/ou d'extermination, sur les prisons et les ghettos, une place particulière est prise par les pièces de théâtre, puisque l'objectif en est non seulement de décrire mais aussi de montrer sur scène les situations dans lesquelles se trouvent confrontés les victimes et les bourreaux.

Les auteurs des pièces dont l'action est située dans ces lieux d'enfermement ont souvent recours au procédé du théâtre dans le théâtre ou spectacle dans le spectacle (*play within a play, Spiel im Spiel*), afin d'obtenir un effet de contraste entre la réalité tragique que vivent les personnages de la pièce "extérieure" et le caractère du spectacle qu'ils donnent. Ce procédé n'est pas nouveau. Déjà Cervantes y recourt, dans *Les bagnes d'Alger (Los baños de Argel)*: les prisonniers espagnols organisent la représentation d'une pièce pastorale de Lope de Rueda.

Ce genre d'ouvrages dramatiques abondent après la Deuxième Guerre Mondiale. Parmi les dizaines de pièces qui associent lieu d'enfermement et théâtre, nous en avons choisi trois, dont chacune se déroule dans un milieu différent.

C'est dans un camp de concentration allemand qu'est située la pièce en trois actes du dramaturge polonais Ireneusz Iredyński *La crèche moderne (Jaseɬka-moderne*, 1962). Sur l'ordre du commandant du camp, un groupe de huit prisonniers prépare le spectacle de la Nativité, dont la trame et les allusions (partisans, gendarmerie, agents secrets, visas, cinéma, généraux fomentant un attentat contre Hérode) ont été modernisées, tout en gardant le ton et le langage d'un mystère biblique. Parmi les personnages il y a d'un côté Marie, Joseph, l'Enfant (un adolescent de seize ans) et, de l'autre Hérode avec ses acolytes. Le prisonnier chargé de mettre en scène le spectacle prétend en avoir écrit le texte. Cependant le Commandant (qui, autrefois, était acteur dans le cabaret du prisonnier-metteur en scène) révèle que c'est lui qui en est l'auteur.

Au fur et à mesure des répétitions, le texte de la pièce sur le Nativité se désintègre, les interprètes perdent leur identité, ils échangent leurs rôles. Les répliques prononcées au cours des répétitions constituent la moitié de la pièce d'Iredyński, toutefois le spectacle n'aura pas lieu. Les chars de l'armée libératrice s'approchent, les gardes s'enfuient, nos acteurs sont parmi les derniers prisonniers qui restent encore dans le camp, avec le Commandant. Celui-ci abat, un par un, les membres de la troupe, avant de se suicider. Il épargne un seul, Hérode, un proxénète emprisonné pour meurtre. Ce dernier, resté seul, ramasse le casque du Commandant et le met sur sa tête—c'est l'image final de *La crèche moderne*.

Situé dans une réalité que connaissent les survivants de la Deuxième Guerre Mondiale, la pièce de l'auteur polonais a cependant un caractère métaphorique ou allégorique. L'une de ses idées principales est exprimé par le Commandant, dans la dernière scène:

> J'étais autrefois dans un pays étranger (...) où j'ai vu un garçon avec une crèche en carton et papiers de couleurs. (...) C'était une petite scène sur laquelle évoluaient les maladroites figurines en bois représentant Marie et Joseph, l'enfant Jésus et les bergers, Hérode dans un rouge manteau royal et la Mort telle que l'imaginaient les gens du Moyen Age: squelette avec la faux, une couronne sur la tête. Le garçon promenait sa crèche d'une maison à l'autre et, avec sa voix muée d'un enfant, il mettait en scène ce grand et vieux spectacle, il était Marie et Joseph, l'Enfant et Hérode, il était aussi la Mort. (...) Je regardais ce monde en plein jeu, ce monde en formation, je regardais ce petit démiurge à voix glapissante et j'étais bouleversé. (...) J'ai compris ce que cela voulait dire être dieu (...), un dieu conscient de sa divinité,

quand tous les autres ne sont que des voix de dieu, ses intonations. (...) Je voulais reconstituer ce divin mécanisme de la crèche. (...) J'attendais le jour où je pourrais me métamorphoser en dieu (...). Ce jour est arrivé et je commence à être dieu.

Le Commandant prononce cette tirade après avoir tué d'un coup de feu le Metteur en scène et avant d'abattre les autres prisonniers (sauf Hérode-le souteneur) et de se brûler la cervelle. Derrière la problématique psychologique du pouvoir et de la tyrannie, on perçoit la grande métaphore du théâtre du monde, exploitée par Calderón et Shakespeare, Panizza et Hofmannsthal. Dans la pièce d'Iredyński, ce théâtre du monde est réduit aux dimensions d'une crèche de Noël et présenté dans un lieu insolite.

Un autre lieu insolite pour la présentation du théâtre dans le théâtre est le ghetto, antichambre de la mort. Lieu où les nazis, dans plusieurs pays de l'Europe occupée, et parfois avec la complicité des collaborateurs locaux, erfermaient la population juive. Lieu qui, souvent, était pire qu'une prison.

L'exemple le plus représentatif d'une telle pièce de théâtre est *Ghetto* de l'auteur israélien Joshua Sobol (né à Tel-Aviv, en 1939). Créé à Haïfa en avril 1984, représenté, deux mois plus tard, à Berlin, *Ghetto* a connu un énorme succès: des dizaines de mises en scènes à travers le monde, surtout en Allemagne et en Autriche mais aussi en Suède, en Norvège, en Italie, en France, en Pologne, en Angleterre, en Lituanie, aux États-Unis, au Canada.

C'est un drame à caractère historique. L'endroit, les événements évoqués, les personnages principaux sont authentiques. Il s'agit de la vie du ghetto de Vilna (selon la graphie habituelle en français) ou Wilno, ville polonaise jusqu'à l'invasion germano-soviétique de septembre 1939, dont la population comprenait alors 66% de Polonais, 28% de juifs et quelques petites minorités (dont 1% de Lituaniens). A la suite du fameux pacte Ribbentrop-Molotov, Staline a offert Wilno à la Lituanie, alors indépendante, avant d'absorber cette petite république tout entière dans l'empire soviétique. Wilno fût baptisé Vilnius par les Lituaniens.[1] L'armée allemande entre dans Wilno en juin 1941 et dès le mois de septembre, la population juive se trouve entassée en enfermée dans le ghetto, avec 1 m² de surface habitable par personne. Les Lituaniens, bien que déçus par le fait qu'Hitler ne leur a pas accordé une autonomie plus large, collaborent massivement avec les nazis et constituent la force principale de la Gestapo; ils sont chargés particulièrement de l'extermination des juifs. Au moment où commence l'action de *Ghetto*, il ne reste à Wilno que seize mille juifs sur une communauté d'environ soixante-dix mille avant la guerre. La pièce évoque des événements survenus dans ce lieu clos, et cela jusqu'en août 1943, à quelques jours de la liquidation totale du ghetto. Ces événements sont présentés à travers l'histoire de son théâtre.

Le chef du ghetto de la part des SS, Hans Kittel, lui-même saxophoniste fanatique qui, avant la guerre, jouait dans des cabarets, voit d'un bon œil la création d'un théâtre. Ce projet est réalisé par le commandant juif du ghetto, Jacob Gens, ancien officier de l'armée lituanienne et originaire de Kaunas (Kovno), capitale de la Lituanie jusqu'en 1939. Les deux piliers du théâtre sont la chanteuse Chaja ou Hayah (dans la vie Luba Lewicka) et le marionnettiste Srulik. Les avis étaient partagés, dans la communauté juive, sur l'opportunité de créer un théâtre dans les conditions de l'époque. La première réaction de Srulik est: "Ce n'est pas le moment de faire du théâtre". "On ne fait pas de théâtre dans un cimetière", était le slogan diffusé par le bibliothécaire et chroniqueur du ghetto de Wilno, le bundiste Hermann Kruk. "Faire du théâtre ici, en ce moment, c'est une honte!", jette-t-il à Gens. Celui-ci réplique, en s'adressant directement aux acteurs:

---

[1] Vilnius est aujourd'hui le nom officiel de cette ville qui reste toutefois imprégnée de culture polonaise et juive. Les graphies Wilno (Vilno) et Wilna (Vilna) existent dans les textes depuis le XIVe siècle et sur toutes les cartes géographiques de cette région de l'Europe dont l'une des plus anciennes et des plus connues, celle d'Ortelius, date de 1570. Les Polonais qui, malgré les déportations, l'exode forcé, la lituanisation et la russification, constituent encore 20% de la population de la ville, l'appellent toujours Wilno. Pour les juifs, dispersés dans le monde, c'est toujours Wilna ou Wilnè. En français, on utilisait la forme Vilna ou Wilna. Notons qu'Henri Reyle, officier de l'armée napoléonienne, qui y a séjourné en 1812, employait la graphie Wilna aussi bien dans ses lettres que dans son journal intime. Et que Romain Gary qui, dans son roman *Éducation européenne*, décrit la période de l'occupation 1942-1943, parle de la Résistance polonaise, du sort des juifs, évoque "le soulèvement des juifs dans le ghetto"—n'emploie que le nom de Wilno.

Nous traversons actuellement une période terrible et je crois que vous êtes les seuls, vous, les comédiens juifs, à pouvoir nous aider à la supporter. Regardez autour de vous. Vous ne verrez que des têtes baisées. Les gens n'ont plus aucune dignité. Vous devez les aider à fortifier leur moral, à reprendre confiance en eux-mêmes, à faire en sorte que chacun se sente redevenir un homme, avec un langage, une culture, un héritage dont nous devons être fiers. Au travail, Srulik. Commence les répétitions.

Voici comment Joshua Sobol rapporte, dans un texte documentaire qui accompagne l'édition française de *Ghetto*, la deuxième représentation de la pièce: "Cette fois, les opposants restèrent silencieux, bien que parmi les invités il y eût des officiers allemands et lituaniens comme l'officier nazi Herring et le commandant des milices lituaniennes de l'Ypatinga, responsables du massacre de dizaines de milliers de juifs à Ponary."

Avec le temps, même l'intransigeant Kruk change d'avis. Il dit à la chanteuse Chaja qui se décide à quitter le ghetto pour rejoindre la lutte armée: "Moi aussi, avant, je pensais comme vous. (...) Maintenant, je vois les choses autrement. (...) Le théâtre et toutes les autres formes d'activités culturelles de ce ghetto font partie de notre combat pour rester des êtres humains."

Les spectacles que l'on voit sur la scène "intérieure" ne sont que des numéros de chansons, de music-hall ou de marionnettes. Cependant le spectacle final, qui constitue la dernière scène de la pièce de Sobol, est une métaphore tragique. Voici quelques fragments des didascalies:

D'un tas de vêtements, plusieurs costumes se soulèvent: un costume de hasside, un costume de femme, suivis d'autres. Ils se mettent debout comme s'ils étaient portés par des personnages invisibles. Aucune tête ni aucune main ne sort. Les costumes se mettent à chanter. Pendant que les comédiens chantent et dansent, l'uniforme d'un officier allemand se soulève du tas. Il manipule une marionnette dont les vêtements rappellent ceux de Gens. (...) Tout en dansant, un couple découvre une armoire. Mais c'est en réalité un tabernacle recouvert d'une étoffe de velours sur laquelle sont brodés les dix commandements. (...) Les costumes courent vers l'échelle qui descend du tabernacle, et commencent à monter. Ils ouvrent la porte du

tabernacle et en font sortir une Torah qu'ils jettent sur le
tas de vêtements. Tous se pressent sur l'échelle pour entrer
dans le tabernacle. (...) L'uniforme les suit et disparaît avec
eux. Les portes du tabernacle se referment.

Le SS Kittel n'apprécie pas cette satir. A la fin de la
scène Kittel s'écarte du groupe, lève sa mitraillette et les
fauche tous d'une longue rafale. Ils tombent. Seuls Srulik et
la marionnette (...) restent debout. Srulik porte encore un
uniforme semblable à celui de Kittel. Kittel semble faire face
à son double. La marionnette continue à chanter. Kittel tire
sur la marionnette qui s'effondre lentement. Les lumières
s'éteignent.

Comme dans *La crèche moderne* d'Iredyński, c'est la fin d'un
théâtre, même si le marionnettiste Srulik se relève. Il est le seul survivant
de la troupe. L'effet du théâtre dans le théâtre est renforcé, dans la scène
finale, par un jeu de miroirs: les deux chefs du ghetto, juif et allemand,
affrontent leurs sosies sur le plateau intérieur. Et c'est Srulik-Kittel qui
en sortira vivant.

Passons de l'univers concentrationnaire nazi à l'univers concentrationnaire communiste, avec la pièce en quatre actes et douze tableaux
d'Alexandre Soljénitsyne, *Le naïf et la fille du bagne* (troisième partie de
la trilogie dramatique *L'année 1945*), pièce rédigée en 1954 et publiée en
1969. Notons qu'il s'agit du premier ouvrage littéraire important du futur
prix Nobel, écrit lorsqu'il a été assigné à résidence au Kazakhstan, après
huit ans de Goulag. Le titre original de la pièce, *Olen i chalachovka*, est
difficile à traduire. Il se rapporte aux deux personnages principaux. *Olen*
signifie cerf, mais au figuré un homme naïf qui se laisse tromper.
Chalachovka est un terme particulier qu'on a cru nécessaire d'expliquer
même dans l'édition russe: "prisonnière de camp, de mœurs légères, prête
à faire l'amour dans des conditions faciles." La "fille du bagne" c'est
Liouba Breslavskaïa, vingt-deux ans, enfant de koulaks déportés et morts
en Sibérie, mariée à deux reprises (la première fois à l'âge de quatorze
ans), condamnée à dix ans d'internement pour "propagande antisovié-
tique" amenée à se prostituer pour survivre dans les camps. Le "naïf", un
homme "aux mains pures", c'est Gleb Nerjine, ex-militaire qui avait
d'abord servi dans la cavalerie, et ensuite a passé quatre ans au front.
Arrivé au grade de capitaine (comme Soljénitsyne), il est arrêté avant la fin
de la guerre (à nouveau comme Soljénitsyne).

L'action se déroule à l'automne 1945. Parmi les différents lieux du Goulag, l'auteur choisit pour le neuvième tableau ("La représentation") une pièce attenante à la salle des fêtes où les prisonniers donnent un spectacle. Au programme, une farce *L'Allemand stupide* avec, comme personnages, un officier allemand et son ordonnance, une vieille femme russe, sa fille, résistante, et son petit-fils. On doit jouer aussi la pièce d'Alexandre Ostrovski, classique du théâtre réaliste russe, *Les loups et les brebis* (1875). Par la porte ouverte nous parviennent des fragments de la farce, on entend l'orchestre, les chansons, beaucoup d'applaudissements, on entend aussi quelques répliques de la pièce d'Ostrovski répétées par les acteurs-prisonniers.

Cette scène est l'occasion d'un rapprochement entre Liouba et Nerjine qui déclare son amour à la jeune fille. Au tableau suivant, après une semaine de liaison amoureuse et devant la menace du transfert des prisonniers dans d'autres camps, Liouba, courtisée depuis longtemps par le médecin de Goulag, propose à Nerjine: "Nous pouvons rester ici tous les deux! Nous pouvons même nous aimer à condition d'être très, très prudents. Seulement promets-moi... dis-moi que tu acceptes... de me partager. Avec le docteur." Nerjine refuse. Et dans la scène finale on voit Liouba frapper à la prote de la "cabine personnelle" du docteur, tandis que le "naïf", victime d'un accident de travail (ou d'une vengeance), est en train de lutter contre la mort.

Si, dans la pièce de Soljénitsyne, le théâtre dans le théâtre dérive de son expérience personnelle, s'il constitue un témoignage véridique de l'ancien prisonnier, les pièces intérieures ne sont pas en relation directe avec l'intrigue de la pièce extérieure. Sauf, peut-être, le titre de la comédie de mœurs d'Ostrovski, *Les loups et les brebis*, qui peut symboliser les rapports entre les deux catégories d'individus vivant dans le camp, même si cette division ne correspond pas toujours à celle entre surveillants et prisonniers.

Mon dernier exemple présente une réapparition de la thématique sous une forme assez surprenante. C'est dans une pièce post-soixante-huitarde, "fable" satirique de René Ehni, *Super-positions* (1970), qui se déroule pendant les répétitions d'un spectacle pornographique, spectacle "marxiste, tendance cul", que nous trouvons une admirable page sur *Hamlet* représenté dans un camp de concentration. Un ancien déporté y relate son expérience personnelle:

Oui, en cette aventure où nous fûmes, (...) il y avait pour maintenir, le théâtre. Ce théâtre était fait de quatre planches: nous montions sur ce radeau et nous disions à nos bourreaux: 'Nous sommes vivants, vous essayez de nous avilir, mais nous sommes vivants, regardez bien: un homme, des hommes refusent les ténèbres, refusent...' Nous avons joué Hamlet. Voyez-vous, Hamlet est une pièce admirable. (...) Nous jouions dans nos tenues rayées. Et cet homme mort depuis des siècles n'avait pensé qu'à nous en écrivant, nous des ténèbres, nous 'sous-hommes': 'Danemark est une prison...' (...) J'étais Hamlet. Il est le seul qui n'accepte pas son rôle. (...) Je disais distinctement le texte et autour de notre radeau ceux qu'on avait décidé 'larves' changeaient: ils refusaient le rôle imposé par le bourreau, ils sortaient de notre théâtre, ah, théâtre cette cabane! des hommes. La race des seigneurs n'était plus dans les miradors.

Le Danemark est une prison. La cour de Danemark est une prison au second degré. *Le meurtre de Gonzague,* joué devant la cour, est donc un spectacle donné dans une prison. Théâtre dans le théâtre, prison dans la prison, c'est chez Shakespeare que l'on trouve l'archétype d'une structure abyssale: théâtre de l'enfermement à la puissance deux.

Tadeusz Kowzan
Caen

Testimony of a Persecuted Romanist: on Victor Klemperer's Diaries

On the third of June, 1920, Victor Klemperer, who was thirty-eight years old then, delivered his inaugural speech at the *Technische Hochschule Dresden*, celebrating his appointment there as "Professor der Romanistik", professor of Romance languages and literatures. Although he had enjoyed the support of his teacher, the famous and very influential Karl Vossler, he had not succeeded in obtaining an appointment at one of the major German universities. This had much to do, as he had reason to assume, with the fact that he was a Jew.

He held his professorship in Dresden until April 1935, when, as a Jew, he was "pensioned off." His dismissal came rather late. Most "retirements" of Jewish professors took place in the first half of 1933. Klemperer enjoyed some respite because he was the bearer of a War Cross and because he was married to what in the unsavory jargon of the period was known as an Aryan woman.[1]

In 1996 *Aufbau Verlag* in Berlin published Klemperer's *Diaries* (*Tagebücher*) 1918-1932, two volumes superbly edited by Walter Nowojski. They deal with the years after the Great War and the period of the

---

[1]   For the early aryanization of the German universities see Friedländer, 1997:49-60.

Weimar republic. His *Tagebücher 1933-1945: Ich will Zeugnis ablegen bis zum letzten*[2] had already been published in 1995. They had made Klemperer famous outside the circle of Romanists and the many admirers of *LTI: Notizbuch eines Philologen*,[3] an analysis of the discourse and "newspeak" of National Socialism. The *Diaries* of the Nazi era take their title from the words written down on June 11, 1942; again and again they are repeated or restated in similar terms, as times get harsher. As he wrote his diaries, Klemperer was fully aware of the risks he was taking in reporting and storing what was happening around him. Still, to write them was his duty, as he more than once tells us. Besides, the work kept him alert and, according to his own confession, it sometimes allowed him to indulge in his vanity.

In this paper I want to single out from these diaries some aspects of Klemperer's study of French literature and his other intellectual activities during the twelve years of the Third Reich, a period of permanent danger, humiliation, worries about money and—later on—of poor housing, hunger, hard labour and the constant threat of death. In the light of such circumstances it might seem frivolous or a mark of professional myopia to focus on literature and literary history; yet in doing so I follow the example of Victor Klemperer, who dedicated every single moment he could spare from his housekeeping and, later on, from his forced labor and the eternal quest for food, to his favorite pastimes: reading, writing, and study.[4] On the last day of 1944, confronted with the necessity to dispel the permanent fear of death, he notes: "Bestes Mittel dafür ist Versenkung ins Studium, so tun, als hätte das Stoffspeichern wirklich Zweck" ("The best remedy is to give oneself over to study, to act as if the collecting of materials were of any use" II/2: 634).[5]

At first Klemperer worked on a history of French literature in the eighteenth century ("mein dixhuitième" as he called it);[6] then, when all possibilities for systematic scholarly work had been taken away from him,

[2] "I will give testimony until the end."

[3] "LTI: (*Lingua Tertii Imperii*) Notebook of a Literary Scholar".

[4] For other aspects of Klemperer's chronicle see the collection of Hannes Heer.

[5] All translations from the German are mine.

[6] The first volume of this history was published in 1954 and is dedicated to his wife Eva. The second volume appeared, posthumously, in 1966.

he occupied himself with his *Vita* and the notes for his *LTI*. During all this time he kept working on his Diaries.

Before further discussing the Nazi period I will shortly consider the diaries of the Weimar period. In these he comments in an intelligent, amusing and mostly open-minded way on his intellectual, social, political, economic and personal life. Central in this personal life is his wife Eva, born in 1881 as Eva Schermer, a musicologist and pianist who at an early age began to suffer from chronic illness, a combination of rheumatic pains and neurological complaints which in the long run obliged her to give up her career. Later, their love and solidarity were to culminate in Eva's resolute anti-nazi stance and her loyalty to her husband, which forced her to share most of the humiliations, the poverty, the bad housing and the hunger of the German Jewry.

Klemperer, so we learn from his *Tagebücher*, obtained his nomination at the *Technische Hochschule* after Ernst Robert Curtius, the first selected candidate, had declined. His inaugural speech was entitled "Gang und Wesen der französischen Literatur" ("Course and Character of French Literature"). He dedicated this lecture to his teacher Vossler, although he had often strongly disagreed on Vossler's exclusively aesthetic-linguistic approach to literature—an approach he once characterized as "reine Formlehre und Aesthetik" ("pure formalism and aestheticism"; *Tagebücher* 2.25.19; I/1: 79). Klemperer's own work joined an interest in the aesthetic qualities of literature to a historical and more psychological approach ("nicht nur aesthetisch, sondern auch menschlich": 3.28.19; I/1: 89). One can read these words also as a kind of program for his wartime diaries, where aesthetic interest always goes together with a humanist and human concern. His scholarly dispute with Vossler led to several, sometimes rather personal, conflicts with his former teacher. Vossler and his favorite Eugen Lerch spoke condescendingly about Klemperer's "Psychologie" or even "Seelenriecherei" ("soul-scenting": 3.10.24; I/1: 794).[7]

During his Dresden years Klemperer continued to look for a chair at a more prestigious university. When, in 1926, he probed his chances for an appointment at the so-called liberal university of Cologne, the Anglicist Herbert Schöffler wrote to him:

---

[7]   For an evaluation of Klemperer's work as a Romanist see Nerlich 1997.

> Nach zwei 'jüdischen' Berufungen würde eine dritte schwer
> sein. Ich stellte für mich die Unterscheidung auf: Es gibt
> reactionäre u. liberale Universitäten. Die reactionären
> nehmen keine Juden; die liberalen haben immer schon zwei
> Juden u. nehmen keinen dritten. (12.26.26; I/2: 312)

> After two 'Jewish' appointments a third one would be difficult.
> For myself I developed this distinction: There are two kinds of
> universities: the reactionary and the progressive one. The
> reactionary ones don't engage any Jews; the progressive ones
> already have two Jews and will not take a third one.

At the same time he never could be completely sure what the real reasons
were. When in 1927 he was passed over at Hamburg, even for the third
place, he wrote in his diary:

> Ich bin also völlig ausgeschaltet. Es ist so unendlich bitter.
> Zumal ich mich immer wieder frage, ob es wirklich die force
> majeure des Antisemitismus ist, oder ob man doch die
> anderen für bedeutender hält als mich. (4.1.27; I/2: 325)

> So I'm completely ousted. It is so infinitely bitter. The more
> so because I always keep asking myself whether it is really
> the force majeure of anti-Semitism, or whether they actually
> judge the others weightier than me.

These are disturbing occurrences for a man who often had a low opinion
of himself, and whom I would characterize as prone to serious depressions.

Klemperer did not really think of himself as Jewish. In 1912 he had
been baptized into the Protestant Church. However, he was hardly a
religious person, not Protestant and certainly not Judaic. In the Great
War he had volunteered for the German army, and for his courageous
behavior he had been decorated with the Bavarian Cross—one of the
reasons why he considered himself a German and nothing else. Like many
Jews he was very proud of his wartime services to his country. But
Klemperer's self-image of a liberal and Protestant German did not prevent
him from being discriminated against as a Jew, and it surely did not stop
the Nazis from persecuting him.

The details of this persecution are contained in his diaries of the
Nazi era. I do not want to give a survey of or even a selection from what

he wrote there about his professional activities. What I will do is *confront* a number of passages, dedicated to his study and writing, with passages about the bare facts of everyday life, in order to show to what extent his scholarly activity was really part of a strategy of survival.

From Michael Nerlich's collection of essays on French Studies in Germany (1977) we learn that since 1870 French studies had always been threatened and were often deemed politically suspect. In the Nazi period the Gymnasium education was reduced from nine to eight years. The teaching of French (and English) was substantially and disproportionally reduced (Kroymann and Ostermann, 1977:155). French and other languages, already a side activity at the *Technische Hochschule*, lost much of their importance there during the Nazi years and were completely dropped in 1942. The content of secondary and academic education was laid down in government rules. In scholarly publications of the period we find a stress on (French) leadership (for instance the Nordic Jeanne d'Arc as a leader against the English), literature about colonies (Nazi Germany badly wanted to have colonies of its own), and racist publications such as "Frankreich und die Rassenfrage" or editions of the French racist novelist Arthur de Gobineau.

In the first year of the Hitler regime Klemperer still had some reviews published, but journals soon began to hesitate or refuse to take contributions from Jewish scholars. In the same early period of nazism Oskar Walzel asked Klemperer's cooperation in editing his *Romanische Literaturgeschichte*, which was rather a courageous act on Walzel's part, even though he also suggested that Italian literature (which Klemperer had wanted to do himself) should be given to someone sympathetic to the new Italy.

Klemperer was soon disgusted by the philological journals and the *Zeitschrift des Hochschulverbandes* that used the new jargon in a way "daß jede Seite Brechreiz verursacht" ("that every page makes one want to vomit" 10.23.33; II/1: 63). Time and again he makes it clear how, from their first days of power, the Party and the government were driven by hatred against "intellectualism", culture and humanistic education. He quotes the words of the Minister of Education, Reichsminister Bernhard Rust, who, in April 1935, speaks about the victory over the "faden Intellektualismus" ("insipid intellectualism") and the priority to be given to "körperliche und charakterliche Fähigkeiten" ("physical and character education": 4.17.35; II/1: 192).

Even in the first year of the new regime Klemperer had been denied the right to examine students. In April 1935 he is dismissed from his post. His commentary is devastating:

> *30 April, Dienstag.* Ich habe einen besonderen koketten Ruhm darein gesetzt, heute eine Seite (Lesage/Marivaux) an meinem 18ième zu schreiben, heute wo ich kein Kolleg zu lesen brauche, weil ich durch die Post meine Entlassungs-urkunde erhielt. (30.4.35; II/1: 195)

> *April 30, Tuesday.* I considered it my coquettish honor to write a page today (Lesage/Marivaux) for my *18ième*, now that I do not need to lecture today, as I received notice of my dismissal through the mail.

During the *Neuphilologenkongreß* in Dresden of October 1935—which he does not attend of course—personal and professional life converge or rather fail to do so:

> Einer sprach über die Religion der Germanen, einer über neusprachlichen Unterricht im nationalsozialistischen Sinn, nicht für 'Geist' und 'Kultur', sondern für 'den deutschen Menschen'. E. von Jan über Frankreichs 'nationale Symbole'—Nicht einer von all den romanistischen Kollegen hat mich aufgesucht; ich bin wie eine Pestleiche. (10.19.35; II/1: 223)

> One lectured about the religion of the ancient Germans, one about modern language teaching in the national socialist way, not for the good of the 'mind' and 'culture', but for 'the New German'. E. von Jan spoke about the 'national symbols' of France.—Not one of all the Romanist colleagues has visited me. I am like the corpse of a plague victim.

The interwovenness of public and private life, the casual way in which he connects the two; his penetrating irony and black humor—all of these characteristic features are present in the following "transit-passages", as I will call them, or transitions from one sphere of life to the other. On October 8, 1937, he writes:

> Das 'Reka', angesehenstes, bestes Warenhaus Dresdens, wurde im vorigen Jahr oder vor zwei Jahren entjudet. Jetzt

macht es Reklame für seinen 'Jubiläumsverkauf: 25 Jahre'. Gleichzeitig hat man auf alle Eingänge gemalt: 'Arisches Geschäft'.

Bei der ungemeinen Verzögerung durch die Grippe bin ich jetzt erst mit dem Morelly völlig druckfertig zu Ende. Nun liegen noch ein paar Tage Haller vor mir, und dann erhebt sich die noch ganz ungelöste Frage nach der Einteilung des Reststoffes. (10.9.37; II/1: 382)

The 'Reka', the most prestigious and best department store of Dresden, was freed from Jews last year or two years ago.[8] Now it advertises its 'Anniversary sale: 25 years'. At the same time signs have appeared at all entrances: 'Aryan Store'.

With the exceptional delay caused by the flue I have only now finished Morelly so that it is ready for press. I still have to work a few days on Haller, and then I will be faced with the yet unsolved question of how to organize the rest of the material.

It will be clear by now that "druckfertig" could only mean "ready for the press in a better future", a future in which most of the time he did not believe, thinking of himself as old and in poor health, and being pessimistic about a possible demise of the Third Reich. In fact, the publication of the Morelly chapter had to wait until 1966, six years after his death.

In the next quote social horror and professional worry add to one another:

[D]ie Zeitung täglich zum Kotzen—heute wieder ein Rasseschänderprozeß [...] Die Berichterstattung darüber stinkt förmlich nach ekelerregender Lüge.

Ich bin schwer deprimiert, da ich auf keine Weise die Weiterdisposition meines Buches finde. (10.29.37; II/1: 384)

The newspaper makes me vomit every day—today another process about interracial rape [...]. The information about it positively smells of nauseating lies.

---

[8] Fortunately the English has no equivalent for the Nazi-words "judenfrei" and "entjudet", both of which mean that either a property has been stolen from its Jewish owner, or, in the case of the deportations, that all the Jews have been "evacuated" from a town or city.

> I am gravely depressed, as I cannot figure out the further
> disposition of my book.[9]

At other times worries about life and work are more explicitly connected:

> Neulich ein Werbebericht der "Wach- und Schließgesell-
> schaft". Aufzählung ihrer Taten im letzten Jahr: x Dieb-
> stähle verhindert, x Brände verhindert, x Straftaten zur
> Anzeige gebracht, eine Rassenschändung.
>
> Im Dix-huitième: Parny ganz fertig; den gräßlichen Lebrun-
> Pindare vorbereitet.[...] Alles wird zu lang, und ich glaube
> ebenso wenig an das Ende dieses Opus wie an das Ende des
> dritten Reichs. (2.23.38; II/2: 398)

> Recently I saw an advertisement of the "House Protection
> Company". They summed up their results of last year:
> prevention of x thefts, prevention of x fires, x criminal
> offenses reported to the police; one interracial rape.

> In my *Dix-huitième*: Parny is completely finished; prepara-
> tory work has been done on the awful Lebrun-Pindare. [...]
> It is becoming far too extended, and I neither believe in the
> end of this work, nor in the end of the Third Reich.

On August 24, 1939, another measure was taken to further the isolation
of the Jews. A man had to take "Israel" as his second name, a woman
"Sara". This second name was obligatory in any official letter or document:

> Morgen die Maschinenreinschrift des Beaumarchais. Ich
> arbeite am Dix-huitième weiter aus reiner Verbohrtheit und
> ohne alle Hoffnung und Illusion. Ich, Victor Israel Klempe-
> rer. (8.24.39; II/1: 421).

> Tomorrow I will type out Beaumarchais in its definite
> version. I continue working on the *Dix-huitième* from pure
> stubbornness, and without any hope or illusion. I, Victor
> Israel Klemperer.

---

[9] The word "Rasseschänderprozeß" is not to be found in a decent dictionary, such as the Oxford
Duden or other post-war German dictionaries. According to the 1936 Nuremberg Laws, non-
Jewish persons who had a sexual engagement with a Jew, or vice versa, were guilty of "violence
against race." I opted for the anachronistic but plastic translation "interracial rape."

Literature as Cultural Memory

On December 2, 1938, Klemperer hears that he no longer can make use of any library facilities. This, to him, means a real "checkmate". The description of how he gets to hear the deeply humiliating and disastrous prohibition to use the library gives us an impression of Klemperer's human quality, and also of some decent behavior on the other side:

> Gestern nachmittag auf der Bibliothek der Ausleihbeamte [..] Ich solle doch mit ihm in das hintere Zimmer kommen. So hatte er mir vor einem Jahr das Verbot des Lesesaals angezeigt, so zeigte er mir jetzt das gänzliche Verbot der Bibliothek, also die absolute Mattsetzung an. Aber es war anders als vor einem Jahr. Der Mann war in fassungsloser Erregung, ich mußte ihn beruhigen. Er streichelte mir immerfort die Hand, er konnte die Tränen nicht unterdrücken. (12.3.39; II/1: 438-439)

> Yesterday afternoon in the library the lending official [...] I should come with him into the back room. In this way, a year ago, he had announced to me the ban on the use of the reading room; in this way he now announced to me the total ban on the library, that means absolute check-mate. But it was different from a year earlier. The man was in a state of bewildered excitement, I had to calm him down. All the time he kept stroking my hand, he could not keep back his tears.

Here, Klemperer the Romanist disappears from the stage for a period of seven years to return to the *Technische Hochschule* of Dresden only in the summer of 1945.[10]

Within a few days, however, he courageously changes his course and, using the diary notes of his early years, starts working on what he calls his *Vita*, his *Curriculum Vitae*. In the first war years he can still read professional books lent to him by friends, but no systematic work is possible any more. He starts reading more or less at random, copying passages and making notes on every book, including even the (often rather uncanonical) novels he daily reads to Eva. For years this has been their favorite pastime and it becomes their only recreation when they can no longer indulge in their passionate love for the cinema, where, from December 1939, Victor is no longer welcome.

---

[10]   Klemperer's re-appointment at the *Technische Hochschule* and his endeavor to upgrade this Polytechnic to a University are described in his 1945 diaries (1996b).

Soon he no longer dares to keep his old diaries, which he needs for his *Vita*, in the house. Writing a diary is now the only creative activity left to him. All the time intellectual work remains his chief remedy against the daily worries, humiliations and the fear of death, which comes home to him again through a report on his failing heart:

> Es erschüttert mich einigermaßen, es ist doch Todesgewiß-heit in sehr absehbarer Zeit [...] Es fällt mir schwer, so weiterzuarbeiten, als wenn mir Zeit bliebe, etwas zu vollenden. Aber Arbeiten ist das beste Vergessen. (3.15.43; II/2: 344)

> It shatters me to some degree, it means certain death within a really short time. [...] I find it difficult to continue working this way, as if there were time left to finish my work. But working is the best way to forget.

From 1941 on, there was the everyday threat of a house search by the Gestapo. One should read the diary entry for of May 22, 1942, to realize on the one hand how thorough, humiliating and threatening a house search can be and, on the other hand, how important his writing was to him. The policemen spat and kicked; they called Eva a *Judenhure*; they stole or even senselessly destroyed the food that had been bought with the scarce ration coupons. The result is appalling:

> Zerrissene Spielkarten, Puder, Zuckerstücke, einzelne Medikamente, Inhalt von Nähkästen dazwischengestreut und eingetreten: Nadeln, Knöpfe, Scherben zerschlagenen Weinachtsschmucks, Pastillen, Tabletten, Zigarettenhülsen, Evas Kleidung, saubere Wäsche, Hüte, Papierfetzen —inextrikabel. [..] Aber das griechische Lexikon mit den letzten Tagebuchseiten war unangetastet [..] Das Tage-buchmanuskript hätte mich fraglos das Leben gekostet. (II/2: 93-94).

> Playing cards, torn to pieces, powder, lumps of sugar, separate pieces of medicine, and the content of the sewing-boxes among them, everything leveled by their feet: needles, buttons, fragments of crushed christmas decorations, pas-tilles, pills, cigarette wrappings, Eva's clothes, clean underwear, hats, scraps of paper—inextricable. [..] But the Greek Lexicon which held the latest diary entries had not

been touched upon [...] The manuscript of the diary surely
would have cost me my life.

On June 1, 1942, he registers the fourth house search within 14 days. It
is mainly because of these house searches that Eva brought all of her
husband's manuscripts to the house of Annemarie Köhler, a physician in
the nearby town of Pirna. Annemarie was their main Aryan friend, who
took great personal risks in hiding the diaries. Every few days Eva transports the newly written diary pages to Annemarie. Eva and Annemarie
stand out as two courageous women, and courageous is also the best word
to describe Victor Klemperer's way of life. Discussing his diary notes he
often says: "This is my heroism: I have to tell what has happened".

In the winter of 1941-1942 Klemperer has to clean the streets from
snow, on several occasions.[11] From April 1943 on he is forced to work in a
herb-tea warehouse and in several paper and cardboard factories in Dresden, often on night shifts. Now Klemperer, who gets exhausted from his
work, even has to force himself to continue his diaries. Yet he never
considers giving up, notwithstanding the exhaustion, notwithstanding the
danger. More than ever the diaries stand for duty and solace.

Often it must have been a bitter solace, as on May 26, 1944, when
he mentions the authoritarian behavior of his overseer in the paper
factory in relation to the appointment of Fritz Neubert to a chair at the
University of Berlin, "diese vollkommenste Mittelmäßigkeit unter den
Romanisten meiner Generation" ("this complete mediocrity among the
Romanists of my generation". II/2: 479):

> Heute, nach langer Pause, wurde ich von Meister Hartwig
> wieder mal furchtbar angebrüllt. Er geht mir sehr auf die
> Nerven. 'Der letzte Mann'—ich denke an den Janningsfilm
> von dem zum Abortdiener degradierten großen Hotelcon-
> cierge. Und ich denke in solchen Momenten der Erniedri-
> gung daran, daß Neubert Ordinarius in Berlin ist. (5.26.44;
> II/2: 522)

> Today, for the first time since long, I was terribly shouted
> at by Master Hartwig. He makes me very nervous. 'Der

---

[11]   Martin Walser, in his novel *Die Verteidigung der Kindheit* (1991) stages a fictional meeting
between the shoveling Klemperer and a 12 year old boy. (Walser 1996: 20; Christmann 1993: 17).

letzte Mann'—I think of the movie with [Emil] Jannings about the concierge of a hotel who has been degraded to lavatory attendant. And at such moments of degradation I think of the fact that Neubert is the new full professor in Berlin.

On June 23, 1944, Klemperer is judged unfit to continue working. In one sense, he is not glad. As long as he had been working he was of some "use" to Germany. Now, more than ever, he has to fear the Gestapo. In another sense, he knows that they have put many useful workers on transport as well. He decides to put all his remaining energy into "real work" again, mainly to dispel the fear of death. On April 29, 1944, he makes a note of some rather disturbing interest for people concerned with Romance philology:

> In der 'Dresdener Zeitung' vom 26.4.44 geschwollenes Referat über die 'Fortsetzung der Vortragsreihe des Sprachamtes Sachsen'. (Dem Sprachamt und seinen Publikationen nachgehen!) [...] Entscheidender Satz: 'Im nationalsozialistischen Staat gilt die Sprache nicht mehr als ein Mechanismus, sondern sie wird erkannt und gewertet als Gestalt von eigenem Wesen, als Ausprägung des Seelen-tums der biologisch-geistigen Gemeinschaft Volk und Mensch'. Sieht man von dem Phrasenschwall ab, so will die neue Sprachphilosophie nichts anderes, als die 'idealisti-sche' Philologie, als Vossler, Spitzer, ich wollen. Nur: Sie *will* unwissenschaftlich sein. Sie will der Politik dienen. [...] Es handelt sich bei den Nationalsozialisten um bewußte Verdrängung und Versklavung der Wissenschaft. (4.29.44; II/2: 507).

> In the 'Dresdener Zeitung' of April 26, 1944, a swollen piece about the 'continuation of the series of lectures of the Language Institute Sachsen'. (Check the Language Institute and its publications!) [...] Most telling sentence: 'In the National Socialist state language is no longer considered a mechanism, but it is recognized and estimated as a struc-ture with its own essence, as the expression of the soul of the biological-spiritual community between the individual and his people'. Apart from the swollen phraseology the modern philosophy of language wants nothing else than the 'idealistic' philology, than Vossler, Spitzer and myself. Only:

this philosophy *wants* to be unscientific, to serve politics.[...]
In the case of the National Socialists the goal consists in the
intentional displacement and slavish repression of scholar-
ship.

Klemperer survived the war; he was never deported due to the fact that
he was married to an Aryan. Near the end of the war he nevertheless had
ample reason to believe that he too would be deported and gassed. Most of
the Jews still remaining in Dresden who were in similar circumstances
were scheduled for deportation from Dresden's Hauptbahnhof on
February 16, 1945. On February 13, Klemperer is ordered to bring around
letters to them. The letters read as orders for "Arbeitseinsatz", forced
labor, but those concerned understand that the real issue is a *Todes-
marsch*. In the evening of the same day he makes his last diary entry
written in Dresden, ending with the ominous words of Kurt Waldmann,
the superintendent of the house on 1-3 Zeughausstraße: "Da stecken
Mordabsichten dahinter [...] Sie werden sehen, ich behalte recht" ("There
is a murderous intention behind this [...] You will see that I am right":
II/2: 661).

The devastating bombardment of February 13 and 14, 1945, paradoxically destroyed the Central Station from where the Jews were to be
deported, thus saving the lives of the few remaining *Sternträger*. During
the bombing Victor was only lightly injured. He fled, tore off the hated
Star of David, and survived. On February 15 and 17, within two days of
the blitz, he writes a report of his flight to a shelter. The first sentence of
this entry reads: "Die erste Wonne war der Riesenkessel Nudelsuppe im
Schlafsaal" ("The first bliss was the huge cauldron of noodle soup in the
dormitory" 2.15/15.45; II/2: 673). Near the end of the same entry he
mentions his losses:

Alle meine Bücher, die Lexica, die eigenen Werke, *ein* Ma-
schinenexemplar des 18ième und des Curriculum. Geschieht
ein Unglück in Pirna, dann ist meine gesamte Arbeit seit
1933 vernichtet. [...] Das alles focht mich nicht übermäßig
an. Das Curriculum würde ich in knapperer und vielleicht
besserer Fassung wiederherstellen. (Bei der [Pearl] Buck
hat mir einmal ein Satz imponiert: 'Darauf zerriß sie alle
Modellzeichnungen, um nun frei gestalten zu können.') Nur
für die Sammlungen zur LTI wäre es ewig schade.—Sooft
ich an den Schutthaufen Zeughausstraße 1 und 3 dachte

und denke, hatte ich und habe auch ich das atavistische Gefühl: Jahwe! Dort hat man in Dresden die Synagoge niedergebrannt. (2.15/17.45; II/2: 674-675).

All my books, the lexicons, my own works, *one* typescript of my *18ième* and of the Curriculum. Should an accident happen in Pirna, then all my work since 1933 will be destroyed. [...] All these things did not trouble me extraordinarily. The Curriculum I would rewrite in a shorter and perhaps improved version. (In [Pearl] Buck I was once impressed by a sentence 'Then she tore up all the drawings to be able to design freely'.) Only for my *LTI*-collection it would be an eternal shame.—As often as I thought and think of the ruins of 1 and 3 Zeughausstraße, I had and have the atavistic feeling: Yahweh! It is there that they burnt down the synagogue in Dresden.

So in the first entry after the Inferno of Dresden the Romanist musings of Klemperer are marked by the Joy of Food and a Jewish atavism connected to his work; by the joy of life and the reluctant recognition of his Jewishness.

Although in his earlier life Klemperer had been fiercely anti-communist and had often equated communism with National Socialism he came to believe in the positive potential of the GDR and communist society. He believed in the determination of the KPD ("Kommunistische Partei Deutschlands") to "muck out" ("ausmisten": Walser, 1996:47) the filth of fascism. He accepted a series of chairs at the East German universities of Dresden, Greifswald, Halle, and Berlin. In 1951 Dresden made him an honorary doctor of pedagogy. It was in this same city that Klemperer died on February 11, 1960.[12]

Jan van Luxemburg
University of Amsterdam

---

[12] For Klemperer's relations with the communist party see Greiner 1997.

Bibliography

Christmann, Hans Helmut. 1993. "Victor Klemperer und sein 'Curriculum vitae'." In: Andreas Kablitz and Ulrich Schulz-Buschhaus. *Literaturhistorische Begegnungen: Festschrift zum sechzigsten Geburtstag von Bernhard König.* Tübingen: Gunter Narr. 17-28.

Friedländer, Saul. 1997. *Nazi Germany and the Jews.* Volume I: *The Years of Persecution 1933-1939.* New York: Harper Collins.

Greiner, Bernd. 1997. "'Zwiespältiger denn je'. Victor Klemperers Tagebücher im Jahr 1945." In: Heer, ed.: 144-151.

Heer, Hannes, ed. 1997. *Im Herzen der Finsternis: Victor Klemperer als Chronist des NS-Zeit.* Berlin: Aufbau.

Klemperer, Victor. 1947. *LTI: Notizbuch eines Philologen.* Berlin: Aufbau.

Klemperer, Victor. 1954 and 1966. *Geschichte der franzözischen Literatur im 18. Jahrhundert.* Two vols. Berlin: Deutscher Verlag der Wissenschaften.

Klemperer, Victor. 1969. [1947]. *LTI: Die unbewältigte Sprache.* München: Deutscher Taschenbuch Verlag.

Klemperer, Victor. 1989. *Curriculum Vitae: Jugend um 1900.* Ed. Walter Nowojski. Two vols. Berlin: Siedler.

Klemperer, Victor. 1995. *Ich will Zeugnis ablegen bis zum letzten: Tagebücher 1933-1945.* Ed. Walter Nowojski. Two vols. Berlin: Aufbau.

Klemperer, Victor. 1996a. *Leben sammeln, nicht fragen wozu und warum: Tagebücher 1918-1932.* Ed. Walter Nowojski. Two vols. Berlin: Aufbau.

Klemperer, Victor. 1996b. *Und so is alles schwankend: Tagebücher Juni bis Dezember 1945.* Ed. Walter Nowojski. Two vols. Berlin: Aufbau.

Kroymann, Maren and Dorothea Ostermann. 1977. "Beitrag zur Untersuchung des Französischunterrichts von 1914-1945". In: Nerlich ed.: 144-167.

Nerlich, Michael, ed. 1977. *Kritik der Frankreichforschung: 1871-1975.* Karlsruhe: Argument.

Nerlich, Michael. 1997. "Victor Klemperer Romanist oder Warum soll nicht einmal ein Wunder geschehen?". In: Heer ed.: 35-48.

Walser, Martin. 1996. "Laudatio auf Victor Klemperer". In: *Literatur als Weltverständnis.* Eggingen: Isele. 19-58.

Les Écrits des prisonniers politiques

La prison politique a existé de tous temps, dans tous les Etats, mais la volonté de rendre témoignage sur sa réalité est un phénomène moderne. Il y a eu quelques textes à l'époque de la Révolution française, fragmentaires, mais aucune œuvre en soi. Le premier grand témoignage apparaît en 1832, lorsque Silvio Pellico publie *Le mie Prigioni,*[1] récit de ses dix années de détention à Venise d'abord, puis dans la forteresse du Spielberg. Ce livre bouleversa l'Europe et jusqu'à l'Amérique. Trente ans plus tard, un autre texte fondamental aura une aussi large audience lorsque Dostoïevsky écrira les *Souvenirs de la Maison des Morts.*[2] Le fait que tous deux aient été des écrivains connus avant leur arrestation a certainement eu une influence sur le retentissement de leur témoignage, mais avant tout leurs lecteurs recevaient le choc d'une réalité brutale qu'ils ignoraient, comme cent ans plus tard ceux de Soljénitsyne.

---

[1]   Pellico Silvio. 1832. *Le mie Prigioni,* Torino, Bocca. Nombreuses rééditions. Trad. française A. de Latour, Paris, Delahaye, 1853, et rééditions.

[2]   Dostoïevskij Fiodor Mikhaïlovič, *Zapiiski iz mertvogo ,* Bazounov, 1862, & *Sobranie socieninij v 10 toma,* Moskva, 1956. 1ère trad. française, Ch. Neyroud, 1866. Cf. trad. E. Mongault & L. Desormonts, in *Œuvres,* Paris, Gallimard, La Pléiade, 6 vol.1950-1972.

Pellico a choisi la forme d'un récit dépouillé à la première personne. Dostoïevsky a opté pour le roman, peut-être pour des raisons personnelles, mais principalement à cause de la censure, qui pouvait accepter un récit se présentant comme une fiction, mettant en scène des détenus de droit commun, mais non un témoignage direct sur le traitement des prisonniers politiques dans l'empire tsariste.

Depuis lors, l'extension mondiale de la prison politique a donné lieu à une très abondante littérature, dans toutes les langues. Qu'elle provienne d'Europe, d'Asie, d'Afrique ou des Amériques, elle a pris essentiellement trois formes: le texte littéraire, fiction ou témoignage direct, œuvre d'écrivains; le récit autobiographique sans aucune prétention littéraire, mais rédigé dans l'urgence de faire savoir la vérité; les lettres, notes, journaux intimes, inscriptions sur les murs des cellules, qui n'étaient pas, à l'origine, destinés à être publiés mais apportent leur confirmation aux autres textes et témoignent d'une très grande richesse humaine dans leur nudité.

Tous ces écrits reprennent les mêmes thèmes, et généralement dans le même ordre: l'arrestation (le choc initial, inoubliable, qui fait basculer toute une vie), les interrogatoires, la torture, la vie quotidienne de la prison ou du camp, les rapports des prisonniers entre eux, la solidarité ou la peur, les rapports avec les gardiens, la présence de la mort et les derniers messages avant l'exécution, la volonté de rester des hommes dans un univers totalement déshumanisé, la libération et, souvent, le difficile retour au monde extérieur.

Dans les prisons et les camps se reconstitue une société, avec ses lois propres et même son langage particulier, société inaccessible du dehors, fondée sur une violence constante faite à chaque individu en même temps qu'à chaque groupe qui la constitue. Une société où n'existent plus que deux catégories d'êtres: les maîtres dotés d'un pouvoir exorbitant, et les esclaves voués à l'obéissance absolue sous peine de perdre le seul bien qui leur soit encore concédé: la vie.

Les auteurs de ces textes s'expriment moins à titre personnel, pour raconter une aventure individuelle, que poussés par l'obligation morale de faire savoir ce qui s'est réellement passé, l'impérieux devoir de témoigner pour ceux qui ne sont pas revenus, d'être "la voix des hommes sans voix", des millions de victimes condamnées au silence.

La comparaison entre les textes fait apparaître une constante: la transposition littéraire ou romanesque devient impossible devant une telle expérience. Même ceux qui, comme Dostoïevsky, ont voulu en faire une fiction, ne sont pas parvenus à s'en détacher, et c'est la voix du détenu politique, et elle seule, qui s'exprime dans leurs pages. La construction, le style de *La Maison des Morts* sont très différents des autres romans de Dostoïevsky. Et l'auteur présumé de ce récit, présenté d'emblée comme un assassin qui a tué sa femme par jalousie, est sans doute le seul personnage dans l'œuvre de Dostoïevsky où abondent, même chez les plus purs, les sentiments de culpabilité, le seul qui se sente totalement innocent. La même impossibilité de transposer en fiction l'expérience carcérale se retrouve chez Soljénitsyne, Victor Serge, Primo Levi ou Jorge Semprun, pour ne citer que quelques exemples plus récents, parce que tous en sont obsédés. Et elle a si profondément et définitivement marqué leur vie qu'elle resurgit toujours, d'une manière détournée ou explicite, dans tous leurs autres romans. Le problème du mal, qui a hanté l'œuvre et la vie de Dostoïevsky, a son origine dans l'expérience du bagne. On retrouve cette hantise chez tous ceux qui sont passés par le même dramatique creuset.

Dans ce monde voué à la destruction, les détenus ont tenté non seulement de survivre, en préservant au maximum leur intégrité physique et morale, mais aussi de combattre l'entreprise d'anéantissement en développant dans la mesure du possible leurs facultés intellectuelles. Entre l'oisiveté totale des prisons et le travail forcé des camps, le principe de la répression politique a toujours tendu à "empêcher les cerveaux de fonctionner", selon le mot du procureur requérant au procès de Gramsci à Rome, en 1928. Le système de défense des détenus a été de faire fonctionner les cerveaux, en dépit de toutes les difficultés, de toutes les restrictions. Ce système de défense a été parfois raisonné, parfois spontané, mais il a toujours eu le même fondement, et il explique la volonté passionnée de connaissances qu'expriment aussi bien les récits que les lettres des détenus.

Dans la solitude de la ségrégation ou la promiscuité des camps, les prisonniers se sont tournés spontanément vers les grandes œuvres du passé pour y trouver une nourriture spirituelle et y puiser la force de résister à l'écrasement de "La Meule". Lorsque les œuvres étaient inaccessibles, ils les ont recherchées en eux-mêmes, faisant jaillir de leur mémoire cette "lecture intérieure" dont Dietrich Bonhoeffer parlait à propos de la musique.[3] La culture des prisons a souvent été une culture sauvage, désordonnée, au hasard des possibilités offertes, des rencontres. Mais elle a été une réalité vivante, essentielle, de cette expérience. Menacé dans son intégrité physique et morale, l'homme enfermé comprend mieux que tout autre ce que signifie l'héritage du passé, et comment ce passé peut se révéler le seul lien encore possible avec la communauté. La culture est source de vie, nourriture, stimulation créatrice pour l'esprit. Elle est une arme défensive, mais elle peut aussi devenir une arme offensive, comme lorsque Martchenko, qui n'avait trouvé qu'en prison le loisir de lire Marx, s'en est servi pour attaquer l'injustice de sa condamnation, embarrassant les autorités du camp.[4]

Mais si les grandes œuvres nourrissent les prisonniers et les aident à survivre, à leur tour ceux-ci redonnent à ces textes une vie, une jeunesse qui ne sont pas sans ouvrir des perspectives nouvelles. Ils sont rares les prisonniers politiques qui ne se sont pas souvenus du "Lasciate ogni speranza, voi ch'entrate" lorsqu'est retombée sur eux "la porte fermée de l'extérieur", et peut-être avec une vérité et une acuité que Dante lui-même n'avait pas prévues. Evguenia Guinzbourg, récitant de mémoire *Eugene Oneguine* dans le train qui la déportait en Sibérie, réussit à fasciner non seulement ses codétenues mais les gardes du convoi.[5] Louis Martin-Chauffier invoquant Mécène dans les vers latins des *Géorgiques* sous les coups de schlague d'un Kapo au camp de Neuengamme,[6] ou Primo Levi expliquant Ulysse et le Chant XXVI de *L'Enfer* à un jeune Alsacien à Auschwitz,[7] donnent eux aussi la mesure de la puissance d'une œuvre d'art dans une situation catastrophique. Le commentaire de Socrate écrit peu de jours avant son exécution, dans une lettre à sa fiancée, par le jeune

---

[3] Bonhoeffer Dietrich. 1970. *Widerstand und Ergebung*, München: Ch. Kaiser Verlag, 1948, Neuausgabe.

[4] Martchenko, Anatoli. 1970. *Mon Témoignage*, trad. Fr. Olivier, Paris, Le Seuil, (1ère ed. en russe en samizdat, puis à l'étranger, London, Pall Mall Press, 1969).

[5] Guinzbourg, Evguenia. 1967. *Le Vertige*, Trad. B. Abbots & J.J. Maris, Paris, Le Seuil. 1ère ed. en *russe, Kritoî Marchrout*, Milano, Mondadori, janvier 1967.

[6] Martin-Chauffier, Louis. 1947. *l' Homme et la Bête*, Paris, Gallimard.

[7] Levi, Primo. 1947. *Se questo è un uomo*, Torino, Da Silva, 1947,& Einaudi 1958.

marin danois Kim Malthe-Bruun,[8] à partir de ce qu'il en avait assimilé au cours d'une très brève existence plus vouée à la marine à voile qu'à la philosophie, mais repensé à travers la terrible expérience de la torture, est, dans sa simplicité, l'un des plus beaux exemples de cette osmose qui s'accomplit entre une œuvre et celui qui la reçoit, non dans la passivité d'une étude imposée, mais comme un don vivant d'un esprit vivant.

Le lien de solidarité si passionnément défendu s'exprime dans cette assimilation des œuvres qui appartiennent à l'humanité tout entière et la représentent. A travers les hommes séparés, la culture se transforme en une force dynamique, salvatrice. Ce ne sont plus les pierres qui sont changées en or dans l'alchimie de la prison. C'est l'or du passé qui se fait chair vivante, sang et sève.

L'énorme masse de témoignages sur les prisons et les camps, dont la publication s'est beaucoup développée depuis un demi-siècle, fait, elle aussi, partie du patrimoine culturel de l'humanité. Cette expérience ne se limite pas à un moment particulier dans l'histoire d'un individu: elle met en jeu toute la vie de l'homme, sa capacité de résistance physique, sa morale et sa culture. Elle est, selon le mot d'Artur London, "l'épreuve d'une vie",[9] mais elle est aussi l'épreuve de toute une société. Elle concerne la morale de cette société et sa culture, tout autant que celles de l'individu et, finalement, la sauvegarde de l'espèce humaine. Son ampleur en a fait un phénomène universel, qu'on ne peut reléguer dans le domaine des "anomalies" de la nature ou de la société, ni dans "les poubelles de l'histoire".

Littérature souvent en marge de la littérature, à la frontière de l'art et du sang, ces témoignages nous demandent de plonger avec ceux qui l'ont subi dans cet univers renversé et déchu où toutes les valeurs qui font la civilisation sont abolies. Ils demandent de ne pas oublier, non seulement au nom des morts et de ceux qui sont encore vivants, mais au nom des générations à venir, puisqu'il est utopique d'espérer qu'elles échappent toutes à cette expérience, comme le prouve le monde actuel.

---

[8] *Kim*, Kim Malthe-Bruun Dagbog og Breve, (Kobenhaven), Thannings & Appels Forlag, 1945. Udgave Poul Kristensen, Herning, 1974. Edition française, *Kim marin danois,* trad. H. Rott de Neufville & A. Synnetsvedt, Paris, E. Gilles, 1953.

[9] London, Artur. 1968. *L'Aveu,* Paris, Gallimard.

Qu'il s'agisse des romans, des témoignages directs, des lettres ou des notes, tous ces textes illustrent les deux situations extrêmes dans lesquelles l'individu se trouve contraint de décider, seul en face de lui-même, de sa morale et de son action: "l'homme est un loup pour l'homme, et "il n'y a pas de plus grand amour que de donner sa vie pour ceux qu'on aime", qui a même été poussé, dans les prisons et les camps, jusqu'à "pour n'importe quel prochain". Les deux concepts de l'Ancien et du Nouveau Testament: "Œil pour œil..." et "Tu aimeras ton prochain comme toi-même..."sont vérifiés, parfois avec une complète concomitance, dans l'univers de la prison et du camp. Les principes du Bien et du Mal, intimement mêlés, éclatent au grand jour dans tous les témoignages, forçant le lecteur à reconsidérer ses certitudes et ses doutes. Aucune existence n'échappe à cet affrontement entre le bien et le mal, mais nulle part ailleurs que dans la détention il ne se pose avec une telle violence et n'exige de façon aussi dramatique une réponse. Tous les régimes ont voulu faire obstacle à la solidarité entre les détenus, en exaspérant les antagonismes nationaux, en mélangeant politiques et droits communs et en donnant à ceux-ci un pouvoir exorbitant sur les politiques, ou comme dans les prisons de la Chine communiste en punissant, même de mort, le moindre geste d'attention envers un autre prisonnier.[10]

La réponse à cet affrontement entre le bien et le mal s'exprime dans les témoignages et elle est aussi ambivalente que la question. Dans cet univers clos, rien n'est insignifiant: le plus petit geste d'altruisme ou d'égoïsme, la moindre faute contre la probité ou la vérité, l'aide la plus minime peuvent avoir des conséquences tragiques ou miraculeuses. Au niveau le plus quotidien la réponse est autant dans la délation, le vol, les coups, l'indifférence à autrui que dans le partage du colis ou de la ration, le don du chandail, l'échange de nouvelles, le signe d'encouragement. Au niveau supérieur elle est tout autant dans le mot terrible de Chalamov: "J'ai vu ce que l'homme ne doit ni voir ni savoir",[11] que dans le "J'aimerais mieux être avec le Christ qu'avec la vérité" de Dostoïevsky. Elle est au

---

[10]   Cf. en particulier: Rissov Constantin, *Le Dragon enchaîné*, Paris, Laffont, 1985 ; Nien Cheng, *Life and Death in Shangai*, London, Grafton Books, 1984; Pasqualini Jean & Chemlinsky Rudolph, *Prisoner of Mao*, New York, Paul R. Reynolds, 1973.

[11]   Chalamov, Varlam. 1969. *Récits de Kolyma*, trad. K. Kerel & O. Simon, Paris, Denoël, 1969. Reéd. augmentée, Paris, Maspero, 1980-86.

même degré dans la "haine très calme" de Victor Serge[12] sortant de la Centrale de Melun que dans le "Il ne faudra pas avoir de haine pour le peuple allemand" de Leone Ginzburg mourant sous la torture de la Gestapo à Rome en 1944[13] comme le demandait déjà Boris Vildé fusillé à Paris en 1942.[14] La réponse est aussi dans le fait d'avoir rendu témoignage pour tous ceux qui ne le pourront plus jamais. Il n'est pas question de faire de tous les détenus politiques des héros ou des saints, mais ceux qui ont pris la peine de parler pour les morts et les muets ont montré que cette réponse à l'affrontement entre le bien et le mal est une part essentielle de notre mémoire culturelle, même si elle n'est pas toujours de la littérature ou de l'art. Ces textes ouvrent sur les capacités de l'homme des perspectives, parfois vertigineuses, sur l'horreur mais aussi sur la beauté. Car si de la nuit où l'on a voulu les engloutir, des voix s'élèvent encore pour tenter, par delà la douleur et l'humiliation, par delà la haine et le pardon, d'en appeler à la conscience, c'est que, en dépit de tout, avec ou sans le secours de Kant, "la loi morale" a survécu au fond des cœurs. Et dans ce choral tragique résonne encore, comme une affirmation de l'humanité sauvée, le défi lancé jadis par Pellico sous les voûtes glacées du Spielberg: "La joie virile de ne pas se confesser vaincu et de tout vaincre".

Bernadette Morand
Paris

---

[12] Serge, Victor. *Mémoires d'un révolutionnaire*, Paris, Le Seuil, 1951. *Les Hommes dans la prison*, in *Romans* , Le Seuil, 1967.

[13] Cf. Ginzburg, Leone. 1964. *Scritti*, Introduzione di Norberto Bobbio, Torino, Einaudi & Pertini, Sandro. 1970. *Sei condamne, due evasioni...*, Milano, Mondadori.

[14] Vildé, Boris. 1988. *Journal et Lettres de prison*, Paris, les Cahiers de l'IHTP, 1988, & Editions Allia,1997.

Le Roi des Aulnes ou le jeu dangereux

- Cher enfant, viens, partons ensemble!
Je jouerai tant de jolis jeux avec toi!
Tant de fleurs émaillent le rivage!
Ma mère a de beaux vêtements d'or.

Dans sa ballade *Le Roi des Aulnes*, écrite en 1782, et qui, comme le souligne Michel Tournier, "a toujours été pour l'écolier français abordant la langue et la littérature allemandes *le* poème allemand par excellence, le symbole même de l'Allemagne" (1977: 118),[1] Goethe présente une scène de séduction et de violence qui se déroule dans un lieu et dans un temps indéterminés.

Chacun connaît ce drame à trois personnes où le père qui chevauche tard dans la nuit avec son fils agonisant ne parvient pas à le protéger contre le Roi des Aulnes, ogre, personnage mystérieux, qui au fond n'est rien d'autre que l'incarnation de la mort. Le Roi des Aulnes invite le gamin à un jeu dangereux à l'issue duquel celui-ci meurt dans les bras de son père désespéré.

---

[1] Il rappelle aussi l'origine danoise du poème et le fait que le titre *Le Roi des Aulnes* est dû à une erreur de traduction de Herder, sous la plume de qui *Eller - les elfes* est devenu *Erlen - les aulnes*, à cause de la spécificité du dialecte qu'on parlait en Prusse-Orientale, à Mohrungen, sa ville natale (cf. Tournier, 1977: 118-9).

Michel Tournier, dans son roman *Le Roi des Aulnes,* couronné par le Prix Goncourt en 1970, dépasse la dimension individuelle, intime, du drame raconté par Goethe. En effet, grâce à sa richesse et sa densité impressionnantes, ce roman se prête aux interprétations les plus diverses, parfois complémentaires et parfois contradictoires, accentuant tantôt les aspects mythologiques ou transtextuels, et tantôt les aspects fantastiques du roman,[2] interprétations qui—faute de temps—il nous serait impossible de rappeler ici. Certes, il met en scène aussi un ogre particulier, Abel Tiffauges, ogre ambigu, déchiré entre le bien et le mal, et dont la vocation ogresse, c'est-à-dire la phorie, est tantôt maléfique, prédatrice, et tantôt bénéfique, salvatrice, à l'instar soit du Roi des Aulnes ou de Gilles de Rais,[3] soit de Saint-Christophe. L'écrivain montre la naissance de cette vocation due à un échec amoureux du héros et à l'accusation trop sincère prononcée par sa maîtresse insatisfaite de leurs rapports sexuels.[4] Bientôt une véritable carrière ogresse d'Abel Tiffauges commence, comme si elle était déclenchée par ces paroles dépréciatives de Rachel, *Tu es un ogre,* paroles par lesquelles d'ailleurs s'ouvre le roman tout entier.

Nous n'allons pas évoquer ici toutes les étapes de cette "carrière" ogresse, qu'une autre femme, ou plutôt une jeune fille, Martine, elle aussi, contribue à provoquer par son accusation injuste. Remarquons seulement que ce qui caractérise l'ogre avant tout c'est son comportement phorique. Le roman de Tournier montre toute l'ambiguïté de la phorie. Abel Tiffauges est partagé entre le désir "d'asservir" et celui de "servir", entre le désir de porter un enfant en le serrant contre soi dans un geste de ravisseur, comme le Roi des Aulnes (surtout l'épisode de la chasse aux garçons pour la Napola), et celui de porter un enfant au-dessus de soi, pour le sauver, tel Saint Christophe chargé du Christ (notamment la scène finale avec Ephraïm, enfant juif). Cette deuxième phorie, phorie bénigne, révèle l'instinct maternel de Tiffauges, et par cela même l'androgynie de ce personnage. Abandonné par une femme, Abel Tiffauges retrouve l'élément féminin en lui-même.[5]

---

[2]   Cf. notamment: Bouloumié, 1988; Degn, 1995: 93-143; Vray, 1997; Koopman-Thurlings M. 1995; Korthals Altes L. 1992.

[3]   Sur *Gilles & Jeanne,* cf. Mrozowicki, 1995: 70-88.

[4]   L'histoire des relations difficiles d'Abel Tiffauges et de Rachel permet à Michel Tournier de présenter toute une théorie de l'opposition de la sexualité masculine et féminine, comme opposition entre l'acte et la puissance. (Cf. 1970: 20-22).

[5]   Cf. Bouloumié, 1988: 102.

Mais Abel Tiffauges, ogre particulier, est doublé, chez Michel
Tournier, et c'est là que réside toute l'originalité de sa version du mythe,
par un ogre "collectif", dont l'activité est située d'une manière précise
dans le temps et dans l'espace,[6] et qui, lui, n'a rien d'ambigu. L'écrivain
donne une image bouleversante de l'un des OGRES de notre époque, dont
la nature maléfique n'est pas sujette à caution, à savoir le régime nazi, qui,
tout comme les autres régimes totalitaires, tels que le communisme, avait
recours à la séduction[7] des jeunes en vue de leur future exploitation,[8]
séduction qui d'ailleurs pour détruire toute résistance éventuelle de la
proie, côtoyait souvent la violence.

L'enquête de Tournier sur le nazisme, décrite amplement dans *Le
Vent Paraclet* (1977: 106-13), lui a révélé la vocation ogresse du régime
nazi, illustrée de la manière la plus éclatante par les cérémonies du 19
avril. Dans *Le Roi des Aulnes*, Abel Tiffauges se rend, le 19 avril 1943, à

---

[6] Cf. Bouloumié,1988: 19. Elle remarque notamment:
"Plus encore que *Vendredi ou les Limbes du Pacifique*, *Le Roi des Aulnes* est ancré dans
l'histoire. Le roman raconte les aventures d'un prisonnier français en Allemagne nazie. Le livre
commence le 3 janvier 1938 et s'achève au mois de mars 1945. Le déroulement du roman suit
celui des événements historiques qui infléchissent le destin du héros: déclaration de guerre en
1939, déroute de l'armée française en juin 1940, déroute de l'armée allemande en janvier 1945.
Abel Tiffauges entre en Allemagne le 24 juin 1940. Il quitte Moorhof, le camp de prisonniers
français en Prusse Orientale où il est d'abord employé à des travaux de drainage, à la suite de
l'opération Typhon déclenchée en octobre 1941 par Hitler contre l'Armée rouge. Il va à
Rominten, la réserve de chasse de Göring, remplacer le fils des domestiques parti pour le front
russe. La défaite de Stalingrad qui amène Göring à réduire les effectifs de la réserve où il se sent
mal protégé des bombardements aériens russes, provoque son départ qui intervient peu après
le 19 avril 1943, veille du jour anniversaire du Führer. Le livre évoque l'Allemagne nazie et les
napolas où le troisième reich forme de jeunes SS. Tiffauges reste plus d'un an à Kaltenborn. Le
chapitre final décrit les derniers combats d'octobre 1944 contre la ville de Goldap, voisine de
Kaltenborn, jusqu'à la nouvelle offensive russe de janvier 1945. Le livre s'achève quand la
citadelle tombe, fin mars, aux mains des Russes".

[7] Michel Tournier, dans son roman, accentue le rôle des cérémonies, des fêtes, des parades
militaires dans la séduction des jeunes par le nazisme. Il en parle dans une de ses interviews:
"Que ce soit celui ou celui de Mussolini, le fascisme est inséparable d'un certain faste
wagnérien avec des défilés, de la musique, des monuments qui se ressemblent tous et des fêtes
nocturnes avec des flambeaux, des projecteurs qui se rejoignent en voûte. Et si vous faites
abstraction de cet aspect du nazisme, vous le dénaturez, vous en donnez une image
imparfaite...C'était une fête nocturne, une fête meurtrière... Ce n'était pas ridicule, c'était
terrifiant... Si on donne une image totale du nazisme, ce que j'ai fait dans *Le Roi des Aulnes*, il
faut décrire sa vitrine, avec ses fêtes, avec ses fastes, toute cette séduction par la violence et en
même temps, naturellement, l'arrière-boutique avec ses camps de concentration et son côté
meurtrier éminent. Les deux choses sont inséparables" (Tournier, 1986: 24).
Cf. aussi Bouloumié, 1988: 106. Sur la séduction dans *Le Roi des Aulnes* de Michel Tournier, lire
aussi Purdy, 1993.

[8] "Le mythe de l'ogre, dans l'œuvre de Michel Tournier, traduit l'angoisse que suscite une
idéologie diabolique". (Bouloumié, 1988: 93).

l'hôtel de ville de Goldap, pour faire renouveler son *Ausweis*. Il y découvre "tout un grouillis de petites filles entièrement nues [qui] égayait le chêne sombre dont l'immense salle était lambrissée" (1970: 367-8). Et il apprend qu'il s'agit des enfants de dix ans qui, la veille de l'anniversaire du Führer, comme tous les ans, passent devant le conseil de révision avant d'être incorporés dans la Jeunesse hitlérienne. Tiffauges, ogre lui-même, mais dont la vocation ogresse, à ce moment-là, était encore loin d'être accomplie, et qui attendait encore ses grands exploits, est visiblement impressionné par ceux de l'Ogre de Rastenburg, maître de tous les Ogres, Ogre Majeur, Adolf Hitler.[9]

> Lorsque Tiffauges reprit le chemin de Rominten, le grand veneur avec ses chasses et ses massacres, ses festins de venaisons et sa science coprologique et phallologique était tombé à ses yeux au rang du petit ogre folklorique et fictif, échappé à quelque conte de grand-mère. Il était éclipsé par l'autre, l'ogre de Rastenburg, qui exigeait de ses sujets, pour son anniversaire, ce don exhaustif, cinq cent mille petites filles et cinq cent mille petits garçons de dix ans, en tenue sacrificielle, c'est-à-dire tout nus, avec lesquels il pétrissait sa chair à canon. (1970: 369)

D'abord prisonnier au camp de Moorhof, et puis garde-chasse dans la forêt de Rominten auprès de Hermann Göring, le grand veneur du Reich, après la défaite des Allemands dans la bataille de Stalingrad qui a provoqué la réduction du personnel de Rominten au strict minimum, le héros du roman de Tournier parvient à être affecté à la Napola de Kaltenborn. C'est là qu'aura lieu la rencontre symbolique d'Abel Tiffauges, ogre individuel, et du système nazi, ogre collectif, tous les deux également fascinés par la jeunesse, voire par les enfants, fascination qui, chez l'un et chez l'autre, tourne à la pédophilie. C'est là que Tiffauges, déchiré par ses penchants vers le mal et vers le bien, au service de l'Ogre Majeur, pourra réaliser la première de ses vocations ogresses, la vocation maléfique.

La napola—on chercherait en vain ce mot dans les dictionnaires français—est un sigle pour *Nationalpolitische Erziehungsanstalt*. Il s'agit d'établissements, créés par Joachim Haupt et August Heissmeyer, installés en général dans des châteaux ou des monastères réquisitionnés,

---

[9]   Cf. Tournier, 1977: 106-7.

et dont la tâche était de former de jeunes SS. Il y avait environ 40 napolas dispersées sur tout le territoire du Reich (cf. Tournier, 1970: 364-5, 411). Celle qui est présentée dans le roman de Tournier est située dans une forteresse purement imaginaire en Prusse-Orientale,[10] mais sa description, s'appuyant sur une enquête scrupuleuse de l'écrivain, est très réaliste. Le romancier cite un fragment du discours d'Adolf Hitler au Reichsparteitag de 1935 où l'Ogre Majeur a parfaitement saisi l'essence du système totalitaire:

> Désormais [...] le jeune Allemand s'élèvera progressivement d'école en école. On le prendra en main tout enfant pour ne plus le lâcher jusqu'à l'âge de la retraite. Personne ne pourra dire qu'il y a eu une période de sa vie où il a été laissé à lui-même. (Tournier, 1970: 379)

L'auteur décrit aussi amplement la structure de l'enseignement de la Jeunesse hitlérienne en Allemagne à partir de 1935, pour se concentrer ensuite sur la structure militaire, les modalités de fonctionnement de la napola et l'emploi du temps que suivaient les Jungmannen, élèves de cette école très spéciale. Ceux-ci, "incorporés à l'âge de douze ans, [...] quittaient l'école à dix-huit ans après avoir acquis d'une part une formation scolaire traditionnelle, d'autre part une formation militaire intense axée, selon leur choix, sur l'armée de terre, la Luftwaffe, la Marine ou les Waffen-SS. C'est à ces derniers qu'allait la faveur de plus de la moitié des Jungmannen" (Tournier, 1970: 379-380).

Ce qui intéresse Michel Tournier tout particulièrement, c'est le recrutement des enfants pour les napolas. Il remarque que

> le recrutement se faisait selon deux voies, les candidatures spontanées et la prospection des écoles communales. Les candidatures auraient certes suffi à remplir les napolas [...] mais les enfants auraient été alors issus en grande majorité de milieux bourgeois—fils de militaires de carrière et de fonctionnaires du parti—, et la philosophie populiste du Reich exigeait une plus vaste ouverture aux couches profondes de la société. Il fallait pouvoir produire des statistiques attestant une proportion convenable de fils

---

[10]   Dans *Le Vent Paraclet*, Tournier remarque la similitude du nom imaginaire de la forteresse de Kaltenborn et de celui de Kaltenbronn, localité réelle dans la région de Baden-Baden (1977: 112).

d'artisans, d'ouvriers et de paysans. A cette fin, les institu-
teurs ruraux étaient invités à présenter à une commission
itinérante les enfants leur paraissant répondre aux normes
de candidature. (1970: 380)

Bref, parmi les Jungmannen des napolas, il y avait des volontaires
et des enfants incorporés de force, enlevés à leurs parents, les uns et les
autres soumis évidemment à un examen racial minutieux, et scrupuleuse-
ment présélectionnés.

Tiffauges, responsable d'abord, dans la napola de Kaltenborn, de
l'approvisionnement, se voit bientôt confier la tâche de recruter des
enfants et se lance à leur poursuite, à travers la campagne, monté sur son
cheval[11] appelé, nomen omen, Barbe-Bleue, accompagné d'une meute de
chiens. Il devient ainsi "l'ogre de Kaltenborn".

Au bout d'un certain temps le ravisseur est identifié par la
population de la Prusse-Orientale, on organise même un attentat contre
lui et on distribue un tract avec le texte suivant reproduit grossièrement
à la machine à photocopier:

Cet avertissement s'adresse à toutes les mères habi-
tant les régions de Gallenburg, Sensburg, Lötzen et Lyck!

Prenez garde à l'Ogre de Kaltenborn!

Il convoite vos enfants. Il parcourt nos régions et vole
les enfants. Si vous avez des enfants, pensez toujours à
l'Ogre, car lui pense toujours à eux! Ne les laissez pas
s'éloigner seuls. Apprenez-leur à fuir et à se cacher s'ils

---

[11] Abel Tiffauges insiste dans ses *Ecrits sinistres* sur l'aspect phorique du cheval: "le cheval n'est
pas seulement l'animal-totem de la Défécation, et la bête phorique par excellence. L'Ange Anal
peut devenir en outre l'instrument d'enlèvement, de rapt, et le cavalier portant phoriquement
sa proie dans ses bras - s'élever au niveau d'une SUPERPHORIE. Mieux encore: le rapt peut
intervenir alors même que la superphorie est déjà acquise, par exemple si un être surhumain
arrache au cavalier l'enfant qu'il emporte, comme dans le poème *Le Roi des Aulnes*. Cette ballade
de Goethe, où l'on voit un père fuyant à cheval dans la lande en serrant sous son manteau son
enfant que le Roi des Aulnes s'efforce de séduire, et finalement enlève de vive force, c'est la
charte même de la PHORIE qu'elle élève à la troisième puissance. C'est le mythe latin de
Christophe-Albuquerque porté à un paroxysme d'incandescence par la magie hyperboréenne"
(Tournier, 1970: 469-470). C'est aussi à un cheval qu'Ephraïm compare Tiffauges dans l'épisode
final de l'astrophorie: "Ephraïm, dit Tiffauges, je n'ai plus mes lunettes. Je ne vois presque plus
rien. Guide-moi. -Ce n'est rien, Cheval d'Israël, je vais te prendre par les oreilles, et te
guider!"(Tournier, 1970: 578). Cf. aussi Tournier, 1970: 15, 75 et Bouloumié, 1988: 58-9.

voient un géant monté sur un cheval bleu, accompagné
d'une meute noire. S'il vient à vous, résistez à ses menaces,
soyez sourdes à ses promesses. Une seule certitude doit
guider votre conduite de mères: Si l'Ogre emporte votre
enfant, vous ne le reverrez JAMAIS! (Tournier: 460-1).

A ce moment, on peut identifier Abel Tiffauges, l'Ogre de Kaltenborn, au Roi des Aulnes de Johann Wolfgang Goethe, qui porte un enfant
en le serrant contre soi dans un geste de ravisseur. Mais les pages suivantes du roman montreront sa conversion,[12] sa transmutation qui se
produit à la suite de son baptême par le sang d'Arnim le Souabe. Comme
le remarque Bouloumié, "Pareil à celui du Christ, le sacrifice d'Arnim
prélude au rachat de l'ogre déchu" (1988: 174).

Cependant c'est surtout la rencontre avec Ephraïm, enfant juif qui
rend possible son inversion bénigne. Maintenant, l'ancien ogre de
Kaltenborn, tel Saint-Christophe, porte un enfant au-dessus de sa tête en
essayant de le sauver. Michel Tournier l'appelle L'Astrophore (tel est le
titre du dernier chapitre du roman), puisqu'il porte sur ses épaules
l'enfant juif porteur d'étoile.

Ce n'était plus la chevauchée tumultueuse qui ramenait
Tiffauges à Kaltenborn après une chasse fructueuse, serrant
dans ses mains une proie blonde et fraîche. Il n'était pas
porté par l'ivresse phorique habituelle qui lui arrachait des
rugissements et des rires hagards. Sur sa tête, le grand
bestiaire sidéral tournait lentement dans le cirque du ciel
autour de l'étoile polaire. La Grande Ourse et son Chariot,
la Girafe et le Lynx, le Bélier et le Dauphin, l'Aigle et le
Taureau se mêlaient à des créatures sacrées et fantastiques,
la Licorne et la Vierge, Pégase et les Gémeaux. Tiffauges
cheminait avec une lenteur solennelle, sentant confusément
qu'il inaugurait une ère absolument nouvelle en accomplis-
sant sa première astrophorie. Sous son grand manteau,
l'enfant Porte-Etoile remuait parfois les lèvres, prononçant
des mots dans une langue inconnue. (Tournier, 1970: 551-2)

---

[12] Michel Tournier et les exégètes du Roi des Aulnes comparent cette conversion à celle de Saul
devenu Paul après la rencontre du Christ sur le chemin de Damas.

L'acte phorique d'Abel Tiffauges, dans ce passage, prend un nouvel aspect mythique, cette fois par la référence à Atlas. Le nom d'Atlas, il est vrai, n'apparaît pas ici, mais on sait bien que c'est lui, géant, fils du Titan Japet et de Clyméné, qui était condamné par Zeus à supporter sur ses épaules le poids de la voûte céleste pour avoir participé à la guerre des Géants contre les dieux.

En s'identifiant à Atlas, grâce à cette ultime phorie, Abel Tiffauges réalise l'un de ses pressentiments dont il parle dans ses *Ecrits sinistres* encore dans le premier chapitre du roman:

> Je m'avise en feuilletant un dictionnaire qu'Atlas portait sur ses épaules—non pas le monde, ni la terre comme on le représente habituellement—mais le ciel. Au demeurant Atlas est géographiquement une montagne, et si l'assimilation d'une montagne à un pilier du ciel a un sens, appliquée à la terre l'image est absurde. Exemple remarquable d'inversion maligne infligée à l'un des plus glorieux héros *phoriques*. Il soutenait de ses épaules les étoiles et la lune, les constellations et la Voie lactée, les nébuleuses, les comètes, les soleils en fusion. Et sa tête plongeant dans les espaces sidéraux se confondait avec les astres. [...] Mais plus j'y pense, plus il me semble qu'Atlas uranophore, Atlas astrophore est le héros mythologique vers lequel devrait tendre ma vie pour trouver en lui finalement son aboutissement et son apothéose. Quoi que je porte à l'avenir, de quelque fardeau précieux et sacré que mes épaules soient chargées et bénies, ma fin triomphale ce sera, si Dieu le veut, de marcher sur la terre avec posée sur ma nuque une étoile plus radieuse et plus dorée que celle des rois mages. (Tournier, 1970: 135-6)

Cette ultime phorie tiffaugéenne, son astrophorie, qui en effet prépare son apothéose finale, est, tout comme celle d'Atlas, une phorie expiatoire. L'enfant juif, porté sur les épaules d'Abel Tiffauges, représente d'une certaine manière toutes les victimes de l'Ogre Majeur à qui, à un certain moment, Abel s'est associé en tant qu'ogre de Kaltenborn. Ephraïm représente toutes les souffrances de ces victimes, tout le mal que le nouvel avatar du Roi des Aulnes leur a infligé. Il ne faut s'étonner, par conséquent, que, dans la scène finale, Tiffauges sentait l'enfant—si mince, si diaphane pourtant—peser sur lui comme une masse de plomb. Il avançait, et la vase montait toujours le long de ses jambes, et la charge qui l'écrasait s'aggravait à chaque pas. (Tournier, 1970: 580-1).

Ephraïm le conduira vers la mort consentie, expiatoire, sacrificielle. Ils s'enfonceront tous les deux dans le limon originel en recevant ainsi une dimension mythique, hors du temps et de l'espace, éternisés par la tourbe[13]. Le lecteur est tenté de les identifier avec les deux corps mystérieux, conservés depuis des siècles[14] (dont l'un sera appelé par les savants *Roi des Aulnes*), exhumés dans les tourbières de Walkenau au troisième chapitre du roman (cf. Tournier, 1970: 290-297).[15]

Avant de conduire Abel Tiffauges vers la mort, avant de rendre possible son passage au mythe, son éternisation par la tourbe, Ephraïm lui révèle ce que Tournier appelle l'arrière-boutique de l'Allemagne nazie ou l'Allemagne souterraine, c'est-à-dire l'univers concentrationnaire, la réalité d'Auschwitz, celle de l'extermination des Juifs et des Gitans, des adultes, mais aussi des enfants, celle des chambres de gaz, des fausses salles de douches, du tissage des cheveux, du supplice des appels "qui pouvaient durer jusqu'à six heures, et pendant lesquels les détenus devaient demeurer debout, immobiles quelle que fût la température" (1970: 557), des chiens dobermans "dressés à pourchasser et à déchiqueter à mort les détenus" (1970: 557), des expériences du Dr Mengele sur les jumeaux ou sur le vide...

---

[13] "Le couronnement de l'œuvre initiatique est la mort du héros. Mais la mort assure la régénération, devient rite de passage à un monde d'être supérieur. Ephraïm est le vrai guide. Le sauvé devient sauveur. La fin du livre suggère une apothéose. L'étoile qui flamboie symbolise cet éveil à la lumière, comme elle le fait rituellement dans les initiations" (Bouloumié, 1988: 174). Une interprétation intéressante du dénouement du livre est donnée par Régnier Pirard (1991:108-9) qui remarque notamment que le dialogue entre Tiffauges et Ephraïm s'oppose en tous points à celui entre le Roi des Aulnes et sa victime dans la ballade de Goethe.

[14] En décrivant la temporalité mythique dans l'œuvre de Michel Tournier, Arlette Bouloumié constate: "Tiffauges s'identifie, finalement, à l'homme des tourbières, baptisé Roi des Aulnes, lorsqu'il s'enfonce dans le marais. La joie paradoxale de Tiffauges ("il persévérait, sachant que tout était bien ainsi" RA 581) vient de la conscience de l'accomplissement de son destin. C'est un exemple d'*amor fati*. La mort est niée par le cycle de l'éternel retour qui abolit le temps. Par cette reproduction d'un acte primordial, Tiffauges retrouve le temps sacré des mythes" (1988: 21).

[15] Une telle interprétation est favorisée par une certaine ressemblance de Tiffauges et du corps exhumé (cf. Tournier, 1970: 290-1).

Cette découverte de la véritable nature de l'Ogre Majeur est, pour Abel Tiffauges, un véritable choc qui renverse complètement sa vision du monde et son système axiologique. Elle est à l'origine de son inversion bénigne.

Les nazis, on l'a déjà montré, étaient axés sur les enfants. Evidemment sur les enfants bien sélectionnés, selon des critères bien précis. Comme le remarque Tournier dans *Le Vent Paraclet:*

> On va s'intéresser désormais aux enfants dès leur plus jeune âge—ce n'est plus seulement des petits soldats que l'on veut, c'est la substance biologique de la nation charnelle qui est en cause—et la juvénophilie tourne à la pédophilie. On avantagera de surcroît certains caractères physiques déterminés. La chair fraîche pour être bonne va devoir être blonde, bleue et dolichocéphale, et il y aura en regard une mauvaise chair, brune, noire et brachycéphale. La suite montra que l'une et l'autre chair sont vouées par le système à la destruction, la mauvaise par voie de massacres, asservissements et autres camps d'extermination, la bonne parce que c'est avec elle que l'on pétrit la chair à canon du Reich millénaire. (1977: 106)

En effet, si l'Ogre Majeur soigneusement distingue ses enfants (les enfants de sa race), et les enfants de l'ennemi (les enfants de l'autre race), le sort qu'il réserve aux uns et aux autres est le même, la mort. Et c'est ce que le dernier chapitre du *Roi des Aulnes* de Michel Tournier montre impitoyablement, en présentant d'abord le massacre des Jungmannen de la napola de Kaltenborn, et tout de suite après, rétrospectivement, dans le récit d'Ephraïm, celui d'enfants juifs à Auschwitz.

Sans doute, les enfants n'étaient jamais épargnés pendant la guerre. Mais c'est au XXe siècle que la guerre a manifestement cessé d'être affaire des adultes. Et de nos jours, de plus en plus souvent, ce sont des enfants qui sont invités à ce jeu dangereux par de nouveaux avatars du Roi des Aulnes.

Le rapprochement de la guerre et du jeu apparaît explicitement dans le roman de Tournier. L'analyse que nous citons amplement ci-dessous est placée dans les Ecrits Sinistres d'Abel Tiffauges, mais indéniablement Tiffauges transmet ici fidèlement le point de vue de l'écrivain lui-même:

Pour scandaleuse qu'elle puisse paraître au premier abord, l'affinité profonde qui unit la guerre et l'enfant ne peut être niée .[...] L'enfant exige impérieusement des jouets qui sont fusils, épées, canons et chars, ou soldats de plomb et panoplies de tueurs. On dira qu'il ne fait qu'imiter ses aînés, mais je me demande justement si ce n'est pas l'inverse qui est vrai, car en somme l'adulte fait moins souvent la guerre qu'il ne va à l'atelier ou au bureau. Je me demande si la guerre n'éclate pas dans le seul but de permettre à l'adulte de faire l'enfant, de régresser avec soulagement jusqu'à l'âge des panoplies et des soldats de plomb. Lassé de ses charges de chef de bureau, d'époux et de père de famille, l'adulte mobilisé se démet de toutes ses fonctions et qualités, et, libre et insouciant désormais, il s'amuse avec des camarades de son âge à manœuvrer des canons, des chars et des avions qui ne sont que la copie agrandie des joujoux de son enfance.

Le drame, c'est que cette régression est manquée. L'adulte reprend les jouets de l'enfant, mais il n'a plus l'instinct de jeu et d'affabulation qui leur donnait leur sens originel. Entre ses mains grossières, ils prennent les proportions monstrueuses d'autant de tumeurs malignes, dévoreuses de chair et de sang. Le sérieux meurtrier de l'adulte a pris la place de la gravité ludique de l'enfant dont il est le singe, c'est-à-dire l'image inversée.

Si maintenant on donne à l'enfant ces jouets hypertrophiés conçus par une imagination morbide et réalisés par une activité déréglée, que va-t-il se passer? Il se passe, ce dont les hauts de Drossewalde—et avec eux la napola de Kaltenborn, et tout le Reich—nous donnent le spectacle: la phorie qui définit l'idéal de la relation entre adulte et enfant s'instaure monstrueusement entre l'enfant et le jouet adulte. Le jouet n'est plus porté par l'enfant—traîné, poussé, culbuté, roulé, comme le veut sa vocation d'objet fictif, livré aux petites mains destructrices de l'enfant. C'est l'enfant qui est porté par le jouet—englouti dans le char, enfermé dans l'habitacle de l'avion, prisonnier de la tourelle pivotante des mitrailleuses couplées. (Tournier, 1970: 454-6)

Etude sérieuse et exhaustive de l'Allemagne nazie, de ses deux côtés complémentaires, de sa vitrine et de son arrière-boutique, *Le Roi des Aulnes* est aussi quelque chose de plus. C'est une réflexion sur la nature humaine déchirée entre le bien et le mal et en même temps, comme le remarque à juste titre Arlette Bouloumié, "un appel à la vigilance, une mise en garde au lecteur trop confiant en sa raison" (1988:113). Ne laissons pas de nouveaux rois des aulnes séduire nos enfants en les invitant à des jeux dangereux où, au lieu de porter leurs jouets, ils seraient portés eux-mêmes par ces jouets devenus des instruments diaboliques, instruments de la dépravation ou de la mort. Telle est la leçon que Michel Tournier, le plus grand pédagogue de la littérature française contemporaine, nous propose de tirer de sa réactualisation de la ballade de Goethe, de sa réactualisation du mythe de l'ogre, encore plus ancien que cette ballade romantique, mythe issu, comme il se doit, de la nuit des temps.

Michal Mrozowicki
Gdansk

Bibliographie

Bouloumié, A. 1988. *Michel Tournier - Le roman mythologique*. Paris: Corti.

Bouloumié, A. 1991. "Inversion bénigne, inversion maligne." In: *Images et signes de Michel Tournier*, pp. 17-41.

Cloonan, W. 1985. *Michel Tournier*. Boston: Clayne.

Davis, C. 1988. *Michel Tournier — Philosophy and Fiction*. Oxford: Clarendon Press.

Degn, I. 1995. *L'encre du savant et le sang des martyrs. Mythes et fantasmes dans les romans de Michel Tournier*. Aarhus: Odense University Press.

Images et signes de Michel Tournier (1991) - Actes du Colloque du centre Culturel International de Cerisy-la-Salle, août 1990, Paris: Gallimard.

Koopman-Thurlings, M. 1995. *Vers un autre fantastique. Etude de l'affabulation dans l'œuvre de Michel Tournier*. Amsterdam: Rodopi.

Korthals Altes, L. 1992. *Le salut par la fiction? Sens, valeurs et narrativité dans Le Roi des Aulnes de Michel Tournier*. Amsterdam: Rodopi.

Merllié, F. 1988. *Michel Tournier*. Paris: Editions Pierre Belfond.

Mrozowicki, M. 1995. *Michel Tournier et l'art de la concision*. Katowice: Editions de l'Université de Silésie.

Pirard, R. 1991. "Au jeu du Père et de l'impair (paternité et couple)", in: *Images et signes de Michel Tournier* (1991), pp. 87-112.

Purdy, A. 1993. "Séduction et simulation: L'empire des signes dans Le Roi des Aulnes", in: *Revue des sciences humaines* 232, pp. 21-33.

Tournier, M. 1970. *Le Roi des Aulnes*. Paris: Gallimard (Folio 656).

Tournier, M. 1977. *Le Vent Paraclet*. Paris: Gallimard (Folio 1138).

Tournier, M. 1983. *Gilles & Jeanne*. Paris: Gallimard (Folio 1707).

Tournier, M. 1986. "Tournier face aux lycéens", in: *Magazine littéraire* (1986) - Dossier Michel Tournier, n° 226 - janvier 1986, p. 24.

Vray, J.-B. 1991. "La question de l'origine", in: *Images et signes de Michel Tournier* (1991) - Actes du Colloque du centre Culturel International de Cerisy-la-Salle, août 1990, Paris: Gallimard, pp. 57-76.

Vray, J.-B. 1997. *Michel Tournier et l'écriture seconde*. Lyon: Presses Universitaires de Lyon.

Worton, M. 1993. "De la perversion et de la sublimation tourniériennes, ou comment aimer si on n'est pas pervers?", in: *Revue des sciences humaines* 232, pp. 119-131.

Cultural Dormancy and Collective Memory from the Book of Genesis to Aharon Appelfeld

"Our birth is but a sleep and a forgetting ...."
— William Wordsworth, "Ode: Intimations of Immortality from Recollections of Early Childhood" (l.58)

"Autrefois au moment de me mettre au lit, l'idée d'une mort temporaire au sein du sommeil me rassérénait, aujourd'hui je m'endors pour vivre quelques heures."
— René Char, *Feuillets d'Hypnos*, #224

"Sleep faster, we need the pillows."
— Yiddish Proverb, cited by Harold Bloom (23)

To sleep is to forget, so Wordsworth and a chorus of authorities have told us. And conversely, awakening is tantamount to remembering, but the analogy soon begins to unravel, for as Wordsworth and Plato long before him have intimated, life itself may only be a state of sleep and forgetfulness from which we can scarcely awaken. To complicate the issue still further, both "sleep" and "memory" are slippery locutions whose manifold meanings and derivative forms have been classified under varied rubrics subject to debate, refinement, and critique.

Aristotle addresses the question of memory in a section of the *Parva naturalia* that, pertinently enough, precedes his analysis of sleep and waking. At the outset, he draws a firm distinction between memory as recollection and memory as the simple storage of events and images.[1] And so from the start, the analogy between sleep and forgetfulness is compromised because an underlying antithesis—sleep vs. memory—, which is often assumed, is subject to slippage. The condition of dormancy is in fact so broadly inclusive that it accommodates comparison with the idea of memory if not as retrieval, then as storage of information or experience.

— I —

In the interests of illustrating and charting the unusual elasticity of the notions of memory and sleep, the work of pioneer sociologist Maurice Halbwachs, who died in Buchenwald, is of considerable relevance. Founder of what has become the widely circulated concept of collective memory, Halbwachs counters the conventional view that memory/recollection is an individual process, even when the subject is alone and remembers vividly. According to Halbwachs,

> ... nos souvenirs demeurent collectifs, et ils nous sont rappelés par les autres, alors même qu'il s'agit d'événements auxquels nous seuls avons été mêlés, et d'objets que nous seuls avons vus. C'est qu'en réalité nous ne sommes jamais seuls. . . . car nous portons toujours avec nous et en nous une quantité de personnes qui ne se confondent pas" (*La mémoire collective* 2).

---

[1] Wolfgang Kemp (87-90) presents a useful summary of the two dimensions of Aristotelian memory, *mneme* and *anamnesis*, and their evolution in European tradition.

Literature as Cultural Memory

Halbwachs proceeds to give the example of a walking tour of London, a metropolis that one appreciates via the mediation of an architect and others who accompany the tourist physically—or only *in absentia* through a germane text that has been read. The individual subject is in this way able to conjure up a cultural milieu, its past, and its significances.

If memory, then, is a communal effort, what about forgetfulness? Oblivion, claims Halbwachs, results from the separation of the individual from a group and its shared experiences, even when one is surrounded by a crowd. Thus a specific day spent at school or a certain place habitually passed may be unremembered because of an ambience of anonymity. Similarly, the reminiscences of a student who encounters a teacher of years past may reawaken (*"réveillent"* [6]) in the latter no memory of particular lectures and classrooms long ago.

Halbwachs's theory of forgetfulness dovetails with the conventional trope according to which sleep is tantamount to forgetting. This figure can be traced to an ancient perspective on dormancy—explicit in Heraclitus— which foregrounds the psychic retreat or sequestration of the sleeping subject into a domain of instinctual indulgence and the private imagery and narratives of dreams. According to Heraclitus, "To those who are awake, there is one ordered universe common to all, whereas in sleep each man turns away from this world to one of his own" (Frag. 89, Freeman 50). Like Halbwachs's absent-minded professor, the sleeper is assumed to be detached from a matrix of social intercourse and thus from a context within which memory is possible. In keeping with this Heraclitean view, Halbwachs critiques the veracity of dreams, arguing that any event recollected in a dream is tainted by the solipsism of the dormant state and hence unreliably remembered.

This sketch of Halbwachs's theory of memory would be incomplete without calling attention to the modernist tinge often apparent in his writings. Halbwachs's modernism is implicit when he identifies in the workings of collective memory a mode of cultural representation. No doubt, this representational capability functions best in an optimally ordered society. The utopian overtones and the insinuation that there is an aesthetic dimension in one of the basic operations of everyday consciousness align him with the assumptions of a "high" modernism. The imprint of a modernist temperament is also evident in the distinct nature of the newness that Halbwachs forges into the traditional concept of memory. Memory is now collective and not individual, claims Halbwachs.[2]

Yet forgetfulness, though held to be an attribute of the individual psyche, undoubtedly subsists in a collective version as well. Both intuition and astute observation affirm that collective memory cannot escape its counterpart, collective oblivion, which might just as well be termed collective or cultural dormancy. What is not immediately clear—but implied because of a semantic overlap of "sleep" and "memory"—is that cultural dormancy and collective memory in some atypical circumstances can be virtually one and the same.

— II —

With qualification of Halbwachs's dichotomy in plain view, discussion turns to the task of calibrating the primary modalities in which the paired terms, cultural dormancy/collective memory, are manifested. Surely, it is easier to identify instances in which the relation between the two phrases is one of opposition rather than apposition. In the Book of Genesis (49:9), this more salient alternative is prefigured when the dying Jacob prophesies that his son, Judah—as well as, by obvious implication, the tribe that he founds—will achieve preeminence and is like a sleeping lion that no one dares to rouse.

A more evolved, explicit example occurs in Pindar's fourth Isthmian ode. Praising the skill of a certain Melissos as a boxer and wrestler, the poet engages in a bit of self-congratulation while proclaiming that the athlete's victory has led to a wondrous hymn—Pindar's—that awakens the fame of the champion's ancestral line from the slumber into which it had fallen (ll. 19-24). Similarly, at the beginning of *The Faerie Queene*, Edmund Spenser asserts that he will revive Arthurian values and

---

[2] A relevant connection is made by Matt Matsuda, who traces (12-13) the concept of collective memory to a late-nineteenth century, colonialist nostalgia for the perceived cohesiveness of primitive cultures.

celebrate noble deeds that have "slept in silence long" (I Preface.1:6).[3]

In contrast to this scenario of alternation, the simultaneity of collective dormancy and memory is also found. Perhaps the earliest example is an austere and archaic passage in the Book of Numbers (33:1-49), a detailed catalogue of the many encampments that the Israelites occupied during four decades of nomadic life. The plodding catalogues of oral literature are perhaps the nemesis of commentators, but over a period of many centuries, resourceful interpreters have endeavoured to counteract the sense of general aporia that this barren and repetitive passage conveys. Maimonides, for example, saw in the passage an overview of the continuous miracle that ensured the survival of a nomadic people for forty years (Plaut, Bamberger, and Hallo 1240-41).

In the present context, we can concur with Maimonides that the stark catalogue of encampments preserves an aura of the wilderness. In this inhospitable environment, the Israelites, while striving to amalgamate an ethos, wandered after their exodus from Egypt. Amid this tracklessness and at precisely this point in the Old Testament, collective memory is briefly but quite literally manifested as cultural dormancy. Both monotonously factual and peculiarly abstract, the passage in question engraves a textual grid across the vacant areas—the wilderness, desert, or *midbár*—in which the wanderers survived for so long. At the intersections of this grid are located the numerous encampments that were the Israelites' temporary villages.

Within these populated areas suspended in the uncertain matrix of a desert cartography, momentous events and receptions of law surely transpired. At the same time, it is necessary to recognize that—on the most basic level—a residence of any sort is first and foremost a place for repose and sleep (Aubert and White 2:1). This awkward catalogue, then, is a list of what were perhaps the world's first bedroom communities, and

---

[3] Also notable is a strategy of late-nineteenth century Prussian political mythology, the rapprochement of medieval Teutonic grandeur and the modern state, as if the former had fallen asleep only to reawaken into the latter. According to one commentator, "Plus que de la chronologie linéaire, le thème de l'endormissement et du réveil est proche du fonctionnement de la mémoire, où l'on peut en effet s'endormir à volonté pendant de longues périodes, c'est-à-dire les escamoter" (Assmann 48). Thus the act of juggling provides an apt image of a definite form of interaction between the twin phenomena, cultural dormancy and collective memory. One configuration passes unproblematically into another as vibrant fame replaces nostalgia for a defunct era and as the heroic or chivalric values of a superannuated culture are revived with apparent effortlessness.

it is composed of memories of sleep, that fragile condition at the fringe of consciousness. The condition of sleep is also the baseline of human existence, and under some circumstance one of the few reference points amid life's distractions and dislocations. Sleep is thus implied here as a kind of nomadic truth, something verifiable amid vacancy and flux.

— III —

The remainder of this paper is concerned with a uniquely disturbing twentieth-century context in which the interconnections of sleep and memory are surprisingly relevant. At issue is the Holocaust, the program to eliminate Europe's Jews and others deemed undesirable. While memory is obviously germane at this juncture, the claim that sleep has something to do with Holocaust commemoration is sure to elicit scepticism. In both visual and verbal texts, however, there is substantial evidence that sleep, its patterns, and the circumstances under which it occurs, together compose a veracious index of life's attributes during the Holocaust. In a situation in which suffering, dying, and death are the norm, dormancy as the easily permeable frontier between life and its absence becomes a salient vehicle of existential demarcation.

An especially germane illustration of this peculiar dynamics is a frequently reproduced photograph from Buchenwald (see, for instance, Schoenberner 253). The image is one of emaciated prisoners packed in their bunks, and it conveys a singular pathos that even images of the dead sometimes do not. Most of the men are awake and—apparently—very recently liberated, but the metal food bowls that have doubled as pillows and the barrier-like interior framing indicated by the stark outline of the bunks make this a scene of sleep. The ensemble convincingly documents the tragic monotony of innumerable periods of dormancy passed on the threshold of annihilation.

Similarly declarative are the Draconian three-level, shelf-like beds that, now empty, are located in the commemorative museum into which the Majdanek concentration camp has been converted (Gutman I:311). What was it like to sleep under these conditions? Of what quality was the life that subsisted under such circumstances? The barbaric dormitories, even bereft of their occupants, provide an answer, for as mentioned above, we live where we sleep. Our place of residence is intuitively defined as our place of slumber and repose, whether we happen to live on Main Street, under an overpass, in the Faubourg Saint-Germain, on Judengasse, or encamped in the centre of a midbár—a wilderness of the conscience—more desolate than any recorded in Exodus or Numbers.

The psychoanalyst Viktor Frankl, who survived incarceration in Auschwitz, supplies eminently pungent and concise verbal documentation of this facet of the death-camp experience:

> The first night in Auschwitz we slept in beds which were constructed in tiers. On each tier (measuring about six-and-a-half to eight feet) slept nine men, directly on the boards. Two blankets were shared by each nine men. We could, of course, lie only on our sides, crowded and huddled against each other, which had some advantages because of the bitter cold. Though it was forbidden to take shoes up to the bunks, some people did use them secretly as pillows in spite of the fact that they were caked with mud.... (Frankl 15)

This group-portrait of desperately uncomfortable sleepers correlates with the grim evidence of photographic archives. Together, words and images engrave a cultural document that preserves some of the programmatic horror of the Holocaust. This representational success is possible because sleep is a minimal existential mode that somehow remains constant and comprehensible—and in some way exemplary—whatever the milieu in which it occurs. In a context of cultural and political pathology, sleep becomes matter for memory.

Further comments by Frankl and others make clear that the general experience of inmate life can be apprehended as a form of enforced cultural dormancy. Frankl recalls "a 'regression' in the camp inmate—a retreat to a more primitive form of mental life" (27). The phenomenon of regression in turn recalls one of Freud's most widely circulated comments on sleep, his view that dormancy is an enactment of reversion to early stages of psychic evolution. As opposed to interest and involvement in everyday waking life, the somnolent subject reverts to a "state of hallucinatory wish-fulfillment" (Freud 138). If such is the mental landscape of the typical sleeper, then even more so for the inmate of the death-camps, a person whose waking life has become a mixture of apathy, disengagement, and somnambulism (Frankl 27).

The forced labor and incessant hazards are, however, at every moment at odds with this sleep-walking. The inmate can continue to exist only by somehow living against the grain of a narrative of extermination that promises death either quickly or through a slower process of depletion and disease. Nightly repose, however deficient in tranquillity, offers a degree of escape from and resistance to the ominous narrative of waking life.

— IV —

This dynamics of cultural degeneration is presented in lurid depth in the concentration-camp memoirs of Primo Levi. In a lamentational poem, dated January 1946, Shoah commemoration and cultural dormancy overlap in a very notable way. It is with this poem that Levi begins *La Tregua* ("the truce"), which bears in translation the suggestive title, *The Reawakening*. The first of its two stanzas suffices to convey a sense of the severity of Levi's malaise and of the inhumane conditions under which the poem developed:

> Dreams used to come in the brutal nights,
> Dreams crowding and violent
> Dreamt with body and soul,
> Of going home, of eating, of telling our story,
> Until, quickly and quietly, came
> The dawn reveille:
> > *Wstawàch.*
> And the heart cracked in the breast. (*Two Memoirs* 177)

Composed just after the author's liberation and return to his home in Turin, this poem records an environment of enforced dormancy within which the discrete somnolence of the inmate constructs the most fragile of psychic reservoirs, one crowded with visions of the fulfillment of basic desires. At the same time, the persistent day-residues of traumatic waking hours have invaded, *en masse*, the highly permeable enclosure of nocturnal consciousness.

There is also an element of wish-fulfillment in the emphasis on dreams, for while Levi foregrounds the nightmare-filled sleep in the camps, sleep-research has made clear that periods of REM- or dream-generating sleep alternate with those of muted, dreamless slumber.[4] While Levi and Frankl both imply that conditions in the camps prohibited non-REM- (that is, dreamless) sleep, such episodes must have occurred with some regularity—even if undetected. But given the challenges with which individual personhood was confronted, the notion of an even more minimal level of subjectivity (one in which not even an oneiric flicker of consciousness is kindled) is no doubt threatening and not to be entertained.

Whatever the mixture of dreams and vacant slumber, this flimsy defensive envelope is soon perforated by an alien summons, *"Wstawàch"*!—"Awaken!"—, into renewed drudgery and degradation. Exit from the domain of Morpheus is announced with the abruptness and finality of a call to Last Judgment, but the command is a blast from a leaden trumpet, a tocsin, the intimidating initiation of one more intermediary stage in the strategy of a Final Solution.

Equally powerful but from a different perspective is a memory of the harried, diaphanous half-sleep into which Levi was typically submerged. On many occasions, Levi underwent a peculiar, synesthetic dozing in which the sound of his neighbour's breathing became the sound of a train-whistle in a repetitive dream-narrative centred on the work-train that monopolized so many daylight hours. What is most intriguing about this episode is that it provides a clue as to the circumstances under which collective memory and cultural dormancy can be said to coalesce.

The passage is highly reminiscent of an idyllic section of the second part of Proust's *À l'ombre des jeunes filles en fleurs* (*Within a Budding Grove*). It is significant that Levi has drastically reworked Proust's iconic

---

[4]   The breaks in consciousness that occur during dreamless sleep, especially its deeper levels, are lucidly discussed by Hobson (142-45).

modernism. A climax of intertextual tension occurs when Levi retools the account of a rhythmic refrain that the somnolent young Marcel fashions in his mind out of the varied sounds heard while he reclines and awaits sleep aboard a train (Proust 15).

In Levi's death-camp rewriting, Proust's blending of Combray bells and railway noises is metamorphosized into a disturbing synesthesia. Levi's shallow sleep is invaded by:

> ... the whistle of the small-gauge track. ... A long, firm note, then another one a semitone lower, then again the first, but short and cut off. ... we have heard [the whistle] so often associated with the suffering of the work and the camp that it has become a symbol and immediately evokes an image like certain music or smells. (*If This Is a Man* 63-4).

Similarly dominated by a rhetoric of fusion, the two passages are dramatically at variance. The amusing syncopation of Proust, half-controlled by a contentedly drowsy Marcel, has been replaced by a brief, tragic melody carved out of the modernist, twelve-tone scale. "Breve e tronca" (*Se questo è un uomo* 74), "short and cut off," the *leitmotif* of Levi's dream of intrusive authority provides a synopsis of inmate life. The melody also expresses a failed modernism devoid of the utopian mixture of art and nature, machine and self so warmly subscribed to by the generation of Proust. Within Levi's transmutation of modernism, the Proustian ideal of life-into-art plays itself out in a theatre of devastation. Among other negative features, the contemporary paradigm of the coalescence of industry and artistry has degenerated, as never before, into technologies concerned with the infliction of mass suffering.[5]

Levi's portrait of an infernal utopia implicitly emphasizes one dimension of a superannuated modernism more than any other: political imagination gone awry, as opposed to an aesthetic ideal that has slid into trivialized novelty or kitsch. Between the negative energy generated by this debased imagination and the representation of sleep, there would seem to be considerable cognitive distance. A phrase that perhaps bridges

---

[5] As Konnilyn Feig sums it up, "Historians and novelists alike have described the Holocaust as the capstone of modern technology" (28). Particularly relevant details of the application of up-to-date technology to the program of extermination are presented by Jean-Claude Pressac and Robert-Jan van Pelt in "The Machinery of Mass Murder at Auschwitz."

Literature as Cultural Memory

this distance between a decomposed modernism and the tropology of sleep is the locution, *end-phase mentation*. The sense that one lives near the end of a distinct period of history, that a given group of cultural assumptions have realized all of their possibilities—and with some undesirable outcomes—is likely to become prevalent toward the conclusion of any historical era.[6]

End-phase mentation is among the diverse meanings that tend to be expressed *via* depictions of dormancy. As is already evident, some of these significations are virtually the opposite of others. In the writings of Proust, for instance, sleep from almost any perspective is intriguing and is an enticement to artistic innovation. Levi cannot simply discard the modernist tradition of aestheticized introspection perfected by Proust. But by exploiting the representation of dormant states so much a part of Proust's program, Levi is able to foreground this tradition as passé. Its tenuous viability is evident in a bizarre context distinctly ill-suited for assertions of modernist optimism.

Testimonies such as Levi's and Frankl's form a significant portion of the collective memory of the concentration camps. If, along with these accounts of the experience of sleep within the barren bunks, the common waking existence of their denizens can be categorized as a mode of cultural dormancy, it is essential to identify as fully as possible the distinguishing traits of this diurnal slumber. A possible handle on this question is hinted at in Levi's reference to dreams "of telling our story." In *If This Is a Man* (*Se questo è un uomo*), the motif of the tale without a listener or recipient is presented in high relief. Levi mentions his experience of encountering a Yiddish story-teller who visits his barracks and whose melancholy narrative he can only vaguely comprehend (62). The sense of an incomplete or broken cycle of the communication of narrative is transmogrified into keen frustration in a type of recurrent dream that, Levi discovered, was experienced by many other inmates as well as himself: "the ever-repeated scene of the unlistened-to story" (65).

---

[6] Jürgen Habermas calls attention to the term "crystallization" as employed by Arnold Gehlen. Like the phrase "end-phase mentation," the notion of crystallizing indicates a state of overall cultural exhaustion. As quoted by Habermas, Gehlen "calls modern culture 'crystallized' because 'the possibilities implanted in it have all been developed in their basic elements. Even the counterpossibilities and antitheses have been uncovered and assimilated so that henceforth changes in the premises have become increasingly unlikely . . .'" (3).

This blockage of narrative desire correlates significantly with the notion of narrative resistance so often detectable in representations of dormancy. In many contexts, implicitly, the phenomenon of sleep is a roadblock in the way of one narrative or another: of labour, of vigilance, of conformity, or of extermination as in the camps, where dormancy has both ameliorative and unfavourable associations. The dream- and nightmare-narratives that alleviate oppressive conditions are, in turn, among the phenomena that are prey to the resistance of sleep to narrative. For the dreamer typically lacks the volitional sense and the potential for agency that the waking individual possesses. Even in a dream of vividly sensuous wish-fulfilment, the oneiric subject can only perform and enjoy what the dream authorizes *via* its structures of enclosure and sequence.

— V —

This paper closes with discussion of "The Awakening," a brief autobiographical essay in which Aharon Appelfeld comments on his post-Shoah life in Israel. A successful novelist and Holocaust survivor, Appelfeld manages to restore the relation between cultural dormancy and collective memory to what is no doubt a more "natural" configuration, one of alternation or opposition rather than simultaneity. In doing so, Appelfeld delineates a crisis of collective memory. A process of averted recollection, undertaken by Appelfeld and many others with only a liminal degree of conscious volition, became a survival strategy for transition into a new era of selfhood beyond the traumas and tragedies inflicted by European fascism. Appelfeld, an adolescent at the time of his arrival in Israel in 1946, explains that the magnitude of his loss—especially the deprivation of an opportunity to apprehend the freedom and other joys of childhood—"lay dull and quiet, on the bedrock of the soul" (149).

With admirable ingenuity, Appelfeld exploits a tropology of dormancy and awakening to represent the often contradictory impulses to which his generation was subject in Israel over the next several years. He reacts to the awesome cathexis of Holocaust memories and emotions by descending into a "deep sleep" of oblivion: "What could we do, young boys of 12 and 13, with so many memories of death? Tell about them? Relive them? Recall them to memory again?" (149). Thus paradoxically, life in the Jewish homeland becomes, for a period of time, a wilderness area or *midbár*, "that dreadful desert of oblivion and self-alienation" (152). During this peculiar and protracted period of transition, a familiarity with Jewish tradition in general is discarded along with intimate knowledge of the Holocaust in all its harsh particulars.[7]

Dominated by "a turn from historical memory to art" (Hartman 155), this era of retreat and complacency eventually draws to a close, for memories repressed or shunned begin to crowd against the threshold of consciousness. The language is distinctly reminiscent of Halbwachs as Appelfeld enumerates the varied reassertions of personal and cultural history that push him toward a reawakening of collective memory: "parents, images from our childhood, tribal incantations, whether in the form of customs or ancestral faith" (Appelfeld 151).

There is surely no surprise that anyone who has endured trauma as radically distressing as Appelfeld's might embark upon a circuitous psychic itinerary entailing first denial and then recognition of an expansive cultural inventory. It is less obvious how or why—as for Levi—both forgetting and recollection should occur at the same time. In explanation of this paradox, the concept of end-phase mentation is appealing. Whether during his period of forgetfulness or the subsequent era of recollection, Appelfeld—no less than Halbwachs—can be viewed as a social constructivist. But there is a difference: The novelist at each stage possesses an implicit vision of some better world even if—as during the first years in Israel—, his interiorized image is pursued in a way that is unmindful of the past and its ramifications. Halbwachs, on the other hand, is almost programmatically an idealist, clinging to a paradigm of primitive social cohesion even as European culture slides toward dissolution. If Halbwachs, aware of the fact or not, is in some way a spokesman for the utopian communities of high modernism, Levi is deeply suspicious that the prevailing ideals, however enticing or entrenched, will *not* generate a culturally ameliorative program that will in turn institute some better life. Thus the notion of dormancy offers a way to grasp cognitively an entire set

[7]   Ramras-Rauch (8-10) provides insight on this stage of Appelfeld's life. Hartman eloquently compares Appelfeld's retreat to "a magical but recuperative sleep, midway between amnesia and gestation" (90).

of assumptions and mental paraphernalia—or in other words, an *episteme*—that is no longer a library and has become an archive.

Wstawàch

Nathaniel Wallace
South Carolina State University

Bibliography

Appelfeld, Aharon. 1994. "The Awakening." Trans. Jeffrey M. Green. In *Holocaust Remembrance: The Shapes of Memory*. Ed. Geoffrey H. Hartman. Oxford: Blackwell. 149-152.

Assmann, Aleida. 1994. *Construction de la mémoire nationale: une brève histoire de l'idée allemande de Bildung*. Trans. François Laroche. Paris: Maison des sciences de l'homme.

Aubert, Vilhelm, and Harrison White. 1959. "Sleep: A Sociological Interpretation." *Acta Sociologica* 4 (1959). Fasc. 1:46-54 and Fasc. 2:1-16.

Bloom, Harold. 1986. "From J to K, or The Uncanniness of the Yahwist." *The Bible and the Narrative Tradition*. Ed. Frank McConnell. Oxford: Oxford University Press. 19-35.

Char, René. 1956. *Hypnos Waking: Poems and Prose by René Char*. Trans. Jackson Mathews et al. New York: Random.

Feig, Konnilyn G. 1981. *Hitler's Death Camps: The Sanity of Madness*. New York: Holmes & Meier.

Frankl, Viktor E. 1962. *Man's Search for Meaning: An Introduction to Logotherapy*. Trans. Ilse Lasch. New York: Simon and Schuster.

Freeman, Kathleen. 1971. *Ancilla to The Pre-Socratic Philosophers: A Complete Translation of the Fragments*. In: Diels, *Fragmente der Vorsokratiker*. Cambridge: Harvard University Press.

Freud, Sigmund. 1916. "Metapsychological Supplement to the Theory of Dreams". *Collected Papers*. Trans. Joan Rivière. 4 vols. London: Hogarth, 1953. 4:137-51.

Gutman, Israel, ed. 1990. *Encyclopedia of the Holocaust*. New York: Macmillan.

Halbwachs, Maurice. 1969. *La mémoire collective*. 2nd ed. Paris: PUF.

————. 1975. *Les cadres sociaux de la mémoire*. New York: Arno.

Habermas, Jürgen. 1987. *The Philosophical Discourse of Modernity: Twelve Lectures*. Trans. Frederick Lawrence. Cambridge: MIT.

Hartman, Geoffrey H. 1996. *The Longest Shadow: In the Aftermath of the Holocaust*. Bloomington: Indiana University Press.

Hobson, J. Allan. 1988. *The Dreaming Brain*. New York: Basic.

Kemp, Wolfgang. 1991. "Visual Narratives, Memory, and the Medieval *Esprit du Système*." In Susanne Küchler and Walter Melion, eds. *Images of Memory: On Remembering and Representation*. Washington: Smithsonian. 87-108.

Levi, Primo. 1959. *If This Is a Man*. Trans. Stuart Woolf. New York: Orion.

————. 1968. *Se questo è un uomo*. I Coralli 184. Turin: Einaudi.

————. 1967. *La tregua*. I Coralli 176. Turin: Einaudi.

————. 1986. *'Survival in Auschwitz' and 'The Reawakening': Two Memoirs*. Trans. Stuart Woolf. New York: Summit.

Matsuda, Matt K. 1996. *The Memory of the Modern*. New York: Oxford University Press.

Plaut, W. Gunther, Bernard J. Bamberger, and William W. Hallo. 1981. *The Torah: A Modern Commentary*. New York: Union of American Hebrew Congregations.

Pressac, Jean-Claude, and Robert-Jan van Pelt. 1994. "The Machinery of Mass Murder at Auschwitz." In *Anatomy of the Auschwitz Death Camp*. Ed. Yisrael Gutman and Michael Berenbaum. Bloomington: Indiana University Press. 183-245.

Proust, Marcel. 1988. *À la recherche du temps perdu*. Vol. II. Ed. Jean-Yves Tadié, Dharntipaya Kaotipaya, et al. Paris: Gallimard.

Ramras-Rauch, Gila. 1994. *Aharon Appelfeld: The Holocaust and Beyond*. Bloomington: Indiana University Press.

Schoenberner, Gerhard. 1973. *The Yellow Star: The Persecution of the Jews in Europe, 1933-1945*. Trans. Susan Sweet. New York: Bantam.

Mémoires romanesques de la Shoah

Doit-on inscrire dans la mémoire des hommes une Histoire qui repousse les limites du pensable et de l'humain et qui remet en question la notion de "culture" elle-même? La littérature peut-elle rendre compte d'événements qui la "stupéfient"? Ces questions éthiques et esthétiques que débattaient dans les années 50-60 des penseurs humanistes tels que Theodor W. Adorno, George Steiner, Gershom Scholem, des critiques et des écrivains tels qu'Elie Wiesel ou Roland Barthes restent pertinentes mais la vie les a doublées et la littérature qui lui est intimement liée.[1] Aujourd'hui la Shoah est définitivement entrée dans l'Histoire et la mémoire figée des commémorations officielles rappelle périodiquement la réalité de son existence. Cependant le temps a engendré mythes et stéréotypes qui en déforment le vécu. Inscrits dans le langage et la pratique quotidienne ils informent et infirment la mémoire de la majorité que caractérise le désir de se démarquer des prisonniers des ghettos et des camps. L'usage de métaphores inadéquates telles que "l'autre planète" ou "l'enfer" pour désigner les lieux d'extermination pourtant situés sur notre

---

[1]   Adorno, Theodor W. qui jugeait "barbare" une esthétisation de la Shoah (*Noten zur Literatur*, III, Frankfurt am Main, Suhrkamp Verlag, 1966, p. 354) revient sur sa position; cf. "Meditationen zur Metaphysik" in *Negative Dialektik*, Frankfurt am Main, Suhrkamp Verlag, 1966, p. 354. George Steiner qui en 1967 doutait de la capacité de trouver une forme susceptible de décrire l'horreur et s'inquiétait de l'avenir du langage comme porteur de vérité (cf. *Language and Silence*, London, Faber and Faber, 1967) publie un roman mettant en scène Hitler: *The Portage to San Cristobal of A.H*, New York, Simon and Schuster, 1981. Cf. Wardi, Charlotte: *Le Génocide dans la fiction romanesque*, Paris, PUF, 1986.

Terre et où les criminels torturèrent des innocents révèle la crainte ou le refus de cette identification. Ces métaphores comme les expressions "morts" ou "revenants" empruntées aux rescapés qui les emploient faute de mieux pour cerner au plus près leur situation extraordinaire, deviennent alors clichés indécents dans la bouche des autres. Les revenants n'existent que dans les histoires de fantômes et malheureusement les morts ne reviennent pas. Il en est de même des fausses abstractions, des amalgames, des généralisations comme "nous sommes tous des rescapés" ou "nous sommes tous des Juifs allemands" qui, en dépouillant les événements de leur spécificité et de leur historicité, les rendent insignifiants. Quant aux comparaisons parfaitement légitimes entre la Shoah et d'autres catastrophes historiques elles négligent trop souvent d'étudier les différences et se transforment par là en assimilation.

Un fossé qui va se creusant sépare la mémoire banalisée ou pseudo-scientifique de "la mémoire charnelle" des rescapés et de celle absente mais obsédante des enfants des victimes.

"On peut tout dire.... le langage peut tout exprimer... mais peut-on tout entendre, tout imaginer?" écrit Jorge Semprun (*L'Ecriture ou la Vie*, 24). Les auteurs nés après l'ère hitlérienne comme Patrick Modiano (1945) et David Grossman (1954) ou trop jeunes pour comprendre ce qu'ils vivaient comme Georges Perec (1936) se heurtent à cette question parce qu'imaginer l'extermination est pour eux une nécessité existentielle et que sans mémoire il n'est ni identité ni écriture possibles.

Mais comment imaginer "ce qui n'a pas été photographié, archivé, restauré....?" (Perec, *Récits d'Ellis Island,* 28) Comment reconstituer un vécu à partir de bribes, de fugaces émergences d'un refoulé ou d'une connaissance toute extérieure? Comment inventer une écriture capable de suggérer la présence obsédante de l'absence de mémoire?

Les ouvrages *W ou le Souvenir d'enfance* (1975) de Georges Perec, *Rue des Boutiques obscures* (1978) de Patrick Modiano et *Voir ci-dessous: Amour* (1986) de David Grossman, qui forment notre corpus, présentent trois aspects de la mémoire littéraire de la Shoah chez des écrivains concernés mais qui diffèrent par leur situation et les relations affectives et intellectuelles qu'ils entretiennent avec celle-ci.

L'expérience de l'exclusion et de la persécution ou leur découverte a-posteriori rompt à jamais l'harmonie avec le monde. Renvoyés à leurs origines, c'est-à-dire à une langue et une culture qu'ils ignorent, Perec et Modiano ne trouvent que vide et manque mais en même temps prennent conscience de leur vocation d'écrivain et de l'écriture comme moyen de vaincre le néant.

"Je sais que ce que j'écris est blanc, neutre, est signe une fois pour toutes d'un anéantissement une fois pour toutes... j'écris parce que j'ai été un parmi eux, ombre au milieu d'ombres... j'écris parce qu'ils ont laissé en moi leur marque indélébile et que la trace en est l'écriture: leur souvenir est mort à l'écriture; l'écriture est le souvenir de leur mort et l'affirmation de ma vie" (*W ou le Souvenir d'enfance*, 59).

La parution de *W...* en 1975 obligea les critiques à reconsidérer leurs interprétations des œuvres de Perec et suscita de nombreuses études formelles et psychanalytiques.[2] Dédié à E (eux) l'œuvre est une recherche de "l'oublié" ainsi qu'une tentative de le transposer en fiction. Le titre en annonce d'emblée les thèmes, le "W" signifiant, dans la poétique des lettres de l'auteur, la judéité et la vie ainsi que la persécution et la mort.[3] Il indique aussi la structure de l'ouvrage: deux récits alternés l'un autobiographique, l'autre fictif séparés par une typographie différente mais "inextricablement liés" par un réseau de correspondances. Le souvenir de la séparation d'avec la mère les scinde en deux, scission représentée par une page blanche et une autre où seuls figurent entre parenthèses trois points de suspension.

La tentative de reconstituer l'histoire de son enfance à partir de réminiscences dénaturées par l'imagination, du déchiffrement incertain de photos jaunies et de documents "dérisoires" rapportés dans des passages disjoints, échoue comme en témoignent les pages de notes rectificatives aux brèves biographies du père et de la mère, imprimées en caractères gras. Même si, dans la seconde partie, "les souvenirs existent" plus riches en détails, plus développés et d'une écriture plus élaborée ils restent "des morceaux de vie arrachés au vide" (*W...*, 94). Mais ce sont précisément l'impossibilité de réaliser un récit autobiographique classique, les erreurs, les démentis, les failles de la mémoire, celle du narrateur comme celle des témoins, les fantasmes qui voilent les besoins affectifs, les techniques de

---

[2]   Cf. la remarquable étude de la genèse de l'œuvre par Philippe Lejeune: *W ou la Mémoire de l'oblique*, Paris, 1991.

[3]   Bénamou, Marcel: "Perec et la judéité", *Colloque de Cerisy* (1984), *Cahiers Georges Perec*, Paris, P. O. L., 1985 (15-29). Motte, Warren: "Embellir les lettres" (110-124).

style comme la juxtaposition des phrases, l'énonciation impersonnelle dans la seconde partie[4] qui gravent dans le texte l'anéantissement et le déchirement vécu par l'enfant.

La première partie du "roman d'aventures" décrit les circonstances du voyage à "l'Ile W". Cette tentative de transposer le vécu en fiction reprend des éléments du texte autobiographique, les organise en un récit chronologique qui exprime le non-dit de celui-ci, décrit l'absence d'identité, les désirs, les sentiments. L'imagination y comble les lacunes de la mémoire donnant forme au difforme et sens à l'insensé. Ainsi, par exemple, la représentation fictive du naufrage en concrétisant la disparition de la mère la rend moins effrayante et offre une explication rassurante de l'abandon de l'enfant.

Dans cette partie l'auteur met en évidence les liens qui unissent le récit personnel au fictif à l'aide de termes et de thèmes récurrents et des doubles fictifs Gaspard Winckler l'enfant sourd-muet et Gaspard Winckler le déserteur. L'itinéraire de celui-ci qui va du refus de la mémoire à la prise de conscience du devoir de mémoire et à l'écriture est identique à celui du narrateur de l'autobiographie.

Une contre-utopie constitue la seconde partie et la deuxième tentative de transposer le vécu "troué" en fiction. "L'Ile W", située à l'extrémité de la Terre de Feu, est la réalisation d'une idéologie qui prêche le culte exclusif du corps, de la force physique et de la victoire. Elle exploite les instincts les plus primitifs de ses citoyens et ce faisant les anéantit et se détruit elle-même. Régis par l'injustice et l'arbitraire, privés de nom, d'identité et de liberté les hommes y sont réduits à l'état de nature décrit par Hobbes. L'auteur qui a réussi à objectiver l'expérience personnelle, rationalise, analyse et interprète l'injustice, la cruauté, l'arbitraire, le mépris pour la personne humaine inscrites dans les souvenirs et dans l'Histoire. Leur transposition fictive révèle la portée réelle des faits rapportés sans commentaires dans l'autobiographie tels que les changements de nom, de langue, la croix sur la tombe paternelle, la conversion de l'enfant juif ainsi que l'absurde cruauté et la trahison que recouvrent des notations apparemment neutres comme : "... elle pensait que son titre de veuve de guerre lui éviterait tout ennui" ou "ma mère n'a pas de tombe.... Si elle avait été de nationalité française elle aurait eu droit à la mention 'mort pour la France'." (*W...*, 58)

---

[4] Burgelin, Claude: "Perec et la cruauté", *Cahiers Georges Perec* (38).

La contre-utopie adopte la forme d'un rapport d'ethnologue d'une grinçante minutie. L'ironie, parfois légère, parfois caustique, mine les descriptions de la machine à broyer les hommes, les explications logiques, les justifications pseudo-morales et dénonce la perversion du langage à l'origine de l'entreprise et qui en masque le véritable visage. Invité dans la première partie de la fiction à assimiler le narrateur fictif au "je" de l'autobiographie, le lecteur se trouve ici en présence d'une voix narratrice anonyme qui souligne l'écart entre la fiction et l'aventure vécue.

Les références historiques et littéraires comme "l'Autriche", la "Nurnbergstrasse" (il faut remarquer la disparition du E dans l'orthographe de ce nom), le voyage, le naufrage, la gare, les symboles qui, dans la première partie, rattachent la fiction à l'Histoire des Juifs, disparaissent ou acquièrent un sens universel dans la seconde. "L'île", symbole de l'enfermement, de l'exil et de la mort est d'abord l'Ile de la Giudecca à Venise, vide de Juifs sans doute depuis le haut Moyen-Age. Cependant son nom les évoque ainsi que les persécutions et aussi, par association, le dernier cercle de l' Enfer de Dante où croupit Judas. "L'Ile W", en dépit de certains détails, ne représente pas la Shoah ni les camps de la mort nazis dans leur spécificité mais tout régime totalitaire dont les camps sont une partie intégrante comme en témoigne la référence au Chili et à Pinochet. La lettre W y désigne non seulement les Juifs mais les "vaincus" des dictatures en général.

Si l'écriture a mis des "limites au déchiffrement", elle n'a guère résolu le problème de l'identité ni celui de l'absence de mémoire: on ignore le sort de l'enfant sourd-muet. Le décalage entre la banalité du déguisement fictif imité des romans d'aventures et la tragédie vécue dans la première partie, l'universalisation des problèmes, leur impersonnalisation dans la seconde, signifient l'incapacité de la fiction à traduire le drame personnel. Cet échec explique le besoin qu'éprouve Perec d'ancrer la contre-utopie dans la réalité historique en ajoutant un paragraphe détaché où il énumère les objets conservés au Musée d'Auschwitz et que terminent les points de suspension, signes de la disparition de la mère. Si la fiction impersonnelle confère une dimension universelle au vécu de l'auteur, celui-ci donne une dimension humaine à la fiction. Mais seule l'écriture autobiographique par son dépouillement même, expression de la mémoire trouée de l'écrivain, rend visible et lisible l'horreur de l'extermination et la cruauté de l'Histoire, "celle avec sa grande H".

Contrairement à "la mémoire charnelle" de Perec la mémoire de Modiano est essentiellement inventée et livresque. Il vit "de manière hallucinatoire la période 35-45" qui lui permet d'exprimer ses hantises, ses angoisses et sa quête des origines. La découverte de l'antisémitisme notamment celui des "phares" de la culture française qu'il admirait le bouleverse: "Gide disait que les Juifs feraient mieux d'écrire en hébreu. Giraudoux aussi était antisémite... Je cite ces gens parce qu'ils représentent l'humanisme français, la quintessence française. Tout ça je l'ai éprouvé profondément..." Ecrire devient alors pour Modiano, "exilé" de la langue et de la culture natales, un acte de vengeance et de fidélité au père "muet devant les antisémites" à qui il prête sa voix. Il désire exprimer "le sentiment d'étrangeté totale du déraciné". (Modiano, interview, 1975) et servir de mémoire à son temps habile à l'oubli.

L'écriture éclatée, hallucinée des premiers ouvrages dont les titres *La Place de l'Etoile, Les Boulevards de ceinture* et *La Ronde de nuit* (Modiano, 1968, 1969, 1972) dessinent l'enfermement du héros pris au piège de l'Histoire, fait progressivement place à l'écriture "pseudo-classique", dont la clarté masque un message qui la détruit.

Rue des Boutiques obscures, (Modiano, 1978) reprend pour les approfondir les thèmes de la mémoire et de l'oubli déjà abordés dans un récit de *Livret de famille* (Modiano, 1977): "Je n'avais que vingt ans mais ma mémoire précédait ma naissance.... J'aurais tout donné pour devenir amnésique."(Modiano, *Livret de Famille*, 1977, 117) Pour vaincre ce désir Modiano l'incarne dans un personnage: le narrateur de *Rue des Boutiques obscures*. Cet ouvrage est une "Recherche du Temps Perdu" qui se présente comme une enquête objective et systématique. Mais le détective privé qui la mène est amnésique et la reconstitution de son passé, l'objet de la recherche. "Je ne suis rien", dit le narrateur au début du livre. Homme sans identité parce que sans mémoire, il interroge celle des autres et les lieux, témoins supposés de sa vie. Mais la mémoire des gens défectueuse et égocentrique restitue un passé incertain et morcelé, les restaurants et les hôtels, lieux de séjour et de rencontre des exilés changent de nom et de propriétaire. Les êtres tels que le symbolique "homme des plages" disparaissent sans laisser d'autres traces qu'une photo, un nom dans un bottin ou sur un document administratif, seules preuves objectives et tangibles de leur existence mais qui non authentifiées par des témoins ne mènent à aucune certitude. Guy Roland, le narrateur qui ignore son vrai nom, croit successivement se reconnaître en Freddie puis en Pedro qui est vraisemblablement Jimmy Stern. Après l'identification commence le travail de l'esprit et de l'imagination qui regroupe les éléments recueillis, les complète, les organise en un récit logique et aboutit à la reconstitution du passé de Jimmy Stern et de sa femme Denise Coudreuse disparue à la frontière Suisse après la trahison du passeur pendant l'Occupation nazie. L'aventure tragique ainsi reconstituée est à la fois "réelle" puisqu'elle représente des événements historiques et imaginaire comme le passé remémoré de chacun.

Les problèmes de la mémoire et de l'oubli ont acquis dans cette œuvre une dimension universelle. Cependant ce qui pousse l'auteur à écrire est la nécessité de cerner sa spécificité juive que révèle le nom symbolique de "Stern", vrai patronyme du narrateur, qui signifie étoile, étoile jaune comme dans *La Place de l'Etoile* et comme la lumière qui le guide. La quête de l'identité juive s'inscrit encore dans le lieu d'origine où il se rend au terme de son errance: la Rue des Boutiques obscures située en bordure du Ghetto de Rome, symbole des persécutions et de l'exclusion des Juifs mais aussi de la violence contemporaine puisque c'est dans cette rue qu'on trouva assassiné Aldo Moro.

L'écriture claire, sans âge, "amnésique", marque la dissonnance entre la beauté et l'ordre de la forme et le désordre du vécu tragique des déracinés, des traqués et des persécutés dans la France du XXème siècle que retracent les intrigues secondaires du roman.

La réalité y apparaît toute en surfaces, des relations affectives et esthétiques ne pouvant s'établir que dans la durée. La suppression des comparaisons et des nuances qui révèleraient quelque lien entre la subjectivité du héros et le monde ambiant réduit la description des objets à quelques détails plats. Il en va de même des personnages interchangea-bles qui vivent au présent hors de l'Histoire et refoulent la Shoah.

Modiano, dans cet ouvrage, poursuit un dialogue avec Proust et traite avec humour le thème du temps destructeur. L'aspect physique des personnages change en fonction de leur expérience et non de leur âge. Ainsi Mansoure, prisonnier de la mémoire de l'Occupation, double neuro-tique et antithétique du narrateur a les cheveux "blancs, très blancs" alors que celui-ci a l'air d'un enfant malgré ses cinquante ans.

Plus sérieuse est la réfutation de la théorie proustienne de l'incons-cient et de la mémoire. Le narrateur préfère la réalité objective à l'intériorité et le regard à l'odorat "le sens de la mémoire" selon Schopenhauer. Les parfums qui enivraient Proust le mondain, familier des salons, n'évoquent rien pour le héros de Modiano qui a grandi dans la puanteur des villes et la violence des guerres. D'ailleurs désire-t-il vraiment se souvenir ou refoule-t-il le passé parce que l'association fugitive qui, dans "les moments privilégiés", naît d'une intensité particulière de la lumière ou à la vue d'une rue déserte, le remplit d'angoisse?

Modiano ne partage pas davantage la conception proustienne de l'enfance. Deux symboles représentent sa position à cet égard: un château entouré d'herbes folles qui ressemble au "château" de Kafka mais qui de dos rappelle les maisons des villes balnéaires de la fin du XIXème siècle et un "labyrinthe" planté par le grand-père de Freddie. Or le château est du XIIIème siècle, mis "sous séquestre" et administré par "Les Domaines". Quant au narrateur il n'a jamais joué dans le labyrinthe puisqu'il n'est pas Freddie. Il n'y a rien de commun entre la merveilleuse enfance de Proust et celle du fils déraciné de l'expulsion et des persécutions pour qui le Paradis est à jamais perdu. Il ne s'agit pas, par conséquent, de se réfugier dans le passé pour vaincre le temps mais de l'élucider, de l'accepter et de le dépasser afin d'accéder à la connaissance et de donner un sens à l'avenir.

Le dialogue avec Georges Perec, lui, exprime l'adhésion. L'œuvre de Modiano rappelle par son titre *La Boutique obscure* (1973) de Georges Perec où le texte du rêve "devient boutique... lieu de dialogue, d'échange entre les hommes" (12). Mais elle présente aussi de nombreux points de ressemblance avec *W ou le Souvenir d'enfance* comme la nécessité inéluctable de la mémoire du passé et de l'écriture de l'anéantissement, la recherche des traces, l'impossibilité de reconstituer une biographie des disparus qui ne soit en partie imaginaire. Certains éléments tels que le naufrage et la disparition dans une île d'Océanie de Freddie, l'ami d'enfance du narrateur qui, lui, a peut-être choisi de "couper les amarres", semblent parodier la première partie du "roman d'aventures" de Perec tout en soulignant la différence entre l'éclipse volontaire de Freddie et la disparition des victimes de Hitler. La fiction chez Modiano imite une réalité qu'il croit pouvoir capter par l'imagination alors que Perec découvre la pauvreté de celle-ci face à la vie. Modiano dans *Dora Bruder* (1997) où il tente de reconstituer l'itinéraire d'une déportée peu de temps avant la déportation reconnaîtra, lui aussi, ses limites.

On distingue dans *Rue des Boutiques obscures* les éléments constitutifs du Nouveau roman ésotérique des années cinquante: le héros anonyme qui marche, la déréliction kafkaïenne, la figure du labyrinthe, la mise en abîme, l'œuvre s'élaborant à mesure qu'avance l'enquête etc... Modiano qui ne voit pas dans "les recherches formelles... une véritable nécessité d'écrire" (Modiano, interview, 1975) se raille de ces techniques en les utilisant pour réaliser le récit imaginaire d'une tragique aventure "réaliste" engagée dans l'Histoire.

De même les signes freudiens et les symboles surréalistes qui parsèment le texte tournent en dérision la littérature des profondeurs et de la libido jugée inauthentique.

Dès *La Place de l'Etoile* Modiano qui se réclame de Kafka, un des rares écrivains "incarnés", selon lui, a opté pour une esthétique de la vie, de la mémoire et de la fidélité dont témoigne encore *Dora Bruder* (1997). Ecriture—mémoire de l'anéantissement, écriture à jamais inachevée puisque ni l'enquête minutieuse du narrateur ni son identification avec la vie et la souffrance de la déportée ne parviennent à restituer "...ce que l'on ignorera toujours de (sa) vie—ce blanc, ce bloc d'inconnu et de silence." (Modiano, 1997)

Avec David Grossman nous nous éloignons dans l'espace et encore davantage dans le temps. L'auteur n'a connu ni la disparition des siens, ni l'exil culturel et sa perception de la Shoah très présente dans la mémoire du peuple au milieu duquel il vit est moins angoissée, moins aiguë mais plus intime que celle de Modiano.

Voir ci-dessous: Amour (1986) ne décrit ni l'anéantissement ni ne reconstitue la Shoah mais représente les répercussions de celle-ci sur l'évolution intellectuelle et affective d'un "sabra", fils unique de rescapés: Schlomo Efraïm Neuman, tour à tour narrateur, acteur et auteur. L'intrigue complexe de cette vaste symphonie éclatée se développe de manière discontinue sur deux plans étroitement liés: la vie du narrateur depuis la découverte traumatisante, à l'âge de neuf ans, de la mystérieuse "bête nazie" suivie du refus de tout lien affectif par crainte de la souffrance jusqu'à l'acception de celle-ci et de la condition humaine; la vie créatrice depuis la révélation de l'écriture et du dessin comme antidotes contre le mal, l'éveil de la vocation d'écrivain jusqu'à la création originale en passant par l'œuvre désengagée où il se contente de "répertorier les choses", les phases d'identification avec Bruno Schulz et Anshel Wasserman écrivain pour enfants et grand-père mythique du narrateur.

La Shoah sert de point de départ et de pierre de touche à une réflexion sur l'homme, le moi, les rapports avec l'Autre, la condition humaine, l'angoisse existentielle celle de Kafka et de Kierkegaard symbolisée par "Le Cri" d'Edvard Munch. Grossman considère le mal comme une poussée instinctive inhérente à la nature humaine. Bruno Schulz métamorphosé en saumon et réduit à une existence purement biologique l'expérimente même au sein de l'Océan, vaste allégorie de la vie libre et naturelle, où sévissent la mort "Yorik" et les forces destructrices telle que la poussée instinctive qui jette Bruno contre Leprik ou l'arrivée de Gorok qui déchaîne la cruauté et l'instinct de meurtre des saumons et les fait s'entre-déchirer. Le bébé mythique Kazik "foetus du cri" qui, en quelques heures, parcourt le cycle d'une vie connaît lui aussi le mal et la haine. Cependant Grossman qui défend les valeurs humanistes et croit en la liberté, la responsabilité individuelle et la perfectibilité de l'homme condamne toute utopie qui vise à le redéfinir (cf. la parodie de la venue du Messie et de l'avènement de "l'ère du génie" dans "Bruno") et toute tentative scientifique qui métarmorphoserait sa nature (cf. Sergueï le physicien russe "aux mains d'or et au cœur scellé", inventeur du système pour "voler le temps").

Il se livre à une critique de la culture atteinte "d'éléphantiasis", du langage porteur de mort qui permet d'énoncer des phrases telles que: "J'en ai seulement tué deux millions et demi" (Grossman, 203, 111), de l'usage des images et des métaphores à la dangereuse ambiguïté, de la perversion de la parole également dénoncée par Perec comme l'instrument le plus efficace des dictatures. Le choix des articles et des définitions de l'Encyclopédie qui constituent la quatrième partie du roman signifie comme chez Heinrich Böll (*Portrait de groupe avec Dame*) ou chez Romain Gary (*L'Angoisse du Roi Salomon*) la nécessité, après Hitler, d'une mise au point des significations et des valeurs.

Incarnée par de multiples personnages réalistes ou fantastiques, représentée dans les situations, la réflexion de Grossman adopte successivement la forme d'une narration "réaliste" rapportée du point de vue d'un enfant (Momik), celle d'une allégorie (Bruno), d'un conte philosophique (Wasserman) et d'une encyclopédie.

Le narrateur de la première partie, Momik, enfant unique de rescapés, intelligent et sensible, tente de percer le mystère du passé qui obsède ses parents et les retient prisonniers. Le mutisme quasi total de son entourage engendre une situation insupportable: il en sait trop pour ne pas s'interroger et faire taire sa curiosité et pas assez pour assouvir sa soif de savoir et satisfaire le désir de s'identifier aux siens et de les délivrer de "la bête nazie". A travers ce personnage Grossman analyse le problème de la découverte du mal et pose celui de la transmission de l'histoire de la Shoah. Momik incarne la situation du "sabra" obligé d'imaginer celle-ci à partir de bribes de révélations, d'explications tronquées, de lectures désordonnées et d'images terrifiantes. Il se représente un univers angoissant et fascinant dans lequel il s'enfonce et se perd. Si Momik ne parvient pas à extirper la "bête nazie" des animaux enfermés dans la cave il apprend qu'à lutter contre le mal par les moyens du mal on se transforme en bourreau que terrorisent ses victimes.

Cependant le grand-père symbole de la tradition et de l'éthique juives, l'immortel écrivain pour enfants "mort à Treblinka" lui sert de guide. Les héros des "Enfants au cœur vaillant", feuilleton dont il est l'auteur, sont des rescapés des génocides indien et arménien à qui viennent se joindre ceux de la Shoah, "les artistes", silhouettes incarnant la créativité de l'homme. Ils révèlent à Momik les forces positives qui permettent de lutter contre le mal.

Dans cette partie Grossman choisit pour narrateur-témoin un enfant qui confond réel et imaginaire. Ce procédé lui permet d'entraîner l'adhésion du lecteur dont il suscite la crédibilité, la sympathie et une tendresse amusée qui atténue le caractère insoutenable des révélations. La naïveté des réactions enfantines qui investigue ce qu'il ignore à partir de ce qu'il sait, leur naturel et leur sincérité en même temps qu'elles introduisent un certain humour découvrent la perversion de la vision du monde, de la mentalité et du langage nazis.

La pauvreté de l'écriture documentaire d'une part, les images et les métaphores dont l'interprétation littérale par Momik révèle l'ambiguïté et le danger d'autre part, constituent les premiers éléments d'une esthétique, de la quête d'une écriture qui se poursuit dans les autres parties du roman. Ajoutons encore la foi en la vertu thérapeutique de l'Art —Momik corrige les photos afin de soulager la souffrance des victimes —la capacité du récit de créer des liens—c'est en racontant les histoires de Schalom Aleichem apprises à l'école qu'il parvient à communiquer avec ses parents, avec son père qui se met soudain à évoquer les souvenirs heureux de son passé.

Les thèmes de base ainsi posés, s'engage dans les trois parties suivantes le processus de la création pendant que se poursuit l'interrogation sur les questions existentielles. Nous ne pouvons analyser ici toute cette vaste fresque romanesque aux multiples références mythiques et littéraires. Nous nous arrêterons à la troisième partie intitulée Wasserman où Grossman dans le cadre d'un conte philosophique, parodie de Shéhérazade, imagine le dialogue entre le tueur nazi Neigel et sa victime à l'intérieur d'un camp qui, par certains détails, rappelle Treblinka.

Ayant reconnu en Anshel Wasserman—dont le prénom évoque Paul (Amshel) Celan et le nom celui d'un célèbre romancier allemand—l'auteur du feuilleton qui avait fait les délices de son enfance, le Commandant SS lui ordonne d'en poursuivre le récit. En échange il tirera tous les soirs une balle dans la tête du Juif immortel, incarnation des valeurs de son peuple. Ainsi s'engage la lutte de l'esprit et de l'imagination contre la force et le pouvoir, l'affrontement entre le surhomme qui ne croyait pas au pouvoir des mots et l'anti-héros, misérable David, qui n'avait en guise de fronde que des mots creux, éclatés et qui tente par la parole—rien n'est écrit sur les pages du cahier—, dans la meilleure tradition de ses pères, d'inoculer au tueur le "virus d'humanité". Entrecoupée de scènes d'extermination et de torture se poursuit la joute fatale et progressivement l'échange de paroles devient conversation puis dialogue. Pour les besoins de sa thèse—devenir nazi est un choix libre qui engage la responsabilité et non une fatalité biologique—l'auteur prend soin de montrer que les vies des deux hommes se ressemblent par certains côtés mais diffèrent par leurs choix. Lorsque Neigel, abandonné par les siens, découvre la souffrance et la valeur de l'Autre il ne peut plus revenir en arrière. Prisonnier de l'idéologie criminelle qu'il avait librement choisie il en devient la victime et en se tuant reste le serviteur obéissant de Himmler qu'il a toujours été. La mort de Neigel dessine les limites de la réhumanisation du nazi.

La tentative de Grossman rappelle celle de Gary dans *La Danse de Gengis Cohn* mais il n'a pas su, comme celui-ci, éviter les écueils inhérents à la parodie et au comique dans la représentation de l'extermination. Le "Dibbouk" qui hante la conscience du nazi dans l'œuvre de Gary, figure irréelle qui se meut au milieu de ganaches dans une histoire de fantôme essentiellement comique, hors du cadre concentrationnaire, est le seul personnage avec lequel le lecteur puisse s'identifier. Grossman, pour illustrer sa thèse doit étoffer les deux protagonistes et leur prêter une psychologie qui leur confèrent une réalité incompatible avec les silhouettes du conte philosophique. Le lecteur est, de ce fait, invité à s'identifier tantôt avec la victime, tantôt avec le bourreau. Par ailleurs chez Grossman la confrontation se déroule dans le temps et l'espace de l'extermination alors que, dans l'œuvre de Gary, la Shoah n'existe que dans la mémoire du Dibbouk qui lutte, après la guerre, contre le désir de l'oubli du nazi. Le lecteur d'une fiction distingue entre le réel représenté et l'imaginaire et ne peut faire abstraction de Treblinka ce qui rend intolérable le dédoublement de l'identification et tue toute velléité de rire. L'alternance entre les massacres et les rencontres bourreau-victime provoque une rupture dans l'esprit et l'affectivité du lecteur confronté tour à tour à l'invraisemblable et à la réalité, à un humour douteux et au tragique.

Afin de briser l'image mythique qui assimile tout Allemand à un tueur, Grossman esquisse des personnages divers figurant différentes attitudes allemandes envers le nazisme. Dans cette partie du roman il traite également des limites de la torture et de la force physique en inventant deux couples incarnant la relation bourreau-victime: celui de Wasserman et de Neigel où elle est d'emblée réduite à néant par l'immortalité du Juif et son refus d'user de la force ce qui l'établit sur le plan du langage et de la pensée; celui d'Orff et de Ginzbourg ou l'affrontement symbolise la dichotomie corps-esprit. Orff, inspecteur spécialiste des tortures, sérieux et consciencieux, nietzschéen adepte de la volonté de puissance et de la vérité objective, torture Ginzbourg pour qu'il lui révèle son identité. Mais Ginzbourg qui représente l'interrogation sur l'être irréductible au corps ne peut lui fournir la réponse qu'il désire. Stupéfait devant l'inefficacité de ses méthodes le tortionnaire entrevoit son erreur: nul ne peut asservir la liberté de l'Autre ni découvrir le mystère de l'être en torturant la chair.

L'œuvre de Grossman dénonce la Shoah et à aucun moment ne confond les nazis avec leurs victimes ni ne porte atteinte aux aspects éthiques de l'Histoire. On y trouve cependant un défaut commun à la plupart des fictions réalisées par des auteurs qui n'ont pas vécu l'horreur nazie: l'interprétation qui commande le choix des éléments de l'œuvre ne découle pas de celle-ci mais de problèmes relevant de l'actualité qui les préoccupent. La qualité et la signification de la représentation dépendent, dans ce cas, de celles des thèses défendues par les auteurs qui parfois entraînent de fâcheux amalgames et des généralisations hâtives voire des falsifications de l'Histoire.

Mémoire trouée du vécu, mémoire imaginaire ou mémoire critique les œuvres d'écrivains concernés que nous avons examinées témoignent de l'incontournable présence de la Shoah. Georges Perec grave l'anéantissement dans l'écriture elle-même. L'écriture minimaliste de Patrick Modiano crée une ambiance qui le suggère. A l'encontre de ceux-ci David Grossman n'est pas en quête de son identité. Il examine les questions existentielles soulevés par l'extermination dans le cadre de l'actualité israëlienne. La richesse de l'invention et les mobiles de l'écriture ne permettront pas au lecteur qui le désirerait d'approcher par l'imagination et la sensibilité le vécu de l'extermination. Mais de la multiplicité des styles se dégage une esthétique inséparable de l'éthique semblable pour l'essentiel à celles de Modiano et de Perec: le rôle de la littérature et de l'art consiste à dénoncer le mal et à servir de mémoire et de lien entre les hommes.

Charlotte Wardi
Haifa

Bibliographie

Böll, Heinrich. 1971. *Gruppenbild mit Dame*. Köln: Kiepenheuer und Witsch. Traduction française: S. et G. de Lalène: *Portrait de groupe avec Dame*. Paris: Seuil, 1973.

Gary, Romain (Ajar, Emile). 1967. *La Danse de Gengis Cohn*. Paris: Gallimard.

—————. 1979. *L'Angoisse du Roi Salomon*. Paris: Mercure de France.

Grossman, David. 1986. *Ayen erech: Ahava*. Tel Aviv: Hakibboutz Hameouhad. Traduction française de J. Mizrahi et A. Barak: *Voir ci-dessous: Amour*. Paris: Seuil, 1991.

Modiano, Patrick. 1968. *La Place de l'Etoile*. Paris: Gallimard.

—————. 1969. *Les Boulevards de Ceinture*. Paris: Gallimard.

—————. 1972. *La Ronde de Nuit*. Paris: Gallimard.

—————. Interview recueillie par Julien Brünn in *Libération*, 22. 9. 1975.

—————. 1977. *Livret de Famille*. Paris: Gallimard (folio).

—————. 1978. *Rue des Boutiques obscures*. Paris: Gallimard (folio).

—————. 1997. *Dora Bruder*. Paris: Gallimard.

Perec, Georges. 1973. *La Boutique obscure*. Postface par Roger Bastide, Paris: Denoël.

—————. 1975. *W ou le Souvenir d'enfance*. Paris: Denoël.

—————. 1980. *Récits d'Ellis Island*. Paris: Editions du Sorbier.

Semprun, Jorge. 1994. *L'Ecriture ou la Vie*. Paris: Gallimard.

Embarrassing Problems Connected with
Polish Concentration Camp Literature

Countless books, essays and articles have already been written and are still being written about different aspects of the Holocaust. Nevertheless, many points still remain controversial and subject to further discussion. One of the greatest difficulties is probably due to the fact that it seems almost unfeasible to deal with just one, isolated problem regarding the Holocaust, without taking into consideration all its other cultural, social and political aspects. Is it at all possible, for example, without taking into account the anti-Semitic strategies of Communist governments in post-war Poland, the influence played by Polish Church teachings or the historical aspects of Polish-Jewish relations? Such an approach to the problem can be easily contested, so, the reflections presented here are not designed to lead to definite or categorical interpretations, but simply to indicate a particular feature connected with the way in which documentary and literary writings from the concentration camp Auschwitz were received.

The question to consider is the following: in what way and to what extent did Polish writings, novels, and memoirs concerning concentration camps influence the idea of Auschwitz dominant in Polish society? The question itself was generated by my personal experience, when I suddenly realised, some years ago, that my idea of Auschwitz as a place of Polish martyrdom was not quite as obvious as I thought it to be. On discovering such controversies as the argument about situating a Carmelite Convent and a Cross in the death camp, I was at first shocked and confused. I was conscious, of course, of the tragedy of the "Final Solution" and of the extermination of Jews in the gas chambers; I was accustomed, however, to consider Polish Jews as Poles of Jewish origin and Auschwitz as place of martyrdom of the Polish nation. It was an idea which I shared, I would say, with a large part of my generation, who had never had any direct contact with the War and the Holocaust. My idea of the War and of what concentration camps were was formed mainly by Polish writings on this subject, especially the texts I read at school.

Obviously, one must not underestimate the effect of other channels of information about Auschwitz, such as films, television programs and documentaries, press articles, scientific publications, etc. For many years the teaching policy in schools, for example, was that of avoiding awkward problems connected with the Holocaust and of hiding the dark and controversial aspects of Polish-Jewish relations. Therefore, while speaking about concentration camps, teachers tended to underline the general ethical and moral problems of the Nazi strategy of extermination and to describe the sufferings of "victims", of "people", without stressing their nationality and origin. As a result, most scholars were induced to interpret the texts they were reading according to the point of view presented by their teachers.

The same tendency occurs in criticism. Analysis and reviews of literary writings about the death camps were interested, in most cases, in general aspects connected with the description of life in the concentration camps, in the difficulty of the artistic transposition of the inhuman reality experienced by prisoners, in the efficacy—or inefficacy—of different narrative strategies adopted by the authors. The word "Jews", if not quite banished, was certainly used rather reticently, especially while speaking about the mass extermination in gas chambers.[1]

On the other hand, the martyrdom in the camp of a Polish Franciscan, Maksymilian Maria Kolbe, recently canonised by Pope John Paul II,

---

[1]   To give an example: in his monograph on Borowski's narrative about Auschwitz, Andrzej Werner never uses the word "Holocaust" of "Shoah"; the words "Jew", "Jews" appear very rarely and mainly while speaking about individuals. Werner does mention "Endlösung", the mass extermination of Jews planned by the Nazis, but generally he chooses to speak about "people" and "prisoners" and very cautiously hints at the moral problems regarding the different situation of prisoners according to their "Aryan" or "not Aryan" origin. Of course, this strategy must not be attributed only to the personal preferences of the critic, but should be considered in the political context in which the essay was written. (Andrzej Werner, *Zwyczajna apokalipsa. Tadeusz Borowski i jego wizja świata obozów*, Warsaw: Czytelnik, 1981.)

became an essential element of the collective Polish imaginary about Auschwitz and became the subject of literary and cinematographic works.[2]

But leaving aside the tangled web of questions, what image of Auschwitz emerges from Polish writings and memoirs from concentration camps? The literature dealing with this subject is, obviously, very extensive, but I would like to analyse here just a few texts which, in my opinion, have had a major impact on the opinion people in Poland have of Auschwitz and which are, at the same time, examples of the main narrative tendencies characteristic of this kind of writings. I have chosen three books: first, *Byliśmy w Oświęcimiu* (*We were in Oświęcim*, 1946), the short stories of Tadeusz Borowski, prisoner in Auschwitz in the years 1943-44; second, *Dymy nad Birkenau* (*The Smoke over Birkenau*, 1945), memoirs of Seweryna Szmaglewska, prisoner in Auschwitz in the years 1942-45, and third, *Z otchłani* (*From the Abyss*), memoirs of Zofia Kossak-Szczucka, prisoner in the camp in the years 1943-44.

The book of the latter is one of numerous texts which follow a traditional narrative pattern and give a dichotomous, black and white vision of the camps reality.[3] *The Smoke over Birkenau*, although conceived as a piece of documentary writing and thus having many points in common with *From the Abyss*, gives a more penetrating view of prisoners' life in Auschwitz and avoids the risk of one-sided moral judgments.

The most interesting, from both the literary and sociological point of view, are nevertheless the short stories of Tadeusz Borowski, which are half way between fictional and documentary writings.

Borowski's first book, which was published in 1946 and instantly became the subject of a heated discussion, elicited accusations of cynicism with respect to its representation of life in the death camp. In fact, the author broke the taboo of not speaking about the most awkward and dark aspects of the reality of the camp, by showing not only the bestiality of the oppressors, but also the profound and inevitable depravation of the victims.

---

[2] It may be worth remembering the short story of Jan Józef Szczepański, *Święty* (*A Saint*, 1975) and the film of Krysztof Zanussi, *Życie za życie. Maksymilian Kolbe.* (*Life for life. Maximilian Kolbe*, 1991).

[3] Among numerous texts which follow such a pattern, may be remembered *Przeżyłem Oświęcim* (*I survived Auschwitz*) by Krystyna Żywulska (1946), *Dziewczyna z Pól Elizejskich* (*A Girl from the Elysian Fields*) by Gustaw Morcinek (1946), and *Opowiadania Oświęcimskie* (*Stories from Auschwitz*) by Maria Zarębińska-Broniewska (1960).

The vision of the "world of stone", in which traditional moral values have been abolished and forgotten, human dignity has ceased to exist and the most repulsive behaviour was regarded as normal and acceptable, appeared at first too shocking for many readers and critics, who attacked the writer harshly, denouncing his book as "false, cynical, injurious ... memoirs from the camp which strike a blow at the dignity of prisoner and martyr" (Poszumski, 1947). However, the literary and documentary value of *We Were in Oświęcim* was soon recognised and the book has become compulsory reading in Polish schools.

Borowski describes the conditions of life in Auschwitz from the point of view of a prisoner who in order to survive had to live according to the rules dictated by the inhuman reality of the death camp. He shows the moral depravity, the indifference towards sufferings of other people, the bestiality of behaviour caused by the living conditions of the prisoners; all the gruesome aspects of everyday life in a death camp are shown with brutal frankness. His own fate and that of his fiancée, imprisoned in the adjacent camp of Birkenau remains, quite understandably, at the centre of attention, but every story presents also a wide and varied range of other figures. There are German criminal prisoners, Russian soldiers, Gypsies, even Spaniards and Greeks. Obviously, there are also Jews. Speaking about individuals, Borowski usually indicates their origin and nationality; but when he describes the general mechanisms of the extermination system in the death camp, he prefers to speak about just "women", "men", "people". Characteristic, from this point of view, are two short stories dedicated to the most horrible aspect of the extermination industry in Auschwitz: the selection of trainloads immediately after arrival and their passage to the gas chambers. The first of these two stories, entitled "Proszę państwa do gazu" ("Ladies and Gentlemen, I invite you to the gas chamber"), is written from the point of view of a prisoner who is a member of the so-called "Canada" commando. (The "Canada" commando was a group of prisoners employed by the Germans to sort out the goods which people brought to the camp and were forced to abandon when leaving the train.) The story presents the first day of work of the narrator in the commando. Therefore, unlike his colleagues, who are already accustomed to the gruesome reality they are confronted with, he is still capable of reacting with horror and repulsion in front of the machine of death. During the day described in the story, three trains arrive in Auschwitz, all from Sosnowiec-Będzin in Poland. After the selection the majority of the newcomers are sent to the gas chamber. The people brought to the camp in this transport are, undoubtedly, Jews; nevertheless the narrator never uses this word throughout the whole story. While describing the moment of arrival of the train and the incidents during the process of selection of the victims, he speaks about "an old lady", "a young and pretty woman", "an old man in an elegant suit", "a sweet little girl", "a young girl with blond hair" etc. There are only two points in the story at which the Jewish origin of the victims is indicated: a child who has lost its mother shouts "mamełe", which is a typical Jewish word; and one of the members of the "Canada" commando, on discovering that a woman wants to abandon her child in order to survive the selection, calls her "jewriejskaja blad" (Jewish whore). Also, in his general reflection about people sent to the gas chambers of Auschwitz the narrator enumerates "Jews, Poles, Russians, people from the South and from the West, from the continent and from the islands", putting the Jews on top of the list, but underlining the multinational provenance of the victims.

The story "Ludzie, którzy szli" ("The people who were passing by") is based on the contrast of two realities: that of everyday life in the camp and that of the people who are passing through—to the gas chambers. These two realities in fact never meet; the people are being selected for the gas chambers immediately after arrival, they never enter the camp because they go straight to the crematorium. The prisoners in the camp, on the other hand, are engaged in a cruel battle for survival. They have, as the narrator tells us "their own problems". The fact, that they have in a sense become accustomed to the sight of an unending procession of people from every part of Europe on their way to the gas chambers, is maybe the most horrible aspect of the mental degradation caused by life in a concentration camp.

Again, the "people who were passing by" are obviously Jews, but in the text this is not explicitly expressed; the narrator refers to them always as to "those people". Thus, the full meaning of the picture presented in the story is clear only to a reader who is aware of its context. One may assume that in 1946 this context was clear to everybody; it is not so obvious, however, for a person who has no direct recollection of the time of the War. Nowadays the fiction of Borowski has become to a certain extent cryptic, and without a proper explanation part of its message may not come across anymore.

The same tendency is evident in two other books I would like to mention here, *The Smoke over Birkenau* by Seweryna Szmaglewska and *From the Abyss* by Zofia Kossak-Szczucka.

Seweryna Szmaglewska was arrested by the Gestapo in 1942 for conspiracy and spent nearly three years in Auschwitz-Birkenau. Her book, written immediately after her escape from the camp during its evacuation in January 1945 and published as early as the summer of the same year, was the first authentic testimony from the camp to reach the public and became also one of the best known. Until now, it has been through no less than eighteen editions.

The Smoke over Birkenau is a documentary giving an impersonal chronological account of everyday life in Birkenau from 1942 until the end of the existence of the camp. Among the prisoners in the camp there are women of different nationalities: Polish, Czech, Greek, French, Italian, Yugoslavian, and others. The writer speaks also about Jewish women and underlines that their situation was even more desperate than that of other prisoners. However, the narrator describes above all the vicissitudes of life of the prisoners with whom she had direct contact; and because Jews were generally held in separate barracks, the narrator considers them rather as a group and takes the position of an external observer. She also has a tendency to speak of the Greeks rather than of Greek Jews, of the French instead of French Jews, etc.

In the first period of her imprisonment, the crematorium was the prime symbol of the camp and of the futility of the prisoners' existence, threatened by countless perils; it was only in 1943 when the construction of four new crematoria and adjacent gas chambers was finished that the systematic mass murder of Jews began. This new complex of buildings had an independent entrance and was separated from the camp by a fence.

Szmaglewska dedicates one of the chapters of her book to the extermination process in Auschwitz. But again, as in Borowski's stories, the point of view is that of a helpless observer; the women in the camp are only the horrified witnesses of the process of destruction; they are never in direct touch with the people sent to the gas chamber immediately after their arrival in the camp. A few—about one-tenth of every trainload—stay alive after the selection and do not enter the main camp, but are directed to a special, separate department of the camp, called "Mexico". The conditions there are so horrible that the imprisoned women soon die from starvation, cold or sickness.

The narrator does not hide some repulsive examples of behaviour provoked by the arrival in the camp of a variety of goods brought in by the

Jews who are unaware that they were destined for mass execution.

> There is a general opinion, that it is better to take whatever
> is available, instead of leaving it to the Germans. But this is
> only a self-deception, which has to justify the first step to
> greediness. (...) Those who reach for the first time for things
> still warm, for things stained with blood, who find joy in
> getting them, become gradually obsessed by the craving for
> possession. In the hubbub of everyday life in the camp this
> change is at first almost imperceptible, does not disturb. But
> it is growing, growing larger, and infects thoughts and
> people. (Szmaglewska, 1989:217)

Szmaglewska speaks clearly about abuses committed by guards and
prisoners higher up in the camp's hierarchy; she confesses a profound
sense of shame and helplessness in front of homicide. But however
terrifying and gruesome the spectacle of death the prisoners are forced to
witness may be, the difficulty of everyday life in the camp is more
pressing. As a result, after this one specific chapter the narration returns
to the life inside the main camp.

The same narrative pattern may be found in *From the Abyss* by
Zofia Kossak-Szczucka. Her memoirs, first published in 1946, did not
attain the popularity of Szmaglewska's book; nevertheless, since their
author was a well-known writer, they attracted the attention of many
readers and also inspired violent polemics, among others an attack by
Borowski.[4] Kossak-Szczucka was arrested in 1943 for conspiracy and spent
only a few months in Auschwitz. Her description of life in the camp is
therefore more general than the picture presented by Szmaglewska,
although its main elements remain very much the same. The most
relevant difference lies in the ideological position of the narrator. Kossak-
Szczucka makes in fact an attempt to apply traditional Catholic values to
her judgement about the reality of the concentration camp. Unlike
Szmaglewska, she is unable to understand the specificity of psychological
changes caused by life in the camp, and therefore she does not hesitate to
pass moral judgements, which in the given context seem superficial and
naive. She tries for example to convince the readers, that faith and prayer
were the principal source of the courage and resistance of the major part

---

[4]   His article, entitled "Alicja w krainie czarów" ("Alice in Wonderland"), became in its turn the
object of many attacks.

of the Polish prisoners. She endeavours also to explain the differences in the behaviour of different groups of prisoners by invoking their national mentality and character. She praises, for example, the French for their spirit and amiable character and dislikes the Ukrainians for being greedy and primitive. Like Szmeglewska, Kossak-Szczucka dedicates one chapter of her book to the mass extermination of Jews in the gas chambers of Auschwitz. She describes also the terrible fate of those few Jewish girls and women who were spared after the selection and put into the "Mexico" camp. She speaks about them with commiseration and sympathy, marked, perhaps, by some sense of superiority, but after few pages she returns to what is the main object of her narration, which is the fate of her compatriots, the Polish prisoners and their heroic behaviour.

On the whole, the view of Auschwitz presented in the book of Kossak-Szczucka has a striking resemblance to the description of the camp made by Szmaglewska. A very similar picture of Auschwitz emerges also from the major part of other documentary Polish writings from the camp, which usually follow the narrative pattern of Szmaglewska's book rather than that of Borowski. They are intended to be, first of all, a document, without any literary aspirations, even if, after all, the camp reality presented by most of them appears to become somewhat idealised, "softened", especially as far as the relations between the prisoners are concerned. As for Borowski's short stories, the situation is more complicated, because they are half way between document and fiction. It happens, therefore, that they are read and interpreted as a literary work and not as a historical testimony. This is a very important point if we consider that among the younger generations Borowski's stories are often the only ones about concentration camps they ever read.

In spite of the many differences between the three books I have discussed, there are some elements which they all have in common. Firstly, they are all testimonies about the concentration camp Auschwitz, and not about the extermination camp Auschwitz. In fact, Auschwitz was founded in 1940 as a concentration camp similar to Bergen-Belsen and Dachau, and although it became later primarily the place of Shoah, its original function had never ceased to exist. The writings of Polish prisoners present the dimension of the camp in which they were most involved; therefore they describe the extermination of Jews from the outside, from the position of witnesses, horrified, but not directly involved in the spectacle of death they are forced to witness. As a consequence, although all authors underline that Jewish prisoners outnumbered other groups present in the camp, they dedicate much more space to the description of the fate of Polish prisoners.

The second important point is the tendency, which may be noticed in all three books, to avoid speaking about the awkward and controversial aspects of Polish-Jewish relations, either in pre-war Poland or even in the camp. It is quite understandable that the horror of Auschwitz has wiped out most of the former antagonism, nevertheless after having read the book of Szmaglewska or of Kossak-Szczucka the average reader will not be able even to perceive the existence of that problem.

To sum up, the view of Auschwitz that emerges from the three books I analysed here, without being false or insincere is undoubtedly a bit partial and one-sided, a characteristic which they share with many other Polish writings about Auschwitz. Fortunately, the cultural and political situation in Poland has been changing for some years already and the access to writings describing the camp of Auschwitz from a different point of view has become much easier. It is evident that Polish concentration camp literature should not remain the only source of knowledge about Auschwitz and it may be hoped that in the future an understanding of the special meaning which the camp has assumed for the Jewish community will be more widespread in Polish society. This does not diminish, however, the documentary value of Polish writings about Auschwitz; considering that more than 140,000 Poles were imprisoned in the camp during the War and about 70,000 died there, these books give testimony to the fact that Auschwitz was also the place of Polish martyrdom and explain to a large extent why every discussion about Auschwitz in Poland provokes such a strong emotional reaction.

Monika Woźniak
Cracow

Bibliography

Borowski, Tadeusz. 1946. "Alicja w krainie czarów". *Pokolenie*, 1946, 1.

Death Books from Auschwitz. 1. Reports, edited by State Museum of Auschwitz-Birkenau, Munich, 1995.

Drewnowski, Tadeusz. 1972. *Ucieczka z kamiennego świata. O Tadeuszu Borowskim.* Warsaw: Państwowy Instytut Wydawniczy.

Hołuj, Tadeusz. 1947. "Temat Oświęcim". *Twórczość*, 1947, 2.

Jagoda, Zenon, Stanisław Kłodziński, Jan Masłowski. 1981. *Oświęcim nieznany.* Cracow: Wydawnictwo Literackie.

Korotyński, Henryk. 1947. "Kiedy będziemy znali Oświęcim". *Odrodzenie.* 1947, 34.

Kuliczkowska, Krystyna. 1947. "Z dni niewoli". *Odrodzenie.* 1947, 1.

Poszumski, Stanisław. 1947. "Fałsz, cynizm, krzywda...wspomnienia z obozu, godzące w godność więźnia męczennika". *Słowo Powszechne*, 1947, 81.

Werner, Andrzej. 1981. *Zwyczajna apokalipsa. Tadeusz Borowski i jego wizja świata obozów.* Warsaw: Czytelnik.

Wyka, Kazimierz. 1974. *Pogranicze powieści.* Warsaw: Czytelnik.

Literature as Cultural Memory

II. Parting from Communism

Stalinism versus European Cultural Memory in the Poetry of Osip Mandel'štam

While early Russian formalism rejected the inclusion of psychological, philosophical and political implications into the interpretation of literary texts, and structuralism, too, laid the main emphasis on the study of the inherent laws of literature, post-structuralism, without advocating a revival of biographism, does indeed allow taking up once more the topic of subjectivity within the interrelation between author and text.

As the poet in question, Osip Mandel'štam [O. M.] (1891-1938), attracted myths and legends about his person and his work like hardly any other modern Russian author, the interrelation between author, real-life circumstances of his times and text in this case appears to be of an exceptionally complex nature. The myth "Osip Mandel'štam" was created, and further fuelled, by the memoirs of his widow, Nadežda, dedicated to the memory of the poet, and by the informal seminars held in her apartment. It was founded, on the one hand, on the specifically Russian notion of the poet as a prophet, a moral authority, or even a saint and, on the other hand, on the tradition of the Russian poet, dating back at least to Radiščev and the Decabrists at the beginning of the 19th century, as a political renegade and a dissident. Only in the Post-Soviet era, as the conception of the poet-as-saint came under review, the myth was dismantled, or rather to some extent corrected (See the works of Gasparov, Freidin and others).

Nadežda Mandel'štam's approach of linking life to œuvre in the case of O. M. was adopted by many Mandel'štam-scholars, especially when analysing his later poems (Ginzburg 1972, Levin 1978, Dutli 1985).

Although, as Ronen has shown in his theses, all of Mandel'štam's œuvre has to be considered as one single text, one single structure, due to its specific chains of lexical-semantic repetitions and the closely knit web of self-references and quotation-like subtexts (Ronen 1973: 370-371), in view of the limitations of this paper I shall concentrate on one particular part of his works, the *Novye stichi* [New verses] written in 1930-34 in Moscow and later named the *Moscow Notebooks*. These are a product of O. M.'s penultimate creative period which was only followed by the Voronež-period from 1935 to 1937 (O. M. died in 1938 in a prison camp near Vladivostok).

Since 1928 O. M. was being persecuted. In the *Moscow Notebooks* he rediscovers his poetic language and defiantly enters into a dialogue with his epoch ("Now is the time for you to learn: I too am your contemporary"). In 1931, he writes one of his most consequential poems, rejecting the wolfish blood of the century (referring to socialism being perverted to Stalinism in Russia and to the rise of fascism). Along with his open epigram against Stalin, written in 1933 under the impression of the terrible consequences of Stalin's policy of forced collectivisation of peasant land, the poem about the violent *"vek - volkodav"* [century of the wolf-hound] was probably one of the main reasons for Mandel'štam's first arrest in 1934.

Attention should be paid to the fact that in O. M.'s later works both the use of non-poetic vocabulary is radically increased and the phonic instrumentation of the verse becomes more and more semantically charged.

This is the point of departure for my thesis that—especially in the Mandel'štam-poems of the thirties—the lyrical "I", which here has moved extremely close to the real-life and the implied author, inscribes itself into the text in a special, anagrammatically coded manner.

Thus, the function of recurring [*os*]-syllables, for example, is not only, as Levin (1978:164) claims, that of constituting an "internal rhyme", but the phonetic web also contains a semantic significance, which establishes a connection between the implied poet and the lyrical subject and—made possible by the fatal coincidence of names—on the one hand the negative pole of the dictator and executioner [Iosif Stalin] and on the other hand the positive pole of the representatives of world poetry in O. M.'s model of the world:

-		+
Iosif, Os'ka (Stalin)	Osip	Osip, Os'ka (Mandel'štam)
ospa [pox]	os' [axis]	Iosif-plotnik [carpenter]
osa [wasp]		Tasso
Moskva		Ariosto
roskoš [luxury]		Toskana
Osetin [Ossetian]		toska [longing]
groza [thunderstorm; fear]		golos [voice]
strekoza [dragonfly]		sol' [salt]
Assirec [Assyrian]		sol'nce [sun]
vlast' [power]		solovej [nightingale]
maska [mask]		vozduch [air]

Whereas in the Anti-Stalin epigram of 1933 the tyrant is openly denoted by directly branding him, in *hyper*semiosis-style, as a "murderer of souls" and sadistic "slayer of peasants", in numerous poems of that period the cryptic, implied true meaning is accessible only on the deeper level of *hypo*semiosis.

The point in question is the phenomenon of the masking "aesopian language" of O. M., discussed, among others, by Zeeman and characterised, on the basis of a few, mainly later poems, as a complex structure of intertwined "frames of reference". The poet's widow, from her point of view, gives an account of how, in 1937, O. M.—to save his life—forced himself to compose an ode to Stalin, while at the same time writing a cycle of poems, in which he semi-unintentionally formulated "verses pointing in the opposite direction". She also points out that, in the verses of the ode as well as in those of the cycle, the syllable [os] is conspicuously dominant, or rather that a recurrence of [s] is observable. She does not go as far, though, as to draw the adequate conclusions and to attempt an interpretation like the one I intend to put forward, based on the anagrammatic method, which is of such great importance for O. M.'s poetry.

In the same way, that R. Jakobson, in his lectures on O. M.'s poem of 1920 *Voz'mi na radost'* [Take for your joy], pointed out that in the second stanza the name *Charon* seems to be encoded (*uslychat', mecha, stracha*), I would claim, that in numerous Mandel'štam-poems of the thirties the name of *Stalin—Iosif Vissarionovič Džugašvili*—and related terms (*kreml'* [Kremlin], *palač* [executioner], *kazn'* [execution], *krov'* [blood], *volk* [wolf], etc.) are inscribed as an anagrammatic *subtext* by semanticizing phonetic repetitions. This can be considered a perversion of the names of gods and heroes, which were, as F. de Saussure has shown, anagrammatically inscribed into classical prayers, incantations and hymns, with the aim, in accordance with the archaic way of thinking, of enhancing the power of the word. Messages coded like riddles is what the author O. M. lets his *poetic persona* convey to his contemporaries and to posterity, messages about the reigning political horror on the one hand, and messages about a bright world culture and the immortal word of the poet on the other hand. On the basis of a few exemplary poems I intend to prove this thesis. First of all, let us turn to the poem *Polnoč' v Moskve* [Midnight in Moscow], written in 1931.

Polnoč' v Moskve (1931)

1 Polnoč' v Moskve. Roskošno buddijskoe leto.
2 S drobotom melkim raschodjatsja ulicy v čobotach uzkich železnych.
3 V černoj ospe blaženstvujut kol'ca bul'varov ...
4 Net na Moskvu i noč'ju ugomonu,
5 Kogda pokoj bežit iz-pod kopyt ...
6 Ty skažeš' – gde-to tam na poligone
7 Dva klouna zaseli – Bim i Bom,
8 I v chod pošli grebenki, molotočki,
9 To slyšitsja garmonika gubnaja,
10 To detskoe moločnoe p'janino –
11 Do–re–mi–fa
12 I sol'–fa–mi–re–do.

13 Byvalo, ja, kak pomolože, vyjdu
14 V prokleennom rezinovom pal'to
15 V širokuju razlapicu bul'varov,
16 Gde spičečnye nožki cyganočki v podole b'jutsja dlinnom,
17 Gde arestovannyj medved' guljaet –
18 Samoj prirody večnyj men'ševik.

19 I pachlo do otk<u>az</u>y lavro<u>viš</u>nej ...
20 Kuda <u>ž</u>e ty? Ni lavrov net, ni <u>viš</u>en ...

21 Ja podtjany butylo<u>č</u>nuju gir'ky
22 Kuchonnych, krupn<u>oskaču</u>ščich <u>čas</u>ov.
23 U<u>ž</u> do <u>č</u>ego <u>š</u>erochovato vremja,
24 A vse-taki ljublju za chv<u>ost</u> ego lovit',
25 Ved' v bege <u>s</u>obstvennom ono ne vinovato,
26 Da, ka<u>ž</u>etsja, <u>č</u>ut'-<u>č</u>ut' <u>ž</u>ulikovato.

27 <u>Č</u>ur! Ne pr<u>os</u>it', ne <u>ž</u>alovat'sja! Cyc!
28 Ne chnykat'!
29 Dlja togo li r<u>az</u>no<u>č</u>incy
30 R<u>asso</u>chlye toptali <u>sa</u>pogi, <u>č</u>tob ja teper' ich predal?
31 My umrem kak pechotincy,
32 No ne pr<u>os</u>lavim ne chi<u>šč</u>i, ni poden<u>šč</u>iny, ni l<u>ž</u>i!

33 Est' u n<u>as</u> pautinka <u>š</u>otlandskogo starogo pleda.
34 Ty menja im ukroeš', kak flagom voennym, kogda ja umru.
35 Vyp'em, dru<u>ž</u>ok, <u>za</u> na<u>š</u>e ja<u>č</u>mennoe gore,
36 Vyp'em do dna!

37 Iz gu<u>sto</u> otrabotav<u>š</u>ich kino,
38 Ubitye, kak p<u>os</u>le chloroforma,
39 Vychodjat tolpy – do <u>č</u>ego oni ven<u>oz</u>ny,
40 I do <u>č</u>ego im nu<u>ž</u>en ki<u>s</u>l<u>o</u>rod!
41 Pora vam zn<u>at</u>', ja to<u>ž</u>e s<u>o</u>vremennik
42 Ja <u>č</u>elovek èpochi M<u>oskvoš</u>veja, –
43 <u>Sm</u>o<u>t</u>rite, kak na mne topor<u>šč</u>itsja pi<u>dž</u>ak,
44 Kak ja stupat' i govorit' umeju!
45 Poprobujte menja ot veka otorvat'!
46 Ru<u>č</u>ajus' vam – sebe svernete <u>š</u>eju!

47 Ja govorju s èpochoju, no r<u>az</u>ve
48 <u>Du</u>ša u nej pen'kovaja i r<u>az</u>ve
49 Ona u n<u>as</u> p<u>os</u>tydno pri<u>ž</u>ilas',
50 Kak <u>sm</u>or<u>šč</u>ennyj zverek v tibetskom chrame, –
51 Po<u>č</u>e<u>š</u>etsja i v zinkovuju vannu –
52 I<u>z</u>obr<u>az</u>i e<u>šč</u>e nam, Mar' Ivanna.
53 Pust' èto <u>os</u>k<u>o</u>rbitel'no – pojmite:

54   Est' blud truda i on u na̲s̲ v krovi.

55   Už̲e svetaet. Šumjat s̲a̲dy zelenym telegrafom',
56   K Rembrandtu vchodit v go̲s̲ti Rafaèl'.
57   O̲n s̲ Mocartom v Mo̲s̲kve d̲u̲ši ne čaet –
58   Z̲a̲ karij gla̲z̲, z̲a̲ vorob'inyj chmel'.
59   I s̲l̲ovno pnevmatičeskuju počtu
60   Il' studenec meduzy černomo̲r̲s̲koj
61   Peredajut s kvartiry na kvartiru
62   Konvejerom vo̲z̲dušnym skvo̲z̲njaki,
63   Kak ma̲j̲s̲kie studenty-š̲elaputy...

Midnight in Moscow (1931)

1   *Midnight in Moscow. The Buddhist summer is splendid.*
2   *With pattering feet the streets disperse in narrow iron boots.*
3   *The rings of boulevards are blissfull in black pockmarks.*
4   *Even at night Moscow can't settle down.*
5   *When peace runs out from under hooves,*
6   *You'll say – somewhere out there on the firing range,*
7   *Two clowns have set up shop – Bim and Bom,*
8   *And got their little combs and hammers going.*
9   *First you hear the mouth organ,*
10   *Then a child's tiny piano –*
11   *Do-re-mi-fa*
12   *And sol-fa-mi-re-do.*

13   *Time was, when I was younger, I'd go out*
14   *In a patched gum coat*
15   *Into the broad-boughed boulevards,*
16   *Where a little gypsy's matchstick legs beat against long skirts,*
17   *Where the arrested bear strolls –*
18   *Nature's own eternal menshevik,*
19   *And the smell of cherry-laurel overflowing ...*
20   *Where do you think your going! There aren't any cherries or laurels...*

21   *I'll tighten up the bottle weight*
22   *On the wide-swinging kitchen clock.*

23   Time's fur is remarkably rough,
24   But just the same I love to catch it by the tail:
25   After all ist not to blame for its own flight,
26   And I guess it cons us just a tiny bit.
27   Back off! No begging, no complaining! Hush!
28   Don't whine
29   Did the raznochintsy
30   Stamp their cracked boots so that I could betray them now?
31   We'll die like foot soldiers,
32   But we won't glorify greed or day-labor or lies

33   Only a spider web's left of our old Scottish plaid –
34   When I die, you'll wrap me in it like a military flag.
35   Let's drink, old pal, to our barley grief –
36   Bottoms up!

37   From the packed and worn-out movie houses,
38   As if chloroformed, dead
39   Crowds emerge. How veined they are.
40   How badly they need oxygen
41   It's time you knew, I'm a contemporary too,
42   I'm a man of the epoch of the Moscow Garment Combine,
43   See how my Jacket bristles on me,
44   How can I speak and strut!
45   Just try to tear me from the age!
46   I swear you'll end up wringing your own neck!

47   I speak with the age, but does it really
48   Have a hempen soul, was it really
49   Born on the wrong side of the sheets,
50   Like some wrinkled little beast in a Tibetan temple
51   That scratches itself, then hops into its zinc-lined tub –
52   Show us another one, Marya Ivanna!
53   It may offend you – but get this:
54   There's a lechery of labour and it's gotten in our blood

55   It's already getting light. Gardens hum like a green telegraph.
56   Raphael comes to pay a call on Rembrandt.
57   He and Mozart just adore Moscow
58   For its hazel eye, for its summer drunkenness.

59   *And like pneumatic mail*
60   *Or Black Sea jellyfish aspic*
61   *Breezes pass from one apartment*
62   *To the next on aerial conveyer,*
63   *Like May students playing hookey ...*

(Cavanagh: 237-239)

Of great significance here is the recurrence of the syllable [*os*], or its unstressed, so-called *akanje*-form [*as*], which appears in the continuous form [*os*], transposed through inversion [from *os, oz, as, az* to *so, zo, sa, za*], or anagrammatically distributed within a lexeme as [*s..o*], like for instance in *gusto* or *kislorod*, and stands for the phenomenon inscribed into the text in three places [*roskošno* (line 1), *krupnoskačušǎch* (line 22), *oskorbitel'no* (line 53)] in its full form [*oska*] or elsewhere abbreviated to [*osk, sko*] (four times in *Moskva*; also in the lexemes *detskoe* and *majskie*) as Mandel'štam's central coded term: *Os'ka*, the colloquial or pejorative version of the name *Iosif* or *Osip*. An indication that it is primarily Stalin and the Stalin-era which are referred to, is given by the use of lexemes like *ospa* [pox] (Stalin was pockmarked), *roskošno* [sumptuous, opulent], *buddijskoe* [Buddhist] (a mythologem carrying negative connotations for O. M., denoting static, totalitarian types of rule), *polnoč* (midnight is equivalent to the beginning of the hours before the break of dawn, when the demons are about), *arestovannyj medved'* [the arrested bear] (referring to the arrests in Russia), or *ulicy v čobotach uzkich železnych* [streets in tight iron boots], signifying the terror-infested era of *Moskvošveja* [Moscow confection] (cf. also lexemes like *men'ševik* and *lavrovišnej*, or *višen,* all phonetically alluding to *Džugašvili,* i.e. Stalin). Meanwhile, the *sovremennik* [contemporary] of these pestilent times and lyrical subject of the poem, longs for *kislorod* [oxygen; i.e. freedom] and *vozduch* [air] and accompanies Rembrandt and Raphael, the representatives of world culture, when they come to *Moscow v gosti* [on a visit] and on their encounter *s Mocartom* [with Mozart]: He, the speaker, is one of their number – *sol'* [salt] of the earth.

Very similar phonetic-anagrammatic phenomena are to be found in poems like *Koljut resnicy* [My eyelashes sting] (1931), *Kvartira ticha kak bumaga* [The apartment is as quiet as paper] (1933), *10 Janvarja 1934* [January 10th, 1934] (1934) etc .

On the other hand, there are poems from this period, for example *Ariost* and *Drug Ariosta, drug Petrarki, Tasso drug* [A friend of Ariosto, Petrarca and Tasso] (1933/34/35), in which the right-hand pole of the axial diagram is emphasised, through the use of lexemes containing *[os]* and carrying positive connotations, like <u>so</u>*lnce* [sun], *<u>so</u>l'* [salt], *<u>so</u>leno* [salty], *golo<u>s</u>* [voice], *p<u>os</u>ol* [ambassador], *v<u>os</u>torg* [rapture], *zol<u>o</u>ti<u>s</u>tyj* [golden], *ja<u>z</u>yk* [language], *ra<u>ss</u>ka<u>z</u>yvaj* [tell!] and especially *Ari<u>os</u>t* and *T<u>a</u>sso* (directly mentioning their names or alluding to them), with whom the lyrical "I", feasting on the universal language of poetry and glossolalia, hopes to become one, and celebrates the presence of traditional world culture in his times; while in the last line Puškin's presence is invoked by a quotation from his poem *Ruslan i Ljudmila*: *"...I my byvali tam. I my tam pili mëd..."* [We too were there. We too drank mead].

In this text as well as in others lexemes not only *phonetically* (i.e. on the level of expression) but also *semantically* (i.e. on the level of content or meaning) related are attributed to the two poles:

—	+
Stalin, Džugašvili	*Petrarka, Dante*
palač [executioner], *placha* [scaffold], *plata* [pay]	*plotnik* [carpenter], *pletenie* [plait], *prjacha* [spinner]
krov' [blood], *volk* [wolf]	*tkan'* [fabric], *nit'* [thread]
kazn' [execution]	*pesn'* [song, poem]
žrnyj [greasy]	*pet'* [to sing], *povestvovanie* [narrative]
čuma [plague], *čërt* [devil], *smert'* [death]	*pit'* [to drink]
dušno [stifling], *ne dyšat'* [not to breathe]	*mëd* [mead]

In the poem *Sochrani moju reč* [Keep my words in mind] (1931), in which indirectly an alter ego carrying positive connotations in the shape of *Iosif-plotnik* [Joseph, the carpenter] is alluded to (whereby the lyrical subject identifies itself with Christ), an anagrammatic subtext through *l*-instrumentation by use of the syllables [al], [ol], [el], [il], [la], [lo], [le], [li] *palač* [the hangman/executioner] is evoked: *plachi* [execution blocks] - *Stalin*. (This *l*-instrumentation denoting *Stalin* can also be found in poems like *Polnoč' v Moskve, Ariost* (1933), *Oda* (1937) etc., whereas, for instance in the poem *Čarli Čaplin* (1937) the recurrence of [*al*], [*li*] and other *l*-syllables connotates one of the positive counterparts of the "great dictator": the great artist Charlie Chaplin.

1 Sochrani moju reč' navsegda za privkus nesčast'ja i dyma,
2 Za smolu krugovogo terpen'ja, za sovestnyj dëgot' truda.
3 Kak voda v novgorodskich kolodcach dolžna byt' černa i sladima,
4 Čtoby v nej k Roždestvu otrazilas' sem'ju plavnikami zvezda.

5 I za èto, otec moj, moj drug i pomoščnik moj grubyj,
6 Ja – nepriznannyj brat, otščepenec v narodnoj sem'e –
7 Obeščaju postroit' takie dremučie sruby,
8 Čtoby v nich tatarva opuskala knjazej na bad'e.

9 Liš' by tol'ko ljubili menja èti mërzlye plachi!
10 Kak priceljas' na smert' gorodki zašibajut v sadu,
11 Ja za èto vsju žizn' prochožu chot' v železnoj rubache
12 I dlja kazni petrovskoj v lesy toporišče najdu.

The main theme of this artistic as well as enigmatic text is the creative activity and vocation of the poet, whom the death-sentence awaits as a way of paying for the immortality awarded to him through his poetry (cf. also the phonic "equation" *kazn'* – *pesn'* [execution – song, poem] in the *Stichy pamjati A. Belogo* [Poems to the memory of A. Belyj]). To describe this death-centredness, A. Hansen-Löve, very appropriately used the term "thanato-poetics".

And if in the text *Staryj Krym* [The old Crimea] (written in 1933), the subject of which is the death of the peasants in the course of Stalin's forced collectivisation, to which the real-life author O. Mandel'štam was a horrified eye-witness (inscribed in line 8 as *mindal'*, the counterpart of *Stalin*), the recurrence of [*al*], [*ali*], [*sta*], [*sto*], [*ost*], [*a...i*] is conspicuous, this is so, because through this device the culprit, i.e. *Stalin* as the murderer, is hypo-semiotized:

Staryj Krym

1 Cholodnaja vesna. Golodnyj Staryj Krym,
2 Kak byl pri Vrangele – takoj že vinovatyj.
3 Ovčarki na dvore, na rubiščach zaplaty,
4 Takoj že seren'kij, kusajuščijsja dym.

5 Vse tak že choroša rassejannaja dal'
6 Derev'ja, počkami nabuchšie na malost'
7 Stojat, kak prišlye, i vozbuždajut žalost'
8 Včerašnej glupost'ju ukrašennyj mindal'

9 Priroda svoego ne uznaet lica,
10 I teni strašnye – Ukrainy, Kubani ...
11 Kak v tufljach vojločnych golodnye krest'jane
12 Kalitku steregut, ne trogaja kol'ca ...

Breathing is the subject of a number of O. M.'s poems, as a symbol of freedom and poetic licence. The extra-textual reference to the real-life author O. M. is established by the fact that—as his widow testifies—since the political reprisals of the mid-20s he increasingly complained of shortness of breath and suffered from angina pectoris. It is especially in texts like *Koljut resnicy* [The eyelashes sting], *Segodnja možno snjat' dekal'komani* [Today you can make decals], *Ja s dymjaščej lučinoj vchožu* [With a smoking torch I enter] (all written in 1931), that one comes across expressions like *dušno* [stifling], *s každym dnem dyšat' vse tjaželee* [With every day breathing gets harder] and *ja ne dyšu* [I do not breathe], which, on a first level, onomatopoetically recreate the whistling sound associated with shortness of breath, and on a second, deeper level of reference, ana-grammatically inscribe the name of the cause of the breathing difficulties, i.e. *Džugašvili*.

On the other hand, and now the positive pole of the axial diagram representing O. M.'s model of the world is again emphasised, a few deep breaths have a liberating effect, as it says in the first two variations of the twelve *Vos'mistišija* [Octets] (1933-35):

Vos'mistišija (1933/34/35)	Octets (1933/34/35)
1 Ljublju pojavlenie tkani, Kogda posle dvu<u>ch</u> ili tre<u>ch</u>, A to četyre<u>ch</u> zady<u>chan</u>ij Prijdet vyprjamitel'nyj vzdo<u>ch</u>.	**1** I love the appearance of the fabric, When after two or three Or even four gasps The rectifying sigh comes.
I dugami parusny<u>ch</u> gonok Zelenye formy <u>č</u>ertja Igraet prostranstvo sprosonok – Ne znav<u>še</u>e ljul'ki ditja.	And tracing green forms With regattas' arcs, Space plays half-awake – A child that has not known a cradle.
2 Ljublju pojavlenie tkani, Prijdet vyprjamitel'nyj vzdo<u>ch</u> Kogda posle dvu<u>ch</u> ili tre<u>ch</u>, A to četyre<u>ch</u> zady<u>chan</u>ij	**2** I love the appearance of the fabric, When after two or three Or even four gasps The rectifying sigh comes.
I tak <u>cho</u>rošo mne i tja<u>ž</u>ko, Kogda pribli<u>ž</u>aetsja mig, I vdrug dugovaja rastja<u>ž</u>ka Zvu<u>č</u>it v bormortan'ja<u>ch</u> moi<u>ch</u>.	And it's so good and so hard for me When the moment's near, And suddenly an arched extension Sounds in my mutterings.

(Pollack: 46-47)

Taking a few deep breaths results in *pojavlenje tkani,* i.e. the fabric, symbol of poetry, becoming apparent. O. M. also used the metaphor of fabric in his prose-text *Razgovor o Dante* [Conversation about Dante], written in 1933.

Svobody vzdoch [the sigh of relief of freedom], as it is called in one variant of the four paraphrases of Petrarca-sonnets from 1934, is closely associated with *Fran česko Petrarka,* who stands for world-culture and exquisite poetry whose name is frequently inscribed in the sonnets as an almost imploring anagram: *Petrarka* – *reka* [river], *ptachi* [birds], *pernatych* [feathered], *prjacha* [female spinner], *krasy* [colours], *plač* [lament], *prelest'* [grace], and *Fran česko* – *skorb'* [grief], *sokol* [falcon], *solovej* [nightingale], *resničnogo* [pertaining to eyelashes], *česti* [of honour], _noč'_ [night], _ključ_ [key], etc.

Perevody iz Fr. Petrarki

Valle che de' lamenti miei se' piena ...

Rečka, rasbuchšaja ot slëz solenych,
Lechnye ptagi rasskazat' mogli by,
Čutkie zveri i nemye ryby,
V dvuch beregach zažatye zelenych;

Dol, polnyj kljatv i šopotov kalenych,
Tropinok promuravlennych izgybi,
Siloj ljubvi zatveržennye glyby
I treščiny zemli na trudnych sklonach –

Nezyblemoe zybletsja na meste,
I zybljus' ja. Kak by vnutri granita,
Zernitsja skorb' v gnezde bylych veselij,

Gde ja išču sledov krasy i česti,
Isčeznuvšej, kak sokol posle myta,
Ostaviv telo v zemljanoj posteli.

Dekabr' 1933 – janvar' 1934

Quel rosignuol, che si soave piagne ...

Kak solovej, sirotstvujuščij, slavit
Svoich pernatych blizkych noč'ju sinej
I derevenskoe molčan'e plavit
Po-nad cholmami ili v kotlovine,

I vsju-to noč' ščekočet i muravit
I provožaet on, odin otnyne, –
Menja, menja! Silki i seti stavit

I nudit pomnit' smertnyj pot bogini!

O, radužnaja oboločka stracha!
Ėfir očej, gljadevšich vglub' ėfira,
Vzjala zemlja v slepuju ljul'ku pracha, –

Ispolnilos' tvoe želan'e, prjacha,
I, plačuči, tveržu: vsja prelest' mira
Resničnogo nedolgovečnej vzmacha.

Dekabr' 1933 – janvar' 1934

Or che 'l ciel e la terra e 'l vento tace ...

Kogda usnet zemlja i žar otpyšet,
A na duše zverej pokoj lebjažij,
Chodit po krugu noč' s gorjaščej prjažej
I mošč' vody morskoj zefir kolyšet, –

Čuju, gorju, rvus', plaču –i ne slyšit,
V neuderžimoj blizosti vse ta že,
Celuju noč', celuju noč' na straže
I vsja kak est' dalekim sčast'em dyšit.

Chot' ključ' odin, voda raznorečiva –
Polužestka, polusladka, – uželi
Odna i ta že milaja dvulična ...

Tysjaču raz na dnju, sebe na divo,
Ja dolžen umeret' na samom dele
I voskresaju tak že sverchobyčno.

Dekabr' 1933 –janvar' 1934

I di miei piu leggier' che nessun cervo ...

Promčalis' dni moi – kak by olenej
Kosjaščij beg. Srok sčast'ja byl koroče,

Čem vzmach resnicy. Iz poslednei moči
Ja v gorst' zažal liš' pepel naslaždenij.

Po milosti nadmennych obol'ščenij
Nočuet serdce v sklepe skromnoj noči,
K zemle beskostnoj žmetsja. Sredostenij
Znakomych iščet, sladostnych spletenij.

No ta, čto v nej edva suščestvovalo,
Dnes', vyrvavšich naverch, v očag lazuri,
Plenjat' i ranit' možet kak byvalo.

I ja dogadyvajus', brovi chmurja:
Kak choroša? k kakoj tolpe pristala?
Kak tam klubitsja legkich skladok burja?

4-8 Janvarja 1934

Furthermore, by connecting the name of the poet with the metapoetic *tkan'* [fabric]-motive in lexemes like *prjacha* [female spinner] and *spletenie* [interlacing; complexity], an auto-reflexive imitational structure is suggested, which metaphorically represents O. M.'s poetic technique, with its artistic plait of recurring phonemes, semes and lexemes, quotations and self-quotations.

The poems from O. M.'s Moscow-period, which came to an end in May 1934 when he was arrested and subsequently banished to Voronež, distinguished by their central anagrammatic *[os]*-system, culminate in an almost fateful-mythical situation, "*kogda po prikazu odnogo Iosifa (Voždja), drugoj Iosif (ochrannik Os'ka) vezet tret'ego Iosifa (poèta Osipa Mandel'štama) v ssylku*" [when acting on orders from the first Josif (the leader) another Josif (the guard) leads a third Josif (the poet Osip M.) into exile] (Kaciz: 52). In the poem *Kama 1* (1935) this was enigmatically formulated as follows: *I so mnoju žena, pjat' nočej ne spala,/Pjat' nočej ne spala, trěch konvojnych vezla* [And with me my wife – for five nights she did not sleep, five nights she did not sleep – three escorting soldiers she drove]. O. M.'s Moscow-period, when "the figure of Stalin ... came to haunt his verse" (Freidin: 245), can be characterised as a period, in which the lyrical subject inscribes itself in the texts—bound up with the dictator and executioner almost like a dark twin or demonic "other"—and increasingly speaks up with universal authority as an intrepid spokesman of his times: *"Ja govorju za vsech s takoju siloj,/Čtob nëbo stalo nebom, čtoby guby/Potreskalis', kak rozovaja glina"* ["I speak for all with such force, that my palate becomes the sky, and my lips crack, like pink clay", as it says in one of the *Fragments of destroyed poems* (IV)].

Summing up, one can say that it is exactly this specific, almost mytho-poetical contiguity (not mimesis, cf. Lachmann: 385) of life, personality of the poet, events and œuvre of Osip Mandel'štam, which through the "difference between the writing subject as author and its lyrically represented 'I'" (Haverkamp: 348) renders the interrelation of fact and fiction almost abysmal and generates a cryptic and enigmatic form of subjectivity.

Dagmar Burkhart
Mannheim

Bibliography

Mandel'štam, O. 1973. *Stichotvorenija*. Leningrad.

Mandel'štam, O. 1990. *Sočinenija v dvuch tomach*. Moskva, vol. I-II.

***

Aizlewood, R./D. Myers (eds.). 1994. *Mandelstam Centenary Conference* (London 1991). London.

Ajzelvud, R./D. Majers (eds.). 1994. *Stoletie Mandel'štama. Materialy simpoziuma*. London.

Averincev, S.S. 1990. "Sud'ba i vest' Osipa Mandel'štama." In: O. M., *Sočinenija v dvuch tomach*, 1990, vol. I, p. 5-64.

Baines, J. 1976. *Mandelstam: The Later Poetry*. Cambridge, London.

Beljaewa-Konegen, S./D. Prigow. 1991. "Tod des heiligen Schriftstellers." In: *Neue Rundschau*, Jg. 102, Heft 3, 1991, p. 57-66.

Benčić, Ž. "Fügung von Metaphern (bei O. Mandel'štam)." In: Flaker, p. 220-234.

Broyde, S. 1975. *Osip Mandel'štam and His Age*. Cambridge, London.

Burkhart, D. 1996. "Avtor, liričeskij sub'ekt i tekst u Osipa Mandel'štama." In: Markovič, V. M./V. Šmid (eds.), *Avtor i tekst. Sbornik statej*. Sankt-Peterburg 1996, p. 408-428.

Cavanagh, C. 1995. *Osip Mandelstam and the Modernist Creation of Tradition*. Princeton.

Dutli, R. 1985. *Ossip Mandelstam. "Als riefe man mich bei meinem Namen"*. Zürich.

Flaker, A. (ed.). 1989. *Glossarium der russischen Avantgarde*. Graz, Wien.

Frank, M./A. Haverkamp (eds.). 1989. *Individualität*. München.

Freidin, G. 1986. *A Coat of Many Colors. Osip Mandelstam and His Mythology of Self-Presentation*. Berkeley.

Gasparov, M. L.: "Metričeskoe sosedstvo 'Ody' Stalinu." In: Ajzelvud/Majers, p. 99-111.

Gifford, H. "Mandelstam and Soviet Reality." In: Aizlewood/Myers, p. 255-267.

Ginzburg, L. 1972. "Poètika Osipa Mandel'štama." In: *Izvestija AN SSSR, ser. Literatury i jazyka*, Vol. XXXI, Nr. 4, 1972, p. 309-327.

Hansen-Löve, A. 1993. " Mandel'shtams Thanatopoetics." In: R. Vroon/J. E. Malmstad (eds.): *Readings in Russian Modernism. To Honor V. F. Markov*. Moscow 1993, p. 121-157.

Haverkamp, A. "Kryptische Subjektivität – Archäologie des Lyrisch-Individuellen." In: Frank/Haverkamp, p. 347-383.

Immendörfer, H. 1993. "Nadežda Mandel'štams Memoiren. Dichterwitwentum als Lebensform und Schreibanlaß." In: U. Grabmüller/M. Katz (eds.): *Zwischen Anpassung und Widerspruch*, Wiesbaden 1993, p. 187-226.

Kaciz, L. 1991. "Poèt i palač. Opyt pročtenija 'stalinskich stichov'." In: *Literaturnoe obozrenie*, vol. 1, 1991, p. 46-54.

Lachmann, R. 1990. *Literatur und Gedächtnis*. Frankfurt.

Levin, Ju. I./ D. M. Segal/ R. D. Timenčik/ V. N. Toporov/ T. V. Civ'jan. 1974. "Russkaja semantičeskaja poètika kak potencial'naja kul'turnaja paradigma." In: *Russian Literature*, Nr. 7/8, 1974, p. 47-82.

Levin, Ju. I. 1975. "O sootnošenii meždu semantikoj poètičeskogo teksta i vnetekstovoj real'nostju. Zametki o poètiki O. Mandel'štama." In: *Russian literature*, Nr. 10/11, 1975, p. 147-172.

Levin, Ju. I. 1991. "Počemu ja ne budu delat' doklad o Mandel'štame." In: *Russkaja mysl'*, vol. 26. 7. 1991, p.14.

Levin, Ju. I. 1978. " Zametki o poèzii O. Mandel'štama tridcatych godov." In: *Slavica Hierosolymitana*, vol. III, 1978, p. 110-193.

Levinton, G.A./P.D. Timenčik. 1978. "Kniga K. F. Taranovskogo o poèzii O.E. Mandel'štama." In: *Russian Literature*, vol. VI, 1978, p. 197-211.

Mandel'štam, N. 1987. *Kniga tret'ja*. Paris.

Mandel'štam, N. 1970. *Vospominanija*. New York.

Mandel'štam, N. 1982. *Vtoraja kniga.* 3 ed., Paris.

Mess-Bejer, I. 1991. "Ėzopov jazyk v poėzii Mandel'štama 30-ch godov." In: *Russian Literature*, vol. XXIX, 1991, p. 243-393.

Pollack, N. 1995. *Mandelstam the Reader.* Baltimore/London.

Ronen, O. 1983. *An Approach to Mandel'štam.* Jerusalem.

Ronen, O. 1973. "Leksičeskij povtor, podtekst, i smysl v poėtike Osipa Mandel'štama." In: R. Jakobson/C.H. van Schooneveld/D.S. Worth (eds.): *Slavic Poetica. Essays in honor of Kiril Taranovsky.* The Hague, Paris 1973, p. 367-388.

Slawinski, J. 1985. "Über die Kategorie des lyrischen Subjekts." In: *Russian Literature*, vol. XVIII, 1985, p. 311-320.

Starobinski, J. 1980. *Wörter unter Wörtern. Die Anagramme von Ferdinand de Saussure.* Frankfurt.

Taranovsky, K. 1976. *Essays on Mandel'stam.* Cambridge, London.

Vozdviženskij, V.G. 1991. "Mandel'štam v tridcatye gody." In: *Slovo i sud'ba. Osip Mandel'štam. Issledovanija i materialy.* Moskva, p. 271-286.

Zeeman, P. 1988. *The Later Poetry of Osip Mandelstam.* Amsterdam.

Weststeijn, W. "Das lyrische Subjekt." In: Flaker, p. 368-389.

Ziegler, R.: Anagramm. In: Flaker, p. 118-125.

Against Silence:
the Cultural Revolution and Literary Memory

> Remember the days of yore, learn the lessons of
> the generation that came before you.
>
> — Deuteronomy 32:7

— I —

Like Auschwitz and the Gulags, the Cultural Revolution in China has committed unimaginable atrocities to the whole nation. Thousands upon thousands of innocent people died with a raging fanaticism for an equally fanatic cause of unparalleled disaster in human history. The exact death toll of this revolution today still remains a mystery. Much has been written about the dehumanization of the Cultural Revolution, particularly the institutional cause of this disaster (i.e. how Mao Zedong's revolutionary romantic ideas for a communist utopia have resulted in a notorious dystopia, ruining almost the whole country).[1] Soon after the Cultural Revolution Ba Jin (1904-), one of China's best known writers, made a failed proposal to establish a national museum in dishonor of this cultural castration in order to condemn it to the stake of historical infamy.[2] No sufficient attention has so far been directed to the inhumanity committed by man against man, or more precisely, the inhumanity inflicted by the fanaticised masses against themselves during that stretch of Chinese history. While the Party apparatus tries to put this infamous period into oblivion by asking its people to look forward to the future (an unknown one for sure), the people themselves tend to ascribe the national nightmare to the societal system and the ideological establishment. Neglecting this subterranean passage of the past makes it difficult to understand how Mao Zedong turned the Cultural Revolution into a paradigmatic symbol of man's inhumanity in the twentieth century.

My paper purports an epistemological study of the crucial issue of mass inhumanity as reflected in literary memory in the Chinese context. It asks such questions as how did the Chinese totalitarianist policy evolve into the dehumanization of mass movements? How should one evaluate the role of the masses in committing the horror of inhuman atrocities? How is the ghastly event of the Cultural Revolution to be recorded in cultural/literary memory? And how could such a nightmare have happened or could have been allowed to happen in human history? I will first discuss the politics of memory and focus on how literature serves to reconstruct individual memories of those people who do the remembering in order to discover the truth of history. I then study the sociopolitical implications of mass inhumanity by examining the literary records of the Cultural Revolution in the writings of Can Xue, a contemporary Chinese woman writer.[3] My primary concern is to demonstrate how the author illustrates the possibility as well as the necessity of literature as an independent and individual rethinking of the inhumanity in China, not simply as one of the

---

[1] Even incomplete statistics show that dozens of books and monographs have already been written (both in Chinese and other languages) on the Cultural Revolution. Most of them, however, are focused on the societal system and turn to the Communist ideology for an explanation of the cause of this national disaster.

[2] Unfortunately, this proposal only turned out to be wishful thinking due to the hindrance from the authorities. (Ba Jin has been holding the chair of the All-China Writers Association for about two decades.)

[3] Can Xue (1953-) is the author of *Dialogues in Paradise* and *Yellow Mud Street*. Can Xue is a pen name, meaning literally "old snow." Her real name is Deng Xiaohua.

totalitarian regime against man, but more significantly as one of the masses against themselves. In the third part I will examine the work of Yu Hua, one of the leading contemporary Chinese writers,[4] in terms of (1) his dialectic of violence and the logic of torture and self-torture to illustrate how violence is exploited as a means of self-identification in the midst of inhumanity, and (2) his understanding of the necessity of reading aesthetic and politics together towards a symbolic resistance to the "metanarrative," which tries to conceal not only the institutional inhumanity, but first and foremost the fundamental issue of mass inhumanity.

— II —

All values, either historical, ideological, aesthetic, or ethical, reside in the remembrance of things past, because the profound human experience is by nature retrospective. Very often the most immediate experiences in our lives become the least recognized because their immediacy does not readily allow for any metaphysical retrospection. The same is true of aesthetic appreciation which becomes possible only by keeping a certain distance. Memory is part of human history as it tries to determine which facts and events are historically true and revealing. To say this is of course not to deny that there exist multiple versions of historical facts and events and one should therefore be wary of any claim to possessing the 'true' or 'authorized' version.[5] But we can legitimately argue that while it is important to distinguish true historical accounts from false ones, what matters more in literary studies is how narrative as a discourse of memory functions to make sense of reality--be it, in Mitchell's words, "the factual reality of historical events or the moral, symbolic reality of fictions."[6] Literature offers one of the most important ways in which human

---

[4] Yu Hua (1960-) is the author of the short story collection *The Past and the Punishment*, trans. Andrew F. Jones (Honolulu: University of Hawaii, 1996).

[5] For an extended discussion of truth-verification in memory and remembrance, see W.J.T. Mitchell, "Editor's Note: On Narrative", *Critical Inquiry*, 7, No. 1 (Autumn, 1980), 1-4.

[6] Ibid., 2.

experience and perceptions are expressed; it is in literary writings that everyday realities are most powerfully encoded and rendered profoundly influential. In a sense, literature is concerned with how narrative discourse may lead to a better understanding of humanity.

Broadly speaking, memory could be divided into two categories: social memory and personal memory.[7] While social memory, commonly known as history, tends to take the sociopolitical dimension as an exclusive explanatory perspective on patterns of historic events, personal memory emphasizes difference and is more concerned with what Julia Kristeva calls "lacuna and silence" that fill the historical narrative in order to illustrate the discourse of historicity in contestation with other discursive voices. In other words, in representing the past historically, personal memory does not seek to recognize historical facts and events as they have first appeared. Rather, it tries to come to grips with a reality as it flashes up at a moment of crisis in order to pursue phenomenological concerns to their existential depth.

Literature proides paramount examples of how personal memory intervenes with and reacts to historical "truth." As a form of cultural memory, literature fathoms the magnitude of the horror of dehumaniza- tion by rendering unimaginable atrocities imaginable. Social phenomena reveal their epistemological significance precisely because they are experienced individually, which enable individual persons to make sense of experienced realities in an individual manner. As Bruce Ross puts it: "The past can best be understood and interpreted meaningfully by taking into account the suppositions and beliefs held by the individuals who participated in the events under study."[8] The essence of literature is the expression of memory, especially individual memory of a phenomenal life, one which refuses to be mediated institutionally. As such, literature often serves as a homage to innocent victims by revealing the nature of the human condition. It is in this sense that we say poets and writers perhaps know more about human memories than historians and social scientists do. Mature literature is one that speaks as a voice of human conscience both in relation to and in contest with the dominant tone of the hegemonic

---

[7] In their discussion of "social memory," James Fentress and Chris Wickham define it as follows: "In principle, we can usually regard social memory as an expression of collective experience: social memory identifies a group, giving it a sense of its past and defining its aspirations for the future." James Fentress and Chris Wickham, *Social Memory* (Cambridge: Blackwell, 1992), 25.

[8] Bruce M. Ross, *Remembering the Personal Past* (Oxford: Oxford University Press, 1994), 160.

Literature as Cultural Memory

force, no matter how weak this voice might be. The two contemporary Chinese writers I will discuss in the following pages illustrate the possibility as well as the necessity of literary studies as an independent and individual rethinking of the nature of the mass inhumanity of the Cultural Revolution—a topic that requires considerable moral courage for them to discuss.

— III —

The Cultural Revolution was started by Mao Zedong first as a movement to rectify what he believed was a dominance of bourgeois thinking and revisionism in the sphere of liberal arts. But the movement soon developed into a nationwide political campaign to purge his political rivals, many of whom were once his close comrades-in-arms. For a whole decade (1966-1976), the entire country was thrown into a fanatic limbo, in which history and present, fiction and reality seemed to have merged into the political delirium of torture and self-torture. During that decade China was deliriously worshipping Mao as the demigod for whom the people would be ready to shed their last drop of blood. Across the land, people from all walks of life were engaged to fight for what they believed to be the noble cause of the revolution. The frenzied mass participation of this revolution is without any parallel, either in Chinese history or even in world history.

In the name of defending their great leader, however, the masses sought all possible opportunities to revenge upon their "enemies" for causes as grandiose as political grievance or as trivial as personal spite. The darkest reaches of madness in the political life of contemporary China unleashed a ravening insanity upon its victims only to pay off old grudges. It was a common scene during that stretch of Chinese history that husband and wife betrayed each other, sons and daughters reported on their parents, siblings fought against one another in order to win a political favor. Overnight, friends were turned into mortal enemies and the whole country became a land of no trust and endless hatred. The internationally awarded films such as *To Live* (dir. Zhang Yimou), *Farewell, My Concubine* (dir. Chen Kaige), and *The Blue Kite* (dir. Tian

Zhuangzhuang) are all paradigmatic of this nightmarish period. What was wrong with a nation that boasts of a civilization of more than five thousand years and that is known for excelling in courtesy, etiquette, and manners?

In his devastating criticism of Chinese culture, Lu Xun (1881-1936),[9] the founder of modern Chinese literature, perceived the debased Chinese national character traits as "jealousy," "noise," "self-deception," and "suspicion." He particularly slashed at what he called "the Fun-Watching Complex" (*Qiao renao*). In his autobiographical notes, Lu Xun recalled the slides he watched in Japan in which his fellow people hilariously enjoyed the spectacle of the beheading of a Chinese spy for the Russian army during the Russo-Japanese war at the turn of the century. What enraged him most was the apathy they displayed at the suffering of their fellow people. Lu Xun's conclusion was that the Chinese nation was spiritually diseased and needed to be cured mentally more than physically. The Cultural Revolution seemed to have pushed this gloating-over-others'-misfortune mentality one step further and transformed it into "a torture complex" from which to derive a sickening pleasure. As was mentioned previously, during that stretch of Chinese history the whole nation became a living inferno in which masses themselves inflicted atrocities upon one another, resulting in a death toll perhaps no smaller than that of a civil war in modern Chinese history. We can of course put the whole blame on Mao Zedong and his followers for this dreadful calamity. *And we should.* Nevertheless, when we reflect upon the unparalleled size and scope of this disaster which affected the whole nation, sparing no single individual, we have to ask ourselves this question: Could one individual person have done this all by himself? Shouldn't the masses themselves be also held responsible for the wanton evil they had given their great leader warrant to commit?

The explanation can be found in the feelings and sentiments that created the symbiotic relationship between Mao Zedong and the Chinese people. Their interdependence grew as the great leader insidiously manipulated their revolutionary fervor and anxieties and burdened them with a strong sense of guilt and responsibility for what they did in political life. Without doubt, it is politically correct that history condemns the great leader to the stake of infamy for having single-handedly initiated the

---

[9] Lu Xun is a pen name. His real name is Zhou Shuren.

Literature as Cultural Memory

disaster. But if sociological research loses sight of the role played by the masses during the Cultural Revolution, it is certainly running the risk to "trivialize rather than illuminate" the real cause of the political movement at issue. In her study of the Holocaust, Lucy Dawidowicz made this observation: "The historian will come closer to understanding the German past by investigating the mass pathology that made it possible for the Germans to accept Hitler as their leader."[10] Insofar as historical happenings are concerned (either in the cultural contexts of the East or the West), they could happen only in relation to human beings. In other words, historical phenomena are enacted and rendered meaningful only in an interactive relationship to a human society inhabited by human beings. Historic events, as we have seen them, necessarily involve a participation of large masses. The Cultural Revolution is no exception. "The historian's task," Lucy Dawidowicz reminds us, "is to untangle that meshwork of human character, behavior, and motive whose intertwining creates the very material of history."[11] To study the occurrence of mass delusion and hysteria from a historical perspective would thus shed light on our understanding of the true nature of the mass inhumanity of the Cultural Revolution.

How then did the mass inhumanity manifest itself during this national disaster? C.G. Jung once remarked: "There is in the psyche some superior power, and if it is not consciously a god, it is the 'belly' at least, in St. Paul's words."[12] Interpreted in sociopolitical terms, this "superior power" can be understood as a kind of fanatic zeal for the absolute or the ultimate truth, which, when repressed, would "push the person into a psychic unshelteredness and instability..." And the latter, as Josel Rudin warns, "will deliver him up to the power of irrational unconscious tendencies and lets him fall victim to the magic of extremes: fanaticism."[13] Mass hysteria, insofar as it commits itself to an absolute enemy-friend schema with an excessive certitude in the absolute rightness and the unchallengibility of the ideas concerned, often resorts to fanaticism as its principle

---

[10] Lucy S. Dawidowicz, *The Holocaust and the Historians* (Cambridge: Harvard University Press, 1981), 41.

[11] Ibid., 146.

[12] C.G. Jung, *Two Essays on Analytical Psychology* (New York: Meridian, 1956) 81, quoted in Josel Rudin, *Fanaticism: A Psychological Analysis* (Notre Dame: University of Notre Dame Press, 1969, 5-6).

[13] Josel Rudin, 5-6.

drive as well as the means of expression. As a social phenomenon, fanaticism is "necessarily multifaceted."[14] In the context of contemporary Chinese sociopolitical realities, this fanatic urge likewise presents itself in many disturbing ways.

First, the communist ideology had inculcated in the people a blind faith in the revolutionary cause embodied personally by Mao Zedong. So demagogic was this ideology and so fervent was this faith that the slightest grievance against the Party apparatus would amount, in the indiscriminate mind of the masses, to a grave challenge of the absolute truths and values long indoctrinated. This rigid orientation of thinking naturally turned the masses into victims of fanaticism whenever they came across an interpretation of social realities different from that of the official ideology.

Second, the treachery of the politics in China brings about a burning sense of insecurity and unshelteredness. Living a life of vicissitude, people have to resort to the instinct of survival, that is, they will attack in the hope of defending oneself. In Michel Foucault's terms, in order to prove one is sane, one needs first to prove that one's neighbour is insane. During the Cultural Revolution many people tried to prove their political correctness by accusing others of being politically disloyal. Betraying and reporting on each other in order to win a political favour was a common scene. "The Fun-Watching Complex" mercilessly criticized by Lu Xun came around in full play during this national nightmare. To watch and, worse still, to make others suffer became a perverse form of entertainment from which the frantic mass obtained diseased pleasures. Anyone who experienced those dark years can testify to the inhuman treatment of the persecuted, which was often rendered in the most theatrical manner.

Thirdly, the "Jealousy Complex" appeared in extreme forms during the Cultural Revolution. The age-old tradition of institutional hierarchy in Chinese society has deprived the socially less privileged of their access to success, both political and material. The sense of instability and being neglected delivered these people to "the power of irrational unconscious tendencies" and made them victims to fanatic zealotry for a change, any change in social status. The political ambiance of the Cultural Revolution was especially conducive to mass epidemics of such fanaticism, as one of the objectives of this revolution was to discontinue the social operation

---

[14] Ibid., 8.

and debunk, if not completely destroy, the institutional hierarchy in order to serve Mao's own political purpose. The symbiotic relationship that connected the German people to Hitler also existed between Mao and the Chinese people.[15] As a resourceful politician, Mao knew only too well how to manipulate the people's feelings for him, particularly how to utilize their "Jealousy Complex" to his full advantage. Mobilizing one faction to attack another was Mao's favorite stratagem, which, however, could not be effective without the masses' being swept up by the lava of fanatic eruptions. One ready example is Mao's often-quoted maxim during the Cultural Revolution—"It is legitimate to rebel"—which was grotesquely popular among the frenzied masses, rebelling against society for their own gains. Historically, the transference of fanatic zeal to masses of people is effected only by mass hysteria and mutual hatred. As Andre Haynal rightly suggests: "Socio-economic factors giving rise to jealousies are doubtless involved: envy and jealousy play a very important role in social life... these mechanisms for fanaticizing the masses are always based on envy, jealousy, and the friend-enemy schema."[16] It is these mechanisms that account for the fact that Hitler so effectively incited an excessive urge among his people, many of whom were well educated ones, turning them into a fanaticised mob capable of believing the most absurd accounts. In their writings Can Xue and Yu Hua illustrate, by means of a metaphorical model, why and how the mechanisms of mass delusion and hysteria have operated in contemporary Chinese society, especially during the Cultural Revolution.

— IV —

Can Xue delivers a disturbing revelation of how self-preservation functions as a model of the mass inhumanity during the Cultural Revolution. By constructing a system of metaphors based upon her poetics

---

[15] For a more detailed discussion of the symbiotic relationship between Hitler and the German people, see Lucy S. Dawidowicz, 34-35.

[16] Andre Haynal, et al., *Fanaticism: A Historical and Psychoanalytical Study* (New York: Schocken Books, 1983), 219-220.

of negation—the notion of the grotesque and chaos, she shows an aesthetic understanding of the human condition: how being dehumanized entails being denatural and how mass hysteria and perverseness shape grotesque realities, in which the displacement of human consciousness tries to reconcile normalcy with paranoia as a way to survive unimaginable inhumanity. In order to reveal this unpleasant truth concealed by the ideological establishment, Can Xue turns to grotesque realism as a challenge at the constraints of the sublime. *Old Floating Cloud (Canglao de fuyun)*, a novella, exhibits an interesting instance of such understanding.[17]

Unlike *Yellow Mud Street*,[18] another story by Can Xue about mass hysteria, which is set explicitly against the backdrop of the Cultural Revolution, *Old Floating Cloud* does not deal with that stretch of Chinese history directly. Instead, it alludes to the Cultural Revolution as a general existential mode in China. The story, which tells of hateful family life and human wickedness, can be read as a satire of modern Chinese society and culture that epitomizes all the debased national character traits censured by Lu Xun. In the narrative, the main characters are bound to each other either by blood ties or by communal linkage. The protagonists, Geng Shanwu and Xu Ruhua, are old neighbors. Both are married yet they are engaged in a fatal liaison with each other. Others such as Lao Kuang (who is Xu Ruhua's husband) and Lao Kuang's ferocious mother and Mu Lan (who is Geng Shanwu's wife), as well as Xu Ruhua's own parents, all stand side by side in opposition to Xu Ruhua, regarding her as a stranger. In the meantime, they also hate and intrigue against one another. The title *Old Floating Cloud,* an image of the transience of life, is an extended metaphor for the impossibility of forming one's self-identity in Communist China, as each of these characters is corrupted and hopelessly trapped in an intriguing meshwork of vitiated human relations.

As the story shows, on the one hand, all of them are excited and agitated by an unquenchable desire to harm others; they seem to derive pleasure in making others suffer, although from this they themselves benefit almost nothing. On the other hand, these characters live in constant paranoia and anxiety that they might be afflicted by others, even though this infliction may be merely imaginary. As a consequence, they all

---

[17]   Can Xue, *Old Floating Cloud*, in *Old Floating Cloud: Two Novellas*, trans. Ronald R. Janssen and Jian Zhang (Evanston: Northwestern University Press, 1991).

[18]   Can Xue, *Yellow Mud Street*, in *Old Floating Cloud: Two Novellas.*

Literature as Cultural Memory

become hypersensitive to harming and being harmed. This hysteria constitutes a basis for the unreasonable hatred entertained by all these characters, which ruins human ties, even turning mother and daughter into mortal enemies. The absurd and paranoid scenes such as these readily remind the Chinese mind of those dark years of revolutionary turmoil.

In the fiction, Can Xue looks into the grotesque mentality of mutual suspicion and persecution by showing how people spy on each other with mirrors: through the holes in a door, from behind a curtain, or even by the cracks on a bathroom wall. For instance, for fear that others might conspire against and inflict harm on him, the protagonist Geng Shanwu keeps a secret watch on people around him with a mirror:

> At home after work, he pretended to trim his beard at the door. With the mirror in his hand, he observed his neighbor's movements behind him. He felt a little relaxed after assuring himself nothing suspicious was going on.[19]

In this case, mirrors become an extension of human eyes to spy on others, thereby providing an illusory sense of security. On other occasions, human beings themselves transform into a metaphorical mirror whereby they watch one another. The family of Xu Ruhua offers a paradigmatic example. The four family members: Xu Ruhua, her father and his second wife, and Xu's fiancée, are emblematic of the poisoned human relations in society. They dislike and slander each other, keeping others under a close surveillance with malicious feelings. To the father, his prospective son-in-law is nothing but a hoodlum, marrying his daughter only for his wealth. But to the daughter, the father married his first wife only to cheat her out of her private money. Distrust and suspicion become the norm in the family. What is even worse is that the whole family is under a close watch by the father's ex-wife: "Turning his head, [father] saw the door again shut tight. A black figure sneaked out from behind the house and hid behind the tree. He saw it was his ex-wife."[20] The world in *Old Floating Cloud* is thus turned into one of tight surveillance, similar to that of Big Brother in *1984*, from which no one can escape. The difference between them lies in that Can Xue's "Big Brother" is not only the reincarnation of a dictatorial party, but, more revealingly, of the hateful masses as well.

[19] Can Xue. *Old Floating Cloud*, 191.

[20] Can Xue, *Old Floating Cloud*, 238.

The author tries to make a point: compared with institutional inhumanity, mass inhumanity can be even worse as no one in Chinese society can possibly stay free from this kind of mass hysteria and delusion.

— V —

While Can Xue debunks the sublimation of the mass dictatorship, Yu Hua demonstrates in his writings how violence and cruelty become a favorite metaphor for the Chinese reality of mass horror. Lu Xun regarded Chinese history as a discourse of spiritual cannibalization, one which can be described with two words: "eating man" (*Chi ren*).[21] Yu Hua further accentuates Lu Xun's critical consciousness of the official Chinese history by exposing its internal mechanism—mass violence and horror which seem to have become a fearful companion of everyday life. A paradigmatic example of a story that reveals this concern both extensively and effectively is afforded by "A Kind of Reality" (*Xianshi yi zhong*), one of Yu Hua's major works.[22] The story is about a family tragedy which takes place in the aftermath of the Cultural Revolution. Two married brothers, Shanfeng and Shangang, live under the same roof with their mother. One day, Shangang's four-year old kid, while playing with his infant cousin, drops him onto the cement ground incidentally and the latter dies instantly. Overgrieved at the sudden death of his baby son, Shanfeng, brutally kicks his nephew to death. Infuriated by this beastly act, Shangang, the boy's father, induces his brother into a willing punishment and tortures him to a most cruel death. Shangang himself is later executed for the crime of murder. Their mother dies mysteriously six days afterwards. The big family thus falls apart. The scene of the playful murder is indeed horrible and deserves our critical attention.

After his son was kicked to a brutal death, Shangang retaliated in an even more beastly and cruel manner. The next day, he seduced his

---

[21]   See Lu Xun's short story "A Madman's Diary" (*Kuangren riji*) which is widely acclaimed as a modern classic in Chinese literature.

[22]   Yu Hua, "Xianshi yi zhong" (A Kind of Reality), *Hebian de cuowu* [Errors by the River] (Wuhan: Changjiang Literature Publishing House, 1992), 50-95.

brother, Shanfeng, into willingly being tied onto a tree, the latter with no idea what would happen next. After binding his brother tightly from feet upwards to the neck, Shangang smeared some pork bone marrow on his feet, right on the underside of the arch. Then he unleashed a hungry dog, which licked joyfully at Shanfeng's bone-marrow-covered feet:

> Soon a strange sensation spread from feet to chest. ... Shanfeng began to laugh madly. He tried to withdraw his legs, but they were unable to bend. ... His body convulsed without, however, being able to make a single movement. So he violently shook his head until he exhausted all his strength. From his mouth came some weird laughter as if two pieces of aluminum were scratching against each other. ... Soon this strange laughter was punctuated with violent belching. Watching his brother suffer, Shangang coldbloodedly put more bone marrow to his feet. As the dog continued licking the delicious marrow on his feet contentedly, Shanfeng began to hiccup in a horrible manner. Shortly, the belch was followed by insufferable heavy breathing. . . . All of a sudden, a frighteningly hilarious laughter exploded from Shanfeng's chest like a whistling wind through a narrow lane at midnight. The laughter lingered in the air for quite a while. Then it stopped just as suddenly as it started. Shanfeng's head hang down listlessly like a bag on his chest and he died.[23]

This is certainly a nightmarish scene of horror. In this fictional scenario one cruel act is followed with another of even more shocking brutality and violence seems to have constituted the whole meaning of human existence. The reader is shocked perhaps more by the incredible composure and seeming indifference with which Shangang is creating his 'artistic' work of cruelty than by the heinous form of the sickening torture itself.

Traditionally, the Chinese place a strong emphasis on family relations and values emphasized by Confucianism. However, Yu Hua aims at exposing the seeds of brutality and evil veiled underneath the garment of civilization. Instead of catering to the reader's curiosity with a sensational account of random episodes, he seems to be more concerned with how deeply hatred and violence are rooted in human relations, even

---

[23]   Yu Hua, "A Kind of Reality" (*Xianshi yi zhong*), 80-82.

those bound by blood. By deconstructing the nuclear family structure, Yu Hua deconstructs the Confucian myth of "the Scripture of Filial Piety" (*Xiaojing*) to lay bare human nature in its naked form.[24] The ending of the story suggests unmistakably the allegorical nature of this narrative. After Shangang is executed for murdering his brother, his testicles are transplanted onto a young man whose reproductive organ is damaged in a traffic accident and the latter gives birth to a baby afterwards. This postmodern playfulness seems to imply that the mechanism of mass horror is self-reproductive and inheritable.

The same existential violence and cruelty is found in Yu Hua's other works such as "The Past and the Penalty," "The Inescapable Fate," "Classic Love," and "Errors by the River," which describe two aspects of human horror: inspiration for artistic creation and the human instinct for self-destruction.[25] The politics of violence necessarily involves the dialectic of dominance and subjugation expressed in the form of torture and self-torture. "1986," another major novella by Yu Hua, is well illustrative of this logic. The story is a disturbing narrative of the victimizing discourse and the subsequent paranoia of self victimizing in China of the 1970s and 1980s. The protagonist, a high school teacher, is driven mad by unbearable tortures during the Cultural Revolution. Before he becomes mad, the school teacher was preoccupied with the fine art of inhuman torture in Chinese history and was particularly fascinated by the five elaborate, almost artistic forms of penalty developed in ancient China. These are "Mo" (branding the face), "Yi" (cutting off the nose), "Fei" (amputating the feet), "Gong" (castration), and "Dapi" (decapitation).

The story begins with the sudden disappearance of the school teacher at the start of the Cultural Revolution. Fortunately, he survives the disaster but returns home a mad man. In 1986, ten years after the end of the Cultural Revolution, the madman returns to his hometown. Life in this small town goes on as if the historical calamity had never happened.

---

[24] For a general discussion of the issue, see Yihen Zhao's article "Yu Hua, Fiction as Subversion," *World Literature Today* (Summer 1991), 415-419.

[25] Yu Hua has been influenced by Nietzsche's perception of the epistemological values of violence. While echoing the Nietzschean notion of violence, more specifically cultural violence, he further accentuates the properties of violence both as inspiration for artistic creation and as revelation of self-destructive human instinct in the context of contemporary China, characterized by the cultural ennui and boredom resulting from an ideological and cultural emasculation. A detailed discussion of Yu Hua's aesthetic of violence is obviously beyond the scope of this article and would require a separate study.

The mad teacher, however, still lives in the dark fantasy caused by the horrible experience. The story records his dark journey into a world of delirium, in which torture and self-torture, executed by and on himself, seem to become the only possible existential mode.

Violence indicates the relation of dominance and subjugation. But the will to violence does not always lead to dominance over others. In the case of the madman, the violence of self-torture reveals a will to dominance over his own fear of becoming vulnerable to torture and suffering all alone in the darkest reaches of nightmare. The idea of suffering with others, or making others suffer, seems to alleviate the actual pain inflicted on himself. This grotesque mentality gives rise to the issue of self-torture as a means of identification with one's fellow people in order to conquer a hidden fear of suffering all by oneself.

Modern psychology reveals that perverse psychic urges such as masochism, sadism, and sadomasochism all pertain to a confused sense of the self. Needless to say, modern man is confronted with problems of various kinds: war, hatred, deception, treachery, betrayal, etc. But the biggest problem he encounters is his own self—the burden of selfhood—in a world of uncertainty and precariousness. To assert the self is to ensure the status of selfhood which is essential to one's existence as an individual being. On many occasions, however, this self-assertion expresses itself in a reversed order. That is, it does not exert a will to power over others but rather over oneself, often on one's own body as found in sadomasochism, so as to secure a sense of self-control. This is because "The self wants to believe itself to be in control of its environment, of its relationships with others, and of *itself*" (emphasis mine).[26] When this self control is at risk or is loosing, one often resorts to illusions for a vicarious control in the hope of reassuring oneself that things are still under control. Self harm, self infliction, self mutilation, and self suffering are some of the grotesque expressions of this illusory self control, which gives the self a make-up belief that at least he/she has the body in his/her own control. In the case of the mad teacher, the more he tortures himself, the stronger a sense of self control (an illusory one for sure) seems to be derived.

However, self control, be it real or illusory, can be acted out only in an interactive relationship to others. In other words, it always goes along

---

[26]   For a general discussion of the topic, see Roy F. Baumeister, *Escaping the Self* (New York: Basic Books, 1991), 5.

with identity, one that can be conceived only in the intricacy of social relations. In *Violence in Modern Philosophy*, Piotr Hoffman discusses the dialectic relation between violence and community. He eloquently argues against the idea of regarding oneself, through the violence of exclusion, as "a particular one ... a self-enclosed, all-encompassing unit." The reason for this is that "Violence alone was able to (brutally) persuade the one that the whole world was not its own private domain. ... violence educates me to the inescapable reality of others; and so I finally begin to view myself as being only one particular self among other selves."[27] This is another way of saying that the individual existence cannot be proved without reference to the existence of others. Hoffman goes on to say: "Violence too is the necessary condition of my emergence as a universal, communal being. For to rise to the level of universality I must, first, gain a perspective broader than, and independent of, my particular self."[28] This reasoning offers a critical mediation of the mad teacher's grotesque logic of torture and self-torture in relation to the paradoxical nature of self control obtained through both self assertion and self abandonment.

The Cultural Revolution is the most horrible anti-humanity disaster in modern Chinese history, which involved almost all Chinese people. While falling prey to the violence performed by Mao Zedong, the fanaticised masses themselves also played the role either of the victimizer/violator, or of the victim/violated, or of both. The whole nation was thrown into a collective delirium in which the light of reason had been extinguished and humanity had been squeezed out. When everyone else suffered the same violence, the very infliction each individual experienced seemed to have lost its intensity of painfulness. One was no more or no less unfortunate than others. Hence, the grotesque mentality of suffering and making suffer altogether. There is one particular scene in "1986" which illustrates well this collective delirium.

After branding his own face with the hot-red iron bar, the mad teacher wanders to a local movie house, where crowds of people attract his attention, exciting his imaginative mind:

---

[27]   Piotr Hoffman, *Doubt, Time, Violence* (Chicago: The University of Chicago Press, 1986), 144.

[28]   Ibid., 144.

He felt the knife twirling in his hands, severing the air around him into fragments. After a spell of twirling, he directed the blade toward their noses. He saw each nose fly up from the knife blade and hover in space. Spurts of blood spouted from the holes where the nostrils had been; flurries of severed noses danced through the air before falling one after another to the ground. Soon, the street was engulfed by the noisy clamor of noses leaping and rolling across the pavement. "Yi" (cutting off the nose), he cried forcefully, limping away.[29]

Thus in a series of ecstasies of fantasy the man performs on imaginary others the five chef types of torture and penalty he learned from history, which in actual reality are executed on his own body. In describing these cruel scenes of self-torture, Yu Hua misses no single detail. His graphic description of the madman's sadomasochism is beyond all measure; it seems to be transfigured as a luxuriant and cathartic eroticism:

[The madman] set the saw blade on his right knee ... let out a great shout, "Fei" (amputating the knee), and started to saw. The skin broke under the teeth, white at first, but gradually growing lustrously red as the blood began to flow from the wound. With a few more strokes, the saw blade hit bone. He stopped sawing and grinned. ... Within a few seconds, his face twisted into another scream. Beads of sweat rolled from his forehead. He gasped for air. The rocking slowed, and his scream faded to an almost imperceptible low wail. His arms fell limply to his sides. The saw chimed on the pavement. His neck tumbled against his chest.[30]

The softhearted reader would certainly faint at the author's seemingly sangfroid account of the madman's cutting off his own knees. The violence of the act as well as the discursive means by which the violence is represented bombards the reader with a brutal force so viciously powerful that there is almost no parallel in contemporary Chinese literature. The story, unparalleled as it is in its expression of violence and horror, seems to have an equivocal misanthropic tinge.

[29] Yu Hua, "1986," in *The Past and the Punishments*, trans. Andrew F. Jones (Honolulu: University of Hawaii Press, 1996), 151.

[30] Yu Hua, "1986," 158-59.

The madman's self-torture is a projection of the hidden fear of vulnerability to violence and cruelty into an imaginary other for paranoid pleasure of counterinvestment. This act of self-victimizing indicates a fanatic desire to dissolve one's particular self in the precarious moment of existential crisis so as to avoid suffering the unbearable blow of violence all by oneself. The darkest reaches of madness in the political life of contemporary China unleash a ravening insanity upon its victims. Self has been alienated and transformed into the imaginary other as an object of torture and self-torture so as to satisfy one's sadomasochistic urges. Much like Lu Xun's madman,[31] this mad teacher becomes a symbol of the persecution complex deeply rooted in the political unconscious of the Chinese mind. His tragic fate is indicative of an existential plight in contemporary China, for which violence and cruelty seem to be the only revealing metaphor.

Chen Jianguo
Michigan State University

---

[31]   Lu Xun is well-known for one of his short stories, a modern classic, entitled "A Madman's Diary" (*Kuangren riji*).

Bibliography

Baumeister, Roy F. 1991. *Escaping the Self*. New York: Basic Books.

Can Xue. 1991. *Old Floating Cloud: Two Novellas,* trans. Ronald R. Janssen and Jian Zhang. Evanston: Northwestern University Press.

Dawidowicz, Lucy S. 1981. *The Holocaust and the Historians*. Cambridge: Harvard University Press.

Fentress, James, and Chris Wickham. 1992. *Social Memory*. Cambridge: Blackwell.

Haynal, Andre, et al. 1983. *Fanaticism: A Historical and Psychoanalytical Study*. New York: Schocken Books.

Hoffman, Piotr. 1986. *Doubt, Time, Violence*. Chicago: The University of Chicago Press.

Mitchell, W.J.T. 1980. "Editor's Note: On Narrative." *Critical Inquiry*, 7, No. 1, Autumn, 1980: 1-4.

Ross, Bruce M. 1994. *Remembering the Personal Past*. Oxford: Oxford University Press.

Rudin, Josel. 1969. *Fanaticism: A Psychological Analysis*. Notre Dame: University of Notre Dame Press.

Yu Hua. 1996. *The Past and the Punishment*. trans. Andrew F. Jones. Honolulu: University of Hawaii.

————. 1992. "Xianshi yi zhong" (A Kind of Reality). *Hebian de cuowu [Errors by the River]*. Wuhan: Changjiang Literature Publishing House.

Zhao, Yihun. 1991. "Yu Hua: Fiction as Subversion." *World Literature Today*, Summer 1991: 415-419.

Fears, Phobias and Hopes in the Dream-books of Polish, Czech and Slovak Dissidents prior to 1989

The topic of my reflections pertains to three works: *Sennik współczesny* (Dream-book for Our Time, 1963) by the Polish author Tadeusz Konwicki, *Český snář* (Czech Dream-book, 1981) by the Czech writer Ludvík Vaculík, and *Písačky* (Writings), a three-volume series of personal confessions by the Slovak man of letters Dominik Tatarka (*Písačky*, 1979, *Sám proti noci*, Alone against the night, 1984, and *Listy do večnosti*, Letters to Eternity, 1988). The bond linking the ideological and aesthetic qualities of these works is the role played by the dream-like visions, daydreams, phobias, nightmares, and fears besetting their authors and created by situations unsolvable on the level of reality.

The domination of dreams over reality is visible already in the titles of the first two volumes; in the work of Tatarka dreams, although absent in the title, actually perform an extremely essential intellectual and constructive role. The structure of all the above mentioned works is similar, and only the arrangement of its dominants differs: the first two examples are situated on the borderline between novel and essay (Konwicki) or novel and diary (Vaculík); the most heterogeneous work (Tatarka) is an amazing collage of the author's personal confessions, intermingled with correspondence, documentary literature, a philosophical essay, and slightly fictional love stories. All three writers inserted distinct autobiographical elements, discernible in the form of confessions which at times are veiled but more frequently prove to be openly exhibitionistic.

Beyond these roughly outlined similarities there stretches an ocean of differences, resulting not only from the artistic distinctness of the particular authors but primarily due to the differences between the historical contexts and the various national traditions to which they belong.

Tadeusz Konwicki (born 1926) comes from the region of Vilno, in the former eastern territories of the Commonwealth of Two Nations (the name given to Poland and Lithuania, connected by a political union). As a boy, he took part in the anti-Nazi partisan movement, guided by the London-based Polish government-in-exile. After the war, membership in this part of the resistance was punishable by death. Konwicki avoided it by joining the party and became a socialist realist writer. His early, oft-awarded books, such as his debut—a classical "production" novel entitled *Przy budowie* (Near the Construction Site, 1950)—were regarded as a veritable nightmare by the then young readers, members of my generation.

Konwicki rapidly parted ways with socialist realism and its schemes because he was simply unable to forget the past. He continued to suffer from a betrayal complex, caused by the transition from one political affiliation to another, although the responsibility for the postwar events was borne by the Yalta-created configuration of forces rather than by its victims in Central-Eastern Europe. Konwicki was forced to flee from his Lithuanian birthplace and the land of his childhood to Poland; hence his second complex pertained to uprootedness and homelessness. These psychological implications as well as experience of the mass-scale deaths of Poles, Lithuanians and Jews, produced the *Dream-book for Our Time* (1963); this implied simultaneously that an *avant la lettre* dissident status was bestowed upon the author. Not until the end of the 1970s, did Konwicki become an outstanding representative of this trend, as the author of *Mała apokalipsa* (Little Apocalypse), *Kompleks polski* (A Polish Complex) and similar works echoing the experiences outlined in *Sennik współczesny*, although arranged in a different pattern.[1]

The events described in the *Dream-book for Our Time* are surrounded by an aura of the extraordinary, and take place along the boundary between reality and dreams, in an unreal reality. The small town, situated on the banks of the river Soła, to be flooded after the construction of a dam, remains unreal, although it is very much present on the map of Poland. Its population,

---

[1]   Możejko, Edward. 1996. "Beyond Ideology: the Prose of Tadeusz Konwicki." *The Review of Contemporary Fiction* 3: 139-155.

whose majority is composed of refugees from the former eastern parts of the country and which constitutes a veritable array of human figures (a Lithuanian count concealing his class origin, an embittered and brutal partisan, an eternally drunk militia-man, battered by his wife, a virtuous old maid from a wondrously backward and no longer existing manor of the gentry, her brother, wasted by serving ever-changing authorities, etc.) is just as unreal although realistic. This gamut of personalities is supplemented by a prewar left-wing teacher who now acts as the leader of a group of Baptists awaiting the end of the world. The local and "imported" communists rule the entire community ruthlessly. The forest, unreal and resembling a bad dream, conceals the mysteries of multiple crimes and murder, and is full of graves, commemorating past insurgents, and former German bunkers. The main hero and narrator—Paweł, a person with a shattered personality, who arrives in the town seventeen years after the war in search of traces of the past— remains a puzzle. His attempted suicide is presented as a search for liberation from the feelings of guilt. The deportees, with whom he is connected by unclear ties, fear that he is an envoy of the Ministry of Security. Here, the war has not come to an end, and the lines of various fronts during this illusory peace remain extremely complicated. The bloody phantom of Huniady, a partisan who continues to carry out death sentences passed against those who had betrayed him, is very much alive.

The plot of the novel takes place upon two levels—contemporary and retrospective. The former constitutes the landscape of daily life, although in the picturesque, surrealistic and grotesque interpretation as proposed by Konwicki, it remains highly unusual. When the awesome partisan "strikes his artificial limb against the top of a table," pickled cucumbers soar into the air, as in Chagall's paintings. A mysterious copper-haired witch named Justyna rambles in the forest. The hero visits "local non-existent villages," and merges "with the shadows of poplars splintered by lightning or missiles." All around, there wander naked corpses with "blood-sealed lips," while the coffin containing the dead communist Szafir "skims across the beer-like greenery like a perch"; and the "town gazes anxiously with its blue windows."[2]

The level of retrospection revives national martyrology, the ever-living memory of the participation of Poles in various insurrections and partisan rebellions; their traces are retained by the "faithful river," whose bed conceals numerous mementos of the deceased: shreds of banners and military iron

---

[2]   Konwicki, Tadeusz. 1964. *Sennik współczesný*. Warsaw: Iskry. 29, 239.

crosses appealing for divine aid. The hero's nightmares recreate the local forest crossed by sleighs carrying the frozen corpses of "young men serving under Kmicic"; they open the doors of a house in which a young partisan is to carry out the death verdict passed by the partisan army upon the pro-communist teacher; they depict the village across which he walks along a "terrible hedge of human eyes," expelled from his unit for insubordination, and portray the old bunker, where in the ashes he discovers the still fresh traces of someone's presence—could they have been left by Korwin, trans-formed into the bloodthirsty avenger Huniady? The strategy employed by Konwicki is not intent on unambiguous answers: the truth about the period could not be disclosed in a country under Soviet domination.

Literary criticism, nonetheless, recognised his strategy, and deciphered Konwicki's novel as a catalogue of national obsessions—*Sennik współczesny* (Dream-book of Our Time) became known as *Sennik polski* (Polish Dream-book).[3]

An entirely different convention and message are to be found in *Český snář*, the "novel-diary" written almost twenty years later (1981) by Ludvík Vaculík (b. 1926), another former communist writer, author of such novels as *Sekyra* (Axe) and *Morčata* (Laboratory Rabbits), one of the leading Czech dissidents after 1968, author of the *Manifesto of 1000 Words*, co-founder of the famous *Charta 77*, and publisher of the underground samizdat series Petlice, whose significance for the development of contemporary Czech literature of dissident origin cannot be overestimated.

The construction of the Czech *Dream-book* is delineated by the autobiographical notes recorded by the author almost daily, from 22th January 1979 to 2nd February 1980. This particular dream-book is peopled by a multitude of prominent members of the Czech and Slovak underground (Karel Kosík, Jiří Gruša, Eva Kanturková, Václav Černý, Jan Vladislav, Pavel Kohout, Karol Sidon, Lenka Procházková, and many others), with whom Vaculík remained in frequent contact, as well as by his family, friends and a varied assortment of police agents. All appear under their own names making the diary particularly attractive for the intellectual elite of the Prague underground, directly linked with the author.

The records are fragmentary, and one is tempted to describe them as a rough copy. They resort to the vernacular and contain a considerable

---

3   Lisiecka, Alicja. 1963. "*Sennik polski.*" *Życie Warszawy* 304:5.

         Literature as Cultural Memory

number of vulgar turns of speech; the recurring descriptions of the occupations of the author are rather monotonous although not without a specific Czech sense of humour. The narrator tries to observe the principles of maximum honesty ad faithfulness as regards facts and words, fearing that excessive stylisation and retouching could deprive his work of authenticity. The first word in the diary is obligation. It is this feeling of duty which turns the narrator into a beast of burden, toiling under the weight of dissident and household obligations; the only respite is offered by his affairs with women.

The feature which appears to strike the reader of the *Czech Dream-book* most is the absence of grand words and a total insensitivity on the part of the author to heroic gestures and poses, both his own and those of others. We are dealing with a purely pragmatic approach to life—a wise understanding of the fact that an isolated, small group of dissidents is insufficient to ensure the survival of a nation, and that heroism is not a prescription suitable for millions. What is the use, asks Vaculík in *Český snář*, of a handful of invincible fighters to glitter, while society as a whole submerges itself in complete disintegration?[4]

A characteristic trait of Vaculík's mode of thought, totally distinct from the Polish and, as we shall see later, the Slovak author, is extreme rationalism and a sober attitude towards life. A positive ethos of work, optimism, a will to survive, a strong feeling of support in his Moravian roots, the land and culture of "positive thinking," combined with an avoidance of posing fundamental ontological questions, are not enough to really free oneself from existential fears. Relegated to the subconscious, they disclose themselves in the dreams of the dissidents. In the *Czech Dream-book*, these fears usually are a direct reaction of the heroes to new threats, constantly produced by the policies pursued by the Czechoslovakian authorities; they echo police repressions, and emerge from fears of mental and physical torture and imprisonment. In accordance with Freudian theories, they are of a diagnostic and therapeutic nature but do not possess a prophetic character, such as the one ascribed to the classical dream-book of the Queen of Sheba. They provide a direct answer to existing threats. When the culmination of the latter reaches its apogee, then Ludvík dreams of the lifeless spaces of Arizona, in whose forests he glides upon mouldy leaves and encounters deadly chasms that open up in front of him, while his wife Madla reacts so violently to daytime threats

[4]   Vaculík, Ludvík. 1990. *Český snář*. Brno: Atlantic. 25.

that in her sleep she slaps imaginary police agents with such force that she awakes with a hand swollen from pain.

These dreams could be used to compose a register of the fears faced by Czech dissidents, different from those of their Polish counterparts but equally disturbing.

The second great theme of the dissident dreams is sex and the ensuing existential hazards.

All the dreams contained in the *Czech Dream-book* are catastrophic, and only the last, which Vaculík recorded under the date of 2nd January, and thus at the very end of his "novel-diary," is optimistic. In this dream, the narrator moves "to a spacious quiet flat in an old, single-storey house," with an abandoned garden nearby, which he is certain to restore to its former grandeur. An additional cause of joy is the fact that his room and that of his wife are located at the extreme ends of the house, and that the distance between them is so considerable that it requires a train journey.

At the end of the novel good signs appear also in reality, forecasting the success of the dissident cause. A group of representatives of the opposition, who travel by train to Brno together with Vaculík, unexpectedly discover that all the train toilets contain hand painted graffiti proclaiming "*Slobodu Chartistom!*" (Freedom to the Chartists!). Nothing could have been a greater source of satisfaction for Czech writers enamoured of Bachtinian descriptions of the lower levels of the body, starting with Hašek and ending with Kundera.

Upon several occasions, fragments of the *Czech Dream-book* referring to the years 1979-1980 mention the name of Dominik Tatarka; at the time, Vaculík was engaged in preparing the Slovak author's *Písačky* for publication. In Vaculík's reminiscences, Tatarka appears predominantly as an object of laborious editorial work conducted by the author of the *Czech Dream-book*, a cause of frequent complaints such as: I am forced to work so hard and to run around town with Tatarka's manuscripts while he spends his time drinking. This rather acrid statement made by Vaculík was not very distant from the truth.

The Slovak author sought oblivion in wine, women and thoughts about death—he remained locked in the embrace of Eros and Thanatos. Tatarka was completely isolated within Slovak society, which was highly conformist, and in which dissidents remained few (while their Czech counterparts numbered thousands). In 1968, he dared to protest publicly against the invasion carried out by Warsaw Pact troops and signed *Charta 77*; during the consecutive historical turmoil, his fate bore a resemblance to that of the biblical Job, and Tatarka became a scapegoat of the community which once elevated him. After all, up to 1968, similar to Vaculík and Konwicki, he was showered with official awards. Some of his books, such as *Farská republika* (Republic of Parsons), *Prútené kresla* (Wicker Armchairs) or *Panna zázračni-ca* (The Miracle-working Maiden) were published in numerous and sizable editions; even *Démon súhlasu* (Demon of an agreement; written during the political thaw of 1956, published in 1963 and containing the first postwar attacks against the aberration of intellectuals serving the Party) was tolerated. After 1968, when, for all practical purposes, the country was ruled by an occupying force relying on specially selected Slovaks, Tatarka was relegated to the margin of society and forced to survive on a starvation-level pension. His books were ejected from libraries and burnt, their further publication was banned, and he was forbidden to enjoy freedom of movement in Czechoslovakia (particular obstacles were created for any contacts with Czech dissidents in Prague). The author remained under incessant police surveillance, and the more he defended his position, the greater the fury of his persecutors.

Tatarka intuitively felt that his individual and, apparently, unique case was a repetition of the well-known scheme of collectively organized violence vis-à-vis the individual.

His trilogy recalls the fate of the executed Clementis, who admitted to non-existent guilt, and the Stalinist condemnation of Gustav Husák, which led to eight years incarceration, a sentence that, however, did not stop the former prisoner from becoming a fervent "normaliser" who in the name of protecting "higher reasons," and without a single word of complaint, passed over the misery of the Stalinist era and his own humiliation.

Up to the very end of his life, Tatarka did not accept the victim's pyre which was set alight both by his foes and false friends. He sought refuge in love and creativity, which appear to be excluded from total enslavement; it is within their range that he wished to construct "the time and space of freedom."[5]

---

[5] Tatarka, Dominik. 1984. *Písačky*. Köln: Index. 41. On the end of the great narratives with reference to Lyotard and Tatarka, see: Janaszek-Ivaničková, Halina. 1996. *Od modernizmu do postmodernizmu*. Katowice: Wydawnictwo Uniwersytetu Śląskiego. 106-125.

Ironically, all of Tatarka's lovers were either police agents or suspected of collaborating with the security forces, a fact which introduced into his works a dose of literary postmodernist irony and authentic suffering, and created a feeling of abasement and ever-present menace.

As in the case of the other two men of letters, protection against fear is offered by dreams. For Tatarka, an ardent admirer of Jung, an enthusiastic reader of the *Musée imaginaire* by Malraux, and a devotee of the anthropology of culture pursued by Lévi-Strauss, the significance of dreams is not restricted to therapy. Dreams are to aid him in a better understanding of himself, in finding his own place among the archetypes of culture: to discover within himself the "Carpathian shepherd" who emerged from ancient tribal wanderings and, at the same time, a European writer of an orientation that cherishes Polish and French traditions. In the wake of the fall of the communist "great narratives," which for Tatarka broke down definitely once his beautiful "Tatrania" was invaded by foreign troops and all hopes for the creation of socialism "with a human face" collapsed, the very concept of time succumbed to a profound change within the writer's consciousness. Linear time, which was to lead to a communist heaven on Earth, failed to pass the test. It became replaced by cyclical, eternal, divine and mythical time, which transcends beyond the here and now, and leads both into an archaic past and into a future that crosses the limits of mundane existence. The author is to be guided towards the archaic past by his relations with women—physical contacts with them are to bring him towards the origin of the world, the forgotten sources of being.

The magnificently stylised dreams depicted by Tatarka, which resort to surrealistic and sophisticated images, frequently contain an animal symbol of manliness (such as the silver moose with powerful jaws created for love) and womanhood (a "doe in heat"). They also include assorted objects endowed with magical properties, such as a sacrificial bowl made of opal which in Indian tantras is the symbol of intercourse, and in Christianity—of the Eucharist.[6] Intercourse is only one step away from the "commune," the most primeval social unit which gives rise to all creative initiatives. Such communes, which Tatarka called "divine," are in his noble utopia to generate a free and democratic Republic, contrasted by the author with a centralised, bureaucratic Party-state organism, which stifles all initiative and gives rise to the monstrosities of power.

---

[6]   Tatarka. *Listy do večnosti*. 1988. Toronto: Sixty Eight Publishers. 67.

Love, friendship and treason perceived from a political and personal point of view constitute three themes present in the writer's dream about three hats, which forms a quasi-fictional canvas for one part of his trilogy— *Sám proti noci* (Alone against the Night). The three hats: that of a peasant, a grey and ordinary brigand's hat inherited from a great-grandfather, and a black velvet hat, worn by the author during the funerals of his friends, symbolise three women who are the object of his sexual yearning and, at the same time, the three "tools of [his] loneliness, betrayal and death."[7] Similarly to the hats of the "simple Simon" from Tatarka's home village, they are also a visible sign of the frenzied despair of both men.

Even in this frenzy and despair, Tatarka does not lose heart. His consciousness stores the recollection of his brave ancestor, who bequeathed the brigand's hat, and constitutes an eternal source of rebellion and protest against national and human enslavement, expressed up to his last days.

Three different national dream-books, three different historical fates, and three varying manners of perceiving the world merge within a Central European triptych—a triptych containing the traumatic experiences that stem from living in a totalitarian system, among the phantoms of violence. Dreams fulfil an essential ideological and aesthetic function—they permit their creators to express, within a given convention which is more beautiful than a wish and more frightening than anxiety, the innermost melody of their souls, by returning to Jungian archetypes of collective consciousness; they revive the feeling of interrupted contact with humankind's ancient past, more permanent and deeper than passing social and political configurations.

Halina Janasczek-Ivaničková
University of Silesia

---

7   Tatarka. *Sám proti noci*. 1984. München: Edice Arkýř. 22.

Visiteurs au village Potemkine

On connaît l'histoire des "villages Potemkine" que le prince Potemkine aurait fait fabriquer, avec des décors de théâtre, pour éblouir la tzarine Catherine II lors de son voyage en Crimée en 1787. Or, cent cinquante ans plus tard, l'esprit Potemkine restait toujours vivant dans l'Ex-Empire russe. Selon Arthur Koestler, lui-même agent du Komintern pendant un certain temps, l'image que la Russie présentait à l'étranger dans les années vingt et trente fut fabriquée de toutes pièces par la propagande soviétique: "C'était l'image d'une super-Amérique, engagée dans l'entreprise la plus gigantesque de l'Histoire, bourdonnante d'activité, d'efficacité, d'enthousiasme."[1] Et une fois que les explorateurs de ce nouveau monde franchirent la frontière de l'Union soviétique pour voir le paradis des travailleurs, le mécanisme Potemkine se déclencha aussitôt pour leur présenter une vue idéalisée du régime stalinien tout en camouflant les aspects inhumains de celui-ci. Durant des visites soigneusement préparées et strictement contrôlées par les autorités locales, les visiteurs restaient isolés de la réalité: ils ne devaient s'apercevoir ni de la dékoulakisation, ni de la famine, ni des atteintes quotidiennes contre les droits humains, ni des procès d'épuration qui se multipliaient à Moscou et ailleurs. Pourtant, et parfois à partir de signes apparemment anodins, les voyageurs sentirent la nature mensongère du village Potemkine qu'on leur faisait visiter et, poussés par une

---

[1]   Arthur Koestler, *Hiéroglyphes*, traduit de l'anglais par Denise Van Moppès, in: *Œuvres autobiographiques*, Édition établie par Phil Casoar, Paris, Robert Laffont, 1994, p.338.

exigence morale, n'hésitèrent pas de la démasquer dans leurs récits de voyage ou dans leurs romans.

"Je livre ici mes réflexions personnelles sur ce que l'U.R.S.S. prend plaisir et légitime orgueil à montrer et sur ce que, à côté de cela, j'ai pu voir"—c'est ainsi que Gide signale d'une manière très subtile, dès le début de son *Retour de l'U.R.S.S.*, les deux sources dans lesquelles il a puisé ses informations souvent contradictoires.[2] Dans ses *Retouches à mon Retour de l'URSS* (1937) écrites dans un souci légitime d'autodéfense, Gide précise que ceux qui, ayant passé quatorze jours en Russie, l'accusent d'avoir menti sur la réalité soviétique, ont pu beaucoup voir, mais rien que ce qu'on leur a montré. Quand on voyage 'accompagné', dit Gide, se souvenant de ses propres expériences au Congo, tout paraît presque merveilleux. Mais il faut quitter la voiture des gouverneurs et parcourir le pays seul, à pied.[3] C'est ce que fit Istrati en Russie, une fois sa visite officielle terminée: "Si j'avais quitté la Russie, au bout de six semaines, comme tous les délégués venus pour le dixième anniversaire, j'aurais écrit des articles dithyrambiques...".[4]

Si l'on ne voyage pas seul, on sera dupé soit par les constructeurs du village Potemkine, soit par son propre enthousiasme et sa propre ignorance. Tel est le cas de Koestler lors de son premier contact avec l'U.R.S.S. Fin juillet 1931 il participa au célèbre voyage du Graf Zeppelin sur l'Arctique et fit escale à Léningrad. Koestler s'émerveilla à la vue des forêts vierges de la Carélie soviétique et s'enthousiasma devant le développement vigoureux du pays: la production de bois en Carélie augmentait au rythme de 40 à 60% par an et le chiffre de sa population était, depuis la révolution, passé de 220.000 à 360.000. Il en rendit compte dans son livre *Nuits blanches, journées rouges*, rédigé en 1933, lors de son deuxième voyage en Russie, et qui parut en langue allemande à Moscou, après avoir été rigoureusement censuré. Vingt ans plus tard, dans son autobiographie, Koestler revient sur sa propre naïveté d'antan: "Ce que je ne savais pas lorsque, en 1933, j'écrivais ce livre, c'est que les agglomérations situées au bord des fleuves dans l'antique forêt avec leurs cabanes de bois grossièrement taillé étaient des camps de concentration; que l'augmentation des chiffres de la population et de la production était presque entièrement due au travail forcé, et que

---

[2]   André Gide, *Retour de l'U.R.S.S.*. Paris, Gallimard, 1936, p.16.

[3]   André Gide, *Retouches à mon Retour de l'U.R.S.S.*, Paris, Gallimard, 1937, p.13.

[4]   Panaït Istrati, *Vers l'autre flamme*, Paris, Les Éditions Rieder, 1929, p.38.

l'étendue de la Carélie que nous survolions à peu près de Pétrozavodsk aux îles Solovetsky est l'une des régions les plus anciennes et les plus notoires de travail forcé de la Russie soviétique, le berceau du futur continent de bagne arctique".[5]

Parmi les centaines de récits de voyage en U.R.S.S., le livre de Gide se distingue tant par la clairvoyance et l'honnêteté intellectuelle de son auteur que par le succès et le scandale que ce livre a suscités dès sa parution. Le *Retour de l'U.R.S.S.* et les *Retouches* ont quasiment éclipsé les autres récits sur la Russie. Pourtant, dès 1927, donc neuf ans avant le voyage de Gide et pour ne mentionner que le domaine français, Georges Duhamel et Panaït Istrati ont très clairement vu les graves problèmes qui menaçaient la liberté de l'homme en Russie.

En parlant de quelques "retours de l'U.R.S.S.", je laisserai de côté les remarques positives, les appréciations et les louanges que ces écrits contiennent, de même que l'expression de la confiance que les auteurs ont, malgré tout, placée dans la grande aventure de l'humanité. Je ne parlerai ici que de critiques dans lesquelles se dégage, au moins pour le lecteur d'aujourd'hui, une tendance inquiétante qui, à partir de petits incidents quotidiens et d'atteintes aux droits de l'homme, mène nécessairement aux procès et aux camps de concentration soviétiques, les goulag.

A l'époque où se font ces voyages qu'on pourrait appeler des pérégrinations, la crise économique bat son plein, le climat politique s'assombrit, l'expansion du fascisme et la menace de l'hitlérisme pèsent sur l'Europe: il n'est nullement étonnant que les esprits inquiets se tournent vers l'utopie et se mettent en route vers l'Union Soviétique, pays où "une expérience sans précédents était tentée" et dont on attendait "un élan capable d'entraîner l'humanité toute entière".[6]

Pourtant, vu de l'intérieur, ce pays est loin d'être l'incarnation de l'utopie millénaire de l'humanité. La construction du socialisme, imposée par une minorité agissante à une majorité hostile, réticente ou simplement passive s'accomplit dans une atmosphère troublée. Vingt ans de luttes intérieures constituent une période tragique dans l'histoire de la Russie, cet ex-Empire devenu en 1922 l'Union des républiques socialistes soviétiques.

[5] Arthur Koestler, *La corde raide*, in: *Œuvres autobiographiques*, pp. 273-274.

[6] Gide, *Retour..*, p.11.

Après une période relativement calme, celle de la nouvelle économie politique (N.E.P.), lancée en 1923 durant laquelle coexistaient encore un secteur capitaliste (l'agriculture) et un secteur étatisé (l'industrie et le commerce extérieur), le premier plan quinquennal annoncé en 1929 imposa une industrialisation accélérée et une collectivisation forcée. Staline élimina successivement l'opposition de gauche et de droite et établit, à partir de 1929, une véritable dictature personnelle. L'assassinat de Kirov en 1934 déclencha une série de grands procès d'épuration: le procès des seize avec, comme accusés principaux Zinoviev et Kamenev, (1936), le procès des dix-sept (1937), et le procès de Boukharine en 1938. Dans la grande purge l'armée fut aussi décimée, et Toukhatchevski fut exécuté en 1937.[7]

Pourtant, la conversion d'une partie importante de l'intelligentsia occidentale au communisme s'effectue au moment même où Staline prend le contrôle du pays[8], car vu de l'extérieur, l'U.R.S.S. représente le grand espoir et l'unique alternative pour ces intellectuels. De surcroît, ce pays devient de plus en plus acceptable pour l'Occident: il est admis à la S.D.N. en 1934 et le pacte franco-soviétique en 1935 le confirme encore dans sa position. Vue de loin, peu à peu, la Russie se polissait.

A partir des années vingt, ce pays fit de gros efforts pour attirer les intellectuels occidentaux et de nombreuses invitations furent adressées à des écrivains et journalistes. Duhamel fut invité par l'Académie des sciences artistiques en 1927. La même année, Istrati participa aux festivités du 10e anniversaire de la révolution. Les écrivains hongrois Gyula Illyés et Lajos Nagy assistèrent au congrès des écrivains soviétiques en 1934. Gide et cinq autres écrivains français, dont Eugène Dabit, furent invités par l'Union des écrivains soviétiques en 1936. Pour ce qui est de Koestler, c'est lui-même qui décida de faire un long séjour en U.R.S.S. en 1932-1933 et obtint un contrat pour écrire *La Russie aux yeux d'un bourgeois.*

Les critiques portent le plus souvent sur les conditions de vie et les droits de l'homme. La plupart des voyageurs soulignent qu'ils ne se servent pas de chiffres, (seul Gide le fera dans ses *Retouches*, pour étayer ce qu'il a décrit dans son *Retour*) tous se fient à leurs expériences directes pour en déduire des conclusions qui sont, pour la plupart, justes.

---

[7]   Voir *Encyclopaedia Universalis*, France, Paris, 1992, tome 23, p.228.

[8]   Roland Quilliot, *Arthur Koestler. De la désillusion tragique au rêve d'une nouvelle synthèse*, Paris, Librairie Philosophique J.Vrin, 1990, p.57.

Gide remarque, dans *Retour de l'U.R.S.S.*, l'uniformisation excessive de la population: "Une extraordinaire uniformité règne dans les mises; sans doute elle paraîtrait également dans les esprits, si seulement on pouvait les voir. (....) A première vue l'individu se fond ici dans la masse, est si peu particularisé qu'il semble qu'on devrait, pour parler des gens, user d'un partitif et dire non point: des hommes, mais: de l'homme".[9] Dans les kolkhozes, il observe une "complète dépersonnalisation" des habitations: dans chacune des pièces "les mêmes vilains meubles, le même portrait de Staline, et absolument rien d'autre; pas le moindre objet, le moindre souvenir personnel."[10]

De cette uniformisation et conformisation excessives il s'ensuit logiquement le manque de liberté d'expression. "Chaque matin, la *Pravda* leur enseigne ce qu'il sied de savoir, de penser, de croire. (..) Songez que ce façonnement de l'esprit commence dès la plus tendre enfance..."[11] "Le citoyen soviétique reste dans une extraordinaire ignorance de l'étranger. Bien plus: on l'a persuadé que tout, à l'étranger, et dans tous les domaines, allait beaucoup moins bien qu'en U.R.S.S."[12] Quant au manque de liberté de parole, Istrati l'observe déjà lors de son voyage en 1927: "...le militant bureaucrate, qu'on appelle là-bas 'militant responsable' va droit son chemin, la tête en avant. Il est le maître de la tribune et de la presse. Seul, il peut parler. Seul, il peut écrire. Il se fabrique un majorité et un présidium, comme il se fabrique un comité de rédaction et une censure. Ainsi, personne ne peut le contredire".[13] Pour ce qui est de la censure, tous les voyageurs se heurtent à un contrôle en ce qui concerne leurs déclarations: Gide devait faire un petit discours, mais on trouva que son texte n'était pas dans la ligne.[14] Quelques années auparavant, Duhamel fut également étonné de se voir censuré: "Bien qu'attendu là-bas avec la plus évidente sympathie, j'ai dû soumettre à la censure les thèmes essentiels de mes conférences. Peine perdue pour tout le monde, car j'ai, dans la suite, parlé

---

[9]   Gide, *Retour..*, p.37.

[10]   *Ibid,* p.47.

[11]   *Ibid.*, p.49.

[12]   *Ibid.*, p.52.

[13]   Istrati, *ouvrage cité*, p.41.

[14]   Gide, *Retour...*, p.87.

d'abondance et négligé mon programme".[15]

Gide s'indigne de la suppression de l'esprit critique: "Ce que l'on demande à présent, c'est l'acceptation, le conformisme. (...) D'autre part, la moindre protestation, la moindre critique est passible des pires peines, et du reste aussitôt étouffé. Et je doute qu'en aucun autre pays aujourd'hui, fût-ce dans l'Allemagne de Hitler, l'esprit soit moins libre, plus courbé, plus craintif (terrorisé), plus vassalisé."[16] "Supprimer l'opposition... il est sans doute heureux que Staline y parvienne si mal"[17]—ajoute-t-il pourtant, non sans naïveté.

Pour ce qui est de la conformisation et de la manipulation des masses, un passage dans le livre de Duhamel est très révélateur. Duhamel qui est médecin fait une visite à l'institut du grand savant Pavlov où on étudie les réflexes de la glande salivaire des chiens et il est surpris d'entendre que "la vie intérieure" des chiens est absolument négligée. Il conclut: "Ce qui me frappe surtout, dans la physiologie moderne, c'est qu'elle peut fournir des exemples, des excuses et des protocoles aux plus austères théoriciens des politiques nouvelles. Ici et là, même rigueur calculatrice en face de la vie, même confiance dans les vertus de la mathématique, même volonté d'abstraire chaque phénomène pour le mieux considérer, même passion simplificatrice, même économie, même dédain, pour tout dire, du seul facteur irréductible à l'analyse, de cette âme insaisissable qui risque de corrompre tout calcul."[18]

Les visiteurs ont fait, évidemment, beaucoup d'observations sur ce que nous appelons aujourd'hui la qualité de la vie, sur les interminables queues devant les magasins (Gide), sur le peu d'intimité dans les habitats (Duhamel). Gide remarque "l'extraordinaire indolence" du peuple de Moscou et se moque du stakhanovisme: une équipe de mineurs français a demandé, par camaraderie, de relayer une équipe de mineurs soviétiques et aussitôt, sans s'en douter, ils ont fait du stakhanovisme—raconte-t-il.[19] Istrati souligne l'incompétence des nouveaux cadres et constate que les

---

[15]   Georges Duhamel, *Le voyage de Moscou*, Paris, Mercure de France, 1927, pp.83-84.

[16]   Gide, *Retour...*, p.67

[17]   *Ibid.*, p.77.

[18]   Duhamel, *ouvrage cité*, pp. 102-103.

[19]   Gide, *Retour...*, pp. 43-44.

entreprises fonctionnent mal car elles sont dirigées par d'incapables communistes.[20]

C'est encore Istrati qui rend compte, d'un ton indigné et ému, de l'affaire Roussakov, beau-père de son ami Victor Serge. Il s'agit, pour ainsi dire, d'un procès avant la date: une syndicaliste désirant s'approprier les quatre pièces que neuf membres de la famille de Roussakov occupent dans un ancien appartement bourgeois, l'accuse de l'avoir insultée: une vaste campagne de presse se déchaînera contre le vieillard et malgré toutes les démarches d'Istrati qui, profitant de ses bonnes relations, essaie de les défendre, les Roussakov seront condamnés à quelques mois de travaux forcés.[21]

Ces critiques dont je n'ai pu donner qu'un aperçu, ont été formulées non sans conflits intérieurs de la part de leurs auteurs. En fait, il est très difficile d'accepter que des illusions longtemps entretenues s'effondrent lors d'une confrontation avec la réalité. Ceux qui gardèrent leur indépendance d'esprit, comme Gide, surent tirer les conséquences de leur déception et n'hésitèrent pas à les rendre publiques. Istrati, le prolétaire anarchiste se proclamant bolchevik, ne sut ni ne voulut se retenir et proclama son indignation, sans tenir compte de la réprobation de ses camarades et de la colère de son menteur et bienfaiteur, Romain Rolland.

Mais c'est Koestler, membre du parti communiste allemand qui eut le plus de mal à faire face à ces expériences déchirantes. Il s'est pourtant tiré d'affaire: "Je réagis au choc brutal de la réalité sur l'illusion, d'une façon caractéristique du vrai croyant. J'étais étonné, éberlué, mais les pare-chocs élastiques que je devais à l'éducation du Parti se mirent aussitôt à opérer. J'avais des yeux pour voir, et un esprit conditionné pour éliminer ce qu'ils voyaient. Cette 'censure intérieure' est plus sûre et efficace que n'importe quelle censure officielle".[22] Et quand il ne pouvait plus rester aveugle devant des évidences bouleversantes, une conviction profonde qu'il partageait avec les autres communistes l'aida à surmonter sa déception. "Ce fut la conviction que la situation était due, non pas à une faute de notre système, mais à l'état arriéré du peuple russe. En Allemagne, en Autriche ou en France, la Révolution prendrait une tout autre forme. Les communis-

---

[20]   Istrati, *ouvrage cité.*, p.15.

[21]   Istrati, *ouvrage cité*, pp. 205-280.

[22]   Koestler, *Hiéroglyphes*, in: *ouvrage cité*, p.340.

tes allemands en Russie se chuchotaient à l'oreille: *Wir werden es besser machen*, nous nous y prendrons mieux".[23] Le compagnon de voyage de Gide, Eugène Dabit qui mourut de la fièvre typhoïde à Sébastopol, a laissé une note qui dévoile quel aurait été le récit de voyage qu'il n'a jamais pu écrire: "Quant à parler de l'URSS en professionnel, avec chiffres, exemples, comparaisons, je ne le puis et ne le veux. D'autres que moi s'en chargent ou s'en chargeront... Quant à parler de la doctrine, du système, il n'en est pas question. Entre plusieurs qui sont proposés aux hommes, entre fascisme et communisme, je n'hésite pas. J'ai choisi le communisme; et quelles que soient les réserves que puissent m'inspirer ce voyage, je m'en tiens fermement à mon choix".[24] Telle devait être l'attitude de la plupart des intellectuels de gauche, et non seulement dans les années trente, mais encore beaucoup plus tard.

Suivons encore l'itinéraire de Koestler. Après le meurtre de Kirov, il y avait eu des actions masquées que la propagande soviétique avait réussi à cacher à une opinion candide et magnétisée. Cependant, tout devait brusquement changer. En août 1936 "les condamnations à mort du 'premier' procès de Moscou marquèrent le passage de la terreur camouflée à la terreur franche et absolue. Mais à cette époque, la guerre civile espagnole avait commencé. La révolte de Franco faisait reculer bien loin les événements intérieurs de Russie, aux yeux des Européens de gauche, moi-même compris. Le jour où les premiers comptes rendus de Zinoviev parurent dans la presse d'Europe, j'étais déjà en route pour l'Espagne, comme agent du Komintern"—raconte Arthur Koestler[25]. La guerre d'Espagne et la guerre mondiale jetèrent le voile de l'oubli sur le village Potemkine et ses malheureux habitants. Ce fut le livre de Koestler, *Le Zéro et l'infini*, qui révéla (non à sa parution en 1940, mais après la guerre) la terrible réalité des procès et des camps dans la "patrie d'élection" des intellectuels de gauche d'Europe.

Judith Karafiáth
Budapest

Avec le soutien de la Fondation Soros, Budapest

---

23   *Ibid.*, p.441.

24   Eugène Dabit, *Journal intime (1928-1936)*, Paris, Gallimard, 1939, p.342. Cité par J.-P.A. Bernard, *Le parti communiste français et la question littéraire 1921-1939*, Presses Universitaires de Grenoble, 1972, p.165.

25   Koestler, *Hiéroglyphes, ouvrage cité*, p.572.

Caryl Churchill's *Mad Forest*: Reconstructing Cultural Memory

Caryl Churchill's *Mad Forest*: *A Play from Romania* began as a workshop project initiated at the Central School of Speech and Drama in London in January, 1990. At this time, Churchill joined director Mark Wing-Davey and a group of ten graduate students on a trip to Bucharest to work with students from the Caragiale Institute of Theatre and Cinema in writing a script representing the confusion of the political changes occurring in Romania between December, 1989 and May, 1990. These dates represent events just prior to the fall of the Ceausescu regime and the election of the National Salvation Front Party. A diary of events preceding the text of *Mad Forest* documents not only the political changes in Romania but also the process of the production of the play. As Donna Soto-Morettini observes, the diary thus represents "a synchronicity of events—revolution and play about revolution happening all at once" (106).

Even before we enter into the action of the play, the title hints at Churchill's attitude towards interpretation, for *Mad Forest* refers to the mythical, impenetrable forest that originally surrounded Bucharest. Churchill informs us that travellers were compelled to go around it, and consequently named the forest Teleorman, or "mad forest" (7). The title thus alludes to the difficulty of finding access to the "paths" of Romania as a subject and relates to the tentative, inconclusive shape the play assumes by "going around the subject" of history and ideology in Romania.

Wing-Davey has pointed out that the play "isn't a documentary," nor are the actors trying to be foreigners, "for much of the play is about being a Westerner in a foreign place," and "the phrase-book sentences that open each of the scenes are there as reminders that this is simply a partial view; it's not the truth" (quoted in Robinson 127).

It is difficult for foreigners entering the mazes of Romania's "mad forest" of political change to determine whether the events represented liberation, revolution, uprising, coup d'état, end of the evil empire, or simply "a change." Churchill's play mirrors the confusion of the characters as they ask themselves whether "the old regime is really dead" (Greenblatt 1):

> Did we have a revolution or putsch? Who was shooting on the 21st? And who was shooting on the 22nd? Was the army shooting on the 21st or did some not shoot or were the Securitate disguised in army uniforms? ... Most important of all, were the terrorists and the army really fighting or were they only pretending to fight? And for whose benefit? And by whose orders? Where did the flags come from? Who put loudhailers in the square? How could they publish a newspaper so soon? Why did no one turn off the power at the TV? Who got Ceausescu to call everyone together? And is he really dead? How many people died at Timosoara? And where are the bodies? Who mutilated the bodies? And were they mutilated after they'd been killed specially to provoke the revolution? By whom? For whose benefit? Or was there a drug in the food at Timosoara to make the people more aggressive? Who poisoned the water in Bucharest? (Churchill 50)

Despite the presumption on Churchill's part to write a play "from" Romania, she avoids constructing meaning from her ethnographic excursion. Instead she uses a number of distancing techniques to question society's assumption of viewing certain relationships as "natural." Among these devices is a self-reflexive presentational technique of doubling or tripling up actors in a number of roles as eleven actors play thirty-seven roles with an age range stretching from eight to over seventy. In addition roles are assigned to "unreal" characters such as an angel, a vampire, a dog, and a ghost. Churchill also relies on many features of Bertolt Brecht's epic-theatre aesthetics of montage for her workshop method. However, if change is the key to Brechtian historicization, Churchill's *Mad Forest* marks a break with the meta-narrative of progress, and instead displays "a universal, diffuse cynicism" (Sloterdijk 3).

In order to compose the semblance of a narrative of a play from Romania, Churchill rearranges and combines recent events from the Romanian history with those that had been left out, put aside, overlooked and forgotten. István Rév observes that

> forgetting is constitutive, an essential element of 'remembering otherwise,' of rewriting history of reconstituting identity. ... By 'remembering otherwise,' the historian constructs an alternative version that liberates one (a person, a group, a nation) from one's past. Forgetting thus has a liberating effect. But what is left out naturally has not been lost forever (9)

Churchill intentionally inserts back into the text of *Mad Forest* traces from the past that had been covered up for the sake of forgetting. Her approach to Romanian history foregrounds that she is a tourist to whom everything seems grotesque and bizarre as she playfully inserts surreal elements into the performance: a vampire, a dog, a rat, a dead grandmother, and a flying angel. These apparitions play a role of revealing that the spectres from the past are not that different from the living ghouls of today. To show how "real" these apparitions are, Churchill does not resort to special effects, for she mentions in the production note that "The Vampire was not dressed as a vampire" and " We didn't use a prop rat" (Churchill 9). Thus, the vampire is just an ordinary Romanian, who having smelled the blood of the revolution from his not so distant past, reappears on the scene of collective vampirism during the December 1989 events, unrecognized by anyone but a starving dog.

Other elements from the past bubble up in a scene in which Churchill conflates the terrorism practised by the Romanian fascist Iron Guard with the repressions practised by Ceausescu's Securitate. The past resurfaces as an "angel" appears out of the "blue" from his not too distant days as a symbol of the Iron Guard to comfort a priest who is ashamed that the Church has not taken a stand against the persecution of its parishioners by Ceausescu's Securitate:

PRIEST: Everyone will think we're cowards.

ANGEL: No no no.

PRIEST: Yes. Yes. Pause. You've never been political?

ANGEL: Very little. The Iron Guard used to be rather charming and called themselves the League of the Archangel Michael and carried my picture about. They had lovely processions. So I dabbled.

PRIEST: But they were fascists.

ANGEL: They were mystical.

PRIEST: The Iron Guard threw Jews out of windows in '37, my father remembers it. He shouted and they beat him up.

ANGEL: Politics, you see. Their politics weren't very pleasant. I try to keep clear of the political side. You should do the same   (Churchill 22).

Each scene of the play's twenty-four scenes is announced by the company reading from a phrasebook as if "for English tourists," first in Romanian, then in English, and once again in Romanian. For example, the first scene opens with the sentence: "Lucia are patru oua. Lucia has four eggs" (Churchill 13). This lesson in Romanian serves both as an indicator that eggs are central to the scene and also points to our limited "vocabulary" in understanding the significance of these eggs. Similarly, in the following scene the question "Who has a match? " announces not only a power failure but also the failure of "illumination" on the part of those participating in the scene. As the play proceeds, the sentences that announce each scene become more complex, but the spectators neither know the situation to which they can apply the phrase, "Ciinelui ii e foame. The dog is hungry" (Churchill 44), nor do they know the rules of grammar in order to construct their own sentences from the very limited vocabulary at the spectators' disposal.

The play is constructed in three acts. Against a many-layered background, Churchill etches the relationships of two families, one accommodating to the Ceausescu regime, and the other divided in its attitude. The first act, entitled "Lucia's Wedding," concerns the lives of the Vladus, representing a working class family , and the Antonescus, representing a privileged, well-educated family of professionals. The second act presents a group of confused speakers consisting of students, workers, and intellectuals as they try to untangle the mazes of the events occurring before their eyes. The last act once again culminates in a wedding, but if weddings represent happy endings, Churchill suggests that the marriage of the once elitist Radu Antonescu to Lucia's sister Florina Vladu is not going to provide the traditional happy closure.

Churchill's reliance on combinations of close-ups and wide-angle snapshots and a reducing or diminishing view through a reversed scope offer the spectator a number of perspectives. The wide angle shot is often accompanied by an alienation technique that could be called "ethonologizing." The plot is intentionally fragmentary in order to reveal what is the same in each of the snapshot-like scenes. The snapshots in the first part include not only close-ups of "familiar" scenes such as family together at home in the evening, but also the trials of everyday life, visits to the doctor, talking to the Securitate, standing in line to buy meat, a classroom scene, two men sitting in the sun, and waiting for the trolley.

Despite her obvious interest in the effect of politics on the individual, Churchill's dramaturgical approach is characterized by a marked absence of any direct portrayal of political events. As Tony Mitchell explains, "By concentrating exclusively on subjects who are not directly connected to the Ceausescu regime, Churchill is still able to portray a representative cross-section of society" (503). The action of the fragmented scenes is linked by a "spectrum of paranoia at one end, stretching through to a very reasonable suspicion at the other " (Mitchell 503). In her portrayal of ordinary Romanians, Churchill focuses on the predicaments and power relations that affect everyday life, and political figures are banished to the background to serve as indicators how the broader political scenario connects to the every-day. In this manner, Churchill illustrates how the power of unseen systems controls human thought and behaviour, and how suppression of political differences regulates, governs and ultimately eliminates resistance.

The many scenes leading up to the first "happy" event of a wedding of Lucia Vladu to an unseen American suggest that Lucia's marriage is an escape from the limited economic possibilities in Romania. This act takes place before the overthrow of Ceausescu and reflects the atmosphere of isolation, mistrust, and deep divisions both within and between the families. While these symptoms in capitalist societies tend to be "private" concerns, Churchill connects these scenes to the practices of Ceausescu's special brand of wholesale repression that operated effectively in both private and public spheres. This is evident in the opening scene when the entire company recites with "smiling" faces a poem in Romanian in praise of Elena Ceausescu while "stirring" Romanian music is played in the background (Churchill 13).

Many of the scenes, particularly those which involve family members with such officials as a doctor or a Securitate man, are conducted as meta-dialogues with a "correct" conversation covering up the real, unspoken business:

> DOCTOR: There is no abortion in Romania. I am shocked that you even think of it. I am appalled that you dare suggest I might commit this crime.
>
> LUCIA: Yes, I'm sorry.
> (LUCIA gives the doctor an envelope thick with money.)
>
> DOCTOR: Can you get married?
>
> LUCIA: Yes. ...
> (The DOCTOR writes again, Lucia nods)
>
> DOCTOR: I can do nothing for you. Goodbye.
> (LUCIA smiles. She makes her face serious again.)
> (Churchill 19)

The conclusions emerging from scenes such as this one inspire questions concerning distinctions whether public and private have meaning in deeply paranoid societies, and also whether, as Soto-Morettini questions, "we can consider the kind of communication we witness here in both government offices and homes to be inauthentic" (107). Only in exchanges between the real and otherworldly characters are questions of authenticity raised. Thus, Flavia's exchange with the ghost of her grandmother suggests that the very life force of Churchill's characters is extinguished:

> GRANDMOTHER: You're pretending this isn't your life. You think it's going to happen some other time. When you're dead you'll realise you were alive now. When I was your age the war was starting. I welcomed the Nazis because I thought they'd protect us from the Russians, and I welcomed the Communists because they'd protect us from

the Germans. I had no principles. My husband was killed. But at least I know that was what happened to me. There were things I did. I did them. Or sometimes I did nothing. It was me doing nothing. ...

FLAVIA: But nobody's living. You can't blame me.

GRANDMOTHER: You'd better start.

FLAVIA. No, Granny, it would hurt.   (Churchill 26)

Unauthenticity in language and, consequently, identity leads for a search for absolutes: freedom, equality, God. Even the confused Priest imagines a certain safety in confiding to an angel floating in "the blue sky" since "no one's ever known an Angel work for the Securitate..." (21). Ultimately, it is the silence of the characters that discloses what cannot be uttered: the fear, paranoia, secret life, and schizophrenia of everyday life. Manea describes the atmosphere of the Ceausescu era as an "insidious, dilated presence of the monster called the Power: in one's home, in one's thoughts, in the conjugal bed" (6). At the same time the isolation that such a system imposes leads to macabre collective pathologies. Thus, fear, apathy and depersonalization ultimately lead to the making of scapegoats. Only when talking to imaginary others or when drunk can the characters voice doubt or dissent. But the dissent is always muted, for even when Radu, Gabriel and Ianos sit down with a bottle of wine, their jokes do not reveal their own beliefs. Thus, despite the liberating moment veiled within the joke, the first act of the play presents the characters "imprisoned within tightly confining ideologies and economic and social structures" (Cousin 20-21).

However, the second act, entitled "December," opens up a new realm of possibilities. This act has the characteristics of a docu-drama and consists of a collection of accounts, observations, and questions by various people designated only by their profession as student, house-painter, doctor, flower-seller, translator, bulldozer driver, and others who witness-ed the events in Bucharest between the 21st and 25th of December. The "speakers" reveal various levels of English usage, thereby demonstrating their inability to describe the events they are recounting coherently. Their reports, presented "as if the others are not there and each is the only one telling what happened" (Churchill 29) point to the limits of political soli-darity. There are utopian moments, however, when this tension evapo-rates and speech and act coincide, albeit fleetingly, to enable the individuals to see themselves as agents of their own liberation. As Mitchell mentions, the discontinuous, interweaving fragments "create a rhythm which builds gradually from fear and anticipation to celebration and joy, and to fear and bewilderment after the Securitate's 'terror shooting' begins" (502). Though Oana-Maria Hock recounts that this was the first time in forty years that "Romanians looked each other in the eyes" (79), Churchill's play suggests otherwise. Consequently, the spoken accounts give the impression of avoidance, confusion, impotence, caution, sporadic joy, withdrawal, and ultimately depression:

> GIRL STUDENT: I'd planned to go to see a film with a friend but in the afternoon my father said I must ring up and pretend to be ill, then my friend rang and said that she was ill. I wanted to go out and my father said I couldn't go alone. I thought of an excuse - - we had to have some bread, so we went out together. There were a lot of people moving from Union Place towards University Place. . . A man came up and asked what was happening but my father pulled me away because he realized the man was a provoker who starts arguments and then reports the people who get involved. My father insisted we go home, I said he was a coward and began to cry. He said if he was single he would behave differently. (Churchill 32)

> FLOWER SELLER: I go to the market to get food and many people are going to the centre. I watch them go by. I am sorry I get married so young. (Churchill 36)

> SOLDIER: They say us it is not Hungarians. It is terroristi. We guard the airport. We shoot anything, we shoot our friend. I want to stay alive. (Churchill 39)

> STUDENT 1: People were shouting. 'Come with us,' but I thought, 'It's a romantic action, it's useless to go and fight and die.' I thought I was a coward to be scared. But I thought, 'I will die like a fool protecting someone I don't know. How can I stop bullets with my bare hands? It's the job of the army, I can do nothing, I will just die.' So I went home. (Churchill 40)

> PAINTER. My girlfriend and I were at the TV station. I didn't know who we were fighting with or how bad it was. I was just acting to save our lives. It is terrible to hate and not to be able to do something real. (Churchill 40)

> STUDENT 2: The train didn't go that day so I stayed at home. I thought, 'This is not my town. I will go to my own town and act there'. (Churchill 42)

> PAINTER. Painting doesn't mean just describing, it's a state of spirit. I didn't want to paint for a long time then. (Churchill 43)

As Mitchell mentions, in the post-production discussions following the premiere of *Mad Forest* in Bucharest, Churchill invoked the Painter's self-reflexive closure to Act II "in reply to an audience member who expressed shame that there was no Romanian play about the events" (502). Though Churchill presents December, 1989 in Bucharest as a potentially liberating moment, one can determine from the "speakers" that their past seems not to make sense anymore.

In the third act, "Florina's Wedding," Churchill focuses once more on the vicissitudes of family life, this time in the aftermath of the tremendous political upheaval, demonstrations, and consolidation of power by the National Salvation Front. These scenes are juxtaposed to parodic, surrealistic, and supernatural scenes. Among the scenes, Churchill presents a highly expressionistic re-enactment of the death of the Ceausescus, and an enactment of one of the character's dreams about a cornered Elena Ceausescu. As Mitchell mentions, "these scenes serve to disrupt and undermine logical paradigms, and establish shifts from objective to subjective viewpoints" (506). Churchill's tight focus on "the micropolitics of the everyday" (Soto-Morettini 106) contributes to a deeper understanding "of the damages, the compromises to the human spirit" (Robinson 127). Though weddings that conclude the dramatic action in drama usually suggest a more happy outcome for the initial complications, the first scene which opens the third act of *Mad Forest* with a Vampire and a hungry dog foreshadows that the upsurge of joy might be arrested and destroyed:

> VAMPIRE: I came here for the revolution, I could smell it a long way off.

> DOG: I've tasted a man's blood. It was thick on the road. I gobbled it up quick, then somebody kicked me. (Churchill 45)

Since several generations had grown up entirely under Ceausescu's myth-making institutional structures, they have no sense of past history. Consequently, *Vergangenheitsbewältigung*, or coming to terms with the past, becomes impossible. In fact the entire country suffers from collective amnesia regarding the truth of the past: "How much worse," comments Rév, if this amnesia "is replaced by false memories, a nonself" (8-9). False memories lead to the writing of history as a triumphant one, or as a story of resistance leading to liberation, or as a memory gap by means of which forty-odd years of Communism have disappeared. Thus, in rewriting their history, the characters of *Mad Forest* place blame on various causalities and scapegoats such as the nomenklatura, informers, Soviet domination, the plots of bordering nations such as Hungary, and ultimately American capitalism and the CIA.

Churchill illustrates the slippage in logic that reveals both the characters' paranoia as well as their inclination toward authoritarianism. This is particularly true of characters such as Bogdan Vladu, a member of the working class and an anti-Front supporter of the *Blut und Boden* platform of the Peasants Party. One of Churchill's methods of revealing his anti-liberalism is to focus on his use of automatic repetitions: "This country needs a strong man" (77, 85). The other is to exhibit the lack of logical links in what he is saying as he argues for privatization on the one hand and support of the Peasants Party on the other. Ultimately, Bogdan's argument is based entirely on nostalgia, ethnic solidarity, and fascist paranoia: "I support the Peasants Party because my father's a peasant. I'm not ashamed of that. They should have their land because their feet are in the earth and they know things nobody else knows. Birds, frogs, cows, god, the direction of the wind " (Churchill 81).

Umberto Eco observes that one of the characteristics of Ur-Fascism is the "privilege to be born in the same country. Since the only ones who can provide an identity to the nation are its enemies, the root of Ur-Fascist psychology is an obsession with a plot, preferably an international one. The followers must feel besieged" (13). This is illustrated by the characters as they attempt to deny the Hungarians and Gypsies in their midst their rights to cultural difference: "If they want to live in Romania they can speak Romanian" (Churchill 83).

As the characters from the two families move out into more public spaces, the silences of the first part are taken over by questions. Each character struggles to ground the confusion in some kind of understanding, and we witness the emergence of suppressed hostility, accusations, and recriminations. Consequently, the characters become increasingly isolated, and even the ghost of her grandmother fails to appear to Flavia to guide her through the unknown straits of what "freedom" represents. Since the characters are unable to verify the reality of political events occurring behind the scenes, suspicion filters down to an intimate level and begins to surround even the most familiar relationships. In addition, their daily communication with each other has been hopelessly damaged by their belief in the authenticity of official language. Consequently, the question that now emerges is how to determine what is "politically correct" in the post-Ceausescu era. This is evident as the once privileged Antonescus continue to reveal their inherent political correctness:

> MIHAI: Radu, I don't know what to do with you. Nothing is on a realistic basis.
>
> RADU: Please don't say that.
>
> MIHAI: What's the matter now?
>
> RADU: Don't say 'realistic basis'.
>
> FLAVIA: It's true, Mihai, you do talk in terrible jargon from before, it's no longer correct. (Churchill 66)

In this scene, Churchill playfully adopts the methodology of writing under censorship by calling attention to words like "human face" or "truth" or "realistic basis" which represent signs of submitting to the paranoia of Ceausescu's regime. After its collapse, these expressions become a means of revealing the continuities of repressive ideology, for language discloses that power is simply continuing in another guise. From these scattered scenes, the spectators can determine that the early scenes of dissidence against Ceausescu—Radu standing in a food line, or the three friends, Radu, Gabriel, and Ianos exchanging subversive jokes while drinking in a bar—seemed to have covered up old ethnic and class hatreds. It is no wonder that Florina says: "Sometimes I miss him" (61).

Ceausescu had provided a united front of fear and hatred, and now the society has fragmented into hate groups in more insidious ways. Radu Antonescu, who seems to despise his father's loyalty to the old regime and holds Mihai's easy redefinition of himself as a liberal democrat in support of the Front in contempt, ultimately uses language as dogmatic as that of

Mihai. Thus Radu, much like his father, is turning into an authoritarian, rigid revisionist. What Churchill reveals is that even the idealistic Radu cannot withstand the "rhinoceritis" of nationalism and fascism. The suspicion generated by the general disillusion and confusion about the fate of the revolution does not only surface between generations but also among classes, nationalities, and minorities. For that reason Radu's and Florina's suddenly "politically correct" marriage is already doomed:

> RADU: Iliescu's going to get in because the workers and peasants are stupid. Pause. Not stupid but they don't think. They don't have the information. Pause. I don't mean your family in particular.
>
> FLORINA: You're a snob like your father. You'd have joined the party.
>
> RADU: Wouldn't you?
>
> FLORINA: Silence."   (Churchill 60)

As the old paranoia begins to overtake the Antonescu and Vladu families, Radu and Florina's wedding celebration ends in a drunken brawl. The guests' collective representativeness justifies their presence at the party, but their individual presences serve only to raise questions about what they collectively represent. Their sporadic interaction displays not so much the convergence but rather the divergence of this group. Julia Kristeva in *Strangers to Ourselves* explains that the cult of origins is a hate reaction. "Hatred of those others who do not share my origins and who affront me personally, economically, and culturally" (2). Within the politics of hate, "a defensive hatred" easily backslides to "a persecuting hatred" and "wounded souls may be seen to turn around and fight their neighbors who are just as hurt as they are—perhaps by the same totalitarian tyrant—but who can easily be taken for the weak link in that chain of hatred, for the scapegoat of one's depression" (Kristeva 2-3). Consequently, the language of the reconciliation scenes leading to the wedding of Radu and Florina are seen to be empty rhetoric:

> IRINA: I don't like seeing you with Ianos.
>
> LUCIA: He's Gabriel's friend.

IRINA: I was once in a shop in Transylvania and they wouldn't serve me because I couldn't speak Hungarian. In my own country.   (Churchill 79)

Other examples illustrate not only the hatred for ethnic minorities such as the Hungarians and the Gypsies but a reversion to prejudice on the part of the educated towards the uneducated:

BOGDAN: Leave my son alone. Hungarian bastard. And don't come near my daughter.

IANOS: I'm already fucking your daughter, you stupid peasant.   (84)

To illustrate the impossibility of constructing meaning out of the elementary situations that Churchill presents for the first-time tourist to Romania, the last scene is spoken entirely in Romanian as the guests at Florina's wedding assault each other with randomly numbered phrases in Romanian that no longer relate to a construction of logical meaning: 1. "This country needs a strong man." 8. "We have to put the past behind us." 14. "You're not going to marry a Hungarian." 9. "I don't care what they're called it's the same people." 14. "But what does it mean? Whose side were they on?" Not only are these sentences overlapping, but at the conclusion everyone is talking all at once, leaving only the vampire's words to be heard as the concluding "moral" of the play: "You begin to want blood. Your limbs ache, your head burns, you have to keep moving faster and faster" (Churchill 85-87).

Churchill's dialogue of overlapping speeches culminates in a near-cacophonic vocalization. The inability on the spectator's part to understand what the characters are saying undermines the possibility of arriving at a single conclusion. Churchill thus demonstrates that the speed and violence of the events prevents any satisfactory resolution. For as Soto-Morettini observes, "we end in circularity, for weddings happy or unhappy will go on. And Angels and Vampires, legendary figures, dance amidst the chaos" (117). Both the Vampire and the Angel have survived not only the revolution but the Iron Guard, the long Ceausescu years, and have come full circle to inhabit yet another period of ethnic hatred and suspicion.

Christine Kiebuzinska
Virginia Polytechnic and State University

Bibliography

Churchill, Caryl. 1990. *Mad Forest*. London: Nick Hern Books.

Cousin, Geraldine. 1989. *Churchill the Playwright*. London.

Eco, Umberto. 1995. "Ur-Fascism." In: *New York Review of Books*. Vol. XLII. No. 11 June 22, 1995:12-15.

Greenblatt, Stephen. 1995. "Jolts." In: *Representations 49*. Special Issue. Identifying Histories: Eastern Europe Before and After 1989. Eds. Stephen Greenblatt, István Rév and Randolph Starn. Winter 1995: 1-13.

Hock, Oana-Maria. 1991. "At Home, In the World, in the Theatre: The Mysterious Geography of University Square, Bucharest." In: *Performing Arts Journal*. 8.2(1991):78-89.

Kristeva, Julia. 1993. *Nations Without Nationalism*. Trans. Leon S. Roudiez. New York: Columbia University Press.

Manea, Norman. 1992. *On Clowns: The Dictator and the Artist*. New York: Grove Press.

Mitchell, Tony. 1993. "Caryl Churchill's Mad Forest: Polyphonic Representations of Southeastern Europe." In: *Modern Drama* 36.4(1993):499-511.

Plesu, Andrei. 1995. "Intellectual Life Under Dictatorship." In: *Representations 49*. Special Issue. Identifying Histories: Eastern Europe Before and After 1989. Eds. Stephen Greenblatt, István Rév and Randolph Starn. Winter, 1995: 61-71.

Rev, Istvan. 1995. "Identity by History." In: *Representations 49*. Special Issue. Identifying Histories: Eastern Europe Before and After 1989. Eds. Stephen Greenblatt, István Rév and Randolph Starn. Winter, 1995: 8-10.

Robinson, Marc. 1991. "Bracing Grace: Wing-Davey's 'Front Foot' Approach to *Mad Forest*." In: *Village Voice*, 24 December, 1991, 127.

Sloterdijk, Peter. 1988. *Critique of Cynical Reason*. London: Verso.

Soto-Morettini, Donna. 1994. "Revolution and the Fatally Clever Smile: Caryl Churchill's *Mad Forest*." In: *Journal of Dramatic Theory and Criticism*. 8.1(1994): 105-118.

'Prague Spring' and the Novels of Milan Kundera

For two decades since 1968 Milan Kundera could never really get over the trauma of the invasion of his country by its 'oversized neighbour.'[1] Kundera would, however, explain his obsession with one "specific historic period" of his country as follows: "... For a novelist a given historic situation is an *anthropologic laboratory* in which he explores his basic question: what is human existence?" (*Life Is Elsewhere* 310-11).

Anyway, the specific 'historic situation' of his novels represented for Kundera an 'unbearable lightness of being'. What he found to be the basic question in Kafka was also his own : "What possibilities remain for man in a world where the external determinants have become so overpowering that internal impulses no longer carry weight" (*The Art of the Novel* 26)?

Kundera's awareness and rejection of this unbearably oppressive life ranks him with Kafka, Orwell, Solzhenitsyn, and others; but he makes his departure from these classic voices of the conscience of mankind in his use of the

---

[1] The deep disturbance of the author as he responds to this 'darkness' may be traced as far back as the early days of communist rule when it had become clear to him that in the coming years Czechoslovakia was going to be "ruled hand in hand by the hangman and the poet" (*Life Is Elsewhere*, 270). In his postscript to the English translation of *Life Is Elsewhere* Kundera remembered his reaction to Paul Eluard's public denouncement of his Prague friend whom Stalinist justice had been sending to the gallows: "This episode hit me like a trauma: when an executioner kills, that is after all normal; but when a poet sings in accompaniment, the whole system of values we considered sacrosanct has suddenly been shaken apart". The phrase occurs in *The Unbearable Lightness of Being* (288).

carnivalesque for recording history and registering his sense of violation. Not that he can always sustain the carnival tone; and his shifts between the moods of sad hilarity and tragic gloom result in an interesting interplay of ribaldry and panic, carnival and nightmare, Rabelais and Kafka. However, it is this element of hilarity that marks him out from the famous dissenters of the century. Orwell had reacted to 'man's inhumanity to man' aggressively, Koestler anxiously, in recent times Tasleema Nasreen and Arundhati Roy (in different contexts) fiercely and sadly. But Kundera tries to respond to his situation with the courage of laughter.

The carnival, originally a device of the underdogs to entertain themselves, was introduced as a literary concept by Bakhtin in *Rabelais and His World*; the concept as proposed by Bakhtin implied a literary mode that parallelled the flouting of authority through the devastating mockery of the carnival season. The carnivalesque in literature included the play of irreverent, parodic, subversive voices.

Greb Nerzhin, the mathematician in the Mavrino prison of Solzhenitsyn's *The First Circle*, used to put away scraps of small paper bit by bit so that one day he should be able to write the true history of his country, —a task Solzhenitsyn himself was to attempt in *The Gulag Archipelago*. Kundera's writing, too, is a struggle against 'forgetting': "The struggle for man against power is the struggle of memory against forgetting" (*The Art of the Novel*, 130). (One is reminded of Orwell's warning against the distortion of historical truth under a totalitarian regime).

As a literary historian of his times and country Kundera captures the spirit of a historical moment; but he does it in a tone of sad comicality that assimilates and absorbs Solzhenitsyn's agony and anger with an almost Rabelaisian spirit of "sunburnt mirth." The struggle against 'forgetting' in Kundera's situation involves an enormous pressure on the mind. We would rather forget the unpleasant and painful like Sabina who dismisses the associations of words like "prisons," "persecution," "banned books," "occupation," "tanks" as "ugly without romance" (*The Unbearable Lightness of Being*, 103); carnival is Kundera's device to negotiate with this pressure, and to bring his reader to face the grim truth. This implies courageous determination on his part since he believes : "By providing us with the lovely illusion of human greatness, the tragic brings us consolation. The comic is crueller: it brutally reveals the meaninglessness of everything" (*The Art of the Novel*, 126).

In the same context Kundera also claims that, though history has always been considered an exclusively serious territory, "there is the undiscovered comic side to history" (*The Art of the Novel*, 126). One may catch the Bakhtinian ring here. In concluding his study of Rabelais, Bakhtin observes: "While analyzing past ages we are too often obliged to ... believe official ideologists. We do not hear the voice of ... a chorus of the laughing people ... (because) not every period of history had Rabelais for coryphaeus"(Bakhtin, 474).

Kundera appears to have devoted himself to this job of the coryphaeus in order to reveal the 'undiscovered comic side' of contemporary history which is, at the same time, evidently, cruel and brutal. Any of his major novels, even if examined in isolation, would bear out the above thesis.

The Unbearable Lightness of Being, for example, recaptures, like many other Kundera novels, the epiphanic historic moment of the Prague Spring of '68 followed by the Russian invasion and the subsequent endless (so it appeared then) 'darkness at noon'. But this dark story of 'panic and emptiness' (Forster's *Howards End*) is narrated so as to focus on some "unexpected realm of the comic" (*The Art of the Novel*, 126). Thus the brief euphoria that preceded the prolonged night is described as "a drunken carnival of hate" (*The Unbearable Lightness of Being*, 26). The history of this period is recorded by means of the dialogic of multiple voices, including the author's own. The author nostalgically recaptures the carnival mood of the first week of Russian occupation[2] when people's hatred took the form of a kind of festivity: "Czech towns were decorated with thousands of hand-painted posters bearing ironic texts, epigrams, poems and cartoons of Brezhnev and his soldiers jeered at by one and all as a circus of illiterates" (26). This is carnival in the age-old sense, the shared irreverence of the folk towards the authority; the shared hatred creating an excitement akin to infectious happiness. Tereza, one of the typically unhappy girls of Kundera's novels, "had spent the whole ... week ... in a kind of trance almost resembling happiness" (25). Tereza shared the merriment of the people she photographed: "Youngmen on motorcycles racing full speed around the tanks and waving Czech flags on long staffs," or, "young girls in unbelievably short skirts provoking the miserable sexually famished Russian soldiers by kissing random passers-by before their eyes" (67). A jovial and reckless way of flouting the authority which the army represented. Another way was poster exhibition where citizens shared a hearty laughter at the 'impostor'. As Tomas sees one of those big posters years later the author also shares his excitement recollected in

---

[2] Ch. 12 of the novel gives a long description of the carnival.

sadness. "That was an excellent joke" (211).[3]

However, "the excellent joke" was also meant to expose a cruel reality and soon this was to be recognised with abject fear and complete silence in the face of increasing oppression and humiliation. Kundera notes in his philosophic way: "No carnival can go on forever" (26).[4] With the collapse of the popular carnival under pervasive terror and hopelessness the author seeks recourse to other forms of the carnivalesque in order to voice his continuing dissent against the absurdity of the situation, which is evident in his faithful pursuit of the anti-'forgetting' mission. Thus he goes on recording an unofficial history of the time in a tone of apparent joviality. In the first week of invasion the Czech photographers had tried to "preserve the face of violence for the distant future" (67); and this is precisely what Kundera does, with the desperate hilarity of a lonely comedian. But apparently this is no easy task. So the grotesque realism of the carnival occasionally becomes merged into horrifying Kafkaesque nightmares.

Thus, in a tone of hilarity tinged with sadness, the author goes on meticulously drawing pictures of tanks, destroyed houses, corpses covered with Czech flags, Russian aeroplanes hovering over the nightsky of a country whose borders had been sealed, the humiliated leader returning from the Moscow prison to address a humiliated nation; Czech painters, philosophers, writers being "relieved of their positions, and become(ing) window-washers, parking attendants, nightwatchmen, boilermen in public buildings, or at best—and usually with pull —taxi driver" (213); a former professor of theology working in the accounting office of a hotel, an ex-ambassador at the reception desk; the increased death-rates accompanying growing hopelessness. Tomas, on being thrown out from the hospital, tries to enjoy his long holiday by going about from house to house and bed to bed as if it were great fun to be reduced from an eminent surgeon to a window-washer. These, and many other details stressing the absurdity of the

---

3   "It was an imitation of a famous recruitment poster from the Russian Civil War of 1918 showing a soldier, red star on his cap and extraordinarily stern look in his eyes, staring straight at you and aiming his index finger at you. The original Russian caption read: 'Citizen, have you joined the Red Army'? It was replaced by a Czech text that read: 'Citizen, have you signed the Two Thousand Words'?
That was an excellent joke: The 'Two Thousand Words' was the first glorious manifesto of the 1968 Prague Spring ... When the Red Army took over this was the typical question asked ... Anyone who admitted to having done so was summarily dismissed from his job." (*The Unbearable Lightness of Being*, 211-12).

4   With Dubcek's return and his "terribly pathetic, stuttering, stammering speech" punctuated by awful pauses, one thing became clear: "the country would have to bow to the conqueror. For ever and ever it will stutter, stammer, gasp for air like Alexander Dubcek. The carnival was over. Workaday humiliation had begun" (26).

system, get aesthetically grafted into the texture as Kundera laughingly (and also tearfully) reconstructs a history different from the official version.

However, some facets of this history appear to be too dark for the tone of mirth so consciously kept up by the author; for example, the 'magic realism' sequence of Petrin Hill (147-49) or the elaborate system of spy-rings that is bent on turning "the whole nation into a single organisation of informers" (163). It is the Kafkaesque world of mysterious files and inaccessible rulers whose personnel watch one through every chink in every door. Yet Kundera generally tries to stress the absurdity more than the horror; hence his emphasis on the comical.

In the course of the philosophical-comical narration the novelist introduces a series of speculations on issues like comicality versus panic, lightness/weight, individuality/uniformity, privacy/concentration camp etc.; the serious issues are treated with a casual amused tone, and often from grotesque angles or odd perspectives. The author often defines the concepts in terms of the body, especially the lower bodily stratum, which is the common realm of the carnivalesque. For example, Kundera's disapproval of the rape of privacy in Czechoslovakia usually finds expression in terms of physical 'obscenity' (stripping the lower body). He uses different voices—scared, serious, angry voices—to comment on the activities of the Secret Police pouncing on one's privacy; this is the *1984* world, the Castle village of Kafka, the 'dark noon' of Koestler, the 'cancer ward' of the 'Gulag' with which the reader is familiar. But then Kundera would surprise and shock the reader by relating this horror to the obscene vulgarity of the naked body in the world of Tereza's mother who did not allow her to close the toilet door, who moved about naked with the windows open, and farted loudly amidst friends. The horrible grotesqueness of the totalitarian system that legitimized "the complete obliteration of privacy" (136), refused to recognize individual differences, and thus turned the entire country into a concentration camp, is comically borne out by its comparison with the world of Tereza's naked mother and the nude family on the nudist beach: "For her the world was nothing but a vast concentration camp of bodies, one like the next, with the souls invisible" (47). Tereza's dream of naked women (57-58) being forced to march and dance to one tune, laughing loudly, may be considered in this light as a reflection on the grotesqueness of the historic situation. Tereza finds the dream horrible, because since childhood nudity had been for her a sign of uniformity and humiliation (137).

Kundera's unashamed references to the bodily lower stratum, including sickness, stomach pain, defecation, pregnancy, urination and infinite copulations, may also be seen in relation to the carnival tradition that stressed the lower part of the body—the belly and the reproductive organs. Kundera exploits in a much more complex context the essential centuries-old link of laughter with the images of the body's lower parts. The 'indecency' and erotic frivolity are used here to make scathing criticism of the ruler's cult of uniformity and the concentration camp system. Again Tomas's excessive sexuality during the period of window-washing is a way of bearing with the grim reality of his dismissal from the hospital; at the same time his obsessive copulation with so many naked bodies whom he cannot even identify afterwards exposes his obsession "with what in each of them is unimaginable ... that which makes a woman dissimilar to others of her sex" (200). So what seems a comic addiction to physical pleasure actually stems from a desire to see the unique individual above the dull uniformity,—a basic theme of Kundera's novels.

It is with the comedian's cruel clarity that the novelist sees through any residual illusions that might be there about the end of the darkness. He knows that after a decade of foreign occupation any protest would be a Kafkaesque "struggle with mute power" (268), and as comic and as disastrous as "the struggle of a theater company that has attacked an army" (268). A typical Don Quixote sequence has been evoked here in order to bring out the despair and the horror implicit in the mechanized system.

Similarly, the 'Grand March' has been ridiculed (though lovingly) through Franz's tragedy as also the 'grand' ideas that have been denigrated to the level of kitsch. Every herd-thought or action that undermines individual freedom is ridiculed by Kundera as kitsch (hypocritical doublespeak), however sacrosanct these might be made to look like by people in power. Kundera's novel is, in a way, a laughing exposure of the totalitarian kitsch:

> Whenever a single political movement corners power, we find ourselves in the realm of totalitarian kitsch ... Everything that infringes on kitsch must be banished for life; any display of individualism (because a deviation from the collective) is a spit in the eye of the smiling brotherhood); every doubt (because anyone who starts doubting details will end by doubting life itself); all irony (because in the realm of kitsch everything must be taken quite seriously) ... In this light we can regard the Gulag as a septic tank used by totalitarian kitsch to dispose of its refuse. (251-52)

The official prohibition of certain kinds of laughter, irony, satire and 'obscenity' was imposed upon the writers of Russia after the revolution. Both

Bakhtin and Kundera may be better understood against this backdrop. During the great terror of Stalinism Bakhtin had written *Rabelais and His World* to remind others how necessary to the pursuit of liberty was the courage to laugh. Rabelais thus emerged in his perception as a kind of historian:[5] "Rabelais's basic goal was to destroy the official version of events ... to break up official lies and the narrow seriousness of the ruling classes" (439). Kundera, like a twentieth-century version of Rabelais as Bakhtin had perceived him, strove to write the true history of his time by means of a penetrating laughter that showed the entire official ideology, politics, arts, thought and ritual (meetings-marches-slogans) in their comic aspect.

As Michael Holquist observes: "Bakhtin's vision of carnival has an importance greater than any of its particular applications (in earlier literatures) ... for the book is finally about freedom, the courage needed to establish it, ... the horrific ease with which it can be lost" (xxi). This is precisely the crux of Kundera's novels. And while in his opening chapter Bakhtin stresses the striking peculiarity of carnival laughter as "its indissoluble and essential relation to freedom" (89), Kundera, in stressing freedom, falls back on the device of laughter.[6]

Before concluding, however, one should mention how difficult it was for Kundera—a lonely merry-maker who trod alone amidst the deserted banquet hall long after the community carnival was over—to keep up a laughing posture. In his own words: "For Rabelais, the merry and the comic were still one and the same ... (but) in the twentieth century Rabelais's merry epic has turned into the despairing comedy of Ionesco, who says, 'There is only a thin line between the horrible and the comic.' The European history of laughter comes to an end" (*The Art of the Novel*, 136).

Yet Kundera tries to keep up laughing though the horrible is always close by and sometimes visibly present. Any authentic laughter is incompatible with dogmatism. Kundera's laughter does not deny the serious; rather he uses it, like Rabelais, to purify the serious from dogmatism, intolerance, fanaticism, pedantry, fear, and intimidation (Bakhtin, 123).

Rama Kundu
Burdwan

---

[5] In contemporary Bengal (India) Gourkishore Ghosh had performed the same role through his *Rupadarshi's Journals* to expose the kitsch of the communist rule in the state by means of the carnivalesque.

[6] Kundera was against 'Infantocnacy'—"the seriousness of a child, the face of the modern era" (*The Art of the Novel*, 133). Naturally he inclined toward the carnival which was not juvenile art, but was indeed very much adult and mature.

Bibliography

Bakhtin, M. 1984. *Rabelais and His World* (trans. Helene Iswolsky), Bloomington: Indiana University Press.

Holquist, M. 1984. 'Prologue.' In: *Rabelais and His World*, Bloomington: Indiana University Press.

Kundera, M. 1992. *The Art of the Novel*, Calcutta: Rupa & Co.

————. 1992. *Life Is Elsewhere*, Calcutta: Rupa & Co.

————. 1992. *Of Laughter and Forgetting*, Calcutta: Rupa & Co.

————. 1992. *The Unbearable Lightness of Being*, Calcutta: Rupa & Co.

(Rupa & Co., Calcutta, published the English translation of Kundera's books by arrangement with Faber and Faber, London.)

Document et anti-utopie dans la littérature roumaine des anciens détenus politiques

Les pages qui suivent n'ont pas la prétention d'être une radio-graphie complète de la littérature roumaine consacrée aux camps et aux prisons communistes. Elles se refusent surtout à des classifications prématurées et à l'hiérarchisation du "matériau" textuel. Le corpus dont nous disposons est à la fois partiel et partial; il nous a semblé toutefois possible d'aborder, à partir de ce nombre restreint de références, des questions essentielles pour la littérature du témoignage en général, et la réponse, plus ou moins spécifique, apportée dans l'espace culturel roumain.

La notion de littérature de témoignage nécessite quelques précisions, dans la mesure où le terme n'a pas encore reçu de consécration univer-selle.[1] Alain Parrau préfère parler de "littérature concentrationnaire," comprenant "l'ensemble des témoignages écrits, dans la forme du *récit*, par les survivants des camps nazis et soviétiques."[2]. Sans prétendre de fixer dans une définition les traits du genre, précisons que par littérature du témoignage nous désignerons le corpus de textes écrits (récits, romans,

---

[1]   Cf. l'intervention de T. Gorilovics p. 207-208 ("Discussions") in C. Comorovski (éd.), *Littérature du témoignage. Europe du Centre et de l'Est.*

[2]   Alain Parrau, *Ecrire les camps*, p. 19.

poèmes...) ou d'interventions enregistrées dans lesquels les survivants des camps et les consciences vivantes du monde figé soviétique parlent, de manière directe ou indirecte, de leur expérience concentrationnaire.[3] Gagnent ainsi droit de cité, à côté des récits *sur les camps*, les œuvres littéraires composées *dans les camps*. Ces poèmes et proses travaillés dans l'enfer concentrationnaire, dont la littérature roumaine est riche, connaissent une élaboration complexe (avant d'être fixées sur le papier les œuvres passent par le filtre de la mémoire de l'auteur, mais aussi de ses camarades de détention),[4] et entretiennent un rapport à part avec l'univers dans lequel elles ont été conçues. L'introduction au *Journal de la félicité* de Nicolae Steinhardt dit la complexité de ce rapport: "Du papier, un crayon, en prison? C'est impossible. Je ne serais donc pas sincère si je prétendais que ce 'journal' a été tenu de manière chronologique. Il a été écrit après coup, fondé sur des souvenirs frais et vivaces. Puisque je n'ai pas pu l'inscrire dans la durée, qu'il me soit permis de le présenter en sautant d'un moment à un autre, comme défilent, dans la réalité cette fois, les images, les souvenirs, les réflexions, dans ce torrent d'impressions que nous nous plaisons à nommer 'conscience'. Le danger est, certes, de produire un reflet plutôt artificiel, mais je me dois d'assumer ce risque."[5]. Quoique l'analyse de ces œuvres écrites dans les camps ne constitue pas le but des pages qui suivent, il convient de retenir leur présence et leur importance dans l'horizon de la littérature du témoignage.

Rien n'est simple dans l'écriture de l'expérience concentrationnaire. Le survivant des camps vit douloureusement les questions du pourquoi et du comment de l'écriture, s'adressant à un récepteur qu'il interpelle à la fois comme instance de jugement et comme inculpé. L'assimilation même du souvenir écrit à la littérature semble problématique, vécue parfois comme négation implicite de la souffrance réelle. Des prises de position

---

[3]   Il convient de préciser que l'existence "libre" dans les pays communistes est parfois ressentie comme similaire à la vie dans une prison. La constatation est faite par Ion Ioanid, par exemple, à sa sortie du camp de travail de Salcia : cf. *Inchisoarea noastra cea de toate zilele* ("Notre prison quotidienne" ; toutes les traductions du livre de Ion Ioanid m'appartiennent), p. 160. Cf. aussi Vasile Gogea, *Frangmente salvate*.

[4]   Ainsi, Nichifor Cranic transmet à travers les murs ses poèmes à un autre détenu, compositeur, frère du peintre Victor Brauner, qui les met en musique (cf. *Memorii*, chapitre "Colaborarea mea cu Harry Brauner"). Lorsque, plus tard, le texte sera imprimé (dans le volume *Soim peste prapastie*), leur dimension musicale sera perdue à jamais.

[5]   *op. cit.*, p. 15.

catégoriques de la part des anciens détenus surgissent périodiquement,[6] condamnant la récupération de leur parole dans le domaine de l'artistique. C'est autour de cette fraternité difficile du document avec le littéraire que notre intervention se structure dans sa première partie, cherchant à l'analyser et à discuter ses raisons. Une deuxième partie tâchera de mettre en évidence la contribution, moins étudiée, des anti-utopies à la littérature de témoignage. Aucune des deux démarches n'est sans doute nouvelle ; aussi s'agit-il plutôt de compléter que de révolutionner. Le terrain roumain reflète, selon des règles qui lui sont propres, les interrogations, les enthousiasmes et les soupçons liés à la littérature du témoignage, et c'est de cette image à la fois particulière et familière qu'il sera question dans ce qui suit.

Littérature et document

Bannie parfois du domaine de la prise de parole sur les camps, au nom d'un respect scrupuleux de la vérité, la littérature s'impose, corrélativement, à d'autres esprits comme unique moyen d'en parler. Sans nous attarder plus longtemps sur les raisons du refus du littéraire, il nous a semblé plus intéressant de faire l'inventaire des motivations contraires, telles qu'elles sont reflétées dans l'espace de la littérature roumaine.

La plupart des auteurs semblent conscients du caractère irrecevable d'un projet stipulant une relation strictement documentaire à la réalité des camps. Il n'existe pas de témoignage objectif, et notre compréhension du

---

[6] Dans son livre, Alain Parrau énumère plusieurs exemples de ces réactions, glanés parmi les interventions des survivants des camps nazis. C'est notamment la représentation *kitsch* de l'enfer concentrationnaire (best-sellers, films à succès) qui réveille les susceptibilités. Sous la forme plus atténuée d'une revendication de scientificité, la méfiance envers la littérature pointe aussi sur le terrain roumain: "Oui. Voyez-vous, pas cet aspect émotionnel. Il faudrait [savoir] sur les camps et les prisons: où ils étaient situés, quelles dimensions avaient-ils, et ensuite en ce qui concerne les camps: qui ont été les commandants, qui les détenus, combien y en avait-il, combien y sont morts? Ensuite: comment recevait-on le détenu, comment se trouvait-il, s'il était en bonne santé ou apte pour le travail, l'alimentation, le contact avec la famille, le comportement envers lui, quel a été le bénéfice financier obtenu par le camp?" etc. (Emil Capraru "Le droit de mourir", interview par Flori Stanescu dans *Arhivele totalitarismului*, p. 175-176, notre traduction).

monde est bâtie sur l'acceptation de cette "distorsion" fondamentale.[7] La condition de vérité "absolue" se trouve, en premier lieu, compromise par l'obligatoire inscription du sujet dans la prise de parole. Tout témoignage, rarement conçu autrement que comme document censé alimenter une analyse historique du phénomène concentrationnaire, dépasse ses motivations documentaires. C'est ainsi que, par exemple, le récit d'Ion Ioanid devient un monument pour la commémoration des morts ("je dédie ce livre de souvenirs à ceux qui sont passés par les prisons communistes et qui ne se trouvent plus parmi nous, pour qu'ils sachent, là où ils sont, que nous ne les avons pas oubliés"[8]), un essai de réflexion sur le bien et le mal ("J'ai parlé aussi longuement de l'attitude des gens avec lesquels j'ai partagé les années de détention, en séparant hommes de caractère et canailles, non pas pour m'ériger en moraliste, mais parce que c'est là que j'ai compris et appris à peser à leur juste valeur les deux notions qui me sont devenues une obsession"[9]) et, surtout, une tentative d'inscription compréhensive du "je" dans la temporalité historique.

S'agissant de la reconstitution du passé, le jeu de la mémoire (deuxième source de subjectivité) y apporte une contribution importante et inéluctable: "Quoique tout ce que j'ai relaté soit la pure vérité sans aucune exagération"—affirme Ion Ioanid—"ceci reste seulement un livre du souvenir, comportant de nombreuses lacunes, des incertitudes et des confusions inhérentes, imputables à l'œuvre impitoyable du temps sur la mémoire."[10]. Raconter pour ne pas oublier ne constitue pas un antidote efficace contre cette distorsion. Hôte involontaire des mécanismes de la création populaire, chaque récit métamorphose subrepticement le témoignage en littérature. Ainsi, selon Paul Goma, le récit le mieux intentionné, qui cherche à coller au plus près à la vérité sans ajouts et sans envolées pathétiques (représentation commune du mécanisme de littératurisation), s'éloigne, à chaque répétition, du premier "jet", de la première prise de parole "objective":

---

[7] Cf. C. J. Coady, *Testimony. A Philosophical Study*, "I.2 What is Testimony?: Formal Testimony/ Natural Testimony".

[8] *op. cit.*, vol. 5, p. 269.

[9] *idem*, p. 264.

[10] *idem*, p. 263.

La mémoire commence à me jouer des tours; *elle ne m'en jouerait peut-être pas autant si je racontais moins souvent.* Mais, insensiblement, à chaque relation la vérité d'origine commence à muer de-ci de-là, si bien qu'après dix versions, la dixième ne ressemble plus à la première. Il est inutile de t'assurer qu'en ce qui me concerne, je me suis à chaque fois efforcé d'être fidèle - tant au fait en question qu'aux versions antérieures. Qui sait, pourtant?... Qui peut savoir si je n'ai pas 'folklorisé'...

- Pas un seul instant je n'ai eu l'impression que tu 'folklorisais'.

- Moi-même je ne m'en rends pas compte... Mais si nous retournions à nos moutons? Je brûle d'impatience de te raconter la, disons, onzième variante de...[11]

Lorsque la plume couche enfin le récit sur la page, les récepteurs successifs y ont presque autant contribué que son auteur initial, par leur méfiance et leurs questions, par leurs demandes de précisions et leurs réflexions. L'œuvre dont les lignes précédentes sont extraites reflète d'ailleurs, dans sa construction même, cette double responsabilité: car il s'agit d'un dialogue, où les répliques de l'ancien prisonnier occupent, naturellement, la place la plus importante, mais dialogue, toutefois, rompant la linéarité du récit avec les questions et les étonnements de l'auditrice. Le témoignage inscrit dans son corps les figures de l'émetteur et du récepteur, et dans ce double "reflet" il convient de placer son impossibilité d'être un simple document.

La littérature du témoignage devient possible sur le fonds de cet impensable accès au document pur. C'est d'abord pour répondre à une certaine usure qu'elle semble recevoir droit de cité. Quelques années seulement après la découverte des camps nazis de concentration, le public semblait, comme remarque Anette Wieviorka[12], saturé de récits crus sur l'horreur de la Shoah. Ce sont les livres d'un Primo Levi, d'un Robert

---

[11]   Paul Goma, *Gherla*, p. 22, c'est moi qui souligne.

[12]   "Le sentiment qui semble dominer dans l'après-guerre n'est pas celui d'un manque d'informations ou de témoignages, mais au contraire celui d'une saturation, souvent exprimée dans les préfaces ou les avant-propos des ouvrages publiés en 1946, alors qu'une trentaine de récits sont déjà parus. Dès le premier trimestre 1946, en effet, les auteurs s'excusent d'ajouter encore un livre à ceux déjà édités [...]" (*Déportation et génocide*, p. 174)

Antelme ou d'un Jorge Semprun qui réussissent, des années plus tard, à faire renaître l'intérêt du public pour une histoire qui, du coup, n'intéresse plus seulement les spécialistes. Les mêmes signes de "fatigue" du récepteur se laissent aujourd'hui détecter à propos des histoires racontées par les survivants du *lager* soviétique, fatigue sans doute renforcée par un certain sentiment de culpabilité et une nécessité incommode de remise en question des croyances et des idéologies. Il est à espérer que les *Récits de Kolyma*, *Contre tout espoir* et d'autres œuvres provenues du monde ex-soviétique réaliseront, à leur tour, cette percée dans l'horizon de la réception.

Le rôle de la fiction ne s'arrête toutefois pas à cette "mise en beauté" des témoignages "bruts", à cette esthétisation destinée à émoustiller, comme un mets raffiné, les papilles gustatives trop habituées aux saveurs. *L'écriture ou la vie* de Jorge Semprun, témoignage tardif qui reflète son propre processus de création, motive ainsi cette nécessaire immixtion de l'art dans le document:

> - Raconter bien, ça veut dire: de façon à être entendus. On n'y parviendra pas sans un peu d'artifice. Suffisamment d'artifice pour que ça devienne de l'art.
> [...]
> J'essaie de préciser ma pensée.
> - Ecoutez, les gars! La vérité que nous avons à dire - si tant est que nous en ayons envie, nombreux sont ceux qui ne l'auront jamais! - n'est pas aisément crédible... Elle est même inimaginable...
> [...]
> - Comment raconter une vérité peu crédible, comment susciter l'imagination de l'inimaginable, si ce n'est en élaborant, en retravaillant la réalité, en la mettant en perspective? Avec un peu d'artifice, donc! [13]

Ainsi, pour être tout simplement intelligible, pour pouvoir transmettre ne serait-ce qu'un sens partiel et confus, le souvenir du camp doit être aménagé, redécoupé selon une temporalité et un ordre spécifiques. C'est notamment le cas des récits sur les camps soviétiques, où à la néces-

---

[13]   *L'écriture ou la vie*, p. 135.

sité de saisir le "mal absolu"[14] s'ajoute la difficulté de dire *la durée.* Certains évitent le danger de répétition par la "systématisation"[15] de l'expérience, d'autres procèdent par des "touches" (relevant des épisodes disparates), d'autres, enfin, mélangent présent et passé, linéarité de la narration (arrestation, enquête, jugement, exécution de la peine, transferts dans différentes prisons et colonies de travail) et divagations, cherchant, tous, à contourner la monotonie de la souffrance journalière.

Mais il existe encore un cercle à franchir pour motiver l' "immixtion" de l'art dans le domaine du témoignage. Car seule la littérature a le pouvoir de dire l'indicible, la force de conjurer l'impuissance des mots, d'approcher ce qui ne se laisse pas nommer et décrire. Le témoin, observe Alain Parrau, n'est jamais témoin de tout et du pire. Son expérience reste limitée et en quelque sorte, privilégiée. Il a pu survivre et parler parce que, d'une façon ou d'une autre, sa vie au camp a été celle d'un "planqué." Comment approcher, dès lors, ce qui s'est passé dans un ailleurs compris à la fois dans l'espace (la chambre à gaz, un autre camp) et subjectivement (la souffrance d'un "musulman", d'un "crevard")? A la littérature de tisser les liens entre la multiplicité des témoignages disparates (c'est ainsi que naît, de cette volonté de totalisation, l'*Archipel du goulag*), de chercher les mots et les images susceptibles de transmettre le non-vu, le non-raconté.

Si la plupart des écrits roumains sur les prisons politiques optent pour la fonction "synthétique" de la littérature (presque tous les témoignages fédèrent des souvenirs communiqués par d'autres camarades de détention), le recours à la reconstitution imaginaire intervient plus d'une fois. C'est ainsi que l'expérience la plus terrible du système concentrationnaire roumain a pu être sauvée d'un oubli presque inévitable: il s'agit du système de "rééducation" mis en œuvre à Pitesti. Comparée par Virgil Ierunca au "lavage de cerveau" pratiqué en Chine, cette soi-disant "réintégration des éléments hostiles au régime communiste" se fonde sur la

---

[14] Que l'on invoque notamment à propos de ce qui s'est passé dans les camps nazis, mais qui désigne de façon aussi légitime l'expérience communiste. Cf. Tzvetan Todorov: "...le régime totalitaire dans lequel j'avais grandi pouvait me servir [...] *d'étalon du mal*" (*L'Homme dépaysé*, p. 25, c'est moi qui souligne).

[15] Il existe ainsi, à côté des chapitres sur le "spécifique" de chaque prison (Cf. Dan M. Bratianu, *Martor dintr-o tara incatusata*: "Les conditions de détention à Pitesti, en 1948", "Les alcôves du Ministère des Affaires Intérieures et un réveillon à Jilava, le 31 décembre 1948", "La prison de Jilava en 1949", etc.), d'autres dédiés aux travaux effectués, aux tortures subies, aux maladies contractées, aux rencontres réalisées (cf. Nichifor Cranic, *Memorii*: "Mes maladies dans la prison", "Les corrections que j'ai reçues dans la prison", "La faim", etc.).

destruction totale de la personnalité: grâce à des raffinements de torture physique et psychologique, le détenu était amené, *par ses camarades mêmes*—et ceci est essentiel—à "s'autodénoncer", à se transformer dans une machine prête à reproduire le discours imposé par le Parti et à torturer ses codétenus qui refusaient de le suivre dans la même voie. A Pitesti, "les victimes de la rééducation", écrit Virgil Ierunca, "avaient été contraintes de devenir à leur tour des bourreaux."[16]

La rareté des témoignages sur Pitesti (un seul détenu, Dumitru Bacu, a osé rompre le silence) s'explique par cette terrible destruction de la légitimité même du témoin, ordinairement fondée, dans les récits sur les camps, sur sa qualité de victime. Ouvrage délicat qui englobe des bribes de confession, des témoignages indirects et des extrapolations à partir de la souffrance personnelle, le roman prend ainsi, naturellement, la place des mémoires. Parler de Pitesti revient presque obligatoirement aux autres, dont l'étrangeté s'avère non pas une source de mensonge romanesque mais l'unique garantie d'un regard capable de saisir l'étendue de l'horreur. Ainsi, assistant à une scène de torture, le narrateur intradiégétique des *Chiens de mort* affirme: "La douleur de Bogdanovici m'est tellement *étrangère* que je la perçois avec plus d'acuité que lui, et je me moque bien du nom porté par le possesseur des lèvres, l'ancien possesseur de la dent."[17]. Le thème du double, familier à la littérature, intervient presque inévitablement pour rendre compte de la métamorphose monstrueuse de la victime en tortionnaire: il structure *Les Chiens de mort ou La passion selon Pitesti*, où Vasile Pop, personnage principal, est arrêté à la place de son frère jumeau Elisav, invoque l'arrivée en justicier de son frère jumeau Elisav, torture, dans l'ultime stade de la rééducation, son frère jumeau Elisav. Fascinante et pesante, la gémellité traduit les contradictions et l'urgence du projet de reconstitution de la parole absente et apparemment impossible.

Si les anciens détenus politiques roumains paraissent accepter comme inévitable la référence à la littérature, pour certains elle constitue non pas le vase d'expansion du témoignage, mais sa limite. Partant de la même prémisse de l'impossibilité de transmettre l'essentiel de l'expérience vécue, un rescapé roumain de l'extermination par le travail ne trouve dans l'expression artistique qu'un pis-aller: "Mais c'est impossible, c'est impos-

---

16   Virgil Ierunca, *Pitesti, laboratoire concentrationnaire (1949-1952)*, p 19.

17   *Les Chiens de mort...*, p. 111, souligné par moi.

sible à communiquer. Moi, si fort que je veuille vous décrire, faire la simple opération de vous informer, je ne peux pas vous rendre sensibles. Les notions ont une capacité limitée d'évocation et de sensibilisation. Non, non, ça ne va pas à l'infini. Je n'en serai jamais capable. [...] *Moi, je peux vous dire un conte.*"[18] L'impossible à dire se résout, provisoirement et incomplètement, dans le dire littéraire. Parler des camps se résumerait, en fin de compte, à une pénible production de littérature...

Littérature et anti-utopie

Elaborée dans la nostalgie du document idéal (parfaitement objectif et parfaitement vrai), la littérature du témoignage s'inscrit également, du moins à l'Est, dans une tradition culturelle. Pour Alain Parrau, *Les souvenirs de la maison des morts* de Dostoïevski et l'*Ile de Sakhaline* de Tchékov informent l'expression de l'expérience du goulag, qu'il s'agisse d'une influence acceptée, comme dans le cas de Soljénitsyne, ou bien d'un héritage refusé, problématique, comme dans le cas de Chalamov. Il existe pourtant une autre référence culturelle dans l'horizon de laquelle les œuvres s'élaborent, notamment dans l'espace roumain: il s'agit du filon des anti-utopies, plongeant ses racines dans l'antiquité grecque et connaissant un développement particulier dans les années '40-'50 de notre siècle.[19]

Livre interdit, livre diffusé sous cape, tout le monde a lu *1984* à l'Est, notamment en Roumanie. Lorsque les premiers récits sur le goulag réussissent à se frayer un chemin, le rapport s'impose dans les esprits: "Orwell avance une prophétie. La lecture de Soljénitsyne en fournit l'illustration, par des faits réels enregistrés en tant que documents de l'his-

---

[18] "Nous ne sommes pas des marchands d'horreurs", interview avec Miltiade Ionescu, p. 178, souligné par moi.

[19] Pour une esquisse de l'histoire des anti-utopies, cf. Eric Faye, *Dans les laboratoires du pire. Totalitarisme et fiction littéraire au XXe siècle* et John Hoyles, *The Literary Underground. Writers and the Totalitarian Experience.*

toire."[20] Ce que l'œuvre de l'un dessine comme dans un cauchemar, le livre de l'autre confirme, discute, corrige parfois. Terme ultime d'une série réunissant le texte utopique et l'anti-utopie, le témoignage apporte le poids du réel dans une confrontation qui le contourne volontairement.

Représenter le lien entre les deux genres comme une correspondance à travers le temps, en-deça et au-delà d'une période historique meurtrière, n'est pas sans certains dangers. Sur une échelle imaginaire de la valeur, l'auteur de témoignages se placerait plus bas que l'auteur d'anti-utopies: le premier ne fait que décrire, le second perce, inspiré, le voile du futur. Mais, comme tout prophète, sa crédibilité dépend de la réalisation de ses prophéties. Ainsi, la valeur de l'anti-utopie serait fondée *a posteriori*, dans la confrontation avec une évolution historique qui remplit, point par point, son programme. Ce serait exclure de la bourse des valeurs, ou du moins ajourner leur cotation, les œuvres de Huxley et celle de Bradbury: la société n'est pas encore arrivée à conditionner ses propres enfants, et les livres sont encore à prix dans notre monde... Et pourtant, *Le meilleur des mondes* et *Fahrenheit 451* ° conservent intact leur intérêt: ce que le lecteur y trouve, c'est moins une description de l'avenir, qu'un avertissement sur le présent. Il convient donc de séparer l'anti-utopie de sa dimension "anticipatrice", et de placer l'essentiel de son projet ailleurs—dans une parole sur le monde immédiat, à portée de la main. L'univers de *1984* existe déjà en 1948,[21] et l'œuvre d'Orwell peut être lue moins comme une fiction cauchemardesque du futur[22] que comme une parabole hyperbolisante du présent.

L'anti-utopie prend ainsi place dans l'horizon de la fable, de l'allégorie; le genre s'ouvre à des œuvres dont la présence aux côtés des "classiques" de cette littérature aurait semblé inappropriée. C'est le cas des romans de Dostoïevski (*Crime et Châtiment*, *Les Démons*), qui ne comportent aucune "anticipation" (dans le sens d'esquisse d'un monde futur

---

[20] Viorica Patea, "Histoire et utopie: Orwell et Soljénitsyne", in C. Comorovski (éd.), *Littérature du témoignage...*, p. 100.

[21] Ancien combattant en Espagne, Orwell a subi personnellement le regard de Big Brother. Le Ministère de la Vérité, le "traitement" par la peur fondamentale et les exercices de haine ne sont que des masques transparents d'institutions soviétiques dont le bruit était parvenu en Occident, même atténué par une volonté tenace de fermer les yeux. Sur les vagues succésives de témoignages sur le système soviétique, cf. Pierre Rigoulot, *Les paupières lourdes. Les Français face au goulag, aveuglements et indignations.*

[22] Définition de l'anti-utopie par Eric Faye, *op. cit.*, "Introduction".

éloigné) mais qui avertissent du danger de préférer les idées aux hommes. Mesuré à l'aune de ces nouveaux exemples, le propre de l'anti-utopie consisterait ainsi dans la réflexion sur les principes fondamentaux des politiques qui promettent, contre des sacrifices présents, des "lendemains qui chantent."[23] Leurs implications meurtrières seraient rendues visibles grâce aux mécanismes de la littérature. A la place d'une réfutation philosophique des idées, l'anti-utopie recourt à la mise en scène, rend vie aux abstractions, oppose le foisonnement du particulier au projet collectif réducteur par sa généralité.

Affirmer la consubstantialité des témoignages, du moins dans leur version "goulaguisante", avec l'anti-utopie frôle, dès lors, l'évidence. La plupart des récits sur le système concentrationnaire soviétique ont été écrits et publiés au moment où le communisme représentait encore, pour la plus grande partie de l'intelligentsia occidentale, la vérité absolue et la pensée la plus progressiste. L'*Archipel du goulag* a été ainsi conçu à la fois comme inventaire du réel et comme dénonciation des idées. "L'œuvre de témoignage"—observe Cornélia Comorovski—"se propose—et propose au lecteur—de réfléchir sur les conditions historiques dans lesquelles *cela* a été possible, mais aussi sur les conditions historiques dans lesquelles *cela* pourrait se répéter—au même endroit ou ailleurs—et sur ce qui, dans la nature humaine, a pu et peut être perverti et mis au service de *cela*."[24]

Les traces de cette réflexion sont détectables jusque dans les témoignages les plus "humbles," les plus proches de ce "document" pur de toute littérature dont on parlait dans la première partie de l'intervention. Les paysans déportés dans le Baragan[25] savent que leur malheur constitue la conséquence du retournement des valeurs fondamentales du monde opéré par le communisme: "Nous n'avons pas mérité tout ceci, nous avons été travailleurs et honnêtes, n'avons offensé personne, mais eux—nous ont chassé et se sont installés dans nos maisons. *Ils disent que c'est correct de*

---

[23] Ou bien, plus généralement, dans la réflexion sur l'essence mécaniciste de la modernité, sur les dangers du progrès sanctifié. Cf., en ce sens, la définition de l'utopie par Fr. Rouvillois *L'Invention du progrès*, p. 90.

[24] "Une introduction à la littérature du témoignage", in C. Comorovski (éd.), *Litterature du témoignage* p. 26.

[25] Plaine fertile mais connaissant des températures extrêmes en été comme en hiver, située au Sud de la Roumanie.

prendre ce qui appartient à autrui, de rendre malheureux son prochain..."[26]
Ils ont la conscience d'une subordination monstrueuse de la vie individuelle à un projet universel absurde: "J'avais un salaire de 600 lei, ce qui
était misérable et *faisait le jeu de la politique de ce temps-là, qui voulait
que tout ce qui est privé soit soumis à l'intérêt collectif.*"[27] Il ne s'agit sans
doute pas d'analyses approfondies, de fines distinctions, mais ces illustra-
tions brutales et personnalisées du communisme tissent une dénonciation
efficace de ses idées.

Construit comme une machine de guerre, l'univers des anti-utopies
fait ressortir les véritables "valeurs" centrales promues par l'idéologie
totalitaire. Sur la promesse d'un futur sans malheurs, l'individu est
enrégimenté, standardisé, vidé de toute substance personnelle. Le travail,
l'égalisation vers le médiocre, l'appauvrissement de la parole, la censure
de la pensée[28] constituent autant de moyens employés pour l'édification de
la société future et pour la création de "l'homme nouveau." Mais, en les
employant tous, le système roumain ne peut être réduit à aucun de ces
procédés. La plupart de nos auteurs ressentent d'ailleurs l'inappropriation
fondamentale de ces anti-utopies dans l'explication de ce qu'ils ont vécu.
Chez Paul Goma, par exemple, ce sentiment se traduit dans un refus
ouvert de l'analyse orwellienne: "—Orwell, pas le moindre rapport, dis-je.
O'Brien, qui était de l'autre bord, a définitivement vidé Winston Smith de
sa mémoire, pour le gaver ensuite, définitivement, de paramémoire.
Tandis que nous..."[29]

Le propre de l'expérience roumaine semble ainsi se situer ailleurs.
L'homme nouveau naît de la complicité, obligatoire, des victimes avec les
tortionnaires, projet appliqué non seulement dans la prison de Pitesti,
mais à l'échelle de la Roumanie en son entier. Initié et mis en œuvre sous
la surveillance directe de Nicolski, représentant de la K.G.B. en Roumanie,
cette expérience de perversion morale mène, dans ses variantes "douces,"
appliquées en masse, à des situations tragi-comiques où un ancien
défenseur de la loi, actuellement prisonnier politique, apprend à un

---

[26] Témoignage de Radovan Subin dans M. Milin, L. Stepanov (éd.), *Golgota Baraganului*, p. 45, souligné par moi. Toutes les traductions d'extraits de ce livres m'appartiennent.

[27] Témoignage de Svetislav Scheusan, dans M. Milin, L. Stepanov, *op. cit.*, p. 89.

[28] Pour une énumération complète, cf. Eric Faye, *op. cit.*, chapitre VIII "Univers. Les valeurs dominantes".

[29] Paul Goma *Les chiens de mort*, p. 281.

Literature as Cultural Memory

gardien à enfreindre la loi.[30] A une première vue, le rapprochement entre un épisode semblable et l'enfer subi par les victimes de Pitesti peut paraître abusif. Il s'agit toutefois, au-delà des apparences, de mécanismes similaires: brutalement mis en œuvre dans la Cellule 4 Spital,[31] avec plus de souplesse et de savoir-faire à "l'extérieur." Un conflit de valeurs, destructeur pour la personnalité, est déclenché dans les deux cas, qu'il s'agisse d'un détenu torturant ses camarades de prison ou bien d'un homme jadis intègre amené à corrompre ses gardiens. Ce que cherche le régime communiste roumain, ce n'est pas l'adhésion des opposants à son idéologie et à ses objectifs, mais l'effacement des points de repère moraux, le bouleversement des valeurs personnelles, la création d'un vide axiologique dans lequel ses propres actes soient relativisés. Les paysans déportés dans le Baragan apprennent, avant tout, un savoir-faire fondé sur les petits larcins. "C'est là qu'ils ont appris à voler des produits agricoles,"[32] affirme un commentateur, et cette courte phrase est lourde d'implications pour un connaisseur de la Roumanie des années '80 et '90: voler pour vivre, avec la complicité menaçante des autorités, devient, dans un pays ravagé par l'ambition de Ceausescu de payer les dettes extérieures, une habitude profondément enracinée. Pour imposer le mal, quel moyen le plus efficace que celui de détruire toute légitimité des juges potentiels du mal?

Conclusions

Entre les deux pôles abordés dans cette communication (document et anti-utopie), un centre de gravité se dessine: c'est le rapport du témoignage à la littérature qui constitue le fil rouge de la recherche. Rapport obligatoire, incontournable, selon la plupart des auteurs roumains, et susceptible d'être approché—comme s'efforce de le démontrer, à partir d'un exemple, la deuxième partie—avec les outils du comparatisme et de

---

[30]   Cf. Ion Ioanid, *op. cit.*, tome 5, p. 27: Doru et les sacs de maïs.

[31]   Cette traduction incomplète (Spital = Hôpital) est employée tout au long de la version française du roman de Paul Goma, *Les chiens de mort*, et nous avons préféré la conserver ici.

[32]   Miodrag Milin, "Il faut pardonner, mais s'en souvenir!", *op. cit.*, p. 196.

l'histoire littéraire. Le témoignage sur les camps est un document qui s'écrit avec les instruments de la littérature, dans l'horizon d'une idéologie meurtrière qu'il s'agit de cerner et de dénoncer.

Face à une bibliographie foisonnante sur les camps soviétiques, face aux analyses multiples et variées du nazisme, la littérature roumaine semble à la fois mûre et à peine sortie de la première effervescence. D'un côté, l'enregistrement des souvenirs des anciens détenus politiques et des déportés constitue encore l'essentiel du travail de plusieurs centres de recherche historique. Les romans de Paul Goma, les mémoires de Constantin Cesianu, Ion Ioanid, Dan M. Bratianu, Nichifor Crainic, pour ne citer que les auteurs auxquels il a été fait référence ici, les poèmes (non mentionnés) de Radu Gyr et Nichifor Cranic attestent, d'un autre côté, l'existence d'une préoccupation plus ancienne et plus profonde pour l'expérience concentrationnaire. La réécriture du passé reste toutefois lente et douloureuse, confrontée à un sentiment général de lassitude et de culpabilité dont les origines sont aisément repérables dans la "rééducation" subie sous le communisme. La littérature roumaine du témoignage est ainsi engagée non seulement dans une récupération historique du passé, mais aussi dans le rétablissement des valeurs morales compromises par la formation de "l'homme nouveau." A l'heure des interrogations sur les difficultés de la transition vers une société démocratique, la réponse des témoignages s'avère indispensable pour la compréhension des mécanismes de blocage du processus. Gardienne du passé, instrument d'analyse du présent et garde-fou pour le futur, la littérature roumaine du témoignage remplit triplement sa fonction de conscience de l'humanité.

Ioana Marasescu
Paris IV

Bibliographie

A) Témoignages

*** *Analele Sighet 2*. 1995. *Instaurarea comunismului - între rezistenta si represiune*, Bucuresti, Fundatia Academia civica, collection "Biblioteca Sighet".

Bratianu, Dan M. 1996. *Martor dintr-o tara încatusata*, Bucuresti, Fundatia Academia civica, collection "Biblioteca Sighet".

Capraru, Emil. 1995. "Dreptul de a muri", interview par Flori Stanescu, *Arhivele totalitarismului*, Bucuresti, Institutul National pentru Studiul Totalitarismului, no. 2, an III, pp. 164-176.

Cesianu, Constantin. 1992. *Salvat din infern*, Bucuresti, Humanitas.

Chalamov, Varlaam. 1986. *Récits de Kolyma*, traduit du russe par Catherine Fournier, Paris, La Découverte - Fayard.

Crainic, Nichifor. s.d. *Memorii*, tome 2, Bucuresti, éditions du Musée de la littérature roumaine, collection "Biblioteca «Manuscriptum»".

Goma, Paul. 1976. *Gherla*, traduit du roumain par Serban Cristovici, Paris, Gallimard, NRF.

————. 1981. *Les chiens de mort ou La passion selon Pitesti*, traduit du roumain par Alain Paruit, postface de Virgil Ierunca, Paris, Hachette, collection "Littérature générale".

Ierunca, Virgil. 1996. *Pitesti, laboratoire concentrationnaire (1949-1952)*, traduit du roumain par Alain Paruit, préface de François Furet, Paris, éditions Michalon.

Ioanid, Ion. 1996. *Inchisoarea noastra cea de toate zilele*, tome 5, Bucuresti, Albatros.

Ionescu, Miltiade. 1995. "Nu suntem negutatori de orori", interview par Flori Stanescu, *Arhivele totalitarismului*, Bucuresti, Institutul National pentru Studiul Totalitarismului, no. 2, an III, pp. 176-185.

Mandelchtam, Nadejda. 1975. *Contre tout espoir*, traduction par Maya Minoustchine, Paris, Gallimard, collection "Témoins".

Milin, Miodrag, Stepanov, Liubomir (éds.). 1996. *Golgota Baraganului*, traduction du serbe par Ivo Muncean, Timisoara, UDSCR.

Semprun, Jorge. 1994. *L'Ecriture ou la vie*, Paris, Gallimard, NRF.

Soljenitsyne, Alexandre. 1974. *L'Archipel du Goulag*, 3 volumes, Paris, Seuil.

Steinhardt, Nicolae. 1996. *Journal de la félicité*, traduit du roumain et annoté par Marily Le Nir, préface d'Olivier Clément, Paris, Arcantère Editions, Editions UNESCO, collection UNESCO d'œuvres représentatives.

Todorov, Tzvetan. 1992. *L'homme dépaysé*.

Zamiatine, Evgueni. 1979. *Nous autres*, traduit du russe par B. Chauvet-Duhamel, préface de Jorge Semprun, Paris, Gallimard, collection "L'imaginaire".

B) Références critiques

Coady, C.J. 1992. *Testimony. A Philosophical Study*, Oxford: Clarendon Press.

Comorovski, Cornélia (éd.). 1992. *Littérature du témoignage. Europe du Centre et de l'Est*, actes du colloque d'Angers des 3 et 4 avril 1992, Presses de l'Université d'Angers.

Faye, Eric. 1993. *Dans les laboratoires du pire. Totalitarisme et fiction littéraire au XXe siècle*, Paris, José Corti.

Hoyles, John. 1991. *The Literary Underground. Writers and the Totalitarian Experience, 1900-1950*, New York, London, Toronto, Sydney, Tokyo, Singapore, Harverster Wheatsheaf.

Kogan, Emil. 1983. *Du bon usage de Soljénitsyne. Essai de psychologie politique*, traduit du russe par Mireille Broudeur-Kogan, Paris, Maurice Nadeau, Papyrus.

Parrau, Alain. 1995. *Ecrire les camps*, Paris, Belin.

Pontuso, James F. 1990. *Solzhenitsyn's Political Thought*, Charlottesville, London, University Press of Virginia.

Rigoulot, Pierre. 1991. *Les Paupières lourdes. Les Français face au goulag: aveuglement et indignations*, Paris, éditions Universitaires, collection "Documents".

Rouvillois, Frédéric. 1997. *L'invention du progrès. Aux origines de la pensée totalitaire* (1680-1730), Paris, Editions Kimé.

Wieviorka, Anette. 1992. *Déportation et génocide. Entre la mémoire et l'oubli*, Paris, PLON, collection "Pluriel".

Perpetual Crisis? Literature and Historical Change: Romanian Literature after the Fall of Communism

One might expect that as soon as literature was liberated from the restrictions and humiliations it had to endure under communism, as soon as it was given the chance to bring in testimony about things impossible to deal with before, it would reach unprecedented vigour. Unfortunately this has not been the case. On the contrary, shortly after the fall of communism, the word 'crisis' began to be repeatedly used in connection with literature. I shall try to give a few hints which might explain this surprising turn. When I refer to 'literature' I do not mean just an inventory or a corpus of related texts, but a kind of activity, implying a network of cooperating actors and intertwining relationships. This is a tortuous path to follow. I have just picked up a few conspicuous land-marks: the status of literature, cultural environment, reading public, genre configurations and thematic repertoires.

The fate of literature under the communist dictatorship was obviously not a happy one, though both troubles and relative benefits varied in nature and degree over almost half a century. In a first radical stage, writers had either suffered severe persecution or enjoyed weighty material advantages and high social status, provided they strictly followed the propaganda line of the party. This stage turned gradually, during the

1960s, into a more 'liberal' epoch, granting considerable creative freedom and a socially acknowledged sense of professional dignity. Many young writers stepped, full of hope, into the arena, building up what came to be called the generation of the 60s. The promise of both creative freedom and professional dignity proved to be delusive during the next decade. By and large, in the last stage of Romanian communism the political leadership gave up attempts to win the writers' support, harassing them instead with all sorts of weapons, be they censorship, secret police, institutional threats or punishments, and bureaucratic or financial boycott.

In spite of the indisputable, often dramatic nuisances caused by the totalitarian regime, literature also profited, in ways commonly unavailable to democratic societies, from the adverse political circumstances. During the 60s literature was considered one of the most powerful means for regaining freedom of thought, of giving public expression to subjectivity: *scribo, ergo sum*. The limitations of literature's powers, set both by official control over the printed media—e.g. taboo topics—and by the very nature of the literary discourse, were underestimated by readers and writers alike. Moreover, literature appeared to be the obvious means for bridging the gap between present times and the pre-communist cultural tradition, especially when pointing back to the 'golden age' that was interwar Romanian culture. Literature also took advantage of the comparatively stronger ideological pressure exerted upon related fields such as the political sciences, philosophy, sociology, psychology, and even history. Due to the indirect, oblique form of the literary discourse, the writer of fiction, be it in prose, verse or dramatic genre, was supposedly capable of assuming many tasks which the political thinker, the historian, the sociologist, or the psychologist could no longer overtly exert. It was by means of literary elaboration or disguise that attempts to oppose official politics could avoid censorship and reach larger population groups. Even though at times such challenges achieved no more than a 'cathartic' effect through laughter or self-compassion, literature put on a heroic aura which strengthened its prestige.

In short, literature enjoyed a certain hegemonic position among the humanities, being perceived, in a quite contradictory way, both as the less blurred mirror of historical consciousness and the better strategy of cultural survival. The prestige of literature increased alongside with the obviously growing caution and adversity of the officials towards it. One should emphasize the fact that such an esteem is possible in societies that perceive themselves as categorically divided into two groups, following opposite interests and cherishing antinomic values: 'we' and 'they', 'the ruled' and 'the rulers'. A deep historical change was needed in order to realize the ambiguities of this self- perception.

I have insisted on the unusually high status literature had acquired during the communist dictatorship—from the point of view of the writers, literary critics, and theorists, as well as numerous readers. By no means am I trying to imply that the political circumstances enabled this literature to flourish. As a matter of fact, the general assessment of the writings produced and published under the communist regime in Romania is one of the most controversial issues among literary critics nowadays. Some of them consider that a radical revision of the established hierarchy of values is absolutely necessary. Others think that, apart from a few exceptions of circumstantial works doomed to oblivion from the very moment of their publication, writers have been able to produce judiciously received and ranked valuable literature. It is not the quality of literature in the totalitarian age, but its flattering public image, that has greatly faded away shortly after the fall of communism. In my opinion, this fact partly explains the intense frustration occasionally expressed by writers and critics after 1989. Many of them had a hard time to accept that, once the long awaited and dreamt of achievements such as freedom of thought and speech came into being overnight, literature lost its monopoly and gradually withdrew towards peripheral areas of public interest. A new 'crisis' was setting in, engendered this time mainly by wild free-market cultural competition against a background of increasing general poverty.

The first 'free' newspaper—i.e., published with no official authorization —appeared already on the 22nd of December 1989, while the state leader, Nicolae Ceauşescu, had fled and armed street fights broke out in Bucharest and other Romanian cities. Soon after that book publishing attracted plenty of entrepreneurs. In less than a couple of years almost 2,000 publishing houses were registered—many of which were family firms, unable to print more than one or two titles yearly. The book market was soon flooded with 'light' fiction: detective stories, science fiction, thrillers, exotica, parapsychology, esoterica, literary soap opera, up to hard core violence and pornography. Many publishing houses wavered for a while between complete submission to market constraints and cultural state-driven demands. This process was aggravated by tensions between private and state publishers. While the former were able to make their own editorial decisions with no bureaucratic hindrance, the latter were asking for supposedly legitimate, discriminatory financial support from the Ministry of Culture.

At present both the readers' appetite for all sorts of 'light' literature and many established authors' fear of its aggressiveness seem to have decreased. Nevertheless, the very idea that the hierarchy of values should be negotiated with the large reading public seems inappropriate to many writers, critics, and academics. The battle of the canon has not actually begun yet in Romania.

Shortly after the fall of communism, many writers started complaining of the 'betrayal' of the reading public. It is doubtful that what occurred was betrayal; rather it is more reasonable to assume that readers were asking for the books they had been waiting for too long. The most demanded books for a couple of years were nevertheless not just the ones of light fiction. Philosophy and the essay for example took revenge over literature. The works of Romanian personalities who started publishing between the world wars and emigrated afterwards, such as Emil Cioran, Mircea Eliade, and Eugène Ionesco, were published in large editions of up to 200,000 copies, and they are still being reprinted. Strangely enough, translations from such masters of world philosophy as Nietzsche, Heidegger, and Hegel, not to mention modern works of political philosophy, enjoyed an unusual success. The elimination of all forms of censorship allowed for a public feedback, casting a light upon the great variety of reading interests and preferences. Unfortunately, proper instruments to investigate the book market are still lacking.

The system of genres also changed in the post-communist period. After a transitory stage up to the late 60s, in which prose writers had chosen mainly the short story, during the 70s and 80s the novel had become, like everywhere else, the most appreciated literary type. The young writers who made their debut by the beginning of the last decade of the communist regime, building up the so-called generation of the 80s, invigorated again the short story genre. However, this was often considered a preparatory step towards writing novels. Meanwhile, the lyrical genre enjoyed an unusually large audience acknowledgement.

It is typical for modern aesthetics to hold the lyric for literature *par excellence*. In a historical context in which authors could afford to neglect the actual wishes of the reading public, the apology of poetry was remarkably successful. Needless to say, the lyric has lost much of its prestige after 1989.

The most striking transformation to occur in the post-communist period was the rise of non-fictional genres such as diaries, memoirs, testimonies, reports, documental writings, interviews, *entretiens*, debates, commentaries on contemporary life, and other mixed types of discourse, which have no name of their own. These have captivated many former readers of fiction and have driven even writers and specialists away from their reading habits.

Last but not least, many of these new genres interfered with the 'canonical' realm of literature, blurring its borderlines and giving an additional reason to proclaim the 'crisis' of literature. There are critics and academics who fear that the literary discourse would lose its identity were it not defended against intruders. *Casa lui David* ('The House of David', 1996) by Dumitru Nicodim, a captivating true report about the author's family, was challenged by critics for having been announced as a 'novel'. Critics reproached an ingenious novel about Thomas Aquinas, *Patimile sfîntului Tomasso d'Aquino* (1995) by Alex Mihai Stoenescu, for not having followed historical truth, thus misleading young readers. While the relation between fiction and non-fiction has always been disputable, in present-day Romania it seems to be quite a thorny problem. After almost half a century the public discourse has been intoxicated with countless lies, no wonder that, under the new circumstances, borderline fiction may appear either superfluous or even deceitful.

The problem of fictionality gets even more intricate when viewed against the background of the cultural structures prevailing during the last decades. In my opinion, there are two inherited patterns which are still competing in Romanian culture, even though opposite camps have not yet been formed along a clear divide. One of the patterns tends to emphasize the autonomy of cultural values, the other, on the contrary, their heteronomy. This distinction is particularly relevant for literature.

Romanian *belles lettres* have a young history. Their modern status and function were established in the second half of the 19th century, when efforts were made to separate literary discourse from other types of cultural products. The doctrine of aesthetic autonomy remained highly influential until the second world war and was recovered during the 60s as the crucial means of keeping literature safe from official intrusions.

Partly challenged by the generation of the 80s both in literary practice and in a theoretical perspective, the purist nostalgia involved in this doctrine is still extant among Romanian men of letters.

As for thematic repertoires, it is very difficult to identify central topics in literary works published in Romania after 1989. One may notice that writings dealing with the recent past were neither abundant, nor did they have the echo one would have expected. It seems to me quite significant that the best known prose writer after '89, Mircea Cărtărescu (author of *Nostalgia*, 1993—the unabridged edition of his censored *Visul* ['The Dream'], 1989—; *Travesti*, 1994; *Orbitor* ['Blinding'], 1996) has published highly subjective short stories and novels, profuse with imagination, focusing mainly on the psychological depths of the ego.

On the whole, literature proved to be a rather feeble means of confrontation with the trauma of experienced communism. Should the past grow older in order to be restored to our cultural memory?

Liviu Papadima
Bucharest

Bibliography

Călinescu, Matei. 1991. "Romanian Literature: Dealing with the Totalitarian Legacy". *World Literature Today* 64.1 (1991): 244-248

Cărtărescu, Mircea. 1989. *Visul* [The Dream]. Bucureşti: Cartea Românească.

─────. 1993. *Nostalgia* [Nostalgia]. Bucureşti: Humanitas.

─────. 1994. *Travesti* [Travesty]. Bucureşti: Humanitas.

─────. 1996. *Orbitor* [Blinding]. 1st vol. *Aripa stîngă* [Left Wing]. Bucureşti: Humanitas.

Lefter, Ion Bogdan. 1994. "Romanian Literature and the Publishing Industry since 1989: Asymmetries between History and Rhetoric." *Canadian Review of Comparative Literature* 22.3-4 (September/December 1994): 867-879

Marino, Adrian. 1996. *Politică şi cultură. Pentru o nouă cultură română* [Politics and Culture. For a new Romanian Culture]. Iaşi: Polirom, 12-40, 198-219

Nicodim, Dumitru. 1996. *Casa lui David* [The House of David]. Bucureşti: Humanitas.

Papadima, Liviu. 1995. "Postmodernisme littéraire et modèles culturels". *Cahiers roumains d'études littéraires* 1-2: 224-230.

Simuţ, Ion. 1994. *Incursiuni în literatura actuală* [Explorations in Present-Day Literature]. Oradea: Cogito, 384-411.

Stoenescu, Alex Mihai. 1995. *Patimile sfîntului Tomasso d'Aquino* [Thomas Aquinas' Passion]. Bucureşti: Humanitas.

III. Reflecting Apartheid

Telling the 'Truth':
Collective Memory of South Africa's Apartheid Heritage in Oral Testimony and Fictional Narrative

...want wat kan ons meer verbyster as dit wat die een mens in staat is om die ander aan te doen?

As ek 'n boek hiervan moet maak, is ek en hy saam daarin: die polisieman en die skrywer, die swarte en die witte .... Sy geskiedenis is my storie, sy verhaal: my beheptheid.[1]

— John Miles, *Kroniek uit die doofpot.* (1991:16).

'It is a confession I am making here, this morning, Mr Vercueil, ' I said, 'as full a confession as I know how. I withhold no secrets. I have been a

---

[1] "...for what can stun us more than that which one person is capable of doing to another? If I have to make a book out of this, he and I are in it together: the policeman and the writer, the black and the white .... His history is my story, his narrative: my obsession." (My translation.)

good person, I freely confess to it. I am a good
person still. What times these are when to be a
good person is not enough!'

J.M. Coetzee, *Age of Iron.* (1990: 150).

... the Nurse related in detail how this our little
sister died, and her premonitions, and the last
words she uttered, and her final laugh,...

Zakes Mda, *Ways of Dying.*(1995: 38).

1. By Way of Introduction: The Truth and Reconciliation Commission

With hindsight these quotations, taken from recent novels by white
and black South African writers, appear almost prophetic in their anticipation (or in the case of Zakes Mda the reflection) of the twofold objective
of disclosure of the truth and confession of guilt which informed the
establishment of the *Truth and Reconciliation Commission* in 1994. This
commission, commonly referred to as the TRC, represents South Africa's
official attempt at coming to terms with its traumatized past by creating
a public forum both for the individual testimonies of those responsible for
and those who suffered the consequences of gross human rights violations.
There is no doubt that the philosophy underpinning the TRC's endeavours
is laudable, albeit idealistic, in that it underscores the belief that national
reconciliation could be achieved if the full truth about the clandestine
operations of perpetrators or the magnitude of victims' suffering were to
be disclosed and became a question of common knowledge.

The decision to establish a Truth and Reconciliation Commission,
or TRC, was taken during the multiparty negotiations that preceded the
democratic elections in 1994. It was commonly acknowledged by all parties
concerned that the question of how to deal with human rights violations
would be one of the most difficult challenges facing a future Government

of National Unity. The worst scenario imaginable would be something akin to the Nurenberg hearings, but such drastic intervention would be unacceptable on two counts: the country did not have the resources to finance thousands of court cases and it was felt that retribution would not serve the ideal of a future peaceful and just society, then symbolized as a "rainbow nation" by Archbishop Desmond Tutu, currently overseeing the work of the TRC. On the other hand, it would be unrealistic to expect that the past could simply be ignored, or that the countless victims of different manifestations of human rights violations would spontaneously enter into a spirit of forgiving and forgetting. It was also realized that there were just too many ghosts to be laid to rest, and blatantly disregarding them would create serious repercussions. As a result of such deliberations, the parties opted for a compromise in that it was felt that the public hearings, and the envisaged compensation for victims, could be financed without placing too cumbersome a burden on the state's resources. But, more importantly, the idealistic objective was stressed—the envisaged result of a full and public disclosure of the truth, regardless of how appalling or shocking the details might prove to be, would not be retribution but, instead, the testimonies would be seen as part of a process intended to facilitate and foster a spirit of national reconciliation.

The TRC was subsequently officially sanctioned when parliament adopted the Law on Unity and Reconciliation in which a number of scenarios were outlined: firstly, an opportunity for victims to tell what had happened to them and to describe the extent of their suffering; secondly, an opportunity for perpetrators to seek amnesty provided a full disclosure of actions amounting to gross violations of human rights were made; thirdly, an opportunity for the Commissioners to establish an official record of a reliable disclosure of the truth. To expedite its functioning, the TRC was allocated three Official Committees dealing, respectively, with human rights violations, applications for amnesty and submissions for reparation and rehabilitation.

As the TRC's activities are drawing to a close after nineteen months of public hearings in different locations across South Africa, to date approximately 12,000 individuals have come forward to testify before the commission in the first category dealing with gross human rights violations. They are the victims of such heinous deeds as murder, culpable homicide, abduction or extreme torture. Although not adhering to normal court procedure, the TRC has investigation and research teams checking the accuracy of the testimonies offered by individuals.[2] The victim is only allowed to tell his or her story in public if it can be corroborated by independent evidence found in, inter alia, police dossiers or hospital records. Despite efforts to be impartial and evenhanded in the selection of victims allowed the opportunity to testify in public, it would appear that by far the majority of stories told are by those who suffered at the hands of the security forces of the former regime, whereas the testimonies of those who had fallen victim to operations carried out as part of the struggle for freedom, are seldom reported in the public media.[3] Appearances to the contrary notwithstanding, it is argued that the reluctance to come forward is not necessarily an indication of distrust in the activities of the TRC. So, for instance, the commission found that the surviving family members of a white farmer and his son who were killed when their bakkie detonated a landmine on one of the dirt roads on their farm in the Northern Province, refused to testify because they did not wish to relive the agony they had suffered fairly recently, nor were they comfortable with the idea of turning their private grief into a public spectacle. Given the widespread exposure of extracts from TRC hearings in the media, this reluctance expressed by an actual victim, of allowing an intensely private experience to become an object of public scrutiny, is understandable. However, to a "literary" inclined reader, the use of the word "spectacle" would seem to suggest something additional—the possibility of providing an artificial, perhaps even an artistic, context for actual experiences. This is certainly true of the use made of television broadcasts, where the viewer is invariably presented with a sequence of cuts focusing primarily on sensationalist extracts from live hearings of the TRC, thereby leaving him or her with a sense of having been subjected to the contrived exaggerations

---

[2] With regard to the second category, concerning those who have been permitted to apply for amnesty on account of their submissions to the TRC, the burden of evidence is heavier. The law stipulates that amnesty may only be considered in cases where a full disclosure of all relevant facts has been made by the perpetrator, and provided it is found that the actions were either politically motivated, informed by military considerations or carried out as a result of military commands. To date the commission has had to consider 15,000 submissions of which only 1,000 have been recommended as possibly qualifying for amnesty.

[3] The commission acknowledges that the impression of bias (with regard to a so-called witch-hunt against white Afrikaners, for example) cannot always be avoided and that the reality of some political manipulation (as in the power struggle between the ANC and Inkatha in Kwazulu-Natal) has to be accepted. The scepticism reflected by public opinion notwithstanding, one has to accept that, given the historical heritage of apartheid, it was only to be expected that the stories told in the first category would, in an overwhelming measure, refer to black victims, whereas the submissions in the second category would, by the same token, largely concern representatives from the Security Forces who had to implement the policies of the former regime.

Literature as Cultural Memory

more commonly associated with theatre, if not indeed with spectacle.[4]

2. Oral Testimony: The "Truth" Presented as Story

Over the past nineteen months the public hearings in different parts of the country have provided a unique opportunity for turning the hitherto untold personal experiences of victims and perpetrators alike into publicly recorded official documents. Whereas the oral testimonies of perpetrators unfailingly take the form of confessions with regard to gross human rights violations, the countless stories of victims bear witness to the suffering of ordinary South Africans who would have remained anonymous and forgotten were it not for the opportunity to have their experiences recorded and their stories told to the public at large. In both instances the objective remains full disclosure of the truth in an attempt to reach eventual national reconciliation.

Although these hearings concern the bitter history of a deeply divided society, from a literary perspective it is striking that the term "story" has become the overarching term consistently used to describe the oral testimony of victims, whereas the more neutral, or less "literary", term "confession" is retained for the testimony of perpetrators. In this regard it is remarkable that the words uttered by the first person narrator of J.M. Coetzee's novel *Age of Iron*, which was published in 1990, seem to have anticipated almost uncannily accurately the philosophy underpinning the policy of encouraging, if not coercing, beneficiaries under the previous system to tell everything in order to be able to apply for amnesty for past wrongs presumably ascribable to them. The words Coetzee puts into his character's mouth first of all assume that a confession is required and that it has to be a full confession without withholding any secrets. The very

---

[4]   A few examples will suffice to illustrate the approximation to spectacle. During one of the very first broadcasts of the TRC hearings on national television, the camera focused at some length on Archbishop Tutu where he had fallen face forward on the table and was wailing aloud after having had to listen to the testimony of a victim. Similar reactions sometimes came from the audience. In one particularly harrowing instance, viewers could see a mother jumping up, wildly gesticulating with her arms and crying out after she had recognized her son being shot and killed during the showing of a police video presented as evidence in formal testimony. Clearly, for her, there was no "comfort" in the artificial filmic context of her son's shooting.

requirement of a confession, however, presumes an acknowledgement of guilt and indeed, as is suggested by the lament that "to be a good person is not enough", an awareness of personal shortcomings only being truly recognized for what they are in the course of the confession.[5]

If the oral testimonies of actual victims indeed deserve the term "story", a golden opportunity presents itself to compare the "true" stories, or testimonies presented in the form of stories, to the fictional representation of similar stories, in both black and white writing in South African literature. In the novelistic examples quoted above, the role of the author or narrator as *mediator* of a victim's story becomes evident—in Miles's novel it is the author who reflects on the process whereby the policeman's history becomes his story; in Mda's book it is the mediating role of the person designated the honour of recounting the circumstances of the deceased's last moments, that is foregrounded through different voices and shifting narratorial positions throughout the novel. It is interesting that the introductory remarks in the exchanges between members of the TRC and the person or persons who have come to testify, frequently contain a reassurance that somebody has been assigned to help the victim tell his or her story. However, the only function these "mediators" fulfil is to prompt the witnesses, in case some detail or other needs clarification, but the actual accounts of whatever befell them are the stories as told by the victims themselves in their own words, and their actual words are recorded for posterity in the transcriptions of the oral presentations.

These "stories" told by victims, relating to personal harm experienced or to grief suffered as a result of the loss of a close relative, are contained in the literal blow by blow transcription of the questions and answers comprising the submissions to the TRC's Committee for Human Rights Violations.[6] In three of the testimonies referred to in this paper, the perpetrators are the Security Forces of the former government; one relates to the disciplinary measures resorted to by the ANC (African National Congress) in so-called detention camps in neighbouring countries such as

---

[5]   Admittedly, Coetzee's narrator, Mrs Curren, is not a perpetrator in the State's sense of the word, but, in her attempt at "a full confession", she nevertheless seems to have accepted the inevitability of facing the truth of a lifetime's commitment to "goodness" rather than to heroic intervention.

[6]   Although part of public hearings, these transcriptions are not yet being publicly released. For the opportunity to have had insight into some of the transcriptions, I wish to thank Professor Piet Meiring, member of the TRC's Committee for Reparation and Rehabilitation.

Angola and Mozambique; and two involve extreme measures taken within a community against individuals.

Within the question and answer format of the submissions, that part in which the victim is given the necessary scope to describe the events in which he or she was directly or indirectly involved, is consistently referred to as the "story" that has to be heard and duly recorded. Thus the core of every submission is the "story", embedded within questions which occasionally prompt the victim to resort to deliberations about the (apartheid) philosophy underpinning past violence, the present necessity of determining the truth and the future ideal of establishing national reconciliation.

It would appear that for the victims who have come forward to testify, the need to *tell* is overdetermined or overshadowed by the necessity to *know*. Thus a common feature in the stories of victims is that the question *why* is invariably coupled to the demand that the perpetrator be held accountable for actions taken against his or her accuser(s). To a certain extent the question *what* is fully explainable by the victim. However, a satisfactory answer to the question *why*, they seem to believe, can only be provided by the perpetrators themselves. It is probably this belief which compels victim after victim to demand that they be given the opportunity to listen to the testimonies of perpetrators; and even, in some instances, that they be allowed to confront their perpetrators directly.

This desire to be confronted with the person responsible for their suffering is matched by vivid recollections of previous encounters between perpetrators and victims. So, for example, in cases where victim and perpetrator had faced each other during a traumatic incident, the experience seems to haunt the victim, as became clear from the testimony of Mr Motsepe, who, whilst acting as the informal ANC ambassador to the Benelux countries in the 1980s, had survived no fewer than four attempts on his life, presumably carried out by hit squads operating within the security forces of the former government.

> ...So they (i.e. the Belgian police) called me over and they showed me a photograph of this man and this was exactly the man I saw that night when he shot at me because for a split second we looked at each other when he came running to the window and he stood there and I stared into his eyes and he stared at me just for a split second before he drew and he shot. (Motsepe 1996)

In this instance the victim claims to know who the perpetrator is and he is demanding that the TRC subpoena the man in question to appear before the commission. In other instances, such as the case where her father was murdered by youths during the 1976 uprisings, Janet Goldblatt merely wants to understand *why* it had to happen and whether her father, having been known as a benefactor of the underprivileged in Soweto at the time, had been recognized by his attackers before being killed by them.

> I know that nothing here today that I say or do can bring him back to myself and my family, but, obviously, our question has been from the day that we heard this awful news, is why Dr Edelstein. He was not a policeman, he was not involved in the violation of any one's human rights. He loved the people of Soweto almost as he did his own family and we would like to know, if possible, what actually happened on that day. Although, as I say, I know it cannot bring him back, but what took place, you know. If there are any witnesses here today or anybody who could recollect or who was with him at the time. Maybe somebody who knows what his last words were and what actually, you know, happened to my father. (Goldblatt 1996)

As we shall see, the question of witness accounts is mirrored by the role of the Nurse, performed by the last person to have seen a person alive and who was "witness" to his death, in Zakes Mda's novel, entitled *Ways of Dying* (1995). A more explicit link with fictional narrative is found in the self-conscious use of "story" as the medium of expression during the hearings. So, for instance, the parents of a young MK (Umkhonto we Sizwe) commander who was tortured by high-ranking ANC officials in a detention camp in Zambia, explicitly announce their experiences as *story*: "My story is as follows" (Mr Ngwenya), or "Now I am presenting my story" (Mrs Ngwenya). As the father relates first his support of his son's involvement in the struggle, and subsequently the inexplicable deeds inflicted on him by the ANC, it gradually becomes not only the meticulously constructed story of his son's suffering and death, but indeed, as is suggested by the quotation from Miles's novel, *his* (i.e. the *narrator's*) personal account of grief suffered, in this case, as a result of his ineffectual attempts at intervention with regard to his son's alleged torture and poisoning by the ANC security people in the notorious detention camps in South Africa's border countries.

This testimony, submitted first by the father and then complemented by the mother's account, contains a number of typical narrative
strategies reminiscent of the self-conscious constructedness of postmodernist literature: the chronological account of the events making up the son's
story, interspersed with self-reflective deliberations offered by both
narrators (father and mother) on the fate of their son; the digressions
caused by quoting additional texts, such as the praise song, the newspaper
reports and even a political-historical book, written by a high-ranking
ANC-official, in which reference is made to the son's untimely death.
Witness, in this regard, the understated account of the father's sacrificial
and heroic, yet ineffectual, attempts at intervening on behalf of his son:

> One night on television I saw Mr Oliver Thambo coming
> back from a conference in Tanzania. He was at State House
> with Dr Kaunda, and I thought now I will have an opportu-
> nity to meet this gentleman. The following morning, early
> the following morning I went to the ANC headquarters, to
> meet him. He wasn't there, he was at State House. I walked
> because my money had run out, I walked to State House to
> meet them. It was such a distance from that morning until
> I got to the State House, enquiring where he was, walking
> on foot, the conference was over. I could not, I hadn't seen
> Mr Oliver Thambo. I was trying to waylay him, of course.
> (Ngwenya 1996)

And then regard the following understatement after he had learnt more
about his son's death:

> It was very strange. Very sick, a bag of bones, instead of
> being taken to hospital, he is thrown into the street, to look
> after himself. (*Ibid.*)

Again and again the two witnesses (father and mother) raised questions
about the reasons for and the circumstances of their son's death. When the
mother came to testify, her factual account, based on the findings of
independent commissions, are interspersed with laments:

> It is a question mark. Who poisoned my son and why? Who
> poisoned my son and why? In the media it is reported that
> he was poisoned. (*Ibid.*)

And later:

> Again on page 12 of the report, it states that TZ's illness
> progressed over months. Why was he not sent to a hospital
> and why poison the man who is dying? (*Ibid.*)

It should be clear from these few examples that those who chose to testify
before the commission managed not only to state the facts as they could
remember or perhaps as they had discovered them, but that they also
managed to convey their own reading of the situation by asking questions
of the commission in return.

This two-way communication, where the victims' testimonies, as it
were, take on a life of their own, is perhaps the most significant difference
in the representation of similar facts, questions and feelings of fictional
accounts. Nevertheless, interspersed in the transcriptions to which I had
access, one may discover surprising affinities with, for example, Zakes
Mda's remarkable reading of death, or the necessity to come to terms with
death, as a precondition for learning how to live even in the adverse conditions of squatter camp existence, where the harsh conditions of the home-
less are exacerbated by the effects of violence.

3.Fictional Context: "Narrative" Masquerading as "Testimony"

If it is true that the accounts of witnesses before the TRC are
self-consciously presented as "stories", it is also true that some fictional
accounts approximate real events to such an extent that they even gave
rise to investigations by the TRC as happened recently with John Miles's
novel when it was announced that the dossier on which his novelistic
investigation was based, would be re-investigated by the TRC. Disclosing
the truth is undeniably the task the author in the quotation from Miles's
novel set himself. But it is a disclosure that would implicate both victim
and author: the "history" of the black policeman whose execution was
presumably sanctioned and ordered by high-ranking white officers becomes
the "story" the author is compelled to tell, because the exposé of the untold

suffering of the black policeman is the obsessional driving force of his investigative writing. In the quotation from Mda's novel, a similar urge, to tell about a victim's suffering by recording the circumstances of his or her death, is concretized in the role of the Nurse at funerals.

If the self-conscious narrators in both novels apparently fulfil the role of indirect transmitters of victims' experiences, they do so from different perspectives. Whereas Miles's narrator has to assume the role of an investigator to disclose the facts on which the victim's story is based, Zakes Mda's observers of funerals already know all the facts and they, therefore, act as official mourners assigned the task of recording and transmitting the circumstances of each victim's violent death. Also, if Coetzee's character assumes the role of perpetrator, be it by omission rather than actual transgression, in need of amnesty through confession, then the Nurse in Zakes Mda's novel, as the official mediator at the funerals of victims of violence in the black community, poignantly illustrates the burning desire to tell, or to have someone record, the full story of how and why the victim died by vividly recapturing the circumstances leading to and ending in death.

It is this aspect of community "culture" in a black squatter camp that Zakes Mda's novel seeks to portray by exploiting an interesting, if unconventional, narrative strategy whereby chameleon-like narrators set about their task of witnessing, recounting or explaining the everyday existence of black people in a violence-ridden township community on the eve of political change in South Africa. Indeed, so common an occurrence is death in the world of Toloki, the main protagonist in Mda's *Ways of Dying* (1995), that he depends on the regularity of funerals to earn his daily bread, quite literally, by performing as a professional mourner at funerals. In fact, ways of dying have inspired not only him, but also other people in the squatter camps, euphemistically referred to as informal settlements, to find new ways of living. Not only has death become a common occurrence, but its untimeliness has become the norm, so that, of the many "ways of dying" we encounter in Mda's novel, a "natural" death, such as dying as a result of illness or old age, has become the exception to the rule of sudden, mostly deadly, violence.

One could say that Mda's novel provides a kind of fictional counter-foil to the TRC, in that it contains a veritable storehouse of different types of violence exemplifying gross violations of human rights. Not only are there direct and indirect references to hardships suffered by black victims at the hands of white perpetrators, but there are deaths as a result of factional violence or family quarrels within the community; and, most harrowingly of all, the burning alive of two boys by their playmates at the instigation of the so-called Young Tigers representing the faction embodying the struggle in the community. The execution of Noria's boy, commonly known as The Second because he was named after his deceased elder brother Vutha, meaning "a burning fire",[7] forms the main motif of the book and the actual circumstances leading to his cruel fate are only disclosed towards the end of the novel, where the terrible consequences of summary sentences meted out by so-called peoples' courts are recounted. Active participators in the struggle, though only five and eight years old, Noria's son and a playmate pay with their lives for the sin of being tricked into disclosing information about a planned attack on a hostel after the hostel dwellers had first kidnapped and then bribed them with sweets. The manner in which this event is portrayed, which surely represents a violation of human rights of the worst possible kind, clearly shows the advantages of a re-enactment of a scene in fictional narrative, as opposed to the mere telling of it in the oral testimonies or "stories" publicly heard by the TRC. As in the TRC hearings, there are also questions to which truthful answers have to be given in the court held by the Young Tigers in the open field of a squatter camp. But in this court confessing the truth does not hold the possibility of forgiveness, let alone offering a means to escape into amnesty:

> "The hostel dwellers are not your uncles. They cannot just give you sweets for nothing. What did you promise them? What did you tell them?"
> The children had to confess that they told the hostel inmates about the planned ambush. The leaders of the Young Tigers were very angry. They called all the children to come and see what happened to sell-outs. They put a tyre round Vutha's small neck, and around his friend's. They filled both tyres with petrol. Then they gave boxes of matches to Danisa and to a boy of roughly the same age.

---

[7]   The danger of giving Noria's first boy the name of Vutha is couched in almost prophetic terms by an enraged grandmother in an encounter with the boy's father: " ' My grandson shall not be dogged by misfortune just because you want to give him a stupid name that means a burning fire! *Don't you know that the meanings of names are fulfilled?*' " (Mda 1995: 75; italics mine.)

                                         Literature as Cultural Memory

"Please forgive us! We'll never do it again. We are very
sorry for what we did."
"Oh, mother! Where is my mother!"
"Shut up you sell-outs! Now, all of you children who have
gathered here, watch and see what happens to sell-outs.
Know that if you ever become a sell-out, this is what will
happen to you as well. Now you two, light the matches, and
throw them at the tyres."
Danisa and the child who had been given the honour of
carrying out the execution struck their matches, and threw
them at the tyres. Danisa's match fell into Vutha's tyre. It
suddenly burst into flames. His screams were swallowed by
the raging flames, the crackle of burning flesh, and the
blowing wind. He tried to run, but the weight of the tyre
pulled him down. The eight-year-old was able to stagger for
some distance, but he also fell down in a ball of fire that
rolled for a while and then stopped. Soon the air was filled
with the stench of burning flesh. The children watched for
a while, then ran away to their mothers.
Danisa also ran to her home. 'Maleholohonolo was not back
from the city yet. So she ran to Noria's.
"Auntie Noria, I burnt The Second because he is a sell-out."

(Mda 1995: 176-177)

It is not only in the actual re-enactment of instances of violence and death
that fictional narrative differs from oral testimony, presented as the true
"stories" told by victims in testimonial narrative. What also sets Mda's
book apart from the stories told at the TRC hearings is the "solution" to
violence, represented as the power of imagination and the escape found in
creative outlets, such as singing, drawing and sculpture. His strategy of
first showing how Toloki and Noria are able to cope after the burning of
her shack, whilst only gradually disclosing more and more details of
Vutha's execution, has the effect of manipulating the reader into accepting
the possibility of the survival of communities seemingly able to become
"reconciled" to an existence of poverty, violence and death. Service to the
community, such as Noria's devotion to children "dumped" because they
had become orphaned as a result of violence, serves to sensitize the reader
to a spirit of caring and sharing operative in the community. Thus, despite
their apparently unbearable circumstances, where life has to be defined in
terms of death, and despite the protracted suffering to which the community is subjected, Mda's protagonists seem to be at peace with each other and

their actual and constructed environment at the close of the book.

In conclusion, the discerning reader may wonder whether there are any redeeming factors in the testimony to gross human rights violations reflected in the complementary "factual" and "fictional" tales of violence and death briefly referred to in this paper. The answer, surprisingly, apparently has to be *Yes*: the reconciliation envisaged by the TRC finds an equivalent in Toloki's and Noria's acceptance of a very ordinary, yet meaningful existence, amidst the "plentiful" occurrence of death in a community where their meagre existence is governed by the laws of violence. This surprisingly hopeful future, where people have become "reconciled" to their environment, is envisaged in the closing of Mda's novel by the touch of colour amidst the "normality" of a fire which, for once, is not consuming human flesh:

> Somehow the shack seems to glow in the light of the moon, as if the plastic colours are fluorescent. Crickets and other insects of the night are attracted by the glow. They contribute their chirps to the general din of the settlement. Tyres are still burning. Tyres can burn for a very long time. The smell of burning rubber fills the air. But this time it is not mingled with the sickly stench of roasting human flesh. Just pure wholesome rubber. (Mda 1995: 199)

Ina Gräbe
UNISA, Pretoria

Bibliography

Coetzee, J.M. 1990. *Age of Iron*. London: Secker & Warburg.

Mda, Zakes. 1995.*Ways of Dying*. Cape Town: Oxford University Press.

Meiring, P.G.J. 1997. Die Waarheids- en Versoeningskommissie: agtien maande later.(The Truth and Reconciliation Commission: eighteen months later.) Paper read at a meeing of the Interdisciplinary Group of Christians. Pretoria, July 17.

Miles, John. 1991. *Kroniek uit die doofpot. Polisieroman.* Kaapstad & Johannesburg: Human & Rousseau.

Truth and Reconciliation Commission. Human Rights Violations. Submissions - Questions and Answers.

Date: 23/07/1996   Name: Janet Goldblatt
Case Number: Soweto

Date: 26/07/1996   Name: Mr & Mrs P. Ngwenya
CaseNumber: Soweto

Date: 15/08/1996   Name: Godfrey Josiah Madileng Motsepe
Case: JB00606   Pretoria

Date: 24/09/1996   Name: Helena Kroon de Kock
Case: 01563   Klerksdorp

Date: 04/10/1996   Name: Simon Farisani
Case: Venda

Date: 12/11/1996   Name: D. Smith
Case: Krugersdorp

Historical Trauma and the Desire for Absolution: Saying *on the Contrary* to the Commissioning of Truth

1. Introduction

The two texts which I focus on in this paper, namely "The Narrative of Jacobus Coetzee" in *Dusklands* by J.M. Coetzee (1974) and *On the Contrary* by André P. Brink (1993), seem to be tailor-made for a number of already existing problematics such as "Europe and its Other(s)", "postcolonialism" and "colonial discourse theory"—and in the case of this conference, "the conscience of humankind."

Both texts can be called 'historical fiction,' making use of material clearly marked as 'historical' in which intercultural contact and conflict play an important role. The same social conflict, that between European colonist and Khoi in the Western Cape region of South Africa, provides the backdrop for the action in the two novels. Roughly the same historical period is represented in the two novels: *On the Contrary* deals with the fortunes of Estienne Barbier, a rebel or social bandit who arrived at the Cape in 1734 and was executed in 1739; "The Narrative of Jacobus Coetzee" concerns Jacobus Coetzee, Janszoon, who undertakes an elephant hunting expedition beyond the borders of the Cape colony in 1760.[1]

In the course of both texts the central protagonists, both Europeans, engage with aboriginal inhabitants, these engagements forming integral parts of the fictional narratives. Similar events and issues are represented in the course of these engagements, such as humiliation, subjection, injustice, cruelty and atrocity. A similar ironic stance towards Western morality and the authority of the European Enlightenment can be read off both texts, attitudes and perspectives associated with a 'modern' European world-view being implicated in the violent subjection of foreign space and people in both texts.

If one generalises one might say that the texts are part of a corpus characterised by the representation of historical events in which injustice, atrocities, genocide—inhumanity in general—is visited by one group of people on another, usually culturally distinct, group of people.

Over the past few decades the attention has however fallen particularly intensely on one facet of this record of inhumanity, namely that associated with European expansion, roughly from the fifteenth century onwards. The events around which inquiry has concentrated include the following: the Spanish Conquest of South America and the demise of the Aztec Kingdom, the colonisation of North America and Australia associated respectively with genocide of the American Indians and the Australian Aborigines, and the imperial control and management of India, other parts of Asia and Africa in which issues such as subjection, marginalisation and slavery figure largely.

The formulation above also enables one to include literature dealing with other chapters in the history of inhumanity, such as the Gulag literature, the reflections of the Chinese Cultural Revolution, and more recently the literature which has been reaching western readers about

---

[1] "The Narrative of Jacobus Coetzee" in *Dusklands* and *On the Contrary* can be placed next to a text such as *The Savage Crows* by Robert Drewe (1976). A protagonist who closely aligns himself with the plight of Australian Aborigines - placed in a similar position to that of the South African Khoi - namely 'The Conciliator', George Augustus Robinson, also plays a central role in Robert Drewe's novel. The most important compositional device of *The Savage Crows* consists of the juxtaposition of a number of texts (which includes Robinson's story), presided over by the narrator, Stephen Crisp, showing clear similarities to the way "The Narrative of Jacobus Coetzee" and *On the Contrary* are composed.

events in the Far East, such as China, Kampuchea, Vietnam,[2] as well as from the Middle East. But most importantly, the formulation enables the inclusion of Holocaust literature, which has somehow become the model for the representation of sociohistorical trauma (see for example Rosenfeld (1980) and Young (1988)).

At the same time, if all the literature and literary criticism alluded to here deals with similar subject matter (the representation of historical inhumanity), the manner in which the subject matter is approached and problems are raised show great diversity. The main reason for this is that the context within which texts are approached largely determines the issues raised, as well as the manner in which this happens.

With regard to the literature and criticism dealing with European expansion—mainly approached with reference to Europe's relation to its 'other(s)'—the framework(s) in which texts have been placed has largely been influenced by various strains of poststructuralism, as it developed in a number of disciplines such as anthropology, history and especially discourse analysis. With reference to this part of the 'terrain,' two main currents can be discerned, which could also be said to represent opposing tendencies.

On the one hand is a critical thrust which focuses on the various forms of injustice, subjection, marginalisation and destruction of cultural traditions which accompanied European expansion and contact with non-European cultures (e.g. Loomba (1991), Slemon (1987), Goldie (1985), and many more). An off-shoot of this current has as its main objective reparation—the reconstruction, recuperation and rejuvenation of forgotten and marginalised voices, subjectivities and identities.

On the other hand one finds expressions—mainly fictional literary texts—originating from a European location—that is, from the 'coloniser,' the 'oppressor,' the 'imperialist' (as this position is represented from certain anti-Western perspectives). The majority of these expressions, such as in novels and films, are characterised by the placing of the 'other,' or the non-Western culture, under the sign of the autochthonous, the primitive and the natural. In a significant number of these expressions attempts are made to express solidarity and empathy with the victims of European

---

[2] Two novels which seem to have achieved a higher than usual circulation are *Novel Without a Name* by Duong Thu Huong (1995) and *The Sorrow of War* by Bao Ninh (1993).

expansion through various strategies, one of which is the simulated immersion in the foreign culture.

The exemplary literary text in this regard might be Alejo Carpentier's *Los pasos perdidos* (*The Lost Steps*) (1953/1956) in which the central protagonist and narrator, a dissatisfied and middle-aged academic and music composer, undertakes a journey into the South American hinterland to search for an obscure musical instrument. He starts the journey off with his mistress, but loses her along the way and completes the journey with an Indian woman, Rosario. The experience radically changes his perception of Western culture, and of his place therein.

Similar 'partnerships' and identifications with 'autochthony' are found in texts as varied as Wilson Harris's *Palace of the Peacock* (1959), James Vance Marshall's *Walkabout* (1971(1959)), Rudy Wiebe's *The Temptation of Big Bear* (1973), Robert Kroetsch's *Gone Indian* (1973) and *Badlands* (1975), Mario Vargas Llosa's *El hablador* (*The Storyteller*) (1989(1987)), Margaret Atwood's *Surfacing* (1979), Peter Matthiessen's *At Play in the Fields of the Lord* (1991) and David Malouf's *Remembering Babylon* (1994), amongst others. Patrick White's *Voss* (1957) and especially *A Fringe of Leaves* (1976) can also be included in this list. Recent texts from Afrikaans literature in which such a tendency is evident are Dalene Matthee's *Fiela se kind* (1985), André P. Brink's *Die eerste lewe van Adamastor* (1993), Karel Schoeman's *Die uur van die engel* (1995) and *Verkenning* (1996). An earlier 'moment' in this development in Afrikaans literature is represented by Jan Rabie's *Bolandia*-series of historical novels such as *Die groot anders-maak* (1964) and *Waar jy sterwe* (1966).

This second current has been criticised from various quarters as, amongst others, opportunist, exoticist, patronising and stereotypical (e.g. Leggo 1990). When this current is approached from a Western standpoint a simplistic critical dismissal seems shortsighted as the representation of, and especially the usage of cultural material originating from so-called autochthonous or primitive cultures by Europeans is a far from simple matter. Central facets of European culture such as its sense of time, history, causality, agency and indeed its sense of self are implicated in such usage.

In the case of the two South African texts on which this paper focuses, these issues are also present and at stake, but as argued above, placing the texts within the available frameworks might not be enough -

the texts, and the approach taken, need to be contextualised. In this paper I thus present one possible way of contextualising the texts as a contribution to the discussion about the role literature plays in the mediation of cultural, social and ethical conflict—be it as 'conscience.'

2. Contextualisation

One way of doing this is by relating the texts to one of the forms in which the problems associated with (European) injustice or inhumanity has recently been approached in South Africa, namely the Truth and Reconciliation Commission (TRC). As part of the process of the 'reconstruction' of South African society after the abdication of the National Party the TRC has been entrusted with dealing with gross human rights violations committed on 'all sides' during the apartheid era in South Africa.

Even though the South African TRC—dealing with events from the recent past—is not specifically concerned with the historical events dealt with in the two texts, "The Narrative of Jacobus Coetzee" and *On the Contrary*, the manner in which historical trauma, injustice and reparation are dealt with in the texts make it possible to see similarities with the problem the TRC has to grapple with. In both cases the same issues are placed in the foreground, namely in the first instance historical injustice and in reaction to this prior situation, a process of recalling this injustice, all of which can be encapsulated in the word, 'remembrance.' Both share a further moment, namely an attempt to *deal with* the past specifically regarding the legacy of this past in which the idea of 'reconciliation' plays an important role.

Approaching the difficult problematics associated with attempts to deal with a traumatic past by way of a comparison of the TRC and literary expression is a hazardous undertaking because the two terms refer to very diverse and sensitive phenomena. For this reason it is important that I clearly spell out what meaning I attach to the 'TRC.' The representation I give of the TRC in this paper is not based on study from an 'objective' standpoint. The issue(s) dealt with by the TRC actually militates against any attempt to approach it 'objectively.' The remarks that are made about the TRC in this paper are made with the understanding that the process the commission is involved in is complex and intricate. I am fully aware that *people* are involved in the process, people who suffered and people who committed gross deeds. It is however not with the perpetrators and their victims that I am primarily concerned.

I am first and foremost interested in the *communal, collective* or *symbolic* facet of the TRC's activities. It is on this level that the events between perpetrators and victims are 'translated' and mediated into relations between groups. The 'reconciliation' the TRC is aiming for can thus be seen to have at least two dimensions, an individual/empirical and a collective/symbolic one. If perpetrators and victims are in the centre of *individual* reconciliation, the 'category' which can first of all be associated with the collective level of the process, is that of the 'bystander.' It is also on this level that a concept such as 'conscience' can have a bearing on the problem. Such an approach is easily justified, seeing that the objective of the TRC is directed not at some rational endpoint, but at an *emotional* one, namely 'healing' and reconciliation.

3. Two historiographical traditions

Just how different the 'universes' are to which the terms 'TRC' and 'literature' refer becomes clear when one compares the historiographical traditions of which they are respectively part. By virtue of its status as an (accessory) organ of the juridical apparatus, the TRC has inevitably to take the idea of 'truth'—and the idea that it can be established conclusively— seriously. The TRC can be said to be founded on an empiricist epistemology, as one would expect of an organ of the juridical apparatus. It is interested in objective 'evidence' first of all, which it collects by investigations and hearings. As a legalistic organ it is expected to make judgements on the basis of this evidence.

In contrast the perspective on evidence, history, historiography and truth in the two fictional texts belong to a radically different epistemological and ontological domain. This difference is not only because of their being 'literature' but also because of their conception, creation and production within a specific context, one decisively marked by what has become known as poststructuralism. With regard to historiography—and related ideas such as 'truth'—poststructuralism has engendered a thoroughgoing scepticism about the schemes according to which historical events have customarily been reconstructed.

The most telling challenge to traditional historiography has come from analyses of historical discourse which highlighted the rhetorical strategies used in historical texts, in a sense showing that history is nothing more than another form of literature. In literature itself a similar tendency came to be known as 'historiographical metafiction,' referring to literary texts in which use is made of historical events and figures, but in which the constructed, fabricated, *textual* nature of the texts (and by implication history itself) are foregrounded (e.g. Hutcheon (1988).

4. Historiographic metafiction

The two South African literary texts to which I refer in this paper are good examples of this literary current, and are actually veritable storehouses of the various 'postmodernist strategies' used by authors to foreground the fabricated nature of literary and historiographical narratives.

"The Narrative of Jacobus Coetzee" in J.M. Coetzee's *Dusklands* (1974) is composed of three texts juxtaposed to one another, namely a first part narrated in the first person by the main character, Jacobus Coetzee, an "Afterword" and a "Deposition of Jacobus Coetzee." The narrative is presented as a translation by the author of *Dusklands*, J.M. Coetzee, of a text purportedly published in 1951 by his "father," S.J. Coetzee for the Van Plettenberg Society, which consisted of the "Afterword" of "The Narrative of Jacobus Coetzee" in the position of an "Introduction" in Afrikaans, followed by the Deposition in its Dutch form, *Het relaas van Jacobus Coetzee, Janszoon.* The "Introduction" (Afterword in "The Narrative of Jacobus Coetzee") is supposed to be an academic text, written by an Afrikaner historian, *Het relaas van Jacobus Coetzee, Janszoon* the official, objective, authoritative account of Jacobus Coetzee's travels in the interior of the Cape colony.

The juxtaposition of the three texts in "The Narrative of Jacobus Coetzee" can be read in such a manner that it highlights the arbitrary nature of any attempt at a reconstruction of the past. The juxtaposition foregrounds the manner in which various mediatory processes (recording, selection, editing and interpretation) affect the image of the past created by historiographical endeavours.[3]

The official deposition of Jacobus Coetzee, for instance, appears—within the context of "The Narrative of Jacobus Coetzee"—as the most impoverished with regard to the events that 'really' took place. This official deposition might also in fact be the most fanciful of all the statements in "The Narrative of Jacobus Coetzee" and a clear example of how the historical record can be informed, distorted and manipulated by personal interest and emotion. It is probable that—seen in the context of "The Narrative of Jacobus Coetzee"—Jacobus made this deposition (and especially the reference to "people with a tawny appearance and long hair") in order to create enthusiasm for another expedition to the hinterland, under cover of which Jacobus could exact the terrible retribution he desired against his servants who had deserted him.

S.J. Coetzee's 'authoritative' treatise is clearly coloured by its author's need to justify his forebears' colonisation of Southern Africa. He consequently presents Jacobus's activities as part of the process of bringing the indigenous inhabitants of Africa out of 'innocence' and closer towards "citizenship of the world" (117). The empiricist foundation of 'authoritative' historiographic texts such as the "Afterword" is however foregrounded—and parodied—in "The Narrative of Jacobus Coetzee." In a section of the "Afterword" S.J. Coetzee is represented as obsessively recording the 'travails' of bodily matter such as hair, crumbs of ear-wax, pus, sweat, smegma, faecal matter, semen, etc. of members of Jacobus Coetzee's expedition in 1760 (126-127). Such a passage foregrounds the arbitrary selection made from the historical 'record' by historiography, especially when it is placed next to the summary dismissal by S.J. Coetzee, the historian of bodily waste, of the second journey undertaken by Jacobus Coetzee as member of Captain Hop's military expedition, during which he exacts revenge on his servants and during which a number of atrocities

---

[3]   For more extended analyses, see Haarhoff (1991) and Attwell (1993).

take place, such as the rape of children.

The events narrated in the first part of "The Narrative of Jacobus Coetzee," such as the rape referred to above, as well as the murder of a number of people, which the "Afterword" (placed within the new context formed by composition of "The Narrative of Jacobus Coetzee") dismisses as "irrelevant" and "dallying by the wayside" (128), abound in detail, making it seem to be the most complete account of what 'actually' happened. The completeness of this first part of "The Narrative of Jacobus Coetzee", as historical record, extends to the thoughts and world-view of the 'historical' personage, Jacobus Coetzee, as he himself unreservedly and 'innocently' reiterates these facts in the form of a variety of coarse prejudices. The irony here is that this 'complete' record is a fiction and could only have been created as such.

The fictive, textual nature of this first part of "The Narrative of Jacobus Coetzee" is further foregrounded by the nature of the narrator, Coetzee himself. Despite being a rough frontiersman, the language he mouths is a mixture of lyricism, logical argument and metaphysical discourse, with clear echoes from philosophical treatises, such as that of Hegel, which appeared after Jacobus's lifetime. In addition to emphasising the textuality of historical writing, the narrative in this way foregrounds another facet of historiography that has now become an accepted view amongst philosophers of history, namely that historiography is absolutely dependent on anachronism. The past cannot be reconstructed without the use of contemporaneous discursive categories. "The Narrative of Jacobus Coetzee" thus makes it abundantly clear that history cannot do without fiction.

In *On the Contrary* the manner in which the integrity of the historical record is compromised by the interventions of historical personages, accident and other causes is foregrounded in a similar manner. The main character, Estienne Barbier, witnesses the deliberate falsification of the historical record on at least two occasions, first when he is replaced by Otto Mentzel as the scribe of an expedition to the interior because he insists on recording the murder of a Khoi serf (37-39), the second when court documents are copied before being sent to higher authorities (204-206). The implication of such representation is the same as in "The Narrative of Jacobus Coetzee," namely that the 'correct' version of the past is lost in 'history' and can only be found through fictional reconstruction.

Estienne's own status as recorder and as witness is however also presented as highly suspect, his perception decisively coloured by an active imagination and by intense identification with figures from fiction, such as Cervantes' Don La Mancha. This is attested to by his fanciful descriptions of African animals (23-26), his sightings of (and shooting of) a unicorn (28-29) and a hippogriph (30), his witnessing the birth of a woman from an egg (109-110), amongst others. The construction of the text in *On the Contrary* facilitates such a mixing of 'fact' and fancy, because the boundaries between factual and fanciful representations are not clearly 'marked' in the text.

As is the case in "The Narrative of Jacobus Coetzee" anachronism is foregrounded clearly in *On the Contrary*. Estienne is accompanied by Jeanne D'Arc on his adventures in the Cape and at a certain point he uses words spoken by Hanan Mikhail-Ashrawi of the PLO (358). In *On the Contrary* the imagination is shown to play a definitive role in the shaping of the historical record, and consequently with regard to any attempt at reconstruction of the past. Estienne is presented as a compulsive liar and vagabond, cheating on his parents (45), the women in his life and the authorities. Fact and fantasy commingle freely in his thoughts and speech as attested to the various accounts he gives of a number of events, such as his arrival at the Cape (5-6, 62, 132-134), his confrontation with Lieutenant Alleman (145-146, 147), his dealings with the slave-woman, Rosette (53-56, 60-61).

The power of an author or historiographer—and writing—is graphically demonstrated in a similar manner in "The Narrative of Jacobus Coetzee" by way of the alternative versions given of the death of Klawer, the only servant who decided to accompany Jacobus Coetzee on his trip back to the Cape (99-100, 100-101). Such alternative versions clearly demonstrate the power of the one with the capacity to speak, write, record—what is written becomes reality.

5. Literature and the TRC

The foregoing analysis serves not only to emphasise the difference between an empirically based process such as the TRC and an imaginatively based one in the case of literature, but is an essential part of the attempt made in this study to delineate the special, privileged role played by literature with regards to dealing with the past.

Literary critical attention to poststructurally inclined use of historical material in literary texts has largely remained concentrated on the relation between literature and historiography, the postmodernist literary texts analysed as participants and allies of the poststructuralist assault on traditional historiography. The attack on traditional historiography has been presented as in the service of a vague 'freedom,' as resistance to the 'master-narratives' on which traditional historiography and modernist thought in general were dependent.

The simplistic transferral of such an approach to the comparison in this paper between the South African TRC and literary attempts to deal with the past would be an empty and futile exercise, the TRC unavoidably being placed in the position of traditional historiography. Such a transferral would be an example of asking the wrong or inapt question, of confusing dimensions or categories. The 'failure' of the comparison on this point should rather form the basis of a two-pronged analysis where the two terms, the 'TRC' and 'literature,' are so placed that a mutually-reinforcing 'dialogue' is set up between the two terms.

With regard to literature, the comparison provides an opportunity to determine what is (substantively) unique about literature's orientation to the past. The question being addressed in this sense has to do with how literature enables a view (and experience) of the past not easily enabled elsewhere. In this instance the TRC serves as a 'background' against which the unique value of literature can stand out clearer. At the same time, such an approach provides the means whereby an essential critique of the TRC can be carried out. In this instance literature forms the background, foregrounding some of the shortcomings of the TRC, which might not be visible due to the hegemonic discourse of which it forms part. The approach thus has two objectives, showing first of all that literature remains the repository of the ideal of justice, and secondly providing a corrective to any hubris which might be engendered by a process such as the TRC.

6. The TRC and its limitations

The problems which a process such as the TRC are saddled with can be traced to the process through which it was constituted. This has placed definite limits on the workings of the commission, on the terms and meanings it can manipulate, and on the meaning(s) that 'outside' observers allocate to it. The constitution of the South African TRC has first of all been clearly marked by a process of negotiation in which the emphasis fell on reconciliation, rather than retribution. The result of this process has been a theologically tinted juridical apparatus. The eventual framework seems to have been further influenced by psychoanalytic and medical ideas about emotional and social 'health.'

The nature of the objective to be reached by the commission, the manner in which this seems to have been conceived and how this impacts in a formative manner on the working of the commission, is a bit more problematic. The operative perspective here, to repeat once again, is that of the 'bystander.' One way in which the final objective of the commission has been presented is that of "healing the nation." The placing of the activities of the TRC within the ambit of a problematic term such as the South African 'nation' unavoidably sets up an association between itself and the hegemonic social and cultural 'project' which the ANC launched on gaining control of the South African political process, namely 'nation-building.'[4] The placement of the TRC's activities within the frame of nation-building shapes the form of the remembrance and reconciliation that the commission can activate. The memory it aims at will clearly have to be of a unitary ('national') nature.

One of the most important implications which the linking of the commission to the hegemonic striving for 'national' unity has is that it makes the TRC vulnerable to being subsumed (or of being perceived to be) under the ANC's political policy structure, resulting in the blurring of the boundary between the TRC and the ANC government.

Basing itself wholeheartedly on the hegemonic desire for a unitary 'nation' has a number of further important implications. The association

---

4   An early attempt to show just how problematic a discourse of 'nation-building' will be in South Africa, is that of Degenaar (1991).

between the TRC and the ANC causes the terms used by the TRC to lose their original, 'neutral,' morally correct meaning and the commission to be perceived as part of an 'apparatus' in the ideological, political and cultural struggle of one part of the South African society. A second important implication that the objective of the TRC carries, is that it has seriously limited its sensitivity for heterogeneity in the material it has to deal with. The South African TRC's allegiance to the hegemonic 'nationalist' project has actually caused it to be incapable of entertaining a conception of historical memory which is *not* unitary. Unique (minority) perspectives on the past will 'naturally' and 'logically' be experienced by the commission as unsurmountable obstacles.

The manner in which the TRC has approached its objective thus makes difficult, if not impossible, a transcendence of the structures of the past, actually leading to a semantic enrichment of the conceptual structures by which the past is apprehended. The process could actually intensify the white/black dichotomy in the society with its associated dichotomies such as that between oppressor and oppressed. The TRC overlays these dichotomies with theological and medical dichotomies such as that between the guilty and the innocent, the sick and the healthy. As a vehicle for giving shape to the 'conscience of humankind' a process such as the TRC is bound to fail, or at the least to be extremely problematic and controversial.

The situation with regard to literature is much less clear, literary expression being by nature indirect and tangential. As will hopefully be evident from the following interpretation of one of the literary texts referred to earlier in this paper, namely *On the Contrary* by André P. Brink, it is precisely in its 'indeterminateness' that the strength of literary expression lies.

7. Literature as repository of conscience

On the Contrary is structured around a central conceit, namely the search of the main character, Estienne Barbier, for a slave woman, Rosette, whom he first mistreated and then helped to escape, placing himself in peril. In the course of the novel Estienne's mistreatment of Rosette is associated with other injustices which include his treatment of women (74, 196-197, 319-320), his willing participation in an extended cattle raid undertaken by colonists on the Khoi in the Cape hinterland and an atrocity during which defenceless women and children are killed (315-316). As the novel progresses Estienne's sense of guilt and responsibility increases, parallel to an intensification of a need for forgiveness and absolution.

The position he finally finds himself in is doubly contradictory: on the one hand he has placed himself in opposition to Cape officialdom by leading a revolt of colonists against the corrupt rulers of the Cape, and on the other he has placed himself in opposition to the indigenous population by participating in atrocities against them. His relation to the slave woman, Rosette, is similarly contradictory: he first misuses her and then helps her.

The third part of the novel is devoted to Estienne's attempt to deal with the legacy of his actions. This process can however only take place on an imaginary level because he is imprisoned. In the novel Estienne's search for absolution is presented in the form of a 'journey,' the third and final undertaken by him to the 'hinterland' (350). On this journey Estienne first encounters the relations and spirits of the Khoi people wronged by him, eventually reaching Rosette where she is telling tales in the interior of a mountain. Using the words of a representative of the PLO he beseeches the people he has wronged to forgive him and to strive for peace (358).

The manner in which a character's attempt to deal with his past is presented in *On the Contrary* is thus roughly similar to the structure of the process envisaged and instituted by the TRC. The character first commits unjust deeds against fellow humans, realises his guilt, then confesses and asks for forgiveness, with the objective being absolution.

It is however not enough to take these expressions of guilt and remorse at face value. Literary expression forces one to complement attention to thematic expression with analysis of the *form* in which thematic expression takes place. When this is done in the case of *On the Contrary* the real difference between literary expression and a process such as the TRC becomes very clear. It is also precisely at this point that the real strength and value of aesthetic expression with regard to dealing with historical trauma becomes apparent.

In the case of *On the Contrary* the main thrust of the formal frame in which thematic expression is placed is to radically undermine the thematic level. Estienne's 'approach to Rosette,' as well as his apology to the Khoi, are framed by the words with which the novel opens and which are repeated a number of times:

> I am dead: you cannot read: this will (therefore) not have been a letter (3; see also 147-148, 183, 349-350, 370-371).

Estienne, as character in *On the Contrary*, utters these words from an extremely marginalised position: he is cut off from all human contact, has been cast out by his group, he is locked up in complete darkness in the Donker Gat, a cell in the Castle in Cape Town used for solitary confinement. He also has no paper, and no pen to write with. The letter that he writes, which forms the substance of the novel, is thus an 'impossible' letter. He is nothing more than a figment of imagination—his own and others'—as he himself realises at certain points in the novel (183, 349).

This framing of the narrative in *On the Contrary* has a number of important implications. First of all, these words foreground the fabricated, artificial, *textual* nature of the representation in the novel. Because the recording and recalling of the past forms part of the material out of which the novel is constructed, the status of historiography is simultaneously implicated and affected. History becomes nothing more than a narrative, of the same order as the novel, as subject to the wages of the imagination and emotion.

More importantly, however, the words framing the events narrated in the novel imply a peculiar world, an 'alternate universe'—a reality in which 'normal' causality, order and structures are apparently not necessarily valid and can be transgressed with impunity, and transcended. This poststructural-like positioning of the process of dealing with the past shifts the whole exercise onto a virtual or simulated plane. Anything is possible in this universe. Literary expression on this plane is a form of conceptual experimentation through which alternate realities not available to ordinary, pragmatic thought can be created by the use of various techniques such as anachrony, hyperbole, fantasy, paradox, etc.

In the case of the subject of this paper—the 'conscience of humankind'—the most important achievement of such an orientation is that it makes possible a universe in which diametrically opposed perspectives can be contained within the same conceptual or expressive frame. Expression can first of all represent the claims of 'victims' through the representation of injustice, in certain cases in hyperbolic form. Where dependable records of such injustice are not available, literary expression serves the cause of reconstruction and 'remembrance,' serving the cause of the 'victims.'

At the same time this universe makes it possible for Estienne, as 'virtual' representative of white South Africa (or the 'oppressor') to simultaneously confess and apologise for injustices committed in the past and to have this confession simultaneously radically relativised. The resultant expression has something of the following form: "if these unjust things really did happen, I will definitely confess and apologise" or "even though we cannot be sure what actually happened, here is my apology anyway."

It is thus a universe in which the tension between the two 'sides' represented by accusation and denial on the one side and confession and reconciliation on the other can be maintained without privileging either. Both are equally 'compromised' in the process: the 'accused' by being confronted by the 'grossness' of deeds committed; the 'victim(s)' by being confronted with an injunction to consider the possibility that the representations of injustice are necessarily constructed, artificial and therefore subject to manipulation and distortion.

Literary expression can thus enable a gesture in which conflicting perspectives and their associated communities are given simultaneous expression, as such serving as an ideal vehicle to maintain the integrity of conflicting appellations to the conscience. Such maintenance of tension is necessary—especially in heterogenous societies—to prevent the 'conscience of humankind' from becoming a one-dimensional political tool in the hands of one group of people, wittingly or unwittingly fashioned (once again) into part of an apparatus of oppression, to the impoverishment of us all.

Philip John
University of Transkei

Bibliography

Attwell, David. 1993. *J.M. Coetzee. South Africa and the Politics of Writing.* Cape Town: David Philip.

Brink, André P. 1993. *On the Contrary. Being the Life of a Famous Rebel, Soldier, Traveller, Explorer, Reader, Builder, Scribe, Latinist, Lover and Liar.* London: Secker and Warburg. (translated from the Afrikaans *Inteendeel* by the author).

Coetzee, J.M. 1974. *Dusklands.* Johannesburg: Ravan.

Degenaar, Johan. 1991. "Nations and Nationalism. The Myth of a South African Nation." *IDASA Occasional Papers* 40.

Drewe, Robert. 1976. *The Savage Crows.* Sydney: Collins.

Goldie, Terry. 1985. "The Necessity of Nobility: Indigenous Peoples in Canadian and Australian Literature." *The Journal of Commonwealth Literature* 20(1): 131-147.

Haarhoff, Dorian.1991. *The Wild South-West. Frontier Myths and Metaphors in Literature Set in Namibia, 1760-1988.* Johannesburg: Wits University Press.

Hutcheon, Linda. 1988. *A Poetics of Postmodernism. History, Theory, Fiction.* London: Routledge.

JanMohamed, Abdul R. and David Lloyd. 1990. *The Nature and Context of Minority Discourse.* Oxford: Oxford University Press.

Leggo, Carl. 1990. "Who Speaks for Extinct Nations? The Beothuk and Narrative Voice." *Literator* 16(1): 31-50.

Loomba, Ania. 1991. "Overworlding the Third World." *Oxford Literary Review* 13: 164-192.

Rosenfeld, Alvin H. 1980. *A Double Dying. Reflections on Holocaust Literature.* Bloomington: Indiana University Press.

Slemon, Stephen. 1987. "Monuments of Empire: Allegory/Counter-Discourse/Post-Colonial Writing." *Kunapipi* 9(3): 1-16.

Young, James E. 1988. *Writing and Rewriting the Holocaust. Narrative and the Consequences of Interpretation.* Bloomington: Indiana University Press.

Theatre and the Struggle of Memory Against Forgetting in Latin America and South Africa

Introduction

The title of this paper echoes Milan Kundera's oft-quoted lines "the struggle of man against power is the struggle of memory against forgetting" (Kundera 1982: 3). However, a few pages later the same author writes "... ultimately everyone lets everything be forgotten" (7). The tension between remembrance and oblivion, between acknowledging the past and burying it, is particularly taut in those societies which have emerged from authoritarian regimes, characterized by brutal oppression and gross human rights abuse, into a democratic dispensation.

Among the nations in the late twentieth century which have undergone or are still in the process of experiencing radical transition, post-dictatorship Argentina and Chile and post-apartheid South Africa offer examples of different ways in which the recovery of a previously silenced history has taken place. The official truth commissions set up in each of these three countries have investigated past atrocities with varying degrees of openness. The results of the findings have ranged from virtually complete amnesty for the perpetrators to partial justice being served.[1]

On the government level the truth commission reports, imperfect and incomplete though they may be, constitute the official record of past injustices. Are they sufficient to enable society as a whole to come to terms with its traumatic past and to begin the process of healing? What other kinds of writing have a role in this process?

As we know, any textual recovery of extreme events such as genocide, torture and cruel forms of execution carries with it a concern that the reality might not remain irreducible, stable and inalterable beyond the discourse through which it is brought to speech. The literary and in particular the dramatic representation of atrocity is even more subject to reservations about transgression of the 'limits of representation'.[2]

The present study compares plays which focus on the practice of torture of political prisoners. In addition to the general disquiet about the literary representation of this topic—that an authorial voice can represent it in such a way as to evade, neutralize, trivialize or even conceal it—the stage portrayal of torture can veer close to titillation or even pornography. Furthermore, the relationship between victimizer and victim can be resolved too conveniently by a playwright in the quest for aesthetic satisfaction or catharsis. The fictional stories of these individuals can deflect rather than focus attention on the realities of torture, death and disappearance.

With reference to the actual staging of a play, there are problems of a technical and formal nature which should be borne in mind. How is

---

[1] The bibliography on these issues is vast and includes the reports of the commissions in Argentina—*Nunca más* (Never again): *The report of the Argentine National Commission on the Disappeared*. 1986. New York: Farrar, Straus & Giroux—and Chile—*Report of the Chilean National Commission on Truth and Reconciliation*. 1993. Notre Dame: Centre for Civil and Human Rights. The final report on the South African Truth and Reconciliation Commission is expected at the end of 1997. The following South African publications contain useful references about transition in the societies mentioned in this study: *Constitutional Transition. Latin American and Iberian experiences: Relevance for South Africa*. 1993. Pretoria: University of South Africa; *The healing of a nation?* 1995. (Alex Boraine and Janet Levy, eds) Cape Town: Justice in Transition.

[2] A conference in the USA in 1992 on the limits of representation in relation to the Holocaust informs these abbreviated notes. See below Saul Friedlander, Berel Lang and Hayden White in *Probing the limits of representation*. Works by Langer, Todorov and Wiesel were also consulted (see below).

Literature as Cultural Memory

torture to be enacted before a contemporary audience well acquainted with realistic television and film depictions of physical violence? How can the past be inscribed in the present tense of a stage performance without resorting to story-telling devices more appropriate to the narrative genre?

The three plays under discussion are presented in relation to the historical moment of their writing and performance: during the hearings of a truth commission, just after a commission had concluded its findings and seven years afterwards.

André Brink's Die Jogger

Written and staged in 1997 during the public hearings of South Africa's Truth and Reconciliation Commission, André Brink's Die Jogger tells the story of Kilian, a colonel in the apartheid regime's security police who had tortured a black African political dissident and subsequently given false evidence which led to the innocent victim's execution.

The first two scenes of Die Jogger provide the causal link between the colonel's past and present. In scene one Kilian interrogates Vusi, the black prisoner, and carries out his threat to cut off his tongue. This representation of torture contains the signs of both its past reality and continuing recurrence as a dream: still photographs flicker as a backdrop against which the torture takes on a shadowy non-realistic appearance. As the lights dim to black, only a piercing scream can be heard. The cry of the tortured becomes that of the torturer as the next scene reveals Kilian awaking from his nightmare in a psychiatric hospital. The opening scenes suggest that Kilian has been driven mad by guilt over his past evil deed: the monster has turned madman. The ghost of Vusi is present, seen only by Kilian, as the mute victim and accuser. However, the colonel rails and thrashes against him in self-defence. This denial of culpability and responsibility for his past actions now negates the earlier assumption that Kilian's dementia arose from guilt.

Does the play subvert its first plot formation only to project another in which Kilian is brought to confront the truth, deal with its consequences and perhaps be redeemed by an expression of remorse? Through a series of enacted flashbacks in which the colonel's private and professional life is exposed and juxtaposed, the reason for scapegoating Vusi becomes clear: someone had to be found on whom to blame a bomb attack on a building. In the same scene in which Kilian admits to Vusi that he knew him to be innocent, the black man regains his speech and recounts the horrors leading to his execution. However, this intersection with a reality both outside the psychiatric ward and the dramatic world itself—the previously silenced can now speak and be heard in the truth commission—has an uneasy parallel in the final confession and expression of remorse uttered by Kilian. Speaking to his former Minister who no longer exists on a telephone that does not work, about his evil actions, all proof of which has been removed, Kilian ends up a pathetic deranged figure. No one is there to listen to him. The play's ending has been seen by some critics as too reliant on the portrayal of guilt, and Kilian's descent into madness could provide an audience with the dubious satisfaction of a just punishment. The final appearance of the 'jogger'—a metadramatic figure seen running across the stage as a signal of scene changes—would seem to confirm a Sisyphus-like connection to Kilian's perpetual self-castigation for his crimes.

Although the excessive individualization of Kilian may provide closure and thus deflect an audience's attention away from the implications of a broader historical reality, that reality does inhere in *Die Jogger* in what one might call Brink's critique of the legacy of apartheid: its racial and cultural divisiveness and patriarchy. Kilian is an indexical figure to those tenets and his derangement is in no small part due to his sense of betrayal at their collapse. However, it is the relationship between Kilian and Noni, his black nurse, that provokes questions about the past and its consequences in an unstable present, both within and outside the dramatic world. Their interaction has all the hallmarks of the South African racial and cultural divide: he speaks to her in Afrikaans, she to him in English; though dependent on her he treats her as his inferior, while she tolerates this tradition only so far as her professional behaviour allows; they tell each other about past experiences, but, since they do not listen to one another, only the audience knows how much they share. In the final scene Kilian cannot see his reflection in a mirror. Noni recognises what that means because she can refer it to a past experience of her own when she felt divorced from reality. A subsequent explanation which led her to recover that memory was, as she states, "hell to live with" (44). It is this knowledge and awareness which makes Noni's final remark to Kilian a suitably unsentimental statement of fact: "I'm here. We're both here" (82).

In *Die Jogger* both the crime of apartheid as a system as well as the atrocities that were committed in its name are inscribed in the play's fictional world. Despite the fact that Kilian's descent into madness provides a certain distancing from the realities that the former architects, servants and supporters of apartheid face in South Africa today, the story of Noni as told by herself in the play, and the matter-of-fact way she interacts with her patient point to the important and difficult task that all South Africans must share in recuperating memory and rebuilding their lives, without knowing what the outcome will be.

Ariel Dorfman's *La muerte y la doncella*

André Brink's play intersects with the revelations of victims and victimizers that, in 1997, are still emerging from the South African truth commission and amnesty hearings. In *La muerte y la doncella* (Death and the Maiden), by Ariel Dorfman, the characters face the dilemmas of living with the consequences of a completed truth commission. The play was written in 1991, one year after the restoration of democracy and just after the Chilean truth and reconciliation commission had published its report on the atrocities perpetrated during the Pinochet regime. In that document the identities of the victimizers were left undisclosed. Cases of torture which did not end in death or disappearance were also omitted from the investigation. The question of how such victims and their torturers would coexist in the new democracy and how they might respond to a chance meeting with one another constitute the conflict of *La muerte y la doncella*.

In the play Paulina, in her home, comes face to face with Roberto, the man whom she believes was the state doctor who tortured and raped her fifteen years before, when she was a political detainee. Roberto vehemently denies this accusation, knowing that Paulina can never positively identify him. He enlists the help of Gerardo, Paulina's husband and a lawyer for the truth commission, to fabricate a so-called false confession in order to appease Paulina and extricate both men from their situation as her captives. Paulina, victim turned victimizer, has tied Roberto to a chair and threatens to shoot him and her husband if she is not given the opportunity to exact the justice she has been denied: that her torturer confess his guilt and express remorse.

Each character is an index to a complex web of dilemmas that hover between two extremes: victim and victimizer; truth and deceit; justice and reconciliation. The audience is not kept at one remove from these dilemmas. At a crucial moment in the unfolding drama, when Paulina finally confronts Roberto with the truth of his supposedly false confession and is undecided about whether to kill him or set him free, a mirror descends on stage to reflect the faces of the playgoers. What is asked of the public here? To identify Roberto as guilty or innocent? To struggle with competing demands for justice or impunity?

The answers to those questions may not lie exclusively within the text of *La muerte y la doncella*, nor even in a particular production of the play, but rather in where it is performed. In New York the 1992 Broadway production was billed as a 'political thriller' and reviewed as "escapist entertainment about political torture" (Rich 1992: B1). This suggests that the thriller genre in which Dorfman has encased the story of his characters can lead to a trivialization of the facts of atrocity and their consequences. It can also allow for an actor to play Roberto as innocent, which is how Robert Whitehead, the South African actor in the 1992 Johannesburg production of the play, portrayed him.[3] The public's reception of the play in different countries is perhaps the best barometer of whether or not "factuality invades the fiction" (Ibsch 1993: 188) and transforms the 'whodunit' into the more unsettling drama of 'what happens when they get away with it': the closer the truth of human rights violations is to the real world of the public the more they shy away from seeing this play and dealing with the dilemmas it projects.[4]

In addition to the mirror segment, the confession statement and the final concert scene also lead to self-questioning. A tape recorder is the

---

[3]   Confirmed in a private interview at the Market Theatre in September 1994.

[4]   For example, productions in Chile, according to the author himself (Dorfman 1992: 97) and in South Africa, from sources at the Market Theatre, Johannesburg, were not commercial successes in comparison with the reported profitable runs on New York and London stages.

vehicle for both Paulina's statement regarding her torture and rape and Roberto's supposedly 'false' confession. The victim's voice is overlapped by that of the victimizer to the accompaniment of Schubert's "Death and the Maiden". Here attention is drawn not to who is telling the truth but to what constitutes human betrayal. The consequences of such betrayal converge in the last scene of the play, a concert hall performance of "Death and the Maiden" attended by Paulina and Gerardo who seek to recover what this music had once meant to them. However, Roberto, or his spectre, appears at the same concert, serving as a stark reminder to Paulina that this musical piece will always be a sign of past as well as present betrayal. The play leaves its characters and its audience struggling with the questions of how to cope with compromise—Paulina's own and the nation's in letting the guilty go free—and how to repair lives broken by a system of which they were all a part.

Eduardo Pavlovsky's *Paso de dos*

Eduardo Pavlovsky's play *Paso de dos* (Pas de deux) was first staged in Buenos Aires in 1990, seven years after the restoration of democracy in Argentina, a country which had demanded justice by trying and sentencing those ultimately responsible for the abduction, torture and disappearance of thousands of Argentineans during the 'Dirty War'. However, the actual torturers and executioners—lower ranking officers—were neither named nor charged for their offences. In 1989 President Carlos Menem granted the first of his two official pardons which ultimately freed and publicly forgave the military juntas "for all past crimes" (Smulovitz 1995:63). For many Argentineans those pardons signalled that the time had come to forget the past while for others they were a sign that the reinstated armed forces could repeat history.

Paso de dos sees the confrontation of victim and victimizer as they grapple with their past in order separately to understand it and to own it in the present. As the play opens, the victimizer, simply called El (He), describes and acts out a series of confused gestures. While admitting he cannot provide any rationale for his past or present actions, he accepts full responsibility for them but denies feeling any sense of guilt. The strongly suggested identification of El with the unnamed agents of torture in Argentina's 'Dirty War' is both a departure point and a frame for the ensuing interplay with Ella (She), the unnamed victim. The Ella character is split into two: the on-stage figure acts out the relationship wordlessly while her voice is carried by her off-stage counterpart who is seated among the spectators, but at one remove from them. The verbal interaction between El and Ella inscribes courtroom-like procedures: incisive questions interspersed with monologues which alternate between self-revelation and self-justification. Initially it is Ella who wants to know if it was political conviction that brought them together. However, the political is quickly replaced in El by his need to possess Ella, sexually, mentally and emotionally. His dependence on her reaches its extreme in the final sequence as he begs her to name him, to grant him the individual recognition he brutally craves and believes only she can bestow on him. Ella, in going over her past relationship with El, never lets him lose sight of the strength of her convictions. Although she refers to the physical intensity of their sexual encounters, and even admits to feeling uncertain as well as terrified about sexual complicity on her part, she returns to the political, reminding him of his role as interrogator and torturer. She has the last words of the playtext and, accusing El of being a non-entity just like all the other torturers, she condemns him to the imprisonment of her silence by refusing to name him.

Does this condemnatory silence 'speak' for the thousands like Ella who were 'disappeared' and made invisible by the military state? On the level of the discourse between El and Ella it is clear that she has taken control of history and her story. However, the role of the on-stage Ella renders this interpretation problematic. From the beginning her physical appearance is that of a woman tortured to the point of near death. However, in a grotesque parody of the play's title, she alternately seduces and resists her torturer. The sexual encounters are graphically portrayed, as is her death by strangulation. As her body sinks into a pool of mud and disappears, El picks up his military jacket and stands to attention. This is the final portrait of the victimizer: unrepentant but also unreleased from his past. What of the visual image that is projected by the on-stage victim? Has Pavlovsky transgressed in making torture and strangulation a pornographic display in which the spectator is participatory voyeur, and hence also accomplice, in defiling the woman's body?

Although a particular production or a particular audience can radically transform a playtext, a 'reading' of *Paso de dos* would mitigate strongly against seeing it as nothing more than the eroticised torture of the stereotypical woman victim. In keeping with virtually all of Pavlovsky's dramatic works, the ending subverts its prior emplotment, obliging the reader/spectator to resemanticise what has gone before. In the case of *Paso de dos*, there is a return to the torturer's initial self-presentation, now more redolent with the uncomfortable ambiguities caused by his inability to dominate his past. There is also the added realization that the speaking Ella is a voice from beyond death: witness *of* the past, as represented by the on-stage Ella, and at the same time witness *to* the present, as the reembodied voice from that past. The 'silence' to which she condemns her torturer is thus both hers and that of the spectator/reader, but it is not the silence of non-accusation or oblivion, rather that of a silent scream of memory that lies always between victimizer and victim, one that, as the noted Argentine critic Osvaldo Pellettieri has remarked, " in Argentina is a constant and current reality" (Pellettieri 1994: 72).

Concluding remarks

In these plays the referent has been a constant: the practice of torture as a sign of a particularly brutal form of state control, an underlying secret, invisible reality. Each of the playwrights has sought to prevent that past reality from becoming invisible: a fading, abstracted or even an avoided memory. In doing so, they both engage and disengage audiences in relation to the fiction of their characters and their stories. The more the reader/spectator is brought to an awareness of the outside reality intersecting the fiction, of its defictionalizing process, the more he/she becomes involved in a process of questioning: how are victimizers empowered, given the moral purpose to identify, castigate and eliminate victims, how have I been a witness to and therefore perhaps complicit in this, what happens now? The reach and depth of such examination will depend on an audience's perception of its own physical and moral proximity to that reality. However, the plays themselves point to the different ways in which both the playreader and playgoer are led to pertinent interrogations.

In *Paso de dos* the on-stage confrontation between a victim and victimizer of Argentina's 'Dirty War' is a potently concrete attempt to keep visibly and even gruesomely intact what memory can turn into an abstraction. The disappeared victim's rewitnessing her past involves the audience in this visceral revisitation, while at the same time her final words of condemning silence directed at the torturer become those of the public. This is not a triumphant silence over the torturer, who remains unanswerable and unrepentant, but rather one that lies between him and his victim, a metaphor for the uneasy relationship between Argentina's past and present . In Dorfman's *La muerte y la doncella*, the similarly disturbing relationship between Chile's survivors of the past is transformed into the dilemma which arises out of a chance meeting of victimizer and victim. What was publicly denied to both—confession and forgiveness—becomes a dramatized but private truth commission in the play. However, the results of that encounter project back into the Chilean reality of 1991: when Paulina releases Roberto she engages in the politics of compromise and suffers the consequences of living among those whose betrayal of her remains unacknowledged.

In these two Latin American plays the victimizers retain the power to suppress the truth of torture. Yet there is a subversion of this power in the sense that these works open up the truth and place responsibility for it in the mind of the reader/spectator. In the South African play, the victimizer is brought to an admission of his role as an agent of terror, a confession which, as it remains in the realm of the private, leads only to self-annihilation. In *Die Jogger* the victimizer is portrayed as an ordinary human being given the capacity to perpetrate evil. However, it is his evil action that is judged and the ensuing self-punishment allows for a cathartic resolution which the play seeks to deflect by means of another intersecting story. Brink places the atrocity of the victimizer within the context of the evil of apartheid via the relationship between the white torturer and his black care-giver, a relationship which carries the legacy of the past into a changing present.

Taken as a group, the plays in this study show that the reality of human atrocity for political ends does not destroy the possibility of its aestheticization, but rather that the literary dramatic representation of atrocity constitutes an important form of transmission, of entering into the consciousness of the public. In 'writing back'—in seeking to engage with the past horrors of their compatriots, both those who perpetrated them as well as those who suffered them—the three playwrights under discussion have further demonstrated that they also 'write to the future', helping to heal their nations and to rebuild broken lives and communities.

Cathy Maree
UNISA, Pretoria

Bibliography

Albuquerque, Severino J. 1991. *Violent acts. A study of contemporary Latin American theatre.* Detroit: Wayne State University Press.

Bixler, Jacqueline E. 1994. Signs of absence in Pavlovsky's "teatro de la memoria". *Latin American Theatre Review* 28(1): 17-30

Brink, André. 1997. *Die jogger.* Kaapstad: Human & Rousseau.

Dorfman, Ariel. 1992. *La muerte y la doncella.* Buenos Aires: Ediciones de la Flor.

Feitlowitz, Marguerite. 1991. A dance of death: Eduardo Pavlovsky's *Paso de dos. The Drama Review,* 35(2): 60-73.

Friedlander, Saul. 1992. Introduction. In: *Probing the limits of representation.* Cambridge: Harvard University Press: 1-21.

Ibsch, Elrud. 1993. Fact and fiction in postmodernist writing. *Journal of Literary Studies,* 9(2): 185-193.

Kundera, Milan. 1982. *The book of laughter and forgetting.* London: Faber and Faber.

Lang, Berel. 1992. The representation of limits. In: Saul Friedlander (ed), *Probing the limits of representation.* Cambridge: Harvard University Press: 300-317.

————. 1990. *Act and idea in the Nazi genocide.* Chicago: The University of Chicago Press.

Langer, Lawrence. 1990. Fictional facts and factual fictions: History in Holocaust literature. In: Randolf L. Braham (ed), *Reflections of the Holocaust in art and literature.* Boulder: Social Science Monographs and New York: The Csengeri Institute for Holocaust Studies: 117-129.

Pavlovsky, Eduardo. 1990. *Paso de dos.* Buenos Aires: Ediciones Ayllu.

Pellettieri, Osvaldo. 1994. *Paso de dos* de Eduardo Pavlovsky: Un texto dramático remanente y una puesta eficaz. In *Teatro argentino contemporáneo (1980-1990).* Buenos Aires: Editorial Galerna: 63-72.

Rich, Frank. 1992. Police-state crimes and punishment. *New York Times:* March 18, p. B1.

Scarry, Elaine. 1985. *The body in pain.* New York: Oxford University Press.

Smulovitz, Catalina. 1995. Commissions of truth and reconciliation: Argentina. In: A Boraine & J Levy, eds., *The healing of a nation?* Cape Town: Justice in Transition.

Snyman, Wilhelm. 1997. Brinks' topical drama panders to guilt. *The Cape Times:* March 1 (Independent Online: www.2inc.co.za/Archives 9703/1Mar/jog.html)

Taylor, Diane. 1991. *Theatre in crisis: Drama and politics in Latin America.* Lexington: The University Press of Kentucky.

Wiesel, Elie. 1977. The Holocaust as literary inspiration. In: *Dimensions of the Holocaust.* Evanston, Ill: Northwestern University Press.

White, Hayden. 1992. Historical emplotment and the problem of truth. In: Saul Friedlander (ed), *Probing the limits of representation.* Cambridge: Harvard University Press: 37-53.

————. 1987. *The content of the form: Narrative discourse and historical representation.* Baltimore: Johns Hopkins University Press.

Literature as Cultural Memory

Bulldozer: the Edifices of the Social Engineering of Group Areas Apartheid in South African Afrikaans Literature

Those of you who have travelled to South Africa and visited Cape Town, will recall that on the gentle slopes at the foot of Table Mountain in the heart of the city a vast area of open land lies waste. Prime, prime real estate.

And if you had questioned any Capetonian about the fact that this prime city area has not been developed, he or she would probably have told you: that was District Six. The fact that this site was never re-developed after the vibrant community who had lived there for centuries were bulldozed onto the Cape Flats into Council housing and oblivion by Group Areas engineers, remained the conscience of the people: Lest we forget.

Adam Small, an Afrikaans author whose texts will dominate this excursion into the past, writes movingly about the destruction of District Six in the introduction to a collection of superb black and white and sepia photographs by Jansje Wissema simply titled *District Six*.

> Of course the District was a *time*, too: a place and time. A specific context of the life that we call human [before] shortly afterwards the bulldozers and other demolition machines were executing their terrible mission. [...] The constructions of brick and mortar which were the District

have fallen. The literal edifices have crashed down. (Small
1986: 5, 6, 7)

In this paper I shall be looking, albeit in a cursory fashion, at what
happened to District Six in Afrikaans literature between 1956 and 1976,
identifying the extent to which the bulldozers who wiped out a community
of close to 70,000 people after 1966, leaving a scar that is physically visible
today. But it is a scar that can be removed through cosmetic social and
political surgery...

South African literature, and Afrikaans literature in particular, will
need to retain such a site to ensure that the realities of an evil system
remain alive in the memory of its users. For literature is indeed the
conscience of humankind, when history fades after becoming the expedient
tool of those in power.

Hans Robert Jauss in Volume 2 of his *Toward an Aesthetic of
Reception* (1982: 45) argues that the "gap between literature and history,
between aesthetic and historical knowledge can be bridged when it
[literary history] discovers in the course of 'literary evolution' that
properly socially formative function that belongs to literature as it
competes with other arts and social forces in the emancipation of mankind
from its natural, religious, and social bonds."

It is in this formative function that literature can establish itself as
the conscience of mankind. It manages to do this *not* because it mirrors
society or is representative of it, but because "it must be regarded,"
maintains Sinfield (1983: 8), "as the writer's interpretation of and
intervention in the world as he or she perceived it."

Literature is personal and human. It is able, therefore, to confront
its readers at their weakest moments, unprotected by the cocoon of the
political cliché, the politically correct flavour of the month. When they are
not ensconced within the group, but vulnerable as individuals confronted
with a reality they have not experienced or had hoped to bulldoze to
obscurity. An interesting question is why readers actually tolerate this
assault on their privacy. Is it because we are moved by the way in which
the moral tragedy unfolds and takes shape? A first answer may be that it
is not the immorality as a phenomenon which moves the reader, but the
assault on human dignity.

The euphoric transition from the outcast *apartheid* state to a hoped-for model democracy in South Africa is now a thing of the past. The visible remnants of the old regime are fading; the Truth and Reconciliation Commission hearings are succeeding in their reduction of the dehumanising system to specific atrocities by a number of individuals.

The edifices of *apartheid* are indeed fast disappearing, bulldozed into oblivion by the realities and the demands of change and the greed and corruption that so often characterises new-found power. The racial divide is slowly being replaced by a class divide while those who had little or no power before are gradually calling the shots. When anything fails, *apartheid* is to blame, but the metaphorically bulldozed sites are being developed by new social engineers who care little for the real memory of the people.

Of all the dehumanising aspects of *apartheid* the legislation pertaining to "Group Areas" probably directly affected the lives and quality of life of South Africans more than any other facet of the policy. David Kramer's song "Skipskop" captures the essence of this tragedy happening to someone who has no idea why it is happening. His life, his little shack of security, has been bulldozed. It is as simple as that.

The position of Afrikaans (in which "Skipskop" was written and sung), my mother tongue and the subject I teach, is a peculiar one in respect of both the political and the literary systems. Afrikaans developed from 17th-century Dutch spoken at the Cape, being profoundly influenced by the Malay and Portuguese speaking slaves brought to the Cape in the first part of its white colonial history, and by the contact with the Khoi-speakers. Another important factor was its distance from the centre, British occupation and the linguistic colonisation since 1820, and the corresponding geographical isolation of its speakers. Ironically enough the main impetus towards the formalisation of the new language was provided by the needs of the coloured speakers of Afrikaans, both Christian and Muslim, with the result that Afrikaans as a people's language was never Christian or white.

Although race-based policies were not the prerogative of the Nationalist government, the rise of the race-dominated *apartheid* policies ran parallel with the rise of Afrikanerdom and led to the notion, or rather the conviction, that Afrikaans was the language of oppression.

Apartheid gave rise to the ironic situation that many native speakers turned their back on the language, while, at the same time, many profound literary texts attacking and exposing the evils of the system were written, published and performed in Afrikaans. The irony arises from the fact that the oppressed, too, included Afrikaans-speakers, and that holds true especially for the community known in South Africa as "the coloureds." This group grew out of the slave community, the people belonging to the Khoi and the Griqua and, increasingly, the children from relationships between black and white inhabitants of the colonies and later the Union of South Africa. They were the people predominantly living in the old Cape Province and in the District Sixes of the country, and found themselves not belonging anywhere. The outcast brother or child of the Afrikaner family, being marginalised, humiliated and translocated by *apartheid*.

D.J. Opperman, one of the most important Afrikaans poets, wrote an exquisite poem on this terrible situation brought about by this legislation, called "Draaiboek."

Draaiboek

Kiek badkamer, maar swak belig;
wys seun wat aan 'n tou verwurg.

Eine kleine Nachtmusik — verdof.
Wissel flitstonele, huis en hof:

"Waarom het hy dié nag hom opgehang?
Was daar miskien 'n nooi in die gedrang?"

"Nee, al was my oudste in sy fleur,
het hy hom aan g'n nôi gesteur."

"Soms raak 'n vader en sy seun oorhoop.
Het dié hom dikwels deurgeloop?"

"Nee, 'n ware aanspraak sonder gier —
net graag alleen voor die klavier."

"Mevrou, kan u ons waarlik niks vertel?"
"Ag, Edelagbare, dis God se spel!"

"Maar waarom ... waarom so 'n daad verrig?"
"Sy vel was donker, sy broers s'n lig."

Kiek waar vier kinders vroeg opstaan,
drie na wit en hy na bruin skool gaan.

[Screenplay

Take One. A rope-strung boy above
a bath. Dim light. Dissolve.

Eine kleine Nachtmusik - and fade.
Jump cut: a Court room, a house in shade.

"Why did he hang himself that night?
Was there a girl involved, maybe in plight?"

"No, even though being in his teens
my eldest was not into love scenes."

"Sometimes a father and a son, you know,
have differences which comes to blows?"

"No, he was exemplary, I swear —
maybe obsessed with the piano. There."

"But Madam, can't you help explain?"
"Your Worship, this is God's end-game."

"But why, why resort to suicide?"
"His skin was dark, his brothers' light."

Scenes: breakfast banter at the break of day;
his brothers to their school and he another way.]
(All translations are mine.)

Afrikaans forms a very important part of the South African literary system, and I want to be so bold to say that as a corpus it has produced the most profound texts coming from South Africa. While the English literature produced in South Africa carried the burden of not cutting its ties with the colonial empire, and texts in the black indigenous languages were either aimed at religious conversion or a safe and prescribed school market, Afrikaans writers explored the geographical and demographical extremes of the country. They did this within the parameters of an extended family (Dutch and German), renewing their literary language by utilising movements in other European and English literatures, and creating a vocabulary and a rhythm which were distinctly their own. The writers, generally, refused to be co-opted by the political system, which is why we have a corpus of texts that shall remain to serve as the conscience of humankind. Lest we forget.

While fiction in all genres was produced which gave an account of group areas *apartheid*, the strength of the texts in Afrikaans was due to the fact that the voice spoke in Afrikaans, which was the language of the regime. And the more so when the writers themselves were the victims of the system perpetuated by the family of speakers.

Initially Afrikaans literary production was dominated by "white" writers, but in the 1940's one or two coloured or "brown" voices became more prominent. Towards the end of the Seventies this increased dramatically.

In this paper, however, I shall be concentrating on those texts published between 1956 and 1976 dealing with District Six. These dates are political markers: in 1956 the Nationalist Government manipulated the composition of the Senate to disenfranchise the coloured voters; in 1976 the Soweto uprising by black students against school education in Afrikaans signalled the beginning of a new disposition to the language.

Precisely in the middle of this period, in 1966, District Six was declared a "white" area in terms of the Group Areas Act. District Six never played a meaningful role in the South African English literature, as Richard Rive demonstrates in his article "District Six and its literature" (Rive 1987). But one would assume that, given its essentially Afrikaans character, the District (as it was commonly referred to) would be a highly visible factor. This is, however, not the case and anybody familiar with the Afrikaans literary system will probably find the explanation in the absence of "coloured" writers, and the initial reluctance to paint a picture of the District by those who did publish.

Although not failing to criticise the racial prejudice, the initial coloured voices focussed on the earlier rural existence, contrasting it with the hardships in the city. Some favourite techniques employed include juxta-positioning the rather splendid and opulent life enjoyed by the white "masters" with the squalid existence of the coloured labourers, and illustrating the hypocrisy of white men who are entertained by coloured women only to ignore them the following day.

Very pertinent is the reference to family ties, where the coloured or dark-skinned child or cousin is relegated to the outside, while the crossing of the racial divide by the light-skinned (a process called "try-for-white") is also given prominence. Although this form of social-climbing is frowned upon, it is not completely discouraged. The main concern is the immorality of subsequently ignoring your family when encountering them, often in embarrassing situations.

One of the most important markers in respect of the speaker or narrator in Afrikaans literature is the type of Afrikaans used in the text. There are very clear distinctions between what was reckoned to be Standard Afrikaans and the language used by the coloured community. Initially the use of standard Afrikaans dominated, except where the "dialect" was utilised for comic effect. The first generation of coloured writers (S.V. Petersen, P.J. Philander and Adam Small) took great pride in their use of standard or "correct" Afrikaans.

Later Small in particular reverted to a more extensive use of "Kaaps" ("Cape Afrikaans" as he called it) in order to identify with the community. He illustrated this dramatically in his quite marvellous play *Kanna hy kô hystoe* (Kanna comes home). Kanna, who has emigrated to Canada and missed the whole destruction of District Six, returns for the funeral of the mother who adopted and raised him. On his arrival at the airport he is initially embarrassed by the presence of his brothers who have come to pick him up in their donkey-cart. When he realises what a sacrifice this entailed, he switches from his perfect standard Afrikaans to the language of the common people, in the process identifying himself publicly with the "outcasts".

In the emergence of a new group of poets in the late Seventies and in the Eighties (Peter Snyders, Patrick Petersen, Clinton du Plessis, André Boezak and others) the use of Kaaps would become far more prevalent, while the novels also captured the language rebellion in its representation of a changed reality. No trace of this use of the marker can be found in the literature written at the beginning of the two decades which I have demarcated for this paper.

The portrayal of District Six prior to the period of the forced removals initially came mostly from the white Afrikaans poets, who stressed violence, hardship and a happy-go-lucky attitude of the District's inhabitants. Some, like I.D. du Plessis and Uys Krige, exhibited a finer understanding of the soul represented by the people of District Six, people who in many respects found themselves outcasts.

An interesting paradox becomes apparent: the devil-may-care and often decrepit lifestyle is complemented by a firm religious conviction. Both Christian and Muslim elements feature strongly in the verse of these poets.

The Christian characteristics would of course be another factor, besides the language, binding the District Sixers to the very government denying them their birthright, their dignity, their vote and the right to live where they please. Religion and language, therefore, are the two main forces dominating the love-hate relationship which is evident in much of the literature produced in Afrikaans.

Vincent van der Westhuizen, not one of the prominent poets in Afrikaans, is the only poet I found who specifically mentions the disenfranchisement of the coloureds. In a poem called "Bulletin" with the subtitle "[Oktober 1956]" Vincent van der Westhuizen records a farmer listening to a radio news bulletin where world events and sports dominate. A single stanza alerts the attentive reader to the final outcome, the removal of the coloureds from the voters' roll:

En in verband	(And in respect
met die Appèl	of the Appeal
is 'n beslissing	a final verdict
nou gevel	has been cast)

Besides this rather revealing poem I could not find a single reference to the disenfranchising of the "Coloureds" in texts published during the period after this had happened in 1956. Could an explanation be that the writers simply did not see this as eroding the rights of people? How revealing this is when tasking literature with the conscience of human-kind!

On the other hand it is a fair question to ask how a political deed like disenfranchisement could be captured in literature. Its effects are almost invisible, not dramatic and tangible only through reconstruction after an election where it only features in the abstract.

Maybe another poem about news bulletins, N.P. van Wyk Louw's "Nuusberigte: 1956" ("News reports: 1956") written while he was lecturing here in the Netherlands, can help us to understand a poet's anger about the stealth with which a mentality, a mind-set, was taking control of the South African society.

Given that the disenfranchisement was a non-literary event, one would nevertheless hope to find signs of the evil which lurked behind the political action. But even that concern hardly surfaced. The absences, the empty and hollow sites where there should have been edifices, will forever remain an indictment against the Afrikaans writers, both coloured and white. Their silences can be read as compliance—they themselves became part of a system which was gradually destroying the moral fabric of the South African society.

The events ten years later, however, when District Six was declared a white area and evictions and demolitions started, were quite different.

It was a process which carried on for almost seven years, visible and audible to the people of Cape Town, and given prominence in newspapers around the country. The initial reaction from the people of the District was vociferous, but as it became clear that their voices were neither being heard nor articulated by the writers it died down.

The bulldozers triumphed, as they did all over South Africa, as the politicians played their racist games:

op 'n tafel in sy kantoor skuif die Baas
behendig gekleurde blokkies oor
die verdeelde kaarte met sy liniaal 'n stootskraper
wat tradisioneel oordonder oor ander,
hul plakkieplase en hul kleiosplekke in die son.

[on a table in his office the Baas
deftly moves coloured blocks across
the divided maps with his ruler a bulldozer
which traditionally overrules others
their places where they play in the sun.]

Of course forced removals, relocations, had already become a part of South African life, but the events surrounding District Six had a larger impact on the conscience than anywhere else. After all, as Adam Small writes in a long poem ironically called "Hêppie Niewedjaar!" ("Happy New Year!"), the coloured community became the conscience of their white language compatriots.

Searching for District Six in Afrikaans literature, however, is a demoralising and disillusioning experience. Specific references in work published between 1966 and 1976 are limited to the work of Adam Small, and a single poem by Barend J. Toerien.

The general phenomenon of the workings and effects of the Group Areas Act, however, is mentioned by a number of other Afrikaans writers. The tone is generally one of sarcasm, ridiculing the politicians who believe they have the right to decide where people may live. Many more writers, especially novelists, had captured the immorality of legislation prescribing who one may marry and criminalizing sex across the so-called colour line. Is the reason for the latter to be found in the more dramatic individual tragedies which became prominent? Pillars of society caught in the flashlight of torches and cameras? People committing suicide rather than having to face the humiliation and ordeal of a court hearing? Lovers having to leave the country of their birth?

But the early morning knocks on the doors of District Six, the orders to ordinary people to pack their belongings and to vacate the houses to move to little boxes far away from the city, the sound of the bulldozers; in short: the destruction of a whole community is heard almost nowhere in

Afrikaans writing except for the texts of Adam Small.

> o God die brief het van hulle ga-eis
> briek af djulle hys
> briek af djulle hy
> want kyk in God se son se skyn
> is djulle nie wit nie, djulle is bryn
>
> [o God the letter in demanding tone
> break down your home
> break down your home
> because in God's sunlight shining down
> you aren't white, but you are brown]

The only real testament of the bulldozers and District Six in Afrikaans literature before 1976 appears, ironically enough, in a limited-edition coffee-table publication called *Oos Wes Tuis Bes Distrik Ses* (East West Home's Best District Six). It contains black and white photographs by Chris Jansen, illustrated by or supported by poems by Adam Small. The photos are of a much later District than those of Wissema which I have referred to: the latter's District is more vibrant and obviously captures District Six long before the bulldozers rumbled in. (Later on Small translated some of the poems in *Oos Wes Tuis Bes Distrik Ses* into English for the Wissema publication.) By the time of the Small-Jansen publication (1973) the levelling of District Six was almost done, and most of its inhabitants were resettled on the Cape Flats. Life on the Kaapse Vlakte became very prominent in Afrikaans writing after 1976, often with references to the era of the District. But at the time of the bulldozing almost nothing was heard, and Small's verse more or less echoes around deserted and destroyed neighbourhoods.

It nevertheless remains the only edifice standing in Afrikaans literature (and, as a matter of fact: all South African literature of that period) to remind us of what had happened. What immediately strikes the reader is the fact that Small refers to people by *name*, and that the photographer focusses on faces amid the emptiness. Could this be an explanation why the effect of other race laws gained prominence in the Afrikaans literature of the time? Was the bulldozer just a machine and its effects so vast but impersonal that the tragedy of one unknown person, one unidentified house, one unfamiliar home disappeared? And that with such an abstraction, the literature failed to become the consciousness and the conscience it should have been?

In the opening poem Small formulates this duty of the writer to speak on behalf of those who can not:

> as jy die oë, die hande, die liefde en die haat
> van die stommer mense soos klippe laat praat
>
> [when you let the eyes, the hands, the love, the hate
> of the dumber people speak like stones]

and ends the collection referring to them as being faceless, haunted by bad luck:

> - vir hulle, mense met die swart kat op hulle pad
> mense ... sonder gesig
>
> [- for them, people with the black cat on their path
> people ... without a face]

Again the linguistic factor plays an important role. The two poems I have referred to are written in Standard Afrikaans (the language of the bourgeois, the purchasers of that volume) and they frame the other 22 poems in the language of the victims of the actions and silences of the bourgeois.

In a number of poems specific references are made to the bulldozers and the demolition, leaving no uncertainty in the mind of the reader what this is about. Surrounded by four photos of the facades of buildings Small's first poem addresses a "proud old building," at the same time calling it a "pathetic pal.". The abundant use of English in this poem makes it almost understandable to those who don't understand a word of Afrikaans:

> Proud ou gabou
> pathetic pêllie
> stil ou
> djy fancy djy staan nog
> one-way
> djy fancy nog: one day, *one* day?
> 'Is wishful thinking daai

proud ou gabou
pathetic pêllie
quiet ou
djy word gedemolish sê ek vi djou!
Wat was djy?
'n Cash store?
'n Kerk?
Ma daai was once upon a time, pêllie,
once upon a time...
Nou wiet ek nie exactly wát is onse crime
ma ek en djy
is suppose' om te wiet crime doesn' pay!
So pêllie,
dis geskryf en gesign en dis 'n must
djy sil vanish hieso in 'n cloud of dust!

Hoor djy die pêrepote vannie bulldozers?

Ek sil djou mis ...
Nou sak djou kop
Nou briek djou hart
Kô lat ons hyl dan, ma nie te hard nie
oor mense wat mal is, pêllie,
soes djy val ...
dja, mal, pêllie

[Proud old building
pathetic pal
quiet one
you still fancy you are standing
one-way
you still fancy: one day, *one* day?
That's wishful thinking
proud old building
pathetic pal
quiet one
you'll be demolished, that's for sure!
What were you?
A cash store?
A church?
But that was once upon a time, old pal,
one upon a time ...

Now I don't exactly know what's our crime
but you and I
are supposed to know crime doesn't pay!
So pal,
it's written and signed and it's a must
you'll disappear from here in a cloud of dust!

Do you hear the hoofbeats of the bulldozers?

I'll miss you..
Now your head sags
Now your heart breaks
Come, let us cry, but not too loudly,
about people gone mad, old pal,
as you fall...
yes, mad, old pal]

The second poem, flanked by photos of love and caring, recall the happy-go-lucky character of the earlier portrayal of the coloured community in Afrikaans literature. *Carpe diem*, the poem warns the young lovers, because life is like a piece of corrugated iron (used for inexpensive roofing, squatter shacks and blocking windows with no glass) which can be dislodged easily by the bulldozers.

The poem "Oppie top vannie mosque" recalls the strong religious sentiments which also characterised writing from the pre-demolition period: Just remember Mohammed and thank Allah; and again: Think of Jesus, he has come to save Everyman. And they can leave their place of worship and walk through the streets while the contractors are busy tearing down the walls. This, incidentally, is a reference to the fact that none of the churches or mosques in District Six were demolished during its destruction.

The next two poems depart from the impending doom awaiting the community, picturing young children playing and the day-to-day existence of ordinary people. The bulldozers are re-introduced by way of a poem of two sisters chatting. The one has been staying on the Cape Flats ("daa innie Bontehiewel, daa by Lywistown") for a while, and remarks thankfully that at least she has something: a council house. The implied history is what gives this poem its real meaning.

And the history then becomes a case study of "Ismael Moegamat Kassiem" who used to run a hairdressing and shaving salon:

> very much alive
> however
> toe hoor hy daa gan manne ko wat bulldozers kan drive
>
> [very much alive
> however
> and then he heard men will be coming driving bulldozers]

The pathos in this poem is found in the juxtaposition between the notice put up and "still alive", and the shop nailed up like a coffin—the tension between a concrete name and the unknown whereabouts of its bearer.

The last but one poem in this collection is a call by the poet's voice to the community to rise from the dust, to climb out of the rubble which is the trademark of District Six. It is a rallying call to take action, to take a stand, to ensure that we never suffer the same fate again:

> Die bulldozers, hulle't gakom
> romtomtom
> dóm
> was ons mos,
> stóm mos
> al die djare
> Klaar gakom het hulle
> en plat gadonner
> alles hieso
> alles, alles,
> hyse, harte
> die lot,
> alles,
> God!
> — So pêllie,
> Klim yt die klippe yt
> op,
> óp!
> Djy dink sieker ek is cynical?
> God, pêllie, ek is serious
> soes djy nie kan wiét nie
> so serious
> So djy móét my glo

oldou sound ek ridiculous:
Klim yt die klippe yt
óp, pêllie,
Klim yt die klippe yt
óp

[The bulldozers came
with a din and a jeer
stupid of us
dumb of us
all these years.
But they came
and demolished
everything here
everything, all
houses, hearts
the lot,
everything,
God!
— So old pal
Climb up from the stones
up,
up!
You think I'm cynical
God, pal, I'm serious
like you'll never know
that serious
So you *must* believe me
even though I sound ridiculous:
Climb up from the stones
up!]

I would like to end this paper by returning to an earlier poem in *Oos Wes Tuis Bes Distrik Ses*. This poem is set off against the others in two ways: it is printed on a photo (of rows of chimneys against the outline of the mountain) and it is in the poet's own handwriting. The poem is, semiotically, quite unique. For me it encapsulates exactly what I have been trying to say about writing being the consciousness of humankind and the extent to which Afrikaans literature between 1956 and 1976—when tumultuous and terrible things were happening to the speakers of Afrikaans who happened to be of colour—failed to do that.

And by failing to do that, it has created another edifice: one of a void where the bulldozers of authority silenced us into submission. This poem then: Lest we forget.

>Skoorstientjies, djulle't gedisappear
>ma' no fear
>djulle roek nou vir 'n hele age
>djulle staan op memory se page
>vi all time
>en testify:
>Jy is hie!
>Waa daa skoorstientjies was
>daa wassie net klip en concrete nie
>>Mure sonder mense? - Nai...
>>Daa was oek ons
>>*Ons*, dja

>[Little old chimneys, you've disappeared.
>but don't fear
>you're smoking now for a whole age
>you're written onto memory's page
>for all time
>to testify:
>You are here!
>Where there were chimneys
>there was more than stone and concrete to hear.
>>Walls without people? Never, you bet
>>There was also us, why
>>Us, yes.]

Fanie Olivier
University of Venda

Bibliography

Brink, André P. 1983. *Mapmakers: Writing in a State of Siege*. London: Faber & Faber.

Coetzee, Ampie & James Polley (eds). 1990. *Crossing Borders: Writers meet the ANC*. Johannesburg: Taurus.

Jauss, Hans Robert. 1982. *Toward an Aesthetic of Reception Theory and History of Literature*. Minneapolis: University of Minnesota Press.

Kannemeyer, J.C. 1993. *A History of Afrikaans Literature*. Pietermaritzburg: Shuter & Shooter.

Malan, Charles. 1987. *Race and Literature/Ras en Literatuur*. Pinetown: Owen Burgess.

Ndebele, Njabulo S. 1991. *Rediscovering the Ordinary: Essays on South African Literature and Culture*. Johannesburg: Cosaw.

Rive, Richard. 1987. "District Six and its literature". In: Malan 1987.

Sinfield, Alan (ed). 1983. *Society and Literature 1945-1970*. London: Methuen & Co Ltd.

Small, Adam. 1962. *Kitaar my kruis*. Cape Town: HAUM.

————. 1963. *Sê sjibbolet* . Johannesburg: Afrikaanse Pers-Boekhandel.

————. 1965. *Kanna hy ko hystoe*. Cape Town: Tafelberg.

————. 1978. *Joanie Galant-hulle*. Johannesburg: Perskor.

Small, Adam en Chris Jansen. 1973. *Oos Wes Tuis Bes Distrik Ses*. Cape Town: Human & Rousseau.

Small, Adam en Jansje Wissema. 1986. *District Six*. Cape Town: Fontein.

Smit, Johannes A., Johan van Wyk & Jean-Philippe Wade. 1996. *Rethinking South African Literary History*. Durban: Y Press.

Toerien, Barend J. 1960. *Gedigte*. Cape Town: Nasionale Boekhandel Bpk.

————. 1973. *Verliese en aanklagte*. Cape Town: Human & Rousseau.

————. 1975. *Illusies elegieë oorveë transfusies*. Cape Town: Human & Rousseau.

Van Wyk, Johan, Pieter Conradie & Nik Constandaras. 1988. *SA in Poësie/SA in Poetry*. Pinetown: Owen Burgess.

Venter, A.J. 1974. *Coloured: A profile of two million South Africans*. Cape Town: Human & Rousseau.

Watson, Stephen. 1990. *Selected Essays 1980-1990* . Cape Town: Carrefour Press.

Marginalised Early South African Testimonies: "//Kabbo's Intended Return Home" (1873) and *The Conversion: Death Cell Conversations of "Rooizak"* and the Missionaries—Lydenburg 1875

N-ka !xoë e //xara-//kam
"My place is the Bitterpits"
(Specimens of Bushman Folklore, 1911:298)

— I —

Stemming from increasing interest in Holocaust literature, "it has been suggested that testimony is the literary—or discursive—mode par excellence of our times" (Felman & Laub 1992:4). Since November 1995 when the Truth and Reconciliation Commission started its work under Bishop Desmond Tutu, testimony has become part of the fabric of a South Africa trying to come to grips with its past. About this painfully slow process, which some South Africans are beginning to doubt the healing power thereof, a leading South African psychiatrist, dr. Sean Kaliski recently remarked: "It will take decades, generations, and people will assimilate the truths of this country piece by piece" (Krog 1998:5). //Kabbo and Rooizak's testimonies can be seen as part of the truths of South Africa's history. The contending voices and identities encapsulated in these testimonies illustrate something of the historical and socio-political tensions in this multicultural community.

Transcripts of //Kabbo, the Bushman convict's dictation in 1873 was preserved in English and in his home language, /Xam, by the German philologist Wilhelm Bleek in *Specimens of Bushmen Folklore* (1911). The testimony of Rooizak, a Swazi labourer awaiting his death sentence in 1874, was recorded by the missionary Albert Nachtigal in German, and sent to Berlin after his death. A hundred years later Peter Delius found the document in the East Berlin archives and translated it into English. The story of Rooizak's conversion was annotated by the historian and published as *The Conversion. Death Cell Conversations of 'Rooizak' and the Missionaries—Lydenburg 1875* (1984).

The elderly /Xam man with three names—//Kabbo (meaning 'dream'), Jantje or /uhi-ddoro—spent July and August 1873 telling the frail, middle-aged dr. Wilhelm Bleek his life story. After having spent some time in the Breakwater jail in Cape Town for stock theft, and then almost three years in the Bleek household in the suburb of Mowbray with the sole purpose of dictating as much as he could of the narratives and customs of the almost extinct /Xam, //Kabbo was intent on returning home: "Thou knowest that I sit waiting for the moon to turn back for me, that I may return to my place" (Bleek & Lloyd, 1911:299). He left a month and a half later for his "place" at Bitterpits near Kenhardt in the north-western Cape. Two years later both of them had died.

In August 1874 a Swazi migrant labourer, called Rooizak, was arrested on a farm near Lydenburg in the northern Transvaal after a fight with a Pedi man called Majan. Majan died in the fight and although Rooizak protested his innocence claiming that it had been a fair fight, Rooizak was imprisoned. For five months he did hard labour in Lydenburg prison, till the court passed a death sentence in February 1875. For one and a half months he was kept in solitary confinement, awaiting the confirmation by the Executive Council of his death sentence. During this period he tried to hang himself in desperation, but was cut loose:

it is a terrible thing to be condemned to death and to have
to wait so long for execution. I wished to be dead but was
stopped. I don't want to live on like this. I want to die now
(Delius 1984:24-25).

The German missionary Nachtigal started ministering to him, together
with a mission convert who spoke Seswati, John Podumu. Nachtigal kept
notes of Rooizak's spiritual development to send to his Berlin headquar-
ters later. On 19 April the sentence was confirmed and after baptising
Rooizak at 4 am on Thursday 22 April, he was led to the gallows and
executed.

On a factual level the life testimonies of //Kabbo and Rooizak might
seem not to have much in common except that they both originate from
the end of the nineteenth century. Yet close analysis proves otherwise.
They are both colonised subjects under colonial rule, waiting passively (the
one to go home, the other for his death) and in the power of colonisers. In
the interim they give their testimonies, locked up intimately with an
interlocutor of another culture, speaking a different language—the one a
German philologist, the other a German missionary. Both //Kabbo and
Rooizak were illiterate. Their testimonies are, however, preserved in
written form, after having undergone various processes of translation and
mediation. Bleek spoke German and English and was still mastering the
/Xam language.

— II —

In the case of both these testimonies there are interviewers or
interlocutors (philologist and missionary) who elicit responses, and who
mediate the testimony. In both cases translation into a further language
is part of the mediating process.

Stemming from increasing interest in Holocaust literature, "it has
been suggested that testimony is the literary—or discursive—mode par.
excellence of our times" and that "films like *Shoah* by Claude Lanzmann
... or *Hiroshima mon amour* by Marguerite Duras and Alain Resnais,

instruct us in the ways in which testimony has become a crucial mode of our relation to events of our times" (Felman & Laub 1992:4).

With literary studies becoming increasingly interdisciplinary it is not strange that attention is focusing more on forms of cultural discourse such as testimony where one finds a "superimposition of literature, psychoanalysis and history", or phrased differently, elements of the historical, the clinical and the poetical (Felman & Laub, 1992:6 and 41). With reference to Holocaust literature Shoshana Felman remarks how

> The story of survival is, in fact, the incredible narration of the survival of the story, at the crossroads between life and death (Felman & Laub 1992:44).

This remark is equally applicable to the preservation of the /Xam narratives in the Bleek & Lloyd collections of 1911 and later—even with the cautionary reminder of the inevitable loss that must have occurred between transmission from the oral mode into the written, and the mediation processes which the material must have undergone at the hands of Bleek and Lloyd.

Felman and Laub describe the typical conditions of the "testimonial process":

> there needs to be a bonding, the intimate and total presence of an other—in the position of one who hears. Testimonies are not monologues; they cannot take place in solitude. The witnesses are talking to somebody (1992:70-71).

Testimony also foregrounds the role of memory which is essential "in order to address another" and "to appeal to a community" (1992:204). What is normally testified to, is a "limit-experience … whose overwhelming impact constantly puts to the test the limits of the witness and of witnessing" (1992:205). The individual voice of the testifying witness also tends to represent an absent community on whose behalf the testimony is made.

Yet it needs to be stressed also that one must be careful to "politicize the fact of trauma and to broaden, even universalize, the perspective of victimhood" because human life itself can be seen as "an endless adaptation to the 'traumatizing' … which persists from birth to death"

(Hartman 1995:546). Hartman sees the relevance of trauma theory for literary studies in three elements: (a) the grappling with issues of reality, bodily integrity, and identity (1995:547), (b) it concerns itself with "disturbances of language and mind" which are central to literary preoccupations (1995:548) and (c) the entrance of the new ethical theory "tries to break down the reproductive tyranny of the education system" (1995:549).

— III —

I would like to suggest that these testimonies can both be read as sites of conflicting cultural values. //Kabbo structures his narrative around a constant juxtaposition of 'here' in the Bleek household where he is forced to do "women's work" and where the others (servants as well as Bleek family members) do not speak his language, and 'there' where he wants to "sit among my fellow men" and listen to stories. Out of this juxtaposition comes his sense of alienation and yearning to end his last days amongst his own people. In Rooizak's story his incomprehension of the alien legal system and religious ideas suggests the missionary zeal of Nachtigal as an alienating imposition of one culture upon another.

Both testimonies have a prison experience as starting point and cause of trauma. In //Kabbo's case he feels as though he is living in exile. Rooizak's trauma is not only the fear of pending execution, but also the imposition of the evangelising fervour of the missionary, who constantly keeps harping on his sin and his awaiting fate.

"//Kabbo's Intendend Return Home" can be read as quintessentially a text expressing the typical psychological characteristics of the exile. He waits for time to pass so that he may go home: "I sit waiting for the moon to turn back for me, that I may return to my place". In his imagination he travels to his home, so "that I may sitting, listen to the stories which yonder come" (1911:301). Then reality yanks him back to 'here' at Mowbray where he feels alienated, for "I do not obtain stories; because I do not visit...they do not talk my language" (1911:301). This leads him into another fantasy flight to his home and a description of what life is like under his people, the "Flat Bushmen". They go to each other's huts, they smoke and tell stories. What //Kabbo is describing, is a sense of joyful and relaxed community—presumably what he misses most in Cape Town. He states: "I feel this is the time when I should sit among my fellow men" (1911: 303). As an old man, he longs to be with his own people to share communal life before he dies.

Tropes of travelling by road, and of movement then take over as he describes the journey which he envisages back up north. The description ends with the imagined arrival. In the imagined arrival scene //Kabbo describes himself in the third person, suggesting "Entfremdung" of the self:

> He will examine the place...he may examine the water pits;
> those at which he drank. He will work, putting the old hut
> in order. (1911:305)

The visualised arrival ends with //Kabbo seeing himself in the third person as an old man ("he grew old with his wife at the place"). Immediately hereafter he launches into a lengthy flashback. Here he switches back to the immediacy of the first person, and the passage reverberates with vitality as he describes himself:

> I felt that I was still a young man, and that I was fleet in
> running to shoot...For, I was fresh for running; I felt that I
> could, running, catch things. Then, I used to run (and)
> catch a hare. (1911:309)

After the extended flashback //Kabbo reverts back to everyday reality, to 'here' at Mowbray. He expresses intense determination to depart soon: "I do not again await another moon". Now he talks about the boots and gun which Bleek promised him, and he is again conscious of his old age and past hardship:

> starvation was that on account of which I was bound...For
> a gun is that which takes care of an old man...It (the gun) is
> strong against the wind. It satisfies a man with food in the
> very middle of the cold (1911:317).

//Kabbo's trauma is one of lengthy exile and what he describes in his testimony is the condition of exile, an important theme in South African literature of the apartheid era. The central trope in his narrative is that of the "stories" which he misses, which represents communality and social life amongs his kindred. He juxtaposes himself as a fleet-footed, hare-chasing young man with himself as an old man, faced by starvation unless Bleek can send a gun to help provide for food in his old age. The silence in the text is the period of imprisonment at the Breakwater prison. The only reference to this ordeal is the euphemistic word "bound" in the phrase "starvation was that on account of which I was bound".

Rooizak's testimony is even more heavily mediated—first by Nachtigal and a hundred years later by Delius. Upon the missionary's first visit he asks how the prisoner feels. Rooizak formulates his sense of trauma thus: "I am to be executed unjustly and I am filled with horror at the idea of having to die such a demeaning death" (1984:21). Nachtigal expresses his wish to minister to the needs of Rooizak's soul. His response is: "I know nothing of this and I feel nothing for it, but I will listen to what you have to say." It transpires in the conversation that Nachtigal has no interest in or comprehension of the African belief system which Rooizak describes ("Their spirits lived on after their deaths. They are here on earth. But they are capricious and have to be placated by sacrifices" 1984:22). Nachtigal tries to inculcate in Rooizak some concept of his deed as "a grave sin" and that God is like a king who "will forgive". Rooizak misunderstands the forgiveness and says, "Then help me. I will gladly do anything to escape hanging" (1984:22). Soon hereafter he tries to hang himself in his cell. The trope of "hanging" thus becomes central in the narrative. But he is discovered and "from this time onwards...he was chained" (1984:24).

On the missionary's next visit Rooizak eloquently describes the effects of solitary confinement (a central trope in South African prison literature):

> I cannot stand this fear any longer...I am forced to sit here alone. My solitude tortures me and fills me with despair. Some days I sleep to still my mind but then my nights are spent in waking terror. How can they be so cruel as to keep me waiting so long for my death? (1984:25)

When next visited by Jonas Podumu (Nachtigal is said to be incapacitated by "a bout of savage headaches" 1984:29), Rooizak is exceedingly calm because of a vision that he has had: "I dreamt that I was taken away to a beautiful land where, feeling weak and strange, I sat on an anthill". He describes how Jesus appeared to him as a "shimmering white person" who greeted him and told him to go back and "behave well" (1984:31), suggesting a traumatised psyche, obsessed with ideas of guilt. Hartman remarks on the relation between trauma and dream that "In literature especially, shock and dreaminess collude. Where there is dream there is (was) trauma" (1995:546).

Not content with the peace that has descended over the Swazi prisoner, both Podumu and Nachtigal proceed to badger him so as to test whether his newly professed Christian faith rings true. This hectoring in the name of Christianity seems particularly cruel and suggests torture more than anything else.

Upon confirmation of his death penalty we read that "Rooizak was given alcohol to ease his shock. He became drunk and started to dance as best his chains would allow in the confines of his cell" (1984:40). Later he "wished death to all whites". When Nachtigal arrives the next morning Rooizak consciously introduces racial discrimination into the discussion: "Isn't it unjust to sentence me to death in my absence? I am treated like this because I am black" (1984:40). The last vestige of resistance in him comes to the fore in the taunting question: "why is God's word not observed when a white kills a black?" (1984:41). Thereafter he succumbs to the missionaries' ministrations and is baptised at dawn on the morning of 22 April. Echoing one of the dignitaries, Rooizak stated "I will soon be in paradise" just before he was killed.

The whole traumatic process lasted seven months. Rooizak's testimony, like //Kabbo's, thus also entails a long waiting, it entails a journey—but a spiritual journey—from near death through attempted suicide back to life. Through the terror of solitary confinement and back into the momentary release of a vision, and then back to the painful interrogation by the missionaries, until eventually he finds release in death. In the intense dialogue between the Swazi prisoner and the evangelists nothing is more striking than the conflict between their different cultures, different justice systems, different customs and the absolutely powerless situation that Rooizak finds himself in. In spite of the heavily mediated nature of this text it is still one of the most striking South African testimonies of one man's trauma and spiritual torture. It also eloquently illustrates intercultural conflict in action.

— IV —

"To attack and damage the memory of a people means to attack its roots, put its vitality at risk", stated Ferrarotti recently (1994:2). No matter how mediated, or how often translated, in the marginalised testimonies of //Kabbo and Rooizak we find preserved memory as part of South Africa's history and conscience.

Helize van Vuuren
Port Elizabeth

Bibliography

Bleek, W.H.I. & Lloyd, L.C. 1911. *Specimens of Bushman Folklore.* London: George Allen.

Delius, Peter. 1984. *The Conversion. Death Cell Conversations of 'Rooizak' and the Missionaries—Lydenburg 1875.* Johannesburg: Ravan.

Ferrarotti, Franco. 1994. *The Temptation to Forget. Racism, Anti-Semitism, Neo-Nazism.* London: Greenwood Press.

Felman, Shoshana & Laub, Dori. 1992. *Testimony. Crises of Witnessing in Literature, Psychoanalysis, and History.* New York and London: Routledge.

Hartman, Geoffrey. 1995. "On Traumatic Knowledge and Literary Studies." In: *New Literary History* 26(3): 537-564.

Krog, Antjie. 1998. *Country of My Skul.* Johannesburg: Random House.

IV. Reconsidering Ethnicity

The Genealogy of Violence in African-American Literature: Non-Native Sources of *Native Son*

On June 1, 1997, a twelve-year-old boy set fire to his grandmother's New York home; three weeks later she died from the severe burns she received in the blaze. The story would probably have gone unnoticed had it not been for the fact that the boy who set the fire was Malcolm Shabazz, grandson of black nationalist leader Malcolm X, and the boy's grandmother was Dr. Betty Shabazz, Malcolm X's widow and a prominent civil rights advocate and educator in her own right. While admitting that he had committed the act that caused his grandmother's death, the boy denied he had intended the outcome, and pleaded guilty to the juvenile equivalents of second-degree manslaughter and second-degree arson. A Family Court Judge decided to place Malcolm Shabazz in a juvenile detention facility for an eighteen-month term that can be extended until he turns eighteen.

It is tempting to try to account for the tragic event of young Malcolm's arson by tracing it to a history of violent acts and rumored conspiracies. The boy had apparently been the victim of repeated physical and alcohol abuse, and had been living with his grandmother off and on since early 1995 after his mother Quibilah Shabazz was indicted on charges (which were later dropped) of plotting to kill Louis Farrakhan, the leader of the Nation of Islam. (Betty Shabazz had herself accused Farrakhan of playing a role in her husband's 1965 assassination.) The boy told the police that he had set the fire because he was angry at his grandmother and didn't want to live with her, but wanted instead to return to his mother who was living in Texas. In short, it is possible to detect a dark genealogy of violence behind the twelve-year-old boy's apparently senseless act. But although Betty Shabazz has now, like her husband thirty-two years ago, also met a violent end, her agonizing death by a fire set by her grandson strikes us, as Henry Louis Gates and Hendrick Hertzberg have noted, as "more horrifying ... more intimate ... and more incomprehensibl[e]" than that of her husband who "was shot down before her eyes by cultist thugs" (4).

Yet, for all its horror, is young Malcolm's act of violence altogether incomprehensible? Isn't it possible to identify a recurring historical pattern of violence centered on the specific nature and circumstances of young Malcolm's act—an African-American youth setting a fire in the house of his grandmother who perishes as a result? Indeed, this fire has a striking precedent that American analysts and commentators might have noted had they not forgotten their own literary heritage. For young Malcolm's act of arson happens to vividly re-enact the opening scene of Richard Wright's autobiographical work *Black Boy* (1945) in which the author describes one of his earliest memories: how, at the age of four, he inadvertently set fire to his grandparents' Mississippi home. During his rigidly religious grandmother's illness, the bored child amused himself by putting some broom-straw into the fireplace to watch it burn; the idea then occurred to him of touching the blazing straw to the window curtains to see what would happen. Seconds later, the room was ablaze and the frightened and guilty child ran outside and crawled under the house to hide. Fortunately, others were alerted to the fire, Richard's grandmother was carried outside to safety, and his mother and younger brother escaped unharmed.

Despite the differences between the fires set by Richard Wright and Malcolm Shabazz—Wright's grandmother did not die from the blaze as Betty Shabazz did; Richard did not intentionally set fire to the house as Malcolm did, but only touched off the curtains out of what seems idle curiosity; and Richard was only a one-third Malcolm's age at the time of the event— the similarity between the two senseless acts of violence are notable. In each case, the dire consequences of the fires set by two black boys (if not the fire itself) appear to have been an accident: Malcolm maintains he did not intend to kill his grandmother, while Richard insists that "it was all an accident; I had not really intended to set the house afire. I had just wanted to see how the curtains would look when they burned" (5). Yet the accidental nature of the fire started by Richard does not change the fact that Richard's grandmother (not to mention the rest of his family) could easily have met the same gruesome fate as Betty Shabazz; had this happened, the punishment and guilt that Wright would undoubtedly have suffered might well have nipped his creative career in the bud. Instead, this potentially tragic experience, which Wright relates as the opening scene of his autobiography, furnished him with a rich primal memory of the sort of transgression and terror that he experiences time and time again throughout his youth.

What is so significant about this senseless, violent act of a black boy setting fire to his grandmother's house? As accidental and incomprehensible as such acts appear, one is tempted to see in them an impulse to reject or repudiate one's ancestry, embodied in the grandmother's matriarchal persona. The repudiation of one's ancestry is a way of negating a history of oppression and exclusion that continues to impose its burden on the living descendants.[1] One is also tempted to see such youthful acts of arson as random, isolated incidents that nevertheless have the capacity to collectively explode as full-scale riots in which entire communities would burn.

As for Richard Wright, the fact that the episode of setting fire to his grandmother's house was among his earliest memories, which he treated as a key autobiographical moment and literary scene, suggests that well before he became conscious of the racial hatred, inequality, and injustice that would later devastate him, he was already seized by an impulse to reject his past and to revolt against the stultifying circumstances of his existence. As a mature author, Wright would draw upon this primal gesture of revolt in his writings.

Perhaps the clearest instance of this gesture is the horrific scene of the first murder in *Native Son*. In Wright's best known work, which has

[1] It would be interesting to relate the scene of a boy's violence directed against his grandmother as a symbol of the past with the inverse scenes found in Toni Morrison's fiction in which a grandmother's or even a mother's violence (as in *Beloved* and *Sula*) is directed against her descendants. Here again, senseless violence is depicted as a desperate attempt to negate an intolerable condition of oppression.

been called an American *Crime and Punishment*, Bigger Thomas unintentionally murders his employer's daughter Mary Dalton, and then disposes her body by burning it in the furnace at the Daltons' home. Bigger did not intend to kill Mary; he suffocated her accidentally in an attempt to avoid being detected in her bedroom, and he burned her corpse in a similar—albeit ironically unsuccessful—effort to blot out his deed and to escape detection. But behind this violent, fiery image of accidental murder and concealment, there is a primal gesture of revolt—a repudiation of his debased condition—combined with a feeling of fear that echoes Wright's own act of setting fire to his grandmother's house. The fact that Bigger's violence is motivated not only by courage, but by "terrible and justified fear" (Bloom 1990:1), connects him to the four-year-old Wright for whom the sensation of terror that followed his setting the fire overshadowed any sense of remorse he might have felt about his deed. Wright makes it clear that he was affected less by guilt for nearly causing his grandmother's death than by fright at having himself nearly been killed by the beating he eventually received from his mother for having caused the fire: "for a long time I was chastened whenever I remembered that my mother had come close to killing me" (II, 9). As he would later show in the emotionally stunted character of Bigger, Wright as a four-year-old was unable to grasp the violence of his act because he was so overwhelmed by fear.

In his essay "How 'Bigger' Was Born" (published in 1940, the same year that *Native Son* appeared), Wright goes to some length to elaborate the impulse to revolt as Bigger's defining trait. Wright explains that Bigger's character was a composite based on a number of actual individuals (at least one of whom went by this name) whom he had encountered during different phases of his youth in the South. One of Bigger's models was a schoolyard bully who tormented black children, another was an older youth who lashed out against all whites; another violated all laws for no apparent reason. What they all had in common, Wright declared, was the fact that they "were the only Negroes I know of who consistently violated the Jim Crow laws of the South and got away with it, at least for a sweet brief spell," although they were eventually made to "pay a terrible price" by "the whites who restricted their lives" (I, 856-57). When Wright discovered in the 1930s that the exclusion and rebelliousness of Bigger was not only an American, but an international phenomenon, he became "fascinated," as he describes in the essay, "by the similarity of the emotional tensions of Bigger in America and Bigger in Nazi Germany and

Bigger in old Russia," all of whom, "white and black, felt tense, afraid, nervous, hysterical, and restless" (I, 865). The character of Bigger Thomas, the "Negro boy" portrayed by Wright in his novel, may have been "an American product, a native son of this land," but as the "product of a dislocated society," as "a dispossessed and disinherited man," he "carried within him the potentialities of either Communism or Fascism" (I, 866). The only "difference between Bigger's tensity and the German variety is that Bigger's, due to America's educational restrictions on the bulk of her Negro population, is in a nascent state, not yet articulate," while "the difference between Bigger's longing for self-identification and the Russian principle of self-determination is that Bigger's, due to the effects of American oppression, which has not allowed for the forming of deep ideas of solidarity among Negroes, is still in a state of individual anger and hatred" (I, 866-67). And so, with this sociological insight from an international perspective, "with this much knowledge of myself and the world gained and known," Wright describes how he set out, "like a scientist in a laboratory," to "try to work out on paper the problem of what will happen to Bigger" (I, 867).

When we come upon this comparison of fiction writing to a laboratory experiment, and when we recall Wright's emphasis on environmental (if not hereditary) factors, not to mention his use in his novel of details reported in the *Chicago Tribune* about the trial of the real-life killer Robert Nixon,[2] it is no wonder that Wright's novel has traditionally been regarded as an exponent of American naturalism (in the tradition of Dreiser, Farrell, and Steinbeck, as well as Zola in Europe) which offered a means of analyzing the evils of society. But given the scientific determinism of the naturalistic novel, it is odd that Wright should lay such stress on the accidental aspect of Bigger's violence in Mary's killing, or in his own act of setting fire to his grandmother's house. And it is curious that after his extended sociological account of Bigger's character and of his own naturalistic approach, Wright describes the composition of *Native Son* as "an exciting, enthralling, and even a romantic experience" (I, 880). It is also noteworthy that he concludes his article by contrasting his work to that of James, Hawthorne and Poe—as one critic notes, while these "nineteenth-century writers could erect fantasies in the head; Wright was trying to rid himself of the fantasy in his" (McCall 76-77). As Wright

---

[2] However, Wright implies that this was an instance of life imitating art since he "was halfway through the first draft of *Native Son*" when the Nixon case became known (I, 874).

himself declared, "if Poe were alive, he would not have to invent horror; horror would invent him" (I, 881). Despite Wright's emphasis on the difference between himself and these American writers of the previous century, and despite Harold Bloom's claim that "the citation of James, Hawthorne, and Poe is gratuitous" (1988: 3), his reference to these authors actually hints at a gothic subtext in his novel reminiscent of Hawthorne, Poe, and the James of "The Turn of the Screw" that offsets his avowed naturalism. Although a few critics have questioned the naturalism of *Native Son* (its determinism and fatalism) and acknowledged Bigger's strength of character and free will as it is shown to evolve in the work, no one seems prepared to acknowledge this novel's relation to the gothic tradition. Thus Dan McCall affirms "that *Native Son* is no more a Gothic romance than it is a naturalistic novel." (76), and Bloom maintains that the "pathos of fear" that Wright's character Bigger provokes in readers is "a fear too naturalistic to be mistaken as a Gothic pleasure, or an indulgence in nightmare" (1990: 2).[3] I would like to suggest that while *Native Son* may not be a gothic romance, it nevertheless offers a profound realistic reading of gothicism itself. Behind Bigger's violence lies a gothic strain that goes back not only to nineteenth-century American writing, but to an even earlier European literary tradition of rebellious rage and nightmarish horror—a transatlantic gothic strain that has been obscured in Wright's case by the rather arid academic debate as to whether he should be regarded primarily as an exponent of American realism or European modernism.

With its supernatural, uncanny, mythical, larger-than-life associations, the gothic is especially evident in Wright's earliest writing—in a story like "Superstition" (1931), for example, which bears the stamp of an American and a European writer, Poe and Conrad, or in an even earlier unpublished effort known as "The Memphis Monster" in which, like Bigger Thomas, Wright "was haunted by the idea that he was a criminal, guilty of murder and haunted by the police" (Fabre 65). Critics have tended to dismiss such elements, however, as a sign of adolescence that had to be outgrown; Wright's biographer and most prominent commentator Michel Fabre notes that Wright was "tempted ... to sacrifice realism to romanticism in 'Superstition,'" and that "his adolescent penchant for the imaginary and the supernatural gave way to verisimilitude" and to his

---

[3] Elsewhere, however, Bloom acknowledges that Bigger is larger than life, and "can be said to have become a myth without first having been a convincing representation of human character and personality" (1988: 2).

"conversion to realism" in his first novel *Lawd Today* (85-86). This curt dismissal of Wright's gothicism as a youthful folly that had to be abandoned before he could make his mark as an exemplar of realism and/or modernism represents the standard, somewhat one-sided view of Wright's craft, that has informed the reception of his best-known novel. The identification of *Native Son* as either a naturalist or a modernist work with its sources either in America or in Europe overlooks certain unmistakable affiliations with an alternative tradition of the gothic that spans both sides of the Atlantic, and that has become such a distinctive feature of American culture today. Bigger may well be, as Wright says, a "product of a dislocated society," and reading his story may help us to gain an understanding of the warped environment that produced him, but he also appeals to our ghoulish obsessions like so many of today's demonic and demonized, black or white, American media-figures—O.J. Simpson, Timothy McVeigh, Andrew Cunanan, and Theodore Kaczynski—who become occasions for public soul-searching and debate.

It may be the case that in fashioning Bigger Thomas, Wright was giving white Americans what they already knew, what they had in fact constructed—the "bad nigger" as Dan McCall has called it. But what is even more monstrous about Bigger Thomas is the possibility that he shows signs of becoming what novelist Thomas Pynchon has called a "Badass." In his 1984 essay "Is It O.K. to Be a Luddite?," Pynchon portrays this figure as belonging to an anti-rationalist, anti-industrialist gothic tradition exemplified by such European works as Horace Walpole's *The Castle of Otranto* (1765) and Mary Shelley's *Frankenstein* (1818) which feature such formidable, larger-than-life characters as Alfonso the Good and Frankenstein's creature. Pynchon depicts these literary Badasses as fictional variants of the historical personage of Ned Lud, the man who gave his name to the Luddite reaction to the Industrial Revolution after he "broke into a house ... in 1779, in a village somewhere in Leicestershire ... and 'in a fit of insane rage' destroyed two machines used for knitting hosiery" (40). Later immortalized in folk legend as King Ludd, a hero of the victims of industrialism, this frame-breaker is seen by Pynchon as the prototype of the Badass who figures so prominently in gothic or what he calls "Luddite" novels: "He is usually male, and while sometimes earning the quizzical tolerance of women, is almost universally admired by men for two basic virtues: he is Bad, and he is Big" (40).

Although the only twentieth-century example of a Badass figure that Pynchon gives is that of the "classic Luddite saint" as he calls him, King Kong (41), it is worth noting the similarities between King Kong and Bigger which at least one critic, Dan McCall, has pointed out: "Climbing buildings he is the giant darky we blew up onto the screen, the 'Bigger' black man; he stands roaring on the rooftops until white technology sends him plummeting to the streets below." The key difference is that while *"King Kong* ends with the assertion that 'beauty killed the beast' ... *Native Son* shows how the beast—if given a chance—will kill the beauty" (85-86). Such a comparison would seem to support the notion that Wright's protagonist is indeed a twentieth-century Badass in the gothic tradition outlined by Pynchon, perhaps *the* major Badass in American fiction—the isolated, rebellious individual who, as Wright said, is not "organically bad" (I, 857), or as Pynchon explained, "Bad meaning not morally evil, necessarily, more like able to work mischief on a large scale. What is important here is the amplifying of scale, the multiplication of effect" (40). Nowhere is this propensity to excess more evident than in the fact that his murderous violence is not limited to one victim, Mary, but spills over in the novel to a second victim, his girl Bessie. But it is with this second murder that the notion of Bigger as a Badass figure in the gothic/Luddite tradition becomes problematic. With Bessie's slaying, Bigger takes his place with other fictional slayers of two women—Raskolnikov in Dostoevsky's *Crime and Punishment* and the ape in Poe's "Murders in the Rue Morgue"—or in the real-life case of Clinton Brewer, a black man imprisoned for murdering a woman who refused to marry him, who, in an instance of life imitating art, then killed another woman after Wright, based on the prestige he had acquired in the year since *Native Son* appeared, helped to arrange his parole. Yet Bigger's rampage in *Native Son* is a good deal more complex and ambiguous than these fictional and nonfictional parallels.

His bludgeoning of Bessie is a deliberate act, in contrast to his earlier act of suffocating Mary which was an accident. While this seems to make him a kind of Badass—someone who has acquired a strong identity through an act of violence, someone who no longer acts out of fear but who has becomes an object of fear himself, someone who in Pynchon's words is capable of "work[ing] mischief on a large scale"—he deludes himself by believing "not only that he has killed to protect himself but also that he has attacked the entire civilization" (Hakutani 220). The fact that his inadvertent suffocation of a white woman is followed by the willful murder of a black woman hardly qualifies him as a revolutionary scourge of white society. And what sort of a Badass is it, anyway, who fights the machine by taking helpless women as his victims?

Thus it is doubtful wether the Bigger Thomas of *Native Son*—unlike the Bigger Thomas of Wright's essay "How Bigger Was Born"—can fulfill his own yearning for some "black man who would whip the black people into a tight band" so that "together they would act and end fear and shame" (I, 551). Since Bigger's rebellious violence is originally motivated by fear, and since the feeling of fear he evokes in readers outweighs any sense of pity or even awe they might feel, he cannot be considered a tragic victim of fate or a naturalistic victim of his environment, or a charismatic rallying point for the disenfranchised and disinherited. As Fabre says, Wright himself "could not believe in the revolt of the Bigger Thomases, since they were as likely to espouse fascism as socialism" (231). Wright was far more successful in depicting a Badass figure in the year after the publication of *Native Son* in his blues lyric called "King Joe" celebrating boxer Joe Louis; like King Ludd, Wright's King Joe who "wrestled Ford engines," who "turned engine himself and went to the fighting game" where "he's fighting a white man" (Fabre 237) was clearly much more of a Luddite hero than Bigger Thomas. But then it might be expected that the folkloric figure of a "tall tale" form like the blues lyric would prove a much better Badass than the tortured protagonist of a quasi-naturalistic novel. Wright's *Native Son*, in short, presents a sober picture, a realistic critique of the folkloric, gothic, but ultimately rather cartoonish Badass sketched by Pynchon. He is a figure who can only exist in the popular imagination and in the dreams of an oppressed people, but not in the harsh light of reality.

The difficulties that arise with the notion of Bigger as a Badass point up a problem with the concept of the Badass itself. For Pynchon downplays a point that Wright's novel brings to the fore: the *misdirected* nature of the Badass's rage and the *unintended and unforeseen* consequences of his rebellious act. Ned Ludd's rage may have been limited to the destruction of a couple of knitting machines, but this act had violent consequences that he was unable to foresee, much as the deeds of those little Badasses—young Richard's act of setting aflame the curtains in his grandmother's house, or young Malcolm's act of torching the home of his grandmother—had such unintended, unforeseen human costs that made these acts all the more senseless and tragic. The case of Bigger Thomas is especially poignant in this regard, since, after his inadvertent slaying of Mary, he enlists the assistance of a machine—the fiery furnace, which it was ironically one of his tasks to minister—to dispose of her body. It is not only the horror of Bigger's act of decapitating Mary and burning her body that causes the reader to shudder, but the misdirected nature of his violence, and his unholy alliance with the machine against the human. And it is entirely fitting in this regard that this machine soon proves to be Bigger's undoing, that far from covering up his violence, it becomes the means by which his violence is exposed.

A few words might be said in closing about trauma and the Badass. There's no question that both the real-life and historical figures discussed in this paper either have experienced, or are shown to be in the process of experiencing, some type of trauma that continues to haunt them in later life. Despite their destructiveness and their capacity for violence, real-life juvenile arsonists like Richard Wright and Malcolm Shabazz are as much terrorized victims of trauma as they are terrorist figures in their own right. We have seen that Wright presents—or remembers—himself as a child, not as a dangerous aggressor who nearly killed his grandmother, but as a small boy terrified by the beating he received from his mother for having started the fire in his grandmother's house. And from the little we have been able to learn about Malcolm Shabazz, he seems to have experienced a number of traumatic delusions resulting from a history of abuse.[4] In the case of the fictional character Bigger Thomas in *Native Son*, although he is presented as a victim of acute deprivation and poverty—illustrated by the nightmarish encounter with the giant rat at the opening of the novel—he is primarily remembered, especially by white audiences, as a Badass figure who terrorizes others. Wright, in effect, has chosen to present a traumatized youth from the reader's perspective as a traumatizing figure in his own right. The novel is designed in such a way that it is no longer the boy who is portrayed as a traumatized victim, but the reader. Wright wrote *Native Son* with the deliberate intention of terrifying his white audiences as a way of making the "white man listen." He set out to write a work that would be impossible for "bankers' daughters" to "read and weep over and feel good about" as he felt they did

---

[4] A child psychologist specializing in "juvenile fire setters" who interviewed Malcolm Shabazz reports that he has "a longstanding interest in the subject of fire that reaches unusual proportions." When he was three -- a year younger than Wright at the time he set the fire to his grandparents' house -- he set fire to a pair of sneakers in the middle of the night. He also created, and identified with, a fantasy cartoon character called "Sinister Torch" (*The Boston Globe* [July 30, 1997], A5).

in response to his earlier collection *Uncle Tom's Children*. Now he was determined to write a book that "no one would weep over," that "would be so hard and deep that they would have to face it without the consolation of tears" (I, 874). It was by first traumatizing his readers with the terrifying specter of his Badass that Wright could expect those readers—that is, we ourselves—to examine the traumatic condition and sources behind Bigger's own impulsive and excessive acts of violence.

Joel Black
University of Georgia

Bibliography

Bloom, Harold, ed. 1988. *Richard Wright's Native Son*. New York: Chelsea House.

————, ed. 1990. *Bigger Thomas*. New York: Chelsea House.

Fabre, Michel. 1993. *The Unfinished Quest of Richard Wright*. Trans. Isabel Barzun. 2nd ed. Urbana: University of Illinois Press.

Gates, Henry Louis, Jr., and Hendrik Hertzberg. 1997. "Requiem." In: *The New Yorker* (7 July 1997).

Hakutani, Yoshinobu. 1988. "Richard Wright and American Naturalism." *Zeitschrift für Anglistik und Amerikanistik*. 36:3 (1988): 217-26.

McCall, Dan. 1969. *The Example of Richard Wright*. New York: Harcourt, Brace & World.

Pynchon, Thomas. 1984. "Is It O.K. to Be a Luddite?" In: *The New York Times Book Review* (28 Oct. 1984): 1, 40-41.

Wright, Richard. 1991. *Works*. 2 vols. New York: The Library of America.

Literature as Cultural Memory

Tales of Betrayal

J'ai raconté notre histoire.
Je t'ai trompé ce soir avec cet inconnu.
J'ai raconté notre histoire.
Elle était, vois-tu, racontable.

[I told our story.
I was unfaithful to you tonight with this stranger.
I told our story.
It was, you see, a story that could be told.]
— Duras (90, 73)[1]

This is not a story to pass on.
— Morrison (275)

Any story told of the subjective pain caused by traumatic loss can only be an unfaithful translation. The narrator of a past event assumes the position of

---

[1]   Quotations in English are from Marguerite Duras and Alain Resnais, *Hiroshima Mon Amour*, trans. Richard Seaver (New York: Grove Press, 1961); quotations in French are from *Hiroshima Mon Amour* (Paris: Gallimard, 1960).

survivor, a position safely after and outside the painful events recounted. He is enabled to hold this position by a durational temporality, one capable of moving past the event. The mourner, however, is arrested at the moment of trauma and can not assume a third person perspective on pain. He feels it in its immediacy, an immediacy that is lost in any translation into narrative. He fosters this pain, caters to it, because in its medium the lost other seems to maintain a freshness and presentness that allows its loss to be denied. The mourner remains silent so as not to endanger this internalized, phantom other, not to betray it to the story. In so doing, he excludes himself from the communal narrative and its temporality of afterness and confines himself to the arrested moment, to his merger with the incorporated you, and so puts at risk his own ability to live past the event, to survive into the after. Are these then the only two responses possible to a collective trauma: a communal story narrated from the safety of the outside that accepts superficiality for the sake of survival or a faithful but death-tending private commemoration of the loss? Must we choose between an ethics of communal survival, one which clearly sides with the living even if it must betray the dead, and a subjective ethics of absolute fidelity to the dead that threatens the possibility of survival and of representation as such? Does not the former expect too little of humans, the latter too much? Are we human if we can tell the story of horrific events, of the worst injustices with the same equanimity and by the same structures that we tell of any other event? But do we not claim to be more than human, almost godlike, if we deny the limitations posed by loss and by time and pretend to be able to guarantee the existence of another which we harbor in our own interiority? Would not the memory of the lost other be better served if the former guarded against its coarse superficiality and the latter against its potential for arrogant narcissism by transgressing their own individual taboos and entering into dialogue? The mourner, who refuses language as such, must be the first to transgress. The mourners in Alain Resnais' *Hiroshima Mon Amour* and in Toni Morrison's *Beloved* are seduced into a betrayal of their absolute fidelity to the lost other by a you which bears its strong resemblance.[2] In the former, that you reveals the frailty of the incorpo

---

[2]   In *Unclaimed Experience: Trauma, Narrative and History*, a book that has come to my attention since the writing of this paper, Cathy Caruth makes a similar linkage between betrayal and the telling of traumatic experience in *Hiroshima Mon Amour*: "What the woman mourns is not only an erotic betrayal, that is, but a betrayal precisely in the act of telling, in the very transmission of an understanding that erases the specificity of a death" (27). Caruth goes on to argue that real communication of traumatic experience will not be achieved by laying claim to traumatic experience as possessable knowledge, but rather by the mutual acknowledging of the limits of knowability by those engaged in dialogue:
"It is indeed the enigmatic language of untold stories—of experiences not yet completely grasped—that resonates, throughout the film, within the dialogue between the French woman and the Japanese man, and allows them to communicate, across the gap between their cultures

rated other, its vulnerability to time and to narrative, while in the latter, it reveals in that other an unlimited appetite capable, if allowed, of swallowing time whole, an other against which taboos must again be enforced.

At the beginning of *Hiroshima Mon Amour*, the French actress who is its main character herself approaches the horrific suffering of Hiroshima from the safety of the outside. She is in Hiroshima to make a film on peace and while there she has visited all of the museum exhibits, heard all the accounts, seen all the reconstitutions of the devastation caused by the bombing. She has no doubt that she has been able to penetrate the pain of the victims by means of these external memorializations. This certainty is belied by the rhythmic interchange with the Japanese man she has taken as lover, an interchange which punctuates each of her claims to him of having witnessed the horror of Hiroshima:

> Lui: Tu n'as *rien* vu à Hiroshima. Rien.
> [He: You saw nothing in Hiroshima. Nothing.]
>
> Elle: J'ai *tout* vu. *Tout*.
> [She: I saw everything. Everything.] (16, 15)

It is the externality of the French actress's gaze that blinds her. It allows her to comprehend the objective factuality of the event but not to pierce its pain. The danger that memorializations aimed at an external gaze could lead to superficiality and indifference is manifest in the scene in the film in which a smiling hostess takes a bus load of visitors on an atomic tour. Here, that which is intended as memorialization becomes the purest act of forgetting.

---

and their experiences, precisely through what they do not directly comprehend" (56). Though I agree with Caruth that any public discourse that pretends to full possession of the knowledge of traumatic experience in effect merely covers over its truth, I choose in my paper to focus as well on another dangerous claim to full possession, that made by the mourning subject itself. While the communal claim to complete knowledge issues in representation, the mourning subject's desire to protect the wholeness of the internalized other causes it to refuse representation outright. Though the mourning subject believes its refusal of representation to be motivated by the highest ethical aims, by the attempt to maintain sacrosanct the pain of the past through its silent incorporation of the lost other, it too easily falls into using that incorporated other to seal off any opening to the outside and to the living other, to found a narcissistic system (given its close identification with this internalized other) that overexaggerates its own self-sufficiency and allows the sought-after silence to deteriorate into an endless self-referentiality. Only by consenting to betray its most cherished ethical absolute, by running the risk of standing self-condemned of the worst crime it can imagine, that of infidelity to the truth of the past, can the mourning subject rupture this narcissism and allow a new opening to the living other. It is only through such a betrayal that the necessary limits on the mourning subject's own excessive claims to full possession are drawn.

The direct address, the "tu" that is the predominant pronoun in this film, seems to offer some alternative to this callous banality, some more intimate testimony to pain. The you of the French actress's Japanese lover awakens in her memories of her dead German one, an enemy soldier to whom she was secretly engaged and who was killed on the eve of the liberation of her town of Nevers. The film intercuts into the main narrative of her current affair with the Japanese man images of her past one with the German, making the structural parallel between the two clear, as when a shot of the Japanese man lying on his stomach with his hand outstretched is followed by the image of her dead German lover with his hand in much the same position.

The ambiguous attitude of the French actress to this ability of her Japanese lover to invoke memories is clear in her repeated remark to him:

> Elle: Tu me tues.
> Tu me fais du bien.
>
> [She: You destroy me.
> You're so good for me.] (27, 25)

This external "tu" echoes the one she keeps safe within the preserve of her pain, threatens to deprive it of its uniqueness, and tempts her to betray it to the outside, to tell the story of their lost love. In telling her story, she addresses her Japanese lover as if he were the dead German one, employs a "you" that is located at once within and without her narrative, its subject and its addressee. The French actress finally becomes able to speak of her pain only when she has found the proper addressee, an addressee who doubles in externality the you that is embedded and protected within the immediacy of her subjectivity. This doubled you tempts the mourner out of her interiority, allows the dyadic nature of her pain some external expression.

Though this expression first brings her solace and joy at having found someone with whom to share the intimacy of her pain, it is soon followed by the agony of the realization that in committing the memory to narration she has begun to forget it. Her telling of her doomed lover's death, her translation of her private pain into the medium of story, has been doubly unfaithful. She has betrayed the sacredness of her memory and for all that has not managed a faithful translation of its essence into narration. After having revealed her secret memory to her Japanese lover, the French actress is wracked by pain and guilt over having betrayed the sanctity of her memory to story. She bitterly underlines both the ease with which this untellable story was told and the superficiality of the telling by recounting her own story from the third person perspective, as her Japanese lover has understood it in the safety of the outside, using the pronoun she:

> Elle: On croit savoir. Et puis, non. Jamais.
> Elle a eu à Nevers un amour de jeunesse allemand...
>
> [She: You think you know. And then, no. You don't.
> In Nevers she had a German love when she was young...]
> (90, 73)

She also must admit what this telling has cost her, the betrayal of the incorporated you, the loss of the intimacy and immediacy of her memory of her German love. She can no longer taste his presence as she did when she shared with him the anachronistic moment of a pain borne inside. In this external temporality, she is the survivor and he is not and all possibility of intimacy is lost. The pain she now feels guarantees no presence but only loss, a loss which her own seduction into the story helped ensure.

It is this suffering, however, that seems finally to open her up to an understanding of the pain of Hiroshima. The pain to which she gains access is not that of the dead of Hiroshima but that of the survivors, of those who like her have betrayed an absolute memory for the sake of representation. In the final scene, the two lovers, who have remained anonymous through the rest of the film, give one another names:

> Elle: Hi-ro-shi-ma. C'est ton nom.
> [She: Hi-ro-shi-ma. That's your name.]
>
> Lui: C'est mon nom. Oui. Ton nom à toi est Nevers. Ne-vers-en-France.
> [He: That's my name. Yes. Your name is Nevers. Ne-vers-in France.] (102-3, 83)

In this moment of double appellation, each recognizes in the intimacy of the other "tu" the proper vehicle for translating the pain of an experience he could otherwise only know from the outside of an external perspective. The breach between the private and the public has been spanned by the suffering attendant on forgetting. While the objective reconstitutions witnessed by the French actress at the beginning of the film pretended to capture the victim's pain from the safety of the outside and fell far short of the mark, this film, through the suffering of the French actress, registers something of the density of pain by attempting more modestly to capture only the secondary pain of the mourner who violates her own code of absolute fidelity to the incorporated other. The French actress's infidelity to her private memory, her surrendering of it to the story, and her pain at having done so provide a medium by which the agony of a failed public memory can reach representation. In making way for the direct address, in giving predominance to the pronoun "tu", the film has become a medium that, while it can not pierce the pain of the victim, can translate with some legitimacy the secret pain any representation itself harbors over its infidelity to the lost other, however necessary that infidelity might be to its own survival; it expresses a communal guilt that would otherwise remain invisible, hidden away in the confines of each separate subjectivity.

If the French actress is finally forced to pay her debts to time by surrendering the immediacy of her painful memory, Sethe, the main character of Morrison's *Beloved*, owes a debt that is not mediated by time, one that she does not have the coinage to repay. Unlike the French actress, who struggled against her placement in the safely after, Sethe has had to take drastic measures to assure herself a foothold there, to make certain that she and her family would not be reclaimed by the slavers she had fled. For the first few days after her escape, it seemed as if she would be welcomed into the safety of an after presided over by the great heart and ethical authority of her mother-in-law Baby Suggs. An unchurched preacher, Baby Suggs bound the community together by calling its members to a ritual in the Clearing, a communal space where they could safely release the intensity of their pain and hope to find some solace:

> Finally she called the women to her. "Cry," she told them. "For the living and the dead. Just cry." And without covering their eyes the women let loose. (Morrison 88)

Baby Suggs is the central healer figure in the novel, her great heart offering the hope that in the strength of communal bonds even the horrific suffering of slavery could be faced and survived. Her moral philosophy centers around her definition of good: "Good is knowing when to stop" (87). Pain must be acknowledged but within the safety of limits, limits that the community alone can provide. Her own faith in the wisdom of limits is threatened on the twenty-eighth day after the arrival of Sethe and her children when the white slavers come to reclaim them, an example of Baby Suggs's observation that white people "don't know when to stop" (104). Faced with a past that would not stay past, which threatened to inflict on her children the indignities she had endured, Sethe takes a hacksaw to her own children rather than see them returned to slavery. She manages to kill only one, her two-year-old daughter, and it is her bleeding body that she holds up to finally force the slavers to stop, to acknowledge a limit:

> By the time she faced him, looked him dead in the eye, she had something in her arms that stopped him in his tracks. He took a backward step with each jump of the baby heart until finally there were none. (164)

This event seems to destroy any illusion of safety in community and in the acknowledgement of bounds. Baby Suggs doubts of her own philosophy and can neither condemn nor condone Sethe's excessive act because it both transgresses her notion of goodness and nonetheless seems necessary to keep the past past. Under the stress of this suspended judgement, Baby Suggs's great heart collapses and with it the hope for a united communal defense against the past. The community rejects Sethe not just because of her violent act but because she claims to not need its protection, to be able to fend back the past on her own. They detect this arrogant claim to self-sufficiency even at the moment she is being taken away to jail after the murder:

> Was her head a bit too high? Her back a little too straight? Probably. Otherwise the singing would have begun at once, the moment she appeared in the doorway of the house on Bluestone Road. Some cape of sound would have quickly been wrapped around her, like arms to hold and steady her on the way. (152)

Sethe is exiled into the silence of her own pain, an exile which she proudly claims, as mutual resentment drives a wedge between the purely subjective and the communal responses to the past.

Eighteen years after this event, Sethe believes she has finally found the proper "you" to hear her story in Beloved, the mysterious young woman whom she takes in when she suddenly appears on her doorstep. To her, she can tell the painful stories of the past that she can tell no other:

> ... every mention of her past life hurt. Everything in it was
> painful or lost. She and Baby Suggs had agreed without
> saying so that it was unspeakable...
>
> But, as she began telling about the earrings, she
> found herself wanting to, liking it. Perhaps it was Beloved's
> distance from the events itself, or her thirst for hearing
> it—in any case it was an unexpected pleasure. (58)

Sethe eventually recognizes that she has been able to tell her pain to Beloved because she is in fact her murdered baby daughter returned to her. Sethe at first believes Beloved's return frees her from her guilt, her debts to the past:

> I don't have to remember nothing. I don't even have to
> explain. She understands it all. (183)

This "you" to which she addresses her stories, however, differs from the you to whom the French actress had told hers. The doubleness of the latter, its being simultaneously witness and participant, both within and without the story, served as a bridge to externality. It could do so only because some distance was still maintained between the two yous, however similar they might be. There is no such distance in the you which Beloved offers to Sethe. Beloved does not resemble the lost you; she is it. Sethe tells her most unspeakable story, that of her killing of her own daughter, to the very you who did not survive it. This seamless you collapses the roles of external audience and internal addressee and tempts Sethe further inward, away from any safety in the third person perspective and towards the deadly intimacy of the dyadic.

Once the two retire, along with Sethe's living daughter Denver, into impenetrable isolation at 124 Bluestone Road, the danger inherent in the "you" Beloved offers Sethe becomes apparent. If Beloved's promise of healing had always been an ambiguous one, if the unbounded desire she held for Sethe seemed to pose as well a threat, as when in an earlier scene her massage of Sethe's neck turned into a stranglehold, it is now exposed as in fact an impossible demand that can only result in Sethe's death. The extreme dependence Beloved had on Sethe is described throughout the novel in images of eating, of parasitism:

> Sethe was licked, tasted, eaten by Beloved's eyes. Like a
> familiar, she hovered, never leaving the room Sethe was in
> unless required and told to. (57)

In their isolation, that metaphor of parasitism is literalized and Beloved's hunger shown to be insatiable. Sethe starves herself in order to feed Beloved's appetite, shrinks herself to the size of a small child while Beloved fattens, but for all that does not in the least satisfy her hunger. Beloved is the non-survivor, who lives perpetually in the moment of her severance from time. Arrested in that moment of severance, unable to move past it into the security of an after, Beloved can not forgive, no matter how many times or in what ways Sethe tries to explain that she acted out of love, in order to protect. Beloved can only insistently and invariably focus on the moment of her hurt:

> You forgot to smile
> I loved you
> You hurt me
> You came back to me
> You left me (217)

Unable to attain forgiveness, unable to forgive herself, Sethe engages in the constant attempt to meet the impossible demands of Beloved, to remain true to the ethical absolute of an unshakable fidelity to an other who has been arrested forever in time. Denver describes the willing antagonism between the two as follows:

> She had begun to notice that even when Beloved was quiet,
> dreamy, minding her own business, Sethe got her going
> again. Whispering, muttering some justification, some bit of
> clarifying information to Beloved to explain what it had
> been like, and why, and how come. It was as though Sethe
> didn't really want forgiveness given; she wanted it refused.
> And Beloved helped her out. (252)

Sethe in the absoluteness of her guilt and Beloved in the implacability of her need will not know when to stop, not know when to draw a limit to this dangerous colonization. Left to her own devices, Sethe, unable and unwilling to withdraw herself from this cycle of implosion, will end by exhausting all of her existential resources, all that binds her to time and to survivorship, in an effort to placate Beloved, and both, host and parasite together, will die in a lethal embrace.

It is Denver who sees the danger to her mother and makes a link back to the externality of the community, that same community which in exiling Sethe had made this colonization more likely. That community now belatedly extends to Sethe an act of forgiveness and of generosity by drawing the limit she can not draw and exorcizing Beloved. The scene of this exorcism parallels in many ways the original scene of victimization, but with important differences that lead to a re-externalization and reintegration of Sethe. Sethe and Beloved are drawn to the porch of the house, to an intermediary space between the inside of the house and the externality of the community gathered outside, by the sound of the united voices of the women of the neighborhood:

> Sethe opened the door and reached for Beloved's hand. Together they stood in the doorway. For Sethe it was as though the Clearing had come to her with all its heat and simmering leaves, where the voices of women searched for the right combination, the key, the code, the sound that broke the back of words. (261)

As in the earlier scene, Sethe sees a white man approach whom she mistakes for the slaver come again to reclaim her and her children and she again is pushed to violence. This time, however, her aggression is aimed towards the external threat and not towards her own loved ones. Wrapped as she is in the community's vocal embrace, Sethe is this time protected from her own excessiveness as Denver restrains her before she can do any harm. If this recurrence of the traumatic event is mitigated by the passage of time for Sethe, if the differences marked in it provide for her salvation and for her reintegration into the community, a rewriting of her original story, its meaning for Beloved has not changed in the least; she is abandoned a second time to her inconsolable and painful solitude. While her host's attention is distracted by the external threat, Beloved simply disappears.

Though not willing Beloved's departure, Sethe consents to it, for she has done all that she can humanly do to satisfy her impossible needs and it has not been enough, has not in the slightest eased her suffering. She joins with the others in the community in forgetting Beloved, though forgetting here does not, as in *Hiroshima Mon Amour*, lead to an erasure of the once incorporated you. The non-transcendable pain of Beloved remains, always on the outer fringes of representation, always threatening to once again find a willing host:

> Sometimes the photograph of a close friend or relative—
> looked at too long—shifts, and something more familiar
> than the dear face itself moves there. They can touch it if
> they like, but don't, because they know things will never be
> the same if they do. (275)

In the last pages of the novel, a variation on the phrase "This is not a story to pass on" is thrice-repeated, like some incantation or spell meant to ward off any future colonizations of the temporality of the after by this non-transcendable moment of pain. In this consent by Sethe, the novel's most excessive living character, to such a taboo, a consent grudgingly offered only when it became clear that no amount of self-laceration would pay her unredeemable debt, Baby Suggs's moral philosophy of limits is also reaffirmed, as her healing memory is evoked by the references to the voices that had once been raised in the communal space of the Clearing.

And yet, Beloved, literally, gets the final word. The novel ends with a last calling of her name, a last recognition of the inconsolable suffering of those who did not survive. And though her exile was necessary for any healing to occur, no balm could have been applied to those wounds had her coming not exposed them in their nakedness, stripped away all of the protective taboos covering them. A moment of absolute risk must be run if there is to be a possibility for the healing of wounds long buried. And yet that moment must not be allowed to set itself up as a false and death-tending eternity but must be again limited by the communal institution of temporal taboos. If after all we then prove to be survivors capable of telling the story of the past in the security of an after, we will not have simply exploited the mechanisms in objective representation that allow for such a *living past* of traumatic pain, but will have earned the appellation of survivor and gained the rights to the temporal territory of the after by having *lived through* a confrontation with such a pain's impossible demands.

Kimberly McGhee
University of Tennessee

Bibliography

Caruth, Cathy. 1996. *Unclaimed Experience: Trauma, Narrative and History*. Baltimore: The Johns Hopkins University Press.

Duras, Marguerite. 1960. *Hiroshima Mon Amour*. Paris: Gallimard.

Duras, Marguerite. 1961. *Hiroshima Mon Amour*. Trans. Richard Seaver. New York: Grove Press.

Morrison, Toni. 1988. *Beloved*. New York: New American Library.

Toni Morrison's *Beloved*: A Love Story

Literature has always taken upon itself the telling of difficult stories, and, from its beginnings, it self-consciously draws attention to this task. In the Western tradition, for instance, when the hero of Homer's *Odyssey* is asked by the Phaiakians about his sufferings, he ponders how to relate his traumatic experience, aware that a recounting of his trials will cause him to "mourn and grieve even more": "What then / shall I recite to you first of all, what leave till later? / Many are the sorrows the gods of the sky have given me" (9.13-15). As it turns out, Odysseus tells his story with remarkable ease, which is really not so surprising, given that his is a success story, a tale of mastery, indeed, a largely uncontested master narrative. At one point, Odysseus reports his encounter with various inhabitants of the underworld, letting the great heroes speak directly of their trials, but presenting the women's stories—stories often involving the trauma of abduction and rape—through the filter of his own narrative voice. In contrast to this, today's literature offers numerous examples of women themselves telling of things not easily told. Often, as in Toni Morrison's *Beloved*, these are stories of widespread historical oppression, but they include a crucial focus on gender-specific experience.

Like a number of other late twentieth-century works of North American fiction (such as Joy Kogawa's *Obasan*, concerning the wartime internment of Japanese Canadians, to which this paper will make passing reference),[1] Morrison's *Beloved*, which deals with slavery in nineteenth-century America, tells its story not easily, but well, in part by means of a focus on various aspects of women's experience. The problem of how to speak of the unspeakable belongs to both men and women in *Beloved*: there are things neither Sethe nor Paul D "ha[s] word-shapes for" (99). Moreover, although there are things "neither kn[ows] about the other" (99), there is an acknowledgement of their common experience under slavery—"Her story was bearable because it was his as well" (99)—or at least of commensurability: "He wants to put his story next to hers" (273). Nevertheless, Morrison's novel, like other contemporary, female-authored narratives, expresses the importance of positionality, both in traumatic experience and in the subsequent processing of such experience. This focus on what has been identified as a feminist concern (Alcoff 428-36) is ultimately what allows readers to put the various stories within the narrative—stories of women and of men—next to one another, the reader working with the text, as the character Beloved does with Denver, when the latter tells of her own birth, the two doing their best "to create what really happened, how it really was" (78).

This is not to say that *Beloved* pretends to offer some unmediated access to the conditions of slavery. Despite reviews that would suggest both a successfully conveyed and a homogeneous reality—"a milestone in the chronicling of *the* black experience in America" says *Publishers Weekly* of *Beloved*,[2] while the back cover of *Obasan* announces it as "*the* moving story of Japanese Canadians during the Second World War" (emphasis added)—Morrison's narrative, like Kogawa's, refuses such illusions. Both novels offer a powerful sense of shared, but not undifferentiated, experience. In *Obasan*, for instance, Naomi recognizes, as she reads her aunt's journal, that "Aunt Emily's Christmas 1941 is not the Christmas [she remembers]" (79). Both works, moreover, highlight the impossibility of recreating "how it really was," an impossibility underlined, for example, by Ella in *Beloved*, who for more than a year was kept locked in a room by a father and son: "You couldn't think up," she says, "what them two done to me" (119). Thus, the past here—the historical experience of oppres-

[1] Another notable example is Beatrice Culleton's *In Search of April Raintree* (Winnipeg: Pemmican, 1983), which tells of the lives of contemporary First Nations women and men in Canada.

[2] Emphasis added. Excerpts from the review in *Publishers Weekly* and from other reviews serve as endorsements included on the first few pages of the edition cited.

sion—is presented as both unspeakable and unimaginable, beyond our knowing, and yet what else do these imaginative works of fiction *claim* to do but tell, but speak of that past?

This not altogether rhetorical question is worth pursuing, not least because of the insistent focus on the very issue of "claiming" in *Beloved*. The novel's epigraph, like that of *Obasan*, comes from the Bible, and speaks of an act of renaming, recalling, reclaiming: "I will call them my people, which were not my people; and her beloved, which was not beloved." These words from Romans 9.25 themselves recall God's promise of reclamation as described in the second chapter of Hosea (2.23), a vision of future relationships, harmonious and faithful, that actually encompasses the past: God's people, figured as the reclaimed beloved, will in this future of justice and mercy sing "as in the days of her youth, and as in the day when she came up out of the land of Egypt" (Hosea 2.15), where she had been enslaved. Reclamation is similarly linked with liberation in *Beloved*, as over and against the claims of the slaveowners,[3] who exhibit an insatiable appetite and greed, the characters who have escaped to what the novel terms "unslaved life" begin, "[b]it by bit," to claim themselves: "Freeing yourself was one thing; claiming ownership of that freed self was another" (95).

Sethe, of course, goes beyond such concern for herself to make "outrageous claims" (171) on the lives of her children, killing her daughter in order to save the child from slavery, thus calling upon herself widespread condemnation, most devastatingly articulated in Paul D's reaction to "what she claimed": "You got two feet, Sethe, not four" (164-65). Such a binaristic formulation, neatly separating, as it does, the human and the animal, is part of the discourse of slavery; it issues from the mouth of schoolteacher, who instructs his pupils to record Sethe's "human characteristics on the left [side of the page]; her animal ones on the right" (193). While Baby Suggs goes to her grave unable to approve or condemn "Sethe's rough choice" (she is "beaten up by the claims of both," 180), Paul D moves from judging Sethe to caring for her, from counting her feet to massaging them (272), from ventriloquizing schoolteacher to anouncing his own claim, "I'm a take care of you, you hear?" (272). These words form part of a new discourse that miraculously "open[s] [the] mind," as Sethe's

---

[3] Baby Suggs describes how, following Sethe's killing of her child, schoolteacher left town, "Filed a claim and rode on off" (183). This is after the destruction made it clear to him "that there was nothing [in the yard] to claim" (149).

daughter discovers when she hears a neighbour say to her, "Take care of yourself, Denver," and she hears it "as though it were what language was made for" (252). Language, such truly *careful* language, is what Morrison claims—or reclaims—in *Beloved*, offering her readers an orientation toward both the past and the future that resists the effects of oppressive discourses. The latter—most notably associated with schoolteacher—are represented in the novel as leaving Sethe "walk[ing] backward," without even looking behind her "to find out where [she is] headed" (193).

At least one review of *Beloved* regards it as "a love story," "a story about the self-sacrifice of motherhood."[4] While we might easily dismiss the first cliched claim along with the second, I would suggest that what Morrison provides is precisely a story of love, the language she claims being in part the language of such love. The narrative's work of reclaiming "what language was made for" involves a reimagining and reconfiguring of conventional relationships and conceptions of love. Halle, for instance, is said to be "more like a brother than a husband. His *care* suggested a family relationship rather than a man's laying *claim*" (25, emphasis added). This anticipates the position into which Paul D moves at the end of the novel, with his declaration of care. Immediately following Paul D's announcement, Sethe wonders if he will bathe "[f]irst her face, then her hands, her thighs, her feet, her back? Ending with her exhausted breasts? And if he bathes her in sections, will the parts hold?" (272). This explicitly recalls Baby Suggs' loving attention to her daughter-in-law's body on the day Sethe crossed the river: Baby Suggs "bathed her in sections," starting with her face, and then moving to her hands and arms, her legs, her stomach and vagina, and finally to her feet (93). Such echoing of the description of the care extended to Sethe by her mother-in-law, Baby Suggs, marks Sethe and Paul D's love affair as a kind of "family relationship." It is predicated, to be sure, on a man's laying claim, but he claims something for both Sethe and himself, something both the man and the woman, under slavery, have long been denied.

Kogawa's *Obasan* presents comparable descriptions of bathing: Naomi's grandmother "rubs each of [Naomi's] fingers, [her] hands, arms, chest, belly and abdomen, neck, back, buttocks, thighs, legs, ankles, the lines behind the ankles, the soles of the feet, between the toes (49); Naomi herself bathes her aunt's weary body (78); and Sachiko scrubs her grand-

---

4   From a review in the *Orlando Sentinel*, an excerpt included as an endorsement on the third of the opening pages of the edition cited.

father's scarred back, the recipient of her attention "trembling less as the hot water pours over him" (165). As in *Beloved*, the relationships depicted in these scenes of care are both intimate and familial. Moreover, the description in these passages constitutes a reclamation of the *blason*, that traditional mode of describing the beloved, here rid of its idealizing, objectifying effects, conveying instead something of what it might mean, as Baby Suggs puts it, to love flesh, to touch "[f]lesh that needs to be loved" (88). In Morrison's novel, Sethe is thus touched by Amy, by Baby Suggs, and finally by Paul D,[5] becoming indeed the beloved, moving into a position similar to that of the reclaimed woman in Hosea, mercifully delivered "as in the day when she came up out of the land of Egypt." The process of liberation—of reclamation—proceeds gradually, "[b]it by bit" (95), and is literalized in these accounts of careful, physical touching.[6]

The morning after she is delivered by the touch of Amy and of Baby Suggs, Sethe, the beloved, lovingly reclaims her children, entering into a new relationship with them now that they have escaped to the promising side of the river. "Sethe lay in bed under, around, over, among but especially with them all" (93). No longer "need[ing] permission for desire" (162), Sethe and her children explore different possible physical positions —under, around, over, among, with—which reflect different possible configurations of pleasurable, "harmonious" relationships (99), such as we see modelled, for example, in the passage already cited, in which Denver tells Beloved the story of her birth: "The monologue became, in fact, a duet as they lay down together, Denver nursing Beloved's interest like a lover whose pleasure was to overfeed the loved" (78). The image of nursing is used here, as elsewhere in the novel, to suggest a reciprocal relationship, both mother and child ideally being in a position actively to nurse. In this case, the picture of the two women—sisters and more[7] than sisters—as lovers, nursing, suggests the kinds of relationships that in the next chapter we see as perhaps possible in the community Baby Suggs, Ella,

---

[5] Amy "massage[s] [Sethe's] feet" (82); Baby Suggs similarly "attack[s] the unrecognizable feet" (93); Paul D asks if he may heat up some water in order to bathe and "[r]ub [Sethe's] feet" (272).

[6] The role of "touching" in *Beloved* brings to mind a key concept of the contemporary German writer Christa Wolf. Morrison's focus, however, is somewhat different from Wolf's, the latter writer identifying "a specifically female epistemological stance" that is associated with "sisterliness" (Kuhn 13).

[7] Denver acknowledges Beloved as her sister and as "more" (266), which is consistent with the common interpretation of this figure as the embodiment of a collective, traumatic past (see, for instance, Wyatt 479-80).

Stamp Paid, and others have come to know. In such a community, being called to claim ownership of the self, one is freed "along with the others" (95) to invent ways "to love and be loved," "feed and be fed" (177).

While the image of nursing is used to express possibilities for free and loving relationships, it also serves to convey something of the horror of slavery, most notably in the scene in which schoolteacher's boys violate Sethe by holding her down and sucking her breast milk. Pamela E. Barnett has shown how "Morrison revises the conventional slave narrative by insisting on the primacy of sexual assault over other experiences of brutality" (420), rape being suffered by both men and women in the novel. The particular violations Sethe and Paul D experience are "characterized by sucking (being sucked or being forced to suck)," the "eating imagery associated with Sethe's rape reappear[ing]" in the account of Paul D and his fellow prisoners being forced to fellate prison guards who announce this as breakfast (Barnett 422). In thus speaking of both of these unspeakable violations, in connecting or relating Paul D's "unrelatable" experience (Barnett 424) to that of Sethe, the novel succeeds in putting the man's story next to the woman's. Rape comes to be associated with race as well as with gender—in fact, as Barnett argues, race, rather than gender, is foregrounded "as the category determining domination or subjection to rape" (419)—as Morrison, through an initial focus on women's experience—in particular, the taking of Sethe's milk (17)—carefully guides readers to an understanding of Paul D's position as well as of Sethe's.

The novel's sustained attention to positionality reveals the extent to which relationships have been damaged under slavery. The notoriety of Sethe's killing of her child, together with the spiteful ghost and the appearance of Beloved, suggests uniqueness, the unforgettability of the incident in the woodshed at least temporarily obscuring so many other severed relationships, such as those between Baby Suggs and her own offspring, who are taken from her, claimed by people who didn't stop "playing checkers just because the pieces included her children" (23). Her fourth child "she could not love and the rest she would not" (23), it being dangerous, as Paul D recognizes, to love anything more than "just a little bit" (45). This knowledge echoes in Ella's advice to Sethe, "I'd say, Don't love nothing'" (92), as together they peer into the tiny face of the newborn Denver. Sethe herself, the only child her mother named and did not throw away, was separated from that mother after only two or three weeks of nursing (60-62, 201), while Ella, forced to deliver "a hairy white thing," would not nurse it (258). Once again, the focus on women's experience under slavery—in this case, on the prevention of mother-child love and the horrifically abusive disruption of maternal claims—ultimately helps to tell Paul D's story as well. Like the enslaved mothers, he makes himself not love what is "not his" (268), including even the beauty of earth and sky; denied human sexual contact, he loves "small and in secret" (221, 162); and unable to remember either his father or his mother (219), he resigns himself to a life all but devoid of relations, "aunts, cousins, children" (221), though he remains fascinated by large, variously constituted families, "[h]alf white, part white, all black, mixed with Indian," making members of such families, when he meets them, "identify over and over who each [is], what relation, who, in fact, belonged to who" (219).

At first glance, *Beloved* resembles a somewhat conventional love story in its narrative of Paul D and Sethe's attempts to establish a life of relations after all: "When I got here," Paul D tells Sethe, "and sat out there on the porch, waiting for you, well, I knew it wasn't the place I was heading toward; it was you. We can make a life, girl. A life" (46). What emerges, however, is a parodic manipulation of traditional literary forms, as Denver's resistance to her mother's forming a twosome with Paul D (13) creates a love triangle (Denver, Sethe, Paul D), which eventually gives way to the deadly conflicts of the more complicated triangle consisting of Denver, Beloved, and Sethe. Both triangles have an initally promising aspect—the "hand-holding shadows" of Denver, Sethe and Paul D "gliding over the dust" (47) on the way to the carnival, for instance, and later the hand-holding threesome of Denver, Beloved, and Sethe, using one and a half pairs of skates to glide over the ice, each supporting the other two as they "take turns. Two skates on one; one skate on one; and shoe slide for the other" (174). Undermining an optimistic interpretation of either scene, however, is the image of Sethe's two sons, after their sister has been killed, "holding hands in the yard, terrified of letting go" (177); they "stayed that way especially in their sleep" (183). The appearance of a loving or even simply benign relationship, as in Denver's telling Beloved that "she never knew [her brothers] to sleep without holding hands" (120), thus emerges as an example of what Paul D terms "[d]evil's confusion" (7, 271): something bad looking good. Denver, Beloved and Sethe provide another example, forming a deceptively goodlooking triangle, whose intense claims—"You are mine / You are mine / You are mine" (217)— betray a "breakneck possessiveness" (54), an infernal togetherness of the kind Dante so vividly describes in his portrayal of the doomed inhabitants of Hell.[8] Morrison's narrative highlights the devilishly confusing nature of these women's relationships, and reveals in ironic terms the absence of their purported freedom behind the closed doors of 124 Bluestone Road; Sethe's turning of the key literally "locks [them] in a love that [wears] everybody out" (243), leaving them hellishly alone with "unspeakable thoughts, unspoken" (199).

Before Beloved comes to replace the ghost, Paul D does the much-needed work of repositioning at 124, breaking up its triangular possessiveness, "making space" for himself "along with" Denver and Sethe (45), sorting out the devil's confusion that reigns there, so that things suddenly "[become] what they [are]" (39). Beloved soon appears, however, with more powerful claims, which crowd the house again and move both Paul D and Sethe around like "rag doll[s]" (126, 243). This time, the repositioning is women's work, accomplished not by the "bash[ing]" of tables and the "wrecking" of everything (18), as in a man's laying claim, Paul D's belligerent "screaming back at the screaming house" (18), but by Denver's response to her grandmother's call to "go on out the yard" (244) and into the community. Having rallied from the defeat reflected in her last works while alive (89, 104), Baby Suggs speaks to Denver from the other side, from beyond the grave, identifying knowledge of the traumatic past— remembering it, telling of it—as the key to moving toward a new position, here literalized as the ability to "walk down the steps" (244).

Throughout the novel, crowded spaces evoke not only the historical conditions of slavery, but also the subsequent inability to free oneself from slavery's monstrous claims: Sethe, for instance, stands daily at her job "in a space no wider than a bench is long," to do the "serious work of beating back the past" (73). Conversely, open spaces such as the Clearing are associated with freedom, with "room to imagine" and to be "interested in the future" (70). It is in the Clearing that Baby Suggs, the "unchurched preacher" (87), calls upon her people ("O my people," 88), the people she has claimed as her own, lovingly to reimagine and reclaim themselves, this open territory, therefore, being neither an empty nor a private place, but one filled with the communal expression of desire. For a long time, 124 Bluestone Road functioned as a kind of Clearing; Baby Suggs lived in the

---

[8]   See, for instance, Dante's depiction of the lovers Francesca and Paulo in canto 5 of the *Inferno*. Note also the apparently casual mention of the devil in *Beloved* (182), as well as the more explicit reference to the fact that the women finally arrive "at a doomsday truce designed by the devil" (250).

house that nominally belonged to the Bodwins, but was actually possessed by no one, claimed by the community as its own. Significantly, it is in this communal space that even the unspeakable, unimaginable past becomes something other: "124 was a way station where messages came and then their senders. Where bits of news soaked like dried beans in spring water—until they were soft enough to digest" (65).

At a crucial point, however, this open space almost imperceptibly develops into private property, "[Baby Suggs'] yard" (179), the arrival of her more immediate family somehow confused with the staking of an exclusive and "arrogant claim" (249) of love, ownership, and protection. The feast that marks this turning point is miraculous, excessive, something the community cannot claim as its own. Baby Suggs had earlier told her people "that the only grace they could have was the grace they could imagine. That if they could not see it, they would not have it" (88). Even though they are present at this miraculous celebration, it remains something they cannot see. The liberating claims of and within the community are thus set against Sethe's "outrageous claims, her self-sufficiency" (171). Only when Denver reclaims connections to the community is this dichotomy overcome, as her story enables some of the women finally to see themselves in Sethe's position, Ella, for instance, thinking of the dead child she refused to nurse "coming back to whip her" (259). These women respond to Denver's "unmistakable love call" (247) by concocting the second wondrous feast described in the novel, this time, however, it being one truly of their own making, the gifts of food literally named as their own on the slips of paper that accompany each offering. This carefully prepared feast appears not all at once, but rather bit by bit over days and weeks, reminiscent, in its gradual emergence, of the freeing process of reclamation as it is elaborated elsewhere in the novel. The second feast constitutes a sustained expression of the women's "care" (250) and a communal celebration of the grace they together can imagine, can see, and therefore can have.

Space permits only a brief mention of the comparable significance of community in *Obasan*, a work that similarly attends to the role of care in its story of reclamation. In the face of an oppressive placing and naming, Naomi, like Morrison's characters, relocates herself in a communal context. She does not, however, find or position herself solely within the community of Japanese Canadians that some have been "desperat[e]" (186) to keep together, but looks also to shifting communities of political and cultural resistance, which have come into existence with perhaps equal, but differently focused, "desperation" (189). Furthermore, Naomi discovers community in the unlikely person of Rough Lock Bill, an outlaw, in this sense remarkably like Amy in *Beloved*, with whom Sethe unexpectedly joins to do something, as Morrison puts it in typically understated fashion, "appropriately and well" (84-85). Amy's care delivers both mother and child, Sethe and Denver; without her touch, neither one would have made it across the river. Rough Lock Bill is also an outsider who functions as a deliverer; not only does he literally pull the struggling Naomi from the lake, but his company helps to free the child from the silence and isolation in which she is drowning. Both Amy and Rough Lock Bill are unlikely caregivers. The latter's tone of voice, moreover, "neither angry nor kind" (144), is as disarming as the "dreamwalker's voice" (79) in which the former speaks. Indeed, these two characters constitute revisions of traditional figures of care, and even their speech reflects the larger narrative project of linguistic reclamation.

Both *Beloved* and *Obasan*, to be sure, find ways to speak of the unspeakable and tell of things too horrific to be told. Paul D's answer, for instance, to Sethe's "careful" question as to why at a crucial point he said nothing to Halle—"I had a bit in my mouth" (69)—relates without embellishment the unrelatable fact of the matter. In *Obasan*, as well as in *Beloved*, details are apparently interspersed "without chronological consistency" (Kogawa 236), and there is much devil's confusion to be sorted, for these are not stories of linear progression that tell of slavery, war, and dislocation definitively giving way to stability, freedom, and peace. However, often adopting an approach similar to Sethe's—that of "[c]ircling, circling"—these texts undeniably find ways of "getting to the point" (162). But like the Biblical passages they cite, both narratives take as their focus the imagining not of an unimaginable past, but of a future that must be seen—figured—in order to be claimed. As it relates stories of women and men to one another and thereby to the reader, Morrison's novel defamiliarizes slavery, freedom, and love, conveying a powerful sense not only of what these terms might have meant, but also of what they might yet mean. And in its vision of possibilities for reconfigured relationships and communities, *Beloved*, like related texts such as *Obasan*, begins to make us hear "what language was made for."

Jean Wilson
McMaster University

Bibliography

Alcoff, Linda. 1988. "Cultural Feminism versus Poststructuralism: The Identity Crisis in Feminist Theory." *Signs: Journal of Women in Culture and Society.* 13 (1988): 405-36.

Barnett, Pamela E. 1997. "Figurations of Rape and the Supernatural in *Beloved.*" *PMLA* 112 (1997): 418-27.

The Holy Bible. King James Version. Cleveland: World Publishing, n.d.

Homer. 1965. *The Odyssey.* Trans. Richmond Lattimore. New York: Harper & Row, 1975.

Kogawa, Joy. 1981. *Obasan.* Toronto: Penguin, 1983.

Kuhn, Anna K. 1988. *Christa Wolf's Utopian Vision: From Marxism to Feminism.* Cambridge: Cambridge University Press.

Morrison, Toni. 1987. *Beloved.* New York: Plume, 1988.

Wyatt, Jean. 1993. "Giving Body to the Word: The Maternal Symbolic in Toni Morrison's *Beloved.*" *PMLA* 108 (1993): 474-88.

V. Remembering War and Revolution

Hermann Kesten, Georges Limbour :
Visions de l'Apocalypse espagnole

Dans son avant-propos au dossier de *L'Herne* intitulé *Les écrivains et la guerre d'Espagne*,[1] Marc Hanrez soulignait l'impact, sur toute une génération, de cette "dernière 'croisade' où l'Europe se trouva engagée, vis-à-vis d'elle-même comme à la face du monde": les œuvres littéraires évoquant la guerre civile sont pour les lecteurs d'aujourd'hui le témoignage non pas seulement d'une réalité tragique, mais aussi la preuve que "la littérature sait, à l'occasion, se dépasser elle-même et agir sur son temps". Claude Pichois, dans ce même dossier, se donne pour but d'esquisser une "problématique de la guerre d'Espagne"[2]: selon lui, si, dans le cas de la guerre civile espagnole, "la mort, les mutilations, l'injustice" ont pu devenir littérature, c'est, bien au-delà des raisons idéologiques et politiques, parce que cette "dernière guerre romantique en Europe" posait aussi aux intellectuels de tous bords le problème de l'engagement concret et non pas seulement abstrait. La pertinence de cette analyse ne saurait être remise en cause. Cependant, les deux romans que nous nous sommes proposé de comparer n'obéissent pas tout à fait à cette optique particulière—c'est précisément l'une de leurs originalités—, tout simplement parce que l'histoire qu'ils racontent se situe à la fois en dehors et à l'épicentre du conflit: les personnages de *La pie*

---

1   *Cahier de l'Herne*, Paris, Éditions de l'Herne, 1975, p.9.

2   *Ibidem*, p. 13.

voleuse[3] et des *Enfants de Guernica*[4] ne sont pas des belligérants: Kesten aussi bien que Limbour représentent une Apocalypse venue d'un Ailleurs incertain, anéantissant la vie tranquille d'une bourgade repliée sur elle-même, sans que celle-ci ait pu sinon prévenir, du moins comprendre l'origine de ce malheur. Même si la riposte armée des villageois survivants aux attaques des Maures marque la fin du roman de Limbour, comme si le cataclysme subi avait aussi provoqué une sorte de réveil des consciences, le point de vue privilégié dans les deux œuvres, bien qu'elles diffèrent par d'autres aspects, n'est pas tant celui d'hommes ou de femmes engagés corps et âme dans un combat pour la liberté que celui d'enfants et d'adolescents (Kesten), de jeunes gens et de jeunes filles (Limbour) évoluant dans un environnement *a priori* paisible, et soudain confrontés à la destruction et à la mort. Aussi est-ce moins de cet héroïsme populaire souvent décrit dans les œuvres évoquant la guerre d'Espagne que témoignent les deux romans, que d'un massacre des innocents devenu le symbole même de la folie meurtrière, à l'instar de la toile de Picasso exposée pour la première fois à Paris en 1937.

Au fil de notre lecture comparée, nous chercherons à mettre en valeur les aspects essentiels du travail de symbolisation à l'œuvre dans ces textes, sans pour autant gommer les caractéristiques propres à chacun d'entre eux: à cette fin, nous préciserons toutes les relations qu'ils entretiennent avec la réalité historique, puis nous comparerons leur structure et leurs partis pris d'écriture respectifs, ainsi que les modalités descriptives particulières caractérisant dans chaque œuvre l'évocation de la catastrophe finale.

La première partie du roman de Limbour, paru à Paris en 1939, la même année que l'œuvre de Kesten, fut rédigée en 1936, au tout début du conflit espagnol, tandis que la seconde, qui occupe le dernier tiers du récit et évoque la destruction du village par des bombardiers allemands, ne fut écrite qu'après 1937. L'action semble se situer en Catalogne, puisque c'est la "sardane" que dansent les villageois lors de la fête annuelle, dans les collines, avant que ne sonne l'heure fatale. Le village n'est nommé qu'une fois, par le personnage d'Emilia, de retour dans son village natal après une période d'exil volontaire "en ville" (sans précision de lieu), lors de laquelle elle a été confrontée aux horreurs de la guerre civile. Cette invocation lyrique résonne comme une prophétie

---

[3]   Paris, Gallimard, "L'Imaginaire", 1995.

[4]   *Die Kinder von Guernica*, Frankfurt/M.-Berlin-Wien, Verlag Ullstein, 1981 (éd. originale: Amsterdam, Allert de Lange Verlag, 1939) ; trad. française Paris, Calmann-Lévy, 1954 ; le texte n'a pas été réédité en France.

pathétique peu avant la catastrophe finale:

> Carolina, j'ai peur, ô Lissa, bien que la joie ne m'ait pas
> ramenée vers toi, je t'aime, à cause des bocaux, des ballons sur
> la plage, à cause des nénuphars qui ont guéri ma folie. Mais
> quel incendie te menace, quelle destruction, ô mon village.
> Puissent tes draps blancs, toujours lavés, ne pas étancher le
> sang des blessés, la sueur des douleurs, la boue des ruisseaux
> collés aux membres qu'on n'a pas eu le temps de laver!
> Puisses-tu, au milieu du malheur qui nous entoure et nous
> frappe, résister aux pluies de feu que nous enverrons nos
> ennemis, résister à la démence, à la cruauté. Oh! Puissent tes
> pierres rester debout au pied de tes remparts en ruine. (PV,
> p.152-153)

Contrairement à ce qui se passe dans le roman de Kesten, aucune date précise n'est mentionnée dans *La pie voleuse*. L'aspect documentaire ne semble pas intéresser Georges Limbour, qui lui préfère la création d'un microcosme poétique reflétant une vision du monde toute personnelle. Au lieu de notations spatio-temporelles explicites et vérifiables, on trouvera donc dans ce roman des *situations* et des *allusions* à la guerre civile, et cela, exclusivement dans la seconde partie du récit, rédigée après 1937: Limbour y décrit successivement le passage de la "F.A.I." (Federación Anarquista Ibérica), le sac de l'église et l'incendie des chasubles, la destruction du village par l'aviation allemande, et enfin la défense contre les Maures, organisée tant bien que mal par les villageois. Ces faits sont en rapport direct avec une réalité historique brûlante à laquelle l'auteur, qui adorait l'Espagne, ne pouvait demeurer indifférent. Le lieu unique et tragique de l'action est ici le "pueblo" naguère enchanteur, et quasi anonyme, où il semble que n'existent ni radio, ni journaux, ni personnages susceptibles d'établir un lien avec le reste du monde: les paroles d'Emilia citées par nous plus haut ont une valeur symbolique, et non pas référentielle (en revanche, dans le roman d'Hermann Kesten, un certain nombre de personnages secondaires, de passage dans cette petite ville très active qu'était Guernica avant la catastrophe, ont pour fonction d'apporter à la famille Espinosa telle ou telle nouvelle de l' "extérieur"). L'insularité de l'espace où se déroule l'action romanesque est du reste caractéristique du récit limbourien, comme l'a noté Yves Michaud.[5]

Hermann Kesten, né le 28 janvier 1900 à Nuremberg, devint, en 1927, directeur littéraire des éditions Kiepenheuer, à Berlin. En 1933, son opposition

---

[5] V. "Les talismans", *Critique*, août-septembre 1976, p. 835-843.

au nazisme et son rôle dans le courant de la "neue Sachlichkeit" le contraignirent à s'exiler, d'abord en France,[6] puis en Grande-Bretagne et en Hollande, où il travaillera aux éditions Allert de Lange. En 1940, Kesten émigre aux Etats-Unis, dont il devient citoyen. Il y luttera contre le fascisme et pour les droits de l'homme, au sein des groupes d'intellectuels exilés. *Die Kinder von Guernica* a paru chez A. de Lange en 1939. Le cadre du roman, tristement célèbre depuis avril 37, est situé dès le titre: le récit se donne comme le témoignage d'un "enfant de Guernica", Carlos Espinosa, lequel va raconter son histoire à un narrateur premier, personnel et anonyme, d'origine allemande, lui aussi réfugié à Paris, pour des raisons que l'on devine même si elles ne sont pas explicitées: de toute évidence, ce "témoin auditif" n'est autre que le double fictionnel de l'auteur lui-même. Thomas Mann, dans sa préface à la traduction française, n'a pas manqué de souligner, malgré l'hommage rendu par ailleurs à Kesten, l'artificialité du procédé ici utilisé: "faire parler tout au long de 167 pages (...) un gamin de quinze ans, fils d'un pharmacien de Guernica, un garçon comme les autres, beau, jeune, doué certes d'une voix de basse surprenante, aux traits de jeune fille, aux yeux noirs et intelligents, n'est-ce pas un peu *trop* de fiction esthétique?" Mais, comme le souligne un peu plus loin le préfacier, l'enjeu moral excuse le manque d'originalité du procédé: Kesten, par le biais d'un récit attestant l'horreur de la tragédie espagnole, se donne pour but de réveiller la conscience engourdie de ceux qui "traversent le monde en dormeurs",[7] comme le souligne amèrement Carlos. Le récit premier, même si cela n'est pas explicitement précisé, se situe au printemps 1938. Le récit second commence *in medias res,* par une évocation très allusive, pudique, du lundi 26 avril 1937 ("N'oubliez pas cette date", dit Carlos à son interlocuteur, EG, p.7) ; la scène de la cave, qui sera reprise et détaillée beaucoup plus tard dans la narration (EG, p. 149) est ici simplement esquissée: nous comprenons seulement que, parmi les douze personnes qui se réfugièrent ce jour-là dans cet abri précaire, sept ont péri: le père et quatre frères et sœur de Carlos, le préparateur, Soces, et enfin un homme de loi dont nous ne pouvons pour le moment expliquer la présence en ces lieux infortunés. Le chiffre sept est bien évidemment symbolique, d'autant plus qu'avant le drame, la famille Espinosa comptait sept enfants, de sept à dix-sept ans. Commencent ensuite les retours en arrière: une première analepse, d'amplitude très brève, évoque le début de cette après-midi fatale. Une seconde analepse nous ramène quinze mois auparavant, le 18 juillet 1936 à midi (EG,

---

[6]   On trouvera dans l'ouvrage de Soma Morgenstern, *Fuite et fin de Joseph Roth*, Paris, Liana Levi, 1997 (pour la traduction française), divers renseignements sur les relations de l'écrivain autrichien avec le couple des Kesten, notamment durant l'année 1934.

[7]   EG, p. 138.

p.11): au début des troubles politiques, annoncés à la radio devant une famille presque indifférente,[8] correspond le retour du frère prodigue, Pablo, qui depuis vingt ans n'avait donné signe de vie. La collusion symbolique entre date historique et date privée est claire, puisque c'est le 18 juillet 1936 que Franco lança son manifeste contre la jeune république espagnole, donnant ainsi le signal du soulèvement. Cette analepse complète va rejoindre p. 149 le point chronologique où commençait le récit du jeune garçon. La fin du roman constitue une sorte de long épilogue: Carlos évoque son itinéraire ainsi que celui des survivants de sa famille, du 26 avril 1937 au printemps 1938 (EG, p. 161-193). Tout au long du texte, les allusions aux faits historiques sont à la fois nombreuses et fiables, dessinant les grandes lignes d'une toile de fond historique sur laquelle se déroulent des événements privés fictifs mais vraisemblables.[9] Le roman acquiert

---

[8]

EG, p. 17-18: "A ce moment-là notre radio se mit à bourdonner. C'était Ghil qui l'avait branchée. Et tandis que Pablo continuait ses histoires, l'appareil tambourinait, chantait, sifflait en sourdine comme d'habitude. Suivirent des informations que personne n'écouta. Seul Ghil, tout en marchant au pas dans la salle avec une allure de général, répétait certains mots en chantonnant: '- Général Mola... Pampelune... Rébellion... Faites feu!'"

[9]

Nous avons choisi de relever et de préciser ces allusions (la pagination renvoie ici à la traduction française): événements du 18 juillet 1936 (p. 18-20), allusion à Companys, depuis 1931 premier gouverneur civil de Barcelone, et qui parvint le 20 juillet 36 à juguler la rébellion avec l'aide des anarchistes (p. 20); revendications des autonomistes basques, représentés dans le roman par le marchand de poisson Ortueta, nouveau "Roi de Guernica" (p. 36) et allusion aux nombreux groupuscules antagonistes qui se déchireront tout au long de la guerre (p. 37): "Il déclarait n'appartenir ni à la république ni aux généraux. Droite et gauche, communistes, socialistes, républicains, carlistes, phalangistes, requetes, tous avaient le diable au corps! Lui, Evaristo Malax-Etxebaria Ortueta, marchand de poisson, homme du peuple, pensant bien, voulait la grande égalité, le ciel sur la terre. 'Sainte nation basque', proclamait-il, 'suis-moi, moi, ton chef!'"; évocation de la chute de Saint-Sébastien, le 12 septembre 1936, précédée par l'assaut sur Irun, le 3 septembre, lors duquel Beorlegui fut blessé à la jambe: "On racontait qu'Irun était en flammes, que Beorlegui avait une jambe gangrenée, que les commissaires de Saint-Sébastien n'avaient voulu que sauver leur jolie ville du feu, ce pourquoi certains gigotaient déjà, pendus aux palmiers du bord de mer." (p. 74-75: les anarchistes, qui voulaient incendier la ville avant qu'elle fût prise par l'ennemi, furent en effet exécutés.) Ces événements signifiaient pour les Basques la coupure d'avec la France, pays ami: cela explique, dans la diégèse, l'angoisse croissante du père de Carlos, qui veut émigrer, à l'instar d'une famille amie, les Elola, et se heurte à mille obstacles, à commencer par l'impossibilité de vendre la pharmacie pour se procurer l'argent nécessaire. Plus loin, il est fait allusion aux événements de septembre et octobre 1936, à savoir l'avancée des Nationalistes dans le sud de l'Espagne et la proclamation solennelle de la liberté basque, sous l'autorité d'Aguirre, le 7 octobre. Ensuite, les allusions historiques concernent principalement la situation économique, rendant quasiment impossible toute transaction, et le siège de Bilbao (p. 120-123), suivi, le 31 mars 1937, par la destruction de Durango (la date est ici précisée par Carlos, tout comme celle de la destruction de Guernica, alors que les autres événements de la guerre ne font pas l'objet de telles précisions chronologiques. Le père de Carlos ayant été "par hasard" témoin de ce nouveau drame, la menace pesant sur Guernica se précise: de même que dans *La pie voleuse* les événements vécus par Emilia, la destruction d'une ville toute proche a ici valeur prophétique, alors même que les habitants poursuivent leurs tâches ordinaires sans vouloir croire en un danger imminent). Enfin, les événements vécus par Carlos après qu'il a échappé au massacre sont également conformes à la réalité historique (pour plus de précisions, v. notamment l'ouvrage d'Hugh Thomas, *La guerre d'Espagne* (1961)1, Paris, Laffont, 1985.

par là une valeur documentaire, tout en échappant à la neutralité en principe attendue du simple "compte-rendu": la sensibilité du lecteur est en effet constamment sollicitée par le récit pathétique de Carlos, ponctué par des réflexions au présent de vérité générale dans desquelles le jeune garçon interpelle son interlocuteur (et donc, à travers lui, le lecteur potentiel de l'œuvre): ces passages, qui correspondent à des retours à la situation narrative du récit premier, en des moments où le récit second devient particulièrement doulou- reux, sont signalés dans la traduction française par des italiques et des blancs typographiques les isolant du récit second, alors que dans le texte original n'existe aucune séparation de cette sorte entre le récit de Carlos et ce que nous pouvons appeler son "commentaire", fortement marqué par la voix auctoriale. Nous n'en citerons qu'un bref extrait, situé au cœur même de l'évocation du 26 avril 1937, et caractéristique d'une écriture ouvertement "didactique":

> Combien dure une vie humaine? murmura-t-il, puis il poursui-
> vit après un silence: Mieux vaut n'en pas parler. Mais est-ce
> qu'une vie humaine se présente toujours ainsi? Sont-ce là tous
> les secrets, tous les rêves d'une vie? Je me demande si mes
> expériences sont générales... Voilà donc le visage de la gran-
> deur de l'homme? Des êtres humains meurent comme ça? Et
> ils ont vécu comme ça? Pour ça? (EG, p.160 ; KVG, p. 99).

Il semble bien que ce soit dans cette manière particulière de commenter—ou de ne pas commenter—l'horreur du massacre que réside l'une des différences essentielles entre le récit de Limbour et celui de Kesten: on a là deux manières presque antagonistes d'investir le récit fictionnel d'une fonction "idéologique": dans les deux cas en effet, sans conteste possible, c'est bien à une dénonciation de la guerre que nous avons affaire.

On notera tout d'abord que l'on ne saurait trouver dans le roman de Limbour, contrairement à ce qui se passe chez Kesten, la trace d'une intention didactique ouvertement exprimée. Seuls deux brefs passages, au début de la seconde partie de l'œuvre, laissent entendre l'écho de la voix auctoriale: lors du passage des anarchistes, tout d'abord, annoncé par un puissant avertisseur automobile ("Jusqu'alors, sur un tel village, le malheur s'annonçait par la voix des cloches: le tocsin! Et c'était l'incendie, la peste, les sauterelles, la famine, les volcans: les mauvais coups de la nature. Mais la sirène: c'est le fer, le plomb fondu, le pétrole, le gaz: le mal de l'homme: la destruction totale." PV, p.128), puis juste avant l'évocation de l'attaque aérienne ; cette seconde occurrence se fonde sur une allusion métaphorique au supplice infligé aux prisonniers carthaginois, dans l'Antiquité ("De nouveaux suppliciés, sans que leurs paupières aient été coupées, garderont leurs prunelles qu'aucune nuit ne remplira d'ombre, toujours ouvertes sur l'horreur." PV, p.159).

Selon la même logique, confirmant la différence fondamentale entre l'écriture de Kesten et celle de Limbour, alors que Carlos, narrateur-témoin, s'exprime dans une langue extrêmement neutre, simple, "objectiviste", tant dans son lexique que dans sa syntaxe, des plus dépouillées, le récit limbourien, en focalisation zéro, autorise une grande liberté stylistique, en particulier dans l'usage d'un système métaphorique sur lequel repose la cohérence du récit. Par ailleurs, bien que la construction générale des deux textes soit tout à fait similaire, puisque dans les deux cas s'opposent la narration de la période précédant la catastrophe (une année environ, couvrant les trois quarts du récit) et la description de cette dernière, détruisant tout en l'espace de quelques heures, l'opposition symbolique entre deux visions du monde ainsi traduite va renvoyer chez l'auteur allemand à une dimension idéologique, et chez Limbour à une perspective exclusivement poétique.

Dans *Les enfants de Guernica*, s'affrontent non seulement, au tout début du roman, le père de Carlos et certains représentants du village, indépendantistes fervents "excités" par les rumeurs guerrières, mais surtout les deux frères: il s'agit là d'un véritable "topos", traité cependant d'une manière assez originale par l'auteur, qui retarde le moment de l'affrontement "ouvert"[10] et met subtilement en valeur, sans céder aux facilités du manichéisme, les ambiguïtés inhérentes à l'attitude propre à chacun des deux frères. L'un comme l'autre en effet refusent l'engagement armé dans le conflit, et semblent préférer l'individualisme à la défense d'une communauté menacée, même si leurs motivations et leurs tempéraments respectifs diffèrent radicalement: alors que le père de Carlos cherche avant tout à préserver sa famille d'un malheur imminent, et prône une morale de la tolérance, une forme d'humanisme sans nul doute idéaliste, Pablo nous apparaît comme un histrion irresponsable, profondément sceptique, uniquement préoccupé de préserver son propre bien-être, à n'importe quel prix: c'est avec la fiancée qu'il avait vingt ans plus tôt abandonnée sans trop d'arrière-pensées, et devenue la femme de son propre frère, qu'il vivra, après Guernica, le parfait amour. Dans le roman de Kesten s'entrelacent donc étroitement un drame historique, à portée universelle, et un drame familial à valeur symbolique, qui n'est pas sans évoquer les souffrances intimes d'un écrivain lui-même rejeté par sa mère patrie... Le choix ultime de

---

[10] EG, p. 129-134.

Carlos est déterminé par l'ensemble de ces événements, et c'est bien son point de vue à lui et à lui seul que Kesten nous invite à partager en condamnant à notre tour, tout autant que les actes des meurtriers eux-mêmes, l'indifférence égoïste de tous ceux qui "secouent leur terreur comme la poussière de leurs souliers en pensant: 'Est-ce que ça me regarde!'" (EG, p.140)

La première partie du roman de Limbour évoque elle aussi un conflit d'abord latent et insidieux, qui va progressivement éclater au grand jour et se résoudre d'une façon dramatique. Mais il est d'une nature bien différente de celui qu'évoque Kesten. Au petit groupe d'amis formé par Gisèle, Gérard et Geneviève, dont on notera qu'ils ont en commun l'initiale du prénom de Limbour, peuvent être opposés les "notables" d'un village enfoncé dans sa torpeur et ses superstitions. Les premiers ont la jeunesse, la grâce, et le don de la fantaisie, celui-là même que Limbour accorde aux personnages les plus proches de lui. La blonde Gisèle, au charme étrange, semble l'âme du petit groupe ; en son langage tissé de métaphores, elle préserve l'essence d'un monde encore intact. Une poésie fantasque, apparentée au merveilleux des contes, guide et motive ces protagonistes: lorsque Gisèle, avec l'aide de Gérard, dissimule dans la pâte du boulanger les objets dérobés par la pie qu'elle a naguère recueillie, le lecteur songe à Peau d'Ane changeant sa bague en fève, pour un gâteau princier... Mais ici la "farce" dégénère en tragédie: l'infâme et répugnant Cornelius—incarnation de la veulerie, à l'instar d'Ortueta dans le roman de Kesten—, vociférant à la tête d'une cohorte haineuse, mettra sauvagement à mort la "pie voleuse" recueillie par Gisèle, et cette dernière, blessée peu de temps après par de bien symboliques chats noirs, finira par succomber: ce sont ces crimes que le village expie, dans la seconde partie du roman. Dans une atmosphère spécifiquement limbourienne, où les signes du réel, porteurs d'un sens mystérieux, tissent d'étranges réseaux, deux visions du monde s'affrontent: l'une, apparentée au merveilleux, manifeste une harmonie à la fois ludique et poétique entre l'être et les objets du monde, animés ou inanimés. L'autre se fonde au contraire sur un rapport de consommation et d'appropriation, c'est-à-dire de destruction. C'est donc moins l'universalité d'un message humaniste que vise Georges Limbour, que l'expression d'un monde intérieur.[11]

Pour ces raisons mêmes, alors que dans le roman d'Hermann Kesten l'évocation du désastre se voit dépouillée de tout ce qui pourrait apparaître comme une forme d'"esthétisation", elle se fonde chez Georges Limbour sur un réseau d'analogies et d'échos inversés reliant la première et la seconde partie du

---

[11]   Selon Jean-Pierre Barou, "cet écrivain n'a jamais misé sur le triomphe de la réflexion. Il répugne aux clartés trop vives." ("Le don", *Critique*, août-septembre 1976, p. 743.)

récit en une même visée d'abord et avant tout esthétique: à travers ces quelques pages (six pour *Die Kinder von Guernica*, le double pour *La pie voleuse*), nous tenterons pour finir de dégager les caractéristiques essentielles du "vérisme" d'un Kesten, par opposition à la vision essentiellement poétique de Georges Limbour.

L'ancrage de nos deux textes dans une réalité historique douloureuse ayant déjà été commenté, on ajoutera simplement que, dans le cas de Kesten, la référence explicite à Guernica exige à l'évidence une certaine fidélité à la réalité objective des faits, alors que Limbour dispose *a priori* de plus de liberté—celle, en l'occurrence, de son propre imaginaire—dans l'évocation du malheur qui frappe le village de *La pie voleuse*. Du même coup, les modalités de la description diffèrent: alors que les précisions données par Carlos sont exclusivement d'ordre chronologique et topographique, et conformes au déroulement des faits, dont Kesten s'est manifestement très précisément informé, Limbour multiplie les détails d'ordre plastique, en combinant très subtilement les "manières de voir" propres à tel ou tel personnage focal et un réseau métaphorique organisé autour de deux motifs principaux liés à la vie quotidienne du village: la fabrication du pain, d'une part, et le blanchissage du linge, d'autre part. Par ailleurs, un certain nombre d'éléments, communs aux deux textes, relèvent de ce que nous pourrions appeler une topique tristement universelle: le vacarme assourdissant des avions et des bombes éclatant de toutes parts, comparé dans les deux cas au grondement d'un tonnerre, au passage d'un ouragan,[12] l'obscurcissement du ciel,[13] la terreur et l'hébétude commune aux bêtes et aux hommes, indifféremment massacrés et déchiquetés,[14] la mort partout répandue parmi les ruines et

---

[12] EG, p. 161 et KVG, p. 100: "Es donnerte in den Lüften. (...) Rauch, schwarz und gelb. Hitze. Feuer. Die Erde wälzte sich." PV, p. 161: "Alors la première détonation retentit comme si la terre elle-même répondait aux tonnerres célestes par ses propres explosions, que des volcans s'ouvraient dans le village, vomissant de la fumée, de la terre noire et des pierres."

[13] EG, p. 162 et KVG, p. 100: "Da war kein Himmel mehr. (...) Der Taumel, wie blind, wie taub." PV, p. 161: "Le ciel était devenu très sombre où le chien distinguait mal ces grandes bêtes noires (bien que le gris-bleu de leurs ailes métalliques dût scintiller dans le soleil) parce que les fracas battaient si fort les tympans qu'ils mettaient un crêpe dans le cerveau: c'était la nuit et ceux qui se souviennent d'avoir vu, n'ont vu qu'à la lueur du feu."

[14] EG, p. 162 et KVG, p. 100: "Die Flieger schossen auf die Schafe mit Maschinengewehren, begreifen Sie, und die Schafe starben hilflos blökend, wie Kinder. Und die heulenden Hunde fielen um und heulten nicht mehr. Und die Flieger schossen auf das blökende Vieh auf dem Viehmarkt ; (...) Sie schossen auf Menschen wie auf Vieh." PV, p. 160: "Au hurlement du chien, des milliers de cris de surprise et de terreur répondirent dans le village" et 162: "dans le bref temps de cette tempête, la voix unique du village était passée du cri aigu mais bien vivant de la terreur, à la plainte sourde d'où fusaient les hurlements, au long bêlement de la douleur et de l'agonie."

les cendres... Seule la mise en œuvre de ces motifs diffère et obéit aux lois internes de chacune des œuvres. Dans le roman d'Hermann Kesten, le 26 avril 1937 est évoqué par un narrateur qui est à la fois victime et témoin: la loi de vraisemblance psychologique à laquelle est soumis ce personnage lui interdit en quelque sorte de pouvoir faire de son atroce expérience le point de départ d'un "tableau", fût-il destiné à dénoncer l'horreur: cette démarche exigerait un travail de recréation dont la proximité de son deuil le rend incapable; son récit ne constitue dans cette voie qu'une première étape: même si un écart d'ores et déjà sensible existe entre temps de la diégèse et temps de l'énonciation, l'évocation de Carlos demeure surdéterminée par son statut de témoin et d'adolescent: il est des choses qu'il ne *peut* dire, mais dans ces blancs du discours, dans ces pauses frémissantes et pudiques, est cependant *exprimée* l'horreur de visions insoutenables. En outre, la focalisation interne nous place tout au long du texte dans la conscience d'un seul personnage, alors que dans *La pie voleuse* le point focal se déplace: le cataclysme est d'abord pressenti par le chien galeux de Cornelius, qui, sous l'effet d'une violente et instinctive terreur, va recouvrer un instant l'ouïe et la vue, avant d'être tué par une bombe. Le point focal est ensuite déplacé sur le personnage de Geneviève: à demi évanouie pendant le bombardement, elle revient peu à peu à elle et déambule par les rues méconnaissables, à l'instar de Carlos courant sous la mitraille après avoir été arraché à la nuit sépulcrale de la cave. A travers le regard effaré de la jeune femme, nous découvrons le corps atrocement mutilé d'Emilia, dont la description, sur près de deux pages, a pour fonction de contraindre le lecteur à voir lui aussi l'image dont le personnage focal se détourne d'abord avec horreur, sans pouvoir pourtant s'y dérober: le narrateur omniscient prend ici le relais d'un être brutalement confronté à une réalité insoutenable, et qui pourtant va parvenir à dépasser sa répulsion face à la mort, et trouver en lui la force de rendre à ce corps détruit et souillé un ultime hommage: "Ces intestins, ces peaux lisses et fluides, ces parois râpeuses hérissées de petites langues remuantes comme le dessous d'une étoile de mer, c'est toi, Emilia. Il y a en toi des bandelettes assez longues, pour, séchées, t'enrouler comme une momie. Tu n'es pas plus laide que lorsque tu marchais nue dans la nuit d'été, tes pieds salis par la poussière! Humaine et mère! Voilà la paille, voilà le matelas sur lequel ton enfant poussa son premier soupir! C'est le premier grabat de l'homme." (PV, p. 166-167) Enfin, c'est à travers le regard d'un dernier personnage focal, Carolina, ouvrière naguère humiliée et misérable, à laquelle la guerre civile a rendu, pour un temps, la liberté, que nous poursuivons ce chemin de douleur, à travers les décombres. En découvrant et en "adoptant" l'enfant d'Emilia, Carolina confirme le rôle essentiel dévolu par Limbour aux figures féminines.

La "description ambulatoire", présente dans l'un et l'autre texte, n'obéit donc pas aux mêmes exigences. Alors que chez Kesten prime le désir farouche de dénoncer de la façon la plus claire et la plus transparente possible les atrocités commises, en se contentant d'en suggérer les effets (on peut ainsi noter la manière dont Kesten fait décrire par Carlos les maisons éventrées en usant d'un lexique renvoyant à la mutilation d'êtres animés), l'écriture de *La pie voleuse* tire sa puissance de suggestion d'une langue précieuse, incantatoire, féconde en descriptions poétiques et en mystérieuses allégories, et qui, bien plus que celle des surréalistes auxquels Limbour fut un temps apparenté, évoque la parole inspirée de Cassandre, derrière les remparts de Troie.

Comme nous avons pu le voir, les romans d'Hermann Kesten et de Georges Limbour évoquant la guerre d'Espagne sont caractérisés par une opposition structurelle entre un "avant" encore paisible, malgré certains troubles et signes prophétiques, et un "après" dramatique, où semble devoir être anéanti dans le feu et le sang tout espoir d'un bonheur possible. La description de cette Apocalypse constitue donc à la fois le terme et l'enjeu des deux récits ; elle en est aussi, d'un point de vue génétique, la partie la plus délicate, dans la mesure où l'écriture romanesque se voit ici confrontée à une question d'ordre éthique: celui qui n'a pas "vécu" la guerre civile—ou tout autre crime contre l'humanité—, celui qui n'a pas subi dans sa chair les épreuves atroces dont ont été victimes des milliers d'innocents, peut-il prétendre *dire* ce drame sans céder aux "facilités" de sa trop confortable position? L'un des objectifs de ce congrès est sans doute de rappeler la valeur intrinsèque de toute œuvre artistique susceptible de maintenir en éveil la conscience assoupie des hommes, trop prompts le plus souvent à oublier les cauchemars de l'Histoire, lorsqu'ils leur ont échappé. S'il existe encore une forme d'humanisme, sinon d'humanité, c'est peut-être en ces œuvres que nous pouvons la retrouver, et c'est pourquoi leur lecture, ou leur redécouverte, ne peut être, à notre sens, tout à fait inutile.

F. Godeau
Université Jean Monnet

Hermann Kesten, Georges Limbour: Vision de l'Apocalypse espagnole

Bibliographie

Limbour, Georges. 1995. *La pie voleuse*. Paris, Gallimard, collection "L'Imaginaire".

Kesten, Hermann. 1981. *Die Kinder von Guernica*. Frankfurt am Main/Berlin/Wien, Ullstein. (Edition originale: Amsterdam, Allert de Lange Verlag, 1939.) Trad. française: *Les enfants de Guernica*, Paris, Calmann-Lévy, 1954.

Cahier de l'Herne: Les écrivains et la guerre d'Espagne, Editions de l'Herne, Paris, 1975.

Critique. Numéro spécial "Georges Limbour", Paris, août-septembre 1976.

Morgenstern, Soma. 1997. *Fuite et fin de Joseph Roth*, traduit de l'allemand par Denis Authier. Paris, Liana Levi.

Pynchon and Oe:
Contemporary Conspiracies and World War II

In novels by Thomas Pynchon and Oe Kenzaburo, the modern world is rife with conspiracies, cults, and counter-realities. Sinister forces are at work undermining our trust not only in the real world of science, politics, and sex, but also in the "real" world of fiction. It has been observed that the innocent-looking word "plot," a traditional element of narrative, takes on a sinister meaning for the readers of Pynchon. As we follow one plot strand to another, there is the growing suspicion that we have become entrapped by the author or by the same sinister force which has possessed him. One recurring idea though is that the contemporary conspiracies are linked to people and events in World War II. One often has the suspicion, for example, that the novel is written in a code that must be cracked before the bombs fall on one's head.

The fictional world of Oe Kenzaburo as well has been hovering around some secret evil from World War II, some unresolved problem, some unacknowledged guilt and secret identification with the excesses of the war. Oe was about ten years old when the war ended (Pynchon was eight), old enough to see and experience both the reality of the Japanese war and of the American occupation. He has deeply ambivalent feelings about the war: for although he has been considered liberal and even left-wing by many, he has confronted the extremist in himself.

Here I would like to discuss the conspiracies in Thomas Pynchon's *The Crying of Lot 49* (1966) and Oe Kenzaburo's *Man'en Gan'nen no Futtoboru* (1967). They are both structured as detective stories in that they are attempts to pursue conspiracies, the protagonists feel that they are entrapped in conspiracies, and readers may or may not be manipulated into experiencing the text as a game version of some secret, deadly reality. In both novels, the secret evils behind the multiple conspiracies can best be understood as disguised versions of the World War II obsessions, based on the childhood experiences of these two authors which are played out more explicitly in their other novels.

The opening sentence of Pynchon's *The Crying of Lot 49* is as clear and precise and enticingly mysterious as its title:

> One summer afternoon Mrs. Oedipa Maas came home from a Tupperware party whose hostess had put perhaps too much kirsch in the fondue to find that she, Oedipa, had been named executor, or she supposed executrix, of the estate of one Pierce Inverarity, a California real estate mogul who had once lost two million dollars in his spare time but still had assets numerous and tangled enough to make the job of sorting it all out more than honorary. (9)

Oedipa Maas, whose name is no less puzzling than that of her former lover, Pierce Inverarity, is a suburban housewife who is suddenly required to settle the inheritance of this equally stereotypical American capitalist. But, "perhaps," we are told, there was too much kirsch in the fondue. The whole typical and yet bizarre situation alerts readers to the fictionality of the novel, to their roles as players in a precise, clever game that may or may not yield results.

In the novel, there are three overlapping conspiracies concerning: 1) Tristero, an alternate postal or communications system; 2) Oedipa Maas, a character who pursues the truth about her fictional world; and 3) the text which ensnares the readers into playing a game which they must learn as they play. Does Tristero exist? Does it control Oedipa? Does it create or deliver or subvert the text? The whole conspiracy concerning Tristero is actually an overlapping digression which appears suddenly, just as Oedipa sets out on her suddenly imposed duty of sorting out the details of her former lover's inheritance. Beneath the surface success story of this American millionaire are various links to the Tristero postal network, something which eerily reminds us of the internet, which traces its roots to a revolt against the totalitarian monopoly of the official postal system both in Europe and then later in America. This secret but paradoxically omnipresent network is a reflection of our desire to resist the monopoly of truth.

The text of the novel contains various "documentary" facts, obviously fabricated, which entice rather than enlighten us. The Tristero system is thus said to have begun as a counterforce to the monopoly of the postal system acknowledged by "the Protestant noble William of Orange" in the latter half of the sixteenth century. It survived the turmoil of European history for the next two hundred years, surfacing every once in a while whenever a ruler became overly oppressive in a region. Then, it is said, most of the members of the Tristero system fled to America in the 1850s, and since then, it has continued to exist as an underground postal system in America, reflecting the desire to protect their idealistic pursuit of the rights to life, liberty, and the pursuit of happiness. In this sense, Oedipa's investigation of the Tristero system turns out to be a rediscovery of the American spirit. And although neither she nor the reader are ever certain whether the Tristero system exists or not, we do learn of the possibility of such an alternative to the official control of communication, whether it be in cyberspace or in the novels secretly sent to market by a writer who has kept his whereabouts and even his physical appearance a mystery, which only recently seems to be on the verge of full discovery.

Oedipa's quest to settle the affairs of Pierce Inverarity leads her, by way of the Tristero mysteries, to attempt to sort out her own affairs, which remain indeterminate as long as she searches for something she fears—the overriding truth that will put everything in its proper and fixed place. In other words, she fears the discovery of a plot to the novel she inhabits. This paradoxical process can be described as paranoia, but it is playful as well. It is indeed a game which draws the readers into the text, letting them feel at times confident that they know better than Oedipa and at other times confused because they suspect that the joke is on them, that they are "waiting for Godot," that they are taking a joke seriously or completely missing the point.

The Crying of Lot 49, as a whole, conspires against its readers as much as it conspires with them in their search for meaning or for the equally comfortable conclusion that there *is* no meaning. Along the way, Pynchon subverts various strategies of interpretation and investigation such as decoding, conducting research, and systematically explaining texts. The fabrication of the history of the Tristero system shows us that fiction is not merely another way of writing about reality. While historical writing is official and authorized, fictional writing is an unofficial and unauthorized version of the same reality. This relationship parallels that between the authorized monopoly of the postal service and its counterpart, the Tristero system. While historical writings consist of facts, documents, and statistics, fictional writings consist of images, symbols, and other literary codes and signs. Instead of using the official network system of media, fiction passes on its message to people literally by hand, just as the Tristero delivery man hands a letter to each person. As mentioned previously, Pynchon is an extremely secretive author who sends out unofficial messages in the form of fiction.

The English title of Oe Kenzaburo's novel *Man'en Gan'nen no Futtoboru* is *The Silent Cry*, but the original title literally means "Football in the First Year of the Man'en Period (1860)." The original title better reflects the playful, postmodern aspect of the novel. By juxtaposing the historical Japanese period with a modern football game, Oe introduces the reader to the game of history in the novel: fact and fiction about the past and present leading to speculations about or models for the future.

As in *The Crying of Lot 49*, conspiracy is a central theme in this novel: first, there are the literal conspiracies of revolt in the past with parallels in the present; second, the main character suspects that he is not in control of his life and finds out that it is worse than he suspects; and third, the plot of the novel often seems a plot or conspiracy in which the readers find themselves caught up, as they try to play the history game but become suspicious or simply confused as the rules seem to change in the process of the game.

As in *The Crying of Lot 49*, there is a quest here, an obligation or duty that is somehow imposed on the main character Mitsusaburo and his brother Takashi when they return to a village on Shikoku Island because they want to put an end to their present troubles and search for a new life. Both brothers become entangled in the family history which reached a climax in the farmer's revolt of 1860 and its aftermath in 1870. While the younger brother actively engages himself in the present day social problems of his village in emulation of his ancestor, the older brother Mitsusaburo tries to find out just what happened and what it might mean.

Takashi organizes the village youths by playing football and eventually leads them in a final game to a riot against the only supermarket store in the village which Takashi believes has destroyed the self-sufficient village economy through its monopoly of the distribution system. He models the riot on the farmers' revolt in 1860 which was led by his ancestor, the younger brother of his great-grandfather, the village chief. Idealizing the farmers' revolt and identifying himself with its leader, Takashi romanticizes his football riot, which fails, leading him to commit suicide.

Meanwhile, his elder brother Mitsusaburo is rather cynical about Takashi's efforts and increasingly disillusioned with what he finds out from the historical records about the farmers' riot of 1860 and its leader. He attempts to reconstruct the historical truth by sifting through documents and village legends. In the process, he concludes that the revolt was insignificant and its leader a coward. This, of course, parallels his feelings about his brother's activities in the village.

After Takashi's suicide, however, he discovers some old documents in the cellar of the storehouse of their residence, and he is forced to revise his conclusions about the farmers' revolt, his brother's social activities, and his own perspicacity. He learns that the leader of the farmers' revolt had confined himself for the rest of his life in the cellar as a form of self-punishment. However, he did emerge once in 1870 to lead a successful revolt, only to return to his self-imposed imprisonment until he died. Mitsusaburo, humbled by his discoveries, renews his faith in human dignity.

It has been observed that the dates 1860 and 1870 correspond to important events in 1960 and approaching in 1970 in Japan—the riots against the renewal of the US-Japan Security Treaty. The novel was written in 1967, at a time when many Japanese looked back at the failure of the widespread riots in 1960 against the treaty, and looked forward to the possibility of a united resistance in 1970. Both of these treaties were of course based on "security" arrangements imposed on the Japanese after World War II, so here the football riots in the 1960s in the novel and the basically historical farmers' revolts in the nineteenth century should be seen in terms of the pattern of suppression and revolt in the relations between America and Japan since World War II. A current example of this confrontation can be seen in recent events in Okinawa, where the rape of a twelve-year old girl led to the largest and strongest opposition to the presence of American bases in Japan since the 1970s.

Just as Japanese have avoided the main problems—their responsibility in World War II and their relations with the United States since then—the main character heads for Shikoku at the beginning of the novel in order to avoid the main problems in his life. He has lost the sight of one eye in an accident, his first child was born with a serious brain defect, and his close friend went insane and killed himself in a bizarre, humiliating manner. Moreover, his wife has retreated to alcohol, fearing that he will also kill himself. Unable to understand why all of these things have happened to him, he grows paranoid, believing that some power is at work, trying to destroy him. Out of all of these misfortunes, it is the suicide of his friend that obsesses him. Although his friend was not political, he happened to be caught in the midst of the clash between the police and demonstrators against the US-Japan Security Treaty in June 1960. He was struck on the head by a policeman, and since then he suffered from a mental disorder. In an insane asylum, he protested against an oppressive caretaker, however, and was forced to leave. He went back home and killed himself in a humiliating manner.

Perhaps this obsession with the apparently absurd demise of his friend leads Mitsusaburo to criticize his brother's involvement in local grievances and to minimize the farmers' revolt and its leader. Eventually, he realizes that whether you are political or not, you can be the victim of the dominant power in society or worse, its tool. In order to live a dignified life, you must live with that awareness, no matter how terrifying it might be, and you must oppose oppression even if it means death. With this realization, he is able to stop escaping and merely observing, and he resumes his life with this awareness, free from paranoia.

As in *The Crying of Lot 49*, there is a central paradox in Oe's novel: trying to discover, uncover, or establish the absolute truth about a fictional situation. In a sense this is true of all fiction, but these two novels highlight the paradox by mixing fact and fiction in their history, by giving mysterious or preposterous names to characters and events, and by engaging the reader sometimes as an accomplice, sometimes as an outsider in an attempt to play the history game: writing, rewriting, and digressing in fanciful exploits to get at the truth which only the lies of fiction can ever reach.

Naomi Matsuoka
Nihon University

Bibliography

Hite, Molly. 1983. *Ideas of Order in the Novels of Thomas Pynchon*. Columbus: Ohio State University Press.

McHoul, Alec, and David Wills. 1990. *Writing Pynchon: Strategies in Fictional Analysis*. Urbana: University of Illinois University Press.

Oe, Kenzaburo. 1971. *Man'en Gan'nen no Futtoboru* [The Silent Cry]. Tokyo: Kodansha.

Pynchon, Thomas. 1986. *The Crying of Lot 49*. New York: Harper & Row.

Writing War: The Bosnian Conflict in Spanish Literature

Heraclitus, in fragment 53, tells us that "War is the father of all things". This statement can be read as a theory of conflict, and as such it serves as the basis for the influence of Heraclitus in the development of dialectical thought. But the sentence can also be interpreted more literally, as a reference to the role of war in history and culture. War is not only an everyday experience for a large part of humanity, but also a determinant factor in the configuration of collective memory, and of the identities of nations and communities. It is a phenomenon that belongs at the same time to our past and to our present, even if only through the media.

Karl von Clausewitz—the Prussian general, a contemporary of Napoleon, who wrote the most influential theoretical essay on the subject—defined war as the continuation of political intercourse through other means. It is a restricted definition that focuses only on the perspective of the State, leaving aside many other ways in which war affects the functioning of the society and the existence of individuals. On the other hand, if, as the military historian John Keegan argues, "[war] is always an expression of culture, often a determinant of cultural forms, in some societies the culture itself" (1993:12), then this cultural phenomenon leaves traces we constantly read in a multitude of signs and representations: cemeteries, monuments, texts, films... The wound of war leaves a scar, in the flesh or in memory—that is its sign. The question is what are the relations between that sign and the event simultaneously inscribed in it and absent from it.

This unbreachable distance—in Derridean terms a *différance*—between experience and representation is somehow doubled by the view from the outside. We also need to take into account the possibility that the cultural context of the representation may be different from that of the event, in cases where an outsider mediates in its narration—I will later analyze this issue in relation to Juan Goytisolo's writings. Thus the foreigner's narrative allows the ontological split to be reproduced within the text, whereby the cultural difference foregrounds the observer's separation from the event.

In *Murder in Our Midst*, Omer Bartov wonders whether our "massive exposure to images of past violence (in which by definition we can no longer intervene) has accustomed us to view images of present violence *as if* they too were happening in the past", making us confuse not only past and present, but also real and fictitious, authentic and false, "progressively transforming reality into fiction and memory" (1996:10).

The question posed by Bartov makes our own position as addressees of the representation comparable to the viewpoint of the foreign observer, who functions as our proxy within the text. Horror is part of our reading of the images and texts that represent the violence and suffering of war. It does not seem possible to approach and interpret them without taking into account that they refer to a human experience. However, horror is not always a decisive component in the representation of war. We often consume representations of war without being horrified, even as entertainment, for pleasure. I am here not only referring to products such as *Rambo*, but also to the *Iliad*.

The representation of war is a fundamental and foundational act within our culture: Homer's *Iliad* and the Trojan War inaugurate at the same time the epic tradition and an uninterrupted dialogue between narrative discourse and armed conflict. History and literature are mutually influential because, suggests James Tatum, "as wars pass from experience into memory, those who survive them as well as those who come long after them, shape their own discoveries of war into patterns first to be found in Homer" (1986:16).

War is one of the main driving forces in history, just as the epic as a genre has narrated the course of history above all in terms of military exploits. But the view we characterize as epic is ideologically biased, to the extent that it glorifies heroism and other similar values. We could characterize the epic as one of the faces of military propaganda, in the sense that, as Daniel Pick points out, "Battles do not necessarily begin when the first shot is fired. The relationship between language and military deeds must be reconceived. Words, ideas, images constitute the discursive support for military conflict; they should be understood not as though they were mere froth without consequences, but as crucial aspects of the destructive reality of violent conflict itself" (1993:14).

War has framed and made possible two of the most traumatic events in contemporary history: the Holocaust and the deployment of the atomic bomb in Hiroshima and Nagasaki. The question of whether the horror of those experiences can be represented has often been raised. Everything that is traumatic in a war seems to be *domesticated* by literature, the epic being its oldest and most conventional form of domestication.

The same tendency appears in the other arts as well. In the paintings in the Hall of Battles at Versailles, for example, we encounter many versions of the subject in which it is easy to observe the exaltation of heroism and glory as well as the marginal space assigned to suffering and death. It is in opposition to this epic tendency, so characteristic of 19th-century painting, that Goya created his *Disasters of War*. His engravings respond to the urge to give a truthful testimony of what happened, to show the less glorious face of war, which often leads Goya to inscribe in his work the position of the witness, for example in the title of "Yo lo vi" [I saw it]. This documentalist impulse has suggested comparisons between the *Disasters* and war photography, but the same impulse is in fact shared by narratives, memoirs, and films, which set against the epic glorification of war a demand for truthfulness. I quote from a short story about Vietnam by Tim O'Brien, "The Things They Carried":

"A true war story is never moral. It does not instruct, nor encourage virtue, nor suggest models of proper human behavior, nor restrain men from doing the things men have always done. If a story seems moral, do not believe it. If at the end of a war story you feel uplifted, or if you feel that some small bit of rectitude has been salvaged from the larger waste, then you have been made the victim of *a very old and terrible lie*. There is no rectitude whatsoever. There is no virtue. As a first rule of thumb, therefore, you can tell a true war story by its absolute and uncompromising allegiance to obscenity and evil" (1990:76).

This "very old and terrible lie" against which O'Brien is warning us evokes the one in the ending of a well-known poem by Wilfred Owen about the First World War:

... My friend, you would not tell with such high zest
To children ardent for some desperate glory,
The old Lie: Dulce et decorum est
Pro patria mori.

Any allusions to truth and lie in this context bring up the issue of the referentiality of discourse. The desire or the need to account for the experience of war illustrate the tension between history and story, between reality and fiction. Evelyn Hinz remarks that "of all types of literature, war literature seems the most resistant to the notion that literary texts are autonomous constructs without any referential status or grounding in reality" (1990:vii). Maybe we feel that there is something obscene in ignoring the reality of death, that it is an offense inflicted upon the dead themselves. That is why one of the basic conventions of the genre requires establishing whether the author has been an eyewitness to the events, as if narrative responsibility was in this case accompanied by some moral responsibility.

But the veracity of documentary or testimonial discourses can never go unchallenged. Whether in Troy or in Bosnia, by means of film documentaries or photo journalism, of memoirs or novels, the subject of war makes evident the most contested aspects of mimesis. Even for military historians, the "battle piece", the description of the actual engagement, is a narrative genre ruled by conventions that are basically literary, and of questionable reliability as a depiction of the events. As Hinz notes, "Truth is the first casualty of war" (1990:ix). Writing war involves a battle between writing and reality, and requires confronting the conflict inherent in the difference between experience and representation. Because what escapes representation is precisely the *disaster* of war, in the sense used by Blanchot in *The Writing of the Disaster*. One of the common issues shared by studies on war and research on the Holocaust is the view that the horror of the event is beyond words (Cobley 1996:6), and that, I quote from Hinz, "literature invariably distorts and domesticates the violent and irrational nature of war" (1990:vi). In other words, when we examine the tradition of the representation of war we can verify how the conventions of this representation constitute a system of rhetorical figuration which attempts to contain—meaning both to accommodate and to restrain— a chaotic experience and subject it to an order that endows it with meaning.

Assuming that a representation involves an interpretive operation, the one that is mediated by a foreign perspective might be seen as a sort of translation. I will not try to explain why a writer writes about a foreign war, but how: how is his position as an outsider registered in the text? This kind of displacement is typical of the Spanish Civil War of 1936-39, which produced numerous accounts by foreigners such as André Malraux, George Orwell, Ernest Hemingway, W.H. Auden. Spaniards, on the other hand, have rarely ventured out of their own wars in this century. The war in Bosnia is an exception that has left traces in Spanish culture: two fictionalized accounts by journalists who covered the conflict—Arturo Pérez Reverte's *Territorio comanche* and Julio Fuentes's *Sarajevo: Juicio final*—and two books by Juan Goytisolo that will be the focus of my discussion, *Cuaderno de Sarajevo* (1993) and *El sitio de los sitios* (1995). Each follows certain generic conventions, but in this privileged space of interaction between literature, memory, and history (and also journalism) there are slippages between fictional genres and those allegedly anchored in the reference to an experience.

Cuaderno de Sarajevo belongs to a very traditional literary genre: the travel journal—as do Peter Handke's accounts, which, however take quite different positions. *Cuaderno* is the journal of a non-combatant traveler who narrates his visit to Sarajevo during the summer of 1993, following an invitation by Susan Sontag, who was staging *Waiting for Godot* in the besieged city. The account relates immediate facts about the conflict to themes that have concerned Goytisolo for a long time: international passivity is compared with the policy of non-intervention during the Spanish Civil War, which favored Franco then as it did the Serbs later; the strategy of ethnic cleansing is associated with the old persecution of Muslims and Jews in Spain, and with the recent wave of racism spreading throughout Europe. For Goytisolo, behind the figures of murders, rapes, and tortures hides "la memoria del horror" [the memory of horror] (1993:43). Opposed to this memory is the killing of memory, what Goytisolo calls "memoricidio": the cultural genocide symbolized by the destruction of the Sarajevo National Library. Thus the testimony of the book implies a double fight against oblivion: the act of writing is an attempt to give voice to both the present horror and the legacy of the past.

This writing nevertheless reveals itself as insufficient. To start with, it is limited by the point of view; it is the testimony of a passing foreigner who has not suffered the experience and narrates it from the outside. The book consequently needs to incorporate other voices and testimonies, and thus there are abundant quotes from journalists, politicians, and victims. As if this proliferation was not enough, the text overflows its margins by means of glosses and commentaries in the author's handwriting (reproduced in facsimile); in addition, there are photographs with their own captions. Autobiography is fused with autograph and photograph as a form of direct testimony, but this inscription of the author within the text reveals even more clearly his position outside the experience.

The insufficiency of the testimony in *Cuaderno de Sarajevo* is confirmed by the novel *El sitio de los sitios*. In an interview for the newspaper *El País* (4/12/95), Goytisolo explains: "After *Cuaderno de Sarajevo*, after the numerous articles and reports and films I have made from and about the besieged city [...] I understood that only fiction could cure me, that only through an extreme fiction could I exorcise the nightmare" (8). This concept of extreme fiction acquires a specific meaning: *El sitio de los sitios* is a text ruled by indetermination and uncertainty; any possibility of a truthful narration of war is violently questioned.

It is a novel in which the author writes his own death, inscribed in the book through the death in Sarajevo of a character who shares the initials J.G. with the author, but whose identity is a mystery. The strategy of the novel resembles Blanchot's view of the disintegration of the subject, who appears fragmented as an effect of the violence of the traumatic experience: "To think the way one dies: without purpose, without power, without unity" (39). The identification of thought and writing with death is, according to Blanchot, the only way to confront the experience of the disaster: making it equivalent to the experience of writing.

The starting point of the story is the alleged death of J.G., the alleged initials of an allegedly Spanish traveller, in a room of the hotel H.I. in the besieged city of S.—thinly disguised references to the Holiday Inn in Sarajevo. The scene begins when the traveller, watching through the hotel window, sees a passer-by ducking down to elude the snipers, and ends with an explosion. A Spanish commandant with the UN forces, who has been sent to investigate the event, discovers that the corpse has disappeared, but finds among its belongings a book of poems with a homoerotic content, with the initials J.G. on it. He also finds a collection of four stories written in the third person, which make reference to the siege of a district inhabited by immigrants in a city that, although it is not named, we easily identify as Paris. Later a fifth story is found that, according the commandant, "corresponded word for word to the content of the first pages of the present book" (1995:60). How could the mysterious J.G. have written his own death, asks the commandant. And how can the commandant know the content of this book, asks the reader.

The novel is constructed as an intricate puzzle of sites, of viewpoints, of narrators, which the texts itself identifies, following Bakhtin, as a "polyphony of voices" (122). There are numerous textual sources for the multiple discourses woven into the fabric of the novel: short stories, erotic and mystical poems, letters, dream sequences, which seldom refer directly to the actual fighting. *El sitio de los sitios* is thus a labyrinth of fragmented subjectivities. Goytisolo circles around the disaster, writing from its margins and on its margins—as he did in the *Cuaderno*. The characters' dissemination of discourses is part of the inhabitants' fight in the besieged city: "Victims of the brutality of history, we took revenge on her with our stories, woven with concealment, interpolated texts, simulated occurrences: such is the marvelous power of literature" (155).

The confusion generated ends up affecting the very same people responsible for it, who seemed to control the "authorship" of the text. A series of crossings and overlappings, of motifs inexplicably repeated across texts of different and distant origins and sources provoke doubts about who wrote them. Any explanation about the sequence of events is called into question by the process of dispersion and contamination of the texts, to the point that the characters themselves become aware of their own unreality.

Nobody seems to control the narrative, as if it were war itself that writes: "Someone—the warlords and their accomplices—writes the storyline and manipulates us like puppets from their watchtower! Reality has transmuted into fiction: the horror story of our daily existence" (162). The writing of the disaster, following Blanchot, is not only what is written about the disaster, but also what the disaster writes: which is the inscription of disaster in our culture, its imprint, its trace, and its memory. And what Blanchot suggests is that the disaster de-scribes, unwrites (1986:7), because its discourse challenges the capacity of writing to register it, and that of the subject to make sense of it.

Goytisolo resorts to the fictionalization of a very real war in order to fight against its reality. The last chapter, narrated by the so-called "compiler", returns to the initial scene: the traveller's gaze through the hotel window focuses on a woman who is crossing the street, only now she is the one who dies from a sniper's shot. The account is followed by a "Note from the author":

> With average courage and a little public spirit, the writer was twice in Sarajevo during the worst days of the siege: the horror and indignation for what he saw still consume him, and he had to resort to fiction to escape and heal from the images that besieged him. Such is the power of literature.
>
> But the siege continues and three hundred thousand people are still trapped in the formerly beautiful city without any possibility of escape or healing in sight. Such is the final limit of literature. (183)

Two sieges, that of the city and that suffered by the writer, and a limit between both, a frontier of the siege, between an inside and an outside, that also divides reality and literature. *El sitio de los sitios* signifies that siege and that limit, thanks to the proliferation of its meanings. The title of the novel has multiple meanings, hinging on the various senses of the word "sitio": it can be read as the siege of sieges or the site of sites: it is, as a metaphor, a center of condensation and multiplication of meaning. The novel makes use of a siege in Paris as a metaphor of the siege of Sarajevo, which is itself, like Guernica, a metaphor of other places and other conflicts. In the same way as Troy is the siege of sieges and the site of sites: the siege and site that founds all war stories.

The novel becomes the site of the siege of reality by writing. The interaction between literature, history, and memory, and the struggle to re-present an event that belongs to the present as much as to the past, find in the writing of war a double site of conflict: the experience of conflict and the conflict of representation. But if literature can be the repository of cultural memory, it is not only through the epic tradition and the domestication of war, but also because of its capacity to wage war within writing.

Antonio Monegal
Barcelona

Bibliography

Bartov, Omer. 1996. *Murder in Our Midst: The Holocaust, Industrial Killing, and Representation*. New York: Oxford University Press.

Blanchot, Maurice. 1986. *The Writing of the Disaster*. Lincoln: University of Nebraska Press.

Cobley, Evelyn. 1993. *Representing War: Form and Ideology in First World War Narratives*. Toronto: University of Toronto Press.

Fuentes, Julio. 1997. *Sarajevo: Juicio final*. Barcelona: Plaza & Janés.

Goytisolo, Juan. 1993. *Cuaderno de Sarajevo*. Madrid: El País-Aguilar.

—————. 1995. *El sitio de los sitios*. Madrid: Alfaguara.

Handke, Peter. 1997. *Apéndice de verano a un viaje de invierno*. Madrid: Alianza.

—————. 1996. *Un viaje de invierno por los ríos Danubio, Save, Morava y Drina*. Madrid: Alianza.

Hinz, Evelyn J., ed. 1990. *Troops versus Tropes: War and Literature*. Winnipeg, Can: University of Manitoba Press.

Keegan, John. 1993. *A History of Warfare*. New York: Vintage.

O'Brien, Tim. 1990. *The Things They Carried*. New York: Penguin.

Pereda, Rosa. 1995. "Sarajevo estaba sometido no a un sitio, sino a varios (Entrevista)," *El País*, 4-12-1995, 8.

Pérez Reverte, Arturo. 1997. *Territorio comanche*.Madrid: Ollero y Ramos.

Pick, Daniel. 1993. *War Machine: The Rationalization of Slaughter in the Modern Age*. New Haven: Yale University Press.

Tatum, James. 1986. "The *Iliad* and Memories of War," *Yale French Review*, 76.1 (1986), 15-31.

Reverberations of the Battle of Kosovo:
The Mountain Wreath and Ethnic Cleansing

The year 1847 was, as Vasa Mihailovich has aptly called it, "the banner year in Serbian literature" (ix). The Karadjordje uprisings of 1804 and 1814 had, it is true, been suppressed by the Ottomans, but with the final defeat of Napoleon in 1815, the Turks had become wary of renewed Russian capability to support the restive Serb nationalists and so they struck a deal with the rebel leader Obrenović establishing the status of the Belgrade pashalik as an autonomous province. Thus, while Serbia and Montenegro did not win international recognition as independent nation states until 1878, at the Congress of Berlin, the Serb cultural revival was in full swing by mid-century, led notably by the pioneering work of Vuk Karadžić in collecting and publishing the rich trove of Serbian oral epic poems, rendering them accessible to the emerging class of literate intelligentsia and enabling them to play a key role in the new nationalist consciousness (Judah 55). In 1847 Karadžić published another important work, his own translation of the New Testament, into current demotic Serbian; the same year Branko Radičević published his *Poems*, the first collection of Serb lyric poetry in the modern vernacular, and Petar Petrović Njegoš, the Prince-Bishop of Montenegro, published his magnum opus, the verse-drama *Gorski Vijenac* (The Mountain Wreath), inspired by the kind of oral epic poems Karadžić was collecting, and dedicated to the modern Serb freedom fighter Karadjordje.

It is almost impossible to overstate the importance of *The Mountain Wreath* in the landscape of modern Serb culture. As Vladeta Popović's introduction to the 1930 James Wiles' English translation of the work puts it:

> What Shakespeare is to England, Njegoš is to Serbia: her greatest and most nationally representative poet. Njegoš's finest work, *The Mountain Wreath (Gorski Vijenac)*, has had a success unparalleled by any other product of Serbo-Croatian literature, both at home and abroad. English is the tenth language into which it has been translated, the others being Russian, Bulgarian, Czech, Slovene, Italian, German, Hungarian, Swedish, and French. In Serbo-Croatian lands it has had a better fate than classics usually have; it is not admired from a respectful distance, but much and widely read and loved. (Popović 11).

Mihailovich, in the introduction to his own, more recent, English translation concurs, saying, "It epitomizes the spirit of the Serbian people kept alive for centuries; indeed, there is no other literary work with which the Serbs identify more" (Mihailovich ix). The Nobel Prize winning Bosnian Serb novelist, Ivo Andrić, offered his own testimonial to the power and importance of Njegoš and the *Mountain Wreath*; in an article entitled "The Ever-Present Njegoš," Andrić argued that "Njegoš is with us all the time," our teacher and supreme counsellor in "the painful search for the true way" (cited in Zorić 79). Corroboration came in 1988, on the occasion of the 175th anniversary of the birth of Petar Petrović Njegoš, when "throughout Serbia, Vojvodina and Montenegro, people at gatherings carried Njegoš's picture and posters with his verses. This was an unforgettable sight," recalled Pavle Zorić with enthusiasm a year later. "Is there anything more beautiful, more sincere and more profound than those pictures and verses written out from memory, not dictated by learned people or copied out of collected works?" (79).

Specific individual witness is provided by the noted revolutionary dissident Milovan Djilas in his classic *Land Without Justice*, where he records his own intoxication in being caught up in the chanting of the old bardic *guslars*, already a rarity in the land; he goes on:

> I had read most of the folk epics while still in elementary school. Frequently I recited them to the villagers. They liked

most of all to listen to the *Mountain Wreath* by Bishop
Njegoš, not only because they had heard that this was the
greatest Serbian poem, but because they found in it more
than anywhere else the greatest expression of their way of
thinking and feeling. They found in it the essence of their
ancient and still-present struggle for survival and the
honour of their name on a soil that was barren in everything but men. The *Mountain Wreath* contained higher
truths, their truths, truths that they had already anticipated, yet which were narrated in a more concise and lofty
manner. One could stop reciting at any verse, and someone
else would take it up and continue. Sometimes people would
interrupt the narrator to interpret passages, ardently and
long ... They experienced the *Mountain Wreath* as simultaneously loftier and simpler than other literature. It
uncovered for them something untransitory, something that
would last as long as their race and tongue survived. It was
expressed in the language of every day, woven together
powerfully and completely, as though it were not created at
all, but existed simply of itself, like a mountain or the clear
untamed gusts of wind and the sun that played on it. These
people hardly knew the Bible. For them the *Mountain
Wreath* might have served as such a book. (*Land Without
Justice* 130)

Djilas in fact wrote a whole polemical monograph on Njegoš; his
lengthy analysis of the *Mountain Wreath* in that volume concludes with
his own ecstatic effusion:

> *The Mountain Wreath* extends beyond the existence of our
> people. In it is recounted all the suffering, all the spiritual
> beauty, of our life here in the Balkans, all the bloodshed,
> woe, and misfortune, as well as the inextinguishable quest
> for the good and light. ... It will move and inspire anew each
> succeeding generation and every person who enters into its
> beauties and essence.
>
> *The Mountain Wreath* is a poem that has never been
> excelled in our literature, nor can it be, as a conceptual
> synthesis and poetic expression of our destiny: the Serbian
> destiny under absolute laws, human resistance to cosmic
> evil, the lyrical expression of a national drama—our people
> in song.

> In *The Mountain Wreath* and through it the Serbian people
> became conscious of themselves and declared themselves to
> the world. ... *The Mountain Wreath* shall ever remain the
> expression of our own destiny. (*Njegoš* 372)

It is time to ask just how "the Serbian people," as Djilas says, declare themselves to the world in *The Mountain Wreath*; to ask, what, in fact *is* the message of this "mountain gospel of Njegoš," as critic Milan Komnenić calls it (Komnenić 70).

The reader who is not at all or not very familiar with *The Mountain Wreath* might, one imagines, be somewhat shocked to set a first reading, or a fresh rereading, of the poem alongside these extraordinary testimonials. That the work itself is correspondingly extraordinary—of that there is no doubt. As it is a conversation play, with most action offstage, the plot itself can easily be summarized. *The Mountain Wreath* is a kind of docu-drama that conflates a series of characters and situations from the Montenegrin history and, for dramatic unity, concentrates them in a single action, during the episcopacy of Bishop Danilo, set at the beginning of the 18th century, at a time when, as the translator James Wiles himself summarizes the situation, "a number of the Montenegrins themselves, like their cousins in Bosnia, had become perverts to Islam" ("Scope and Setting" 61—this, I wish to emphasize, is how the 20th-century English translator saw fit to articulate it). Another admirer of *The Mountain Wreath*, Ivo Andrić, often taken in literary circles for a cultural liberal, in his 1924 doctoral dissertation on "The Development of Spiritual Life in Bosnia," had commented that "Njegoš, who can always be counted on for the truest expression of the people's mode of thinking and apprehending, portrays in his terse and plastic manner the process of conversion thus: ... The lions turned into tillers of the soil, / The cowardly and the covetous turned into Turks" (Andrić, *Development* 20). It is the very ethnic kinship of the Islamicized Slavs with their Christian neighbours that sets up the "problem" from a Christoslavic viewpoint. The linguistic and folkloric researches of Njegoš's contemporary Vuk Karadžić had a decisive impact on Greater Serbian ideology, as Tim Judah concisely explains: "The thrust of his argument was that the Slavs of the region were not different peoples but rather one people divided by religion—that is, Orthodoxy, Catholicism and Islam. While the Orthodox mostly called themselves Serbs, the problem with the people of the other confessions was that they would not recognize the fact that they too were Serbs. ... but Serbs who refused to acknowledge the fact" (61-62). Michael Sells draws from this the consequent double-bind of Islamicized Slavs:

> As *The Mountain Wreath* and the national mythology it expressed became more popular, Slavic Muslims were placed in a particularly impossible situation. By the linguistic standards of Vuk Karadžić, since the Slavic Muslims spoke South Slavic dialects Vuk Karadžić labelled Serb, they were considered Serbs. But by the standards of *The Mountain Wreath*, all Serbs had to be Christian, and any conversion to Islam was a betrayal of Serb blood and entailed a transformation from Slavic to Turkish blood. Slavic Muslims could not escape being considered Serb because of the Vuk Karadžić linguistic criteria, but as Serbs they had to be considered traitors according to the Njegoš mythology. They were delegitimated as a group and dehumanized as individuals. (43-44)

And this, of course, is exactly how Milovan Djilas, commenting on *The Mountain Wreath*, sees it: as for the "Turkish renegades and those nameless Montenegrins who consort with them," he says, "The hatred expressed for them in *The Mountain Wreath* knows neither measure not limit. They are an evil nurtured in one's own breast. ... For this is the ultimate treason—the acceptance of an alien faith, way of life, and even language, that is, those delights and Turkish expressions that are characteristic of our Moslems" (*Njegoš* 337). As Bishop Popović put it in his very partisan introduction to James Wiles's translation of *The Mountain Wreath*:

> The spread of Mohammedanism among the Montenegrin tribes became a serious danger. Christianity and nationality with more or less primitive people were the same thing. If Christianity went, national customs went with it. Language would remain, but the people would be cut away from the bulk of the Serbian nation, and would feel like a man in a fog. This is what may be seen today [1930] in Bosnia: the Mohammedans speak Serbian and consider themselves as Serbs, but the stream of their energy has been blocked, and, not mingling with the current of Christian Serbia, it is flowing nowhere and it is stagnating. (Popović 22)

[This, incidentally, is the kind of expression that one is likely to find even in academic comments on Serbian national literature.]

In the opening scene of *The Mountain Wreath*, on the eve of the annual Whitsuntide Festival, Bishop Danilo, alone, at night, delivers himself of a long brooding state-of-the-world monologue on the destiny of nations. He contemplates the rising tide of Islam, where "Besides Asia, where their nest is hidden,/ the devil's tribe gobbled up the nations— ... a mosque arises where the broken Cross lies" (*The Mountain Wreath*, trans. Mihailovich ll. 19-20, 59). Some of Bishop Danilo's warriors insist on "cleansing" (*čstiti*) the land of non-Christians (ibid., ll. 93-95, 131-132; and see Sells 41; Bogert 180). Their actions would thereby avenge the ancient defeat by the Turks at the battle of Kosovo in 1389 and follow the example of the self-sacrificing hero Miloš Obilić, who had assassinated Sultan Murad in his tent (ll. 215-248). Then, as the devotees bring their crosses to the summit of Mount Lovćen, a heavenly portent appears: two flashes of lightning form a cross in the sky.

The next series of scenes, making up the bulk of the play, occur during an assembly on the feast day of the Nativity of Mary. The opening Kolo (a circle dance of the folk, used here as a Greek chorus representing the collective voice of the people) rehearses the sufferings of the Serb people, disasters they have brought upon themselves in the past by disunity of the rulers and nobles, culminating in the worst disaster of all, which is that native kinsmen—Montenegrins, Serbs—have defected from Christendom, and become Islamicized:

> The high mountains are reeking with heathens.
> In the same fold are both wolves and sheep,
> and Turk is one with Montenegrin now.
> Hodja bellows on the plain Cetinje!
> A stench has caught the lion in the trap,
> wiped out is now the Montenegrin name,
> no one crosses himself with three fingers.
> (*The Mountain Wreath*, trans. Mihailovich ll. 284-290)

As one of the Montenegrin nobles then sums up the challenge this represents:

> May God remove all the trace of our race
> if we should live in cowardice and disgrace!
> Why the devil in Christian land of ours?
> Who do we feed a snake in our bosom? (ll. 304-307)

But Bishop Danilo, who is "tortured ... by blackish thoughts," sees that this is a much more problematic situation than previous battles, however disastrous, against invading Turks:

> But I do fear the evil at our home,
> Some wild kinsmen of ours have turned Turkish.
> If we should strike at our domestic Turks,
> their Serbian kin would never desert them.
> Our land would be divided into tribes,
> and tribes would start a bitter, bloody, feud. (ll. 530-535)

In typical epic fashion, a great debate ensues, including the Muslim neighbours, who are invited to participate. The most militant Christian nobles insist that the Montenegrin Muslims abjure their faith and return to Christendom, and if not, why then "both our faiths will be swimming in blood./ Better will be the one that does not sink" (ll. 866-867). Interestingly, Njegoš presents the Muslim spokesmen as accommodators who see no need to talk of changing faith: "Aren't we brothers despite differences?/ Didn't we fight the same battles together?/ We share the good and the bad like brothers./ Doesn't both Turkish and Serbian maidens' hair/ cover in grief the graves of slain heroes?" (ll. 969-972); "Though this country is a bit too narrow,/ two faiths can live together side by side,/ just as two soups can be cooked in one pot./ Let us live on together like brothers,/ and we shall need no additional love!" (ll.1019-1023). The debate is inconclusive and interrupted by a series of episodes that each cast a different light on the matter; one is a Muslim wedding party that includes Christian wedding guests, a party that ends in mutual recriminations and leads one of the militant Christian nobles at Danilo's assembly to comment on such dishonourable fraternization: "Shameless, brazen, and stinking-dirty whores!/ Those plate-lickers, bringing us dishonor!/ They know of no dignity of heroes,/ or else they wouldn't hanker after the Turks./ They're more hateful to me than the Turks" (ll. 1896-1900).

The figure who puts an end to these inconclusive proceedings is the aged blind Abbot Stephen. His monologue presumes to rise above mere national interests and pragmatic political calculations and to cut through to the fundamental realities, in this case, that

> A fierce struggle lies ahead of you all;
> Part of your tribe has renounced its own roots
> and is therefore serving the dark Mammon!
> The curse of shame has now fallen on it.
> What is Bosnia and half of Albania? ...
> Your destiny is to bear the Cross
> of the fierce fight against brothers and foes!
> (ll. 2341-2345, 2348-2349)

This leads the assembled Christians to swear an oath to fight to the death to exterminate their Muslim kinsmen from Montenegro and to bring down a terrible curse on anyone disloyal to this commitment:

> may all he has turn to stone and ashes!
> May the Great Lord with his awesome power
> change all the seeds in his fields to pebbles
> and the children in his wife's womb to stone!
> (ll. 2410-2413)

This crusade to exterminate Muslim kinsmen becomes, then, the fulfilment of that "heroic vision" uttered by one of the militant Montenegrins earlier in the poem: "Let the struggle go on without respite./ Let it be what men thought could never be" (ll. 659-659)—about which Ivo Andrić has said, "Nowhere in the poetry of the whole world nor in the destiny of nations have I found a more terrible battle cry ... Yet without that suicidal absurdity, without that stubborn negation of reality and the obvious, no action would be possible, or any thought of any action against evil" (quoted in Djilas, *Njegoš* 339).

Part III takes place almost four months after this oath-taking, on another liturgical occasion, Christmas Eve. It begins with Abbot Stephen, who in Njegoš is more of a philosopher of Christoslavism than he is a churchman, pronouncing he has put this "troublesome world" through the "sieve and colander" of his mind and "drunk to dregs its cup of poison" (ll. 2486-2488). He has learned the Heraclitian lesson that this world is a tyranny, a "work of infernal discord" (ll. 2499-2501), a theatre of endlessly striving dualities, so that the Muslim/Christian conflict by implication is simply one more manifestation of the endless cosmic strife of light against darkness. This sets the stage for the series of announcements that constitute the action of this final movement of *The Mountain Wreath*. These terrible announcements detail, district by district, the extermination of the Muslim (called "Turkish") communities of Montenegro:

> We put under our sharp sabers all those
> who did not want to be baptized by us.
> But all those who bowed to the Holy Child
> and crossed themselves with the sign of Christian cross,
> we accepted and hailed as our brothers.
> We set on fire all the Turkish houses,
> that there might be not a single trace left
> of our faithless domestic enemy...
> Out of their mosque and of a small building
> we made a pile of accursed rubble there,
> as a warning of shame to all people. (ll. 2599-2613)

Bishop Danilo's reaction to this news is unambiguous: "You have brought me great gladness, my falcons,/ great joy for me. Heroic liberty!" (ll. 2614-2615). Abbot Stephen then dispenses communion and the assembly celebrates with Christmas Eve festivities, including the dancing of the kolo and the distribution of the folk dish of cooked wheat mixed with pomegranate seeds and topped with wine and honey. This action is reprised in a following scene on New Year's Day as another messenger announces yet another extermination of a Muslim community, following the death of two Christians who had challenged them to "spit at the Koran"; now "They are razing the town of Obodnik/ with its Turkish towers and single mosque,/ so our market will not reek of heathens" (ll. 2704-2706). And in another town, after a bloody fight with many Christian casualties, finally, "we did kill all Turks in Crmnica/ and Besac fort we levelled to the ground,/ there is no trace of e'en one single Turk/ if you did search our entire district now,/ save for headless corpses or a ruin" (ll. 2720-2724). This time Bishop Danilo is moved to weep because of all the Christian deaths, but Abbot Stephen can only laugh in exaltation:

> Yes, I grasped it, but I still cannot weep.
> If I only knew how to weep for joy,
> my weep would be sweeter than e'er before.
> It's so with me, when my soul is singing,
> my tears dry up from joy and happiness. (ll. 2728-2732)

Milovan Djilas's gloss on this passage is: "The Abbot seems to say that evil and good each come in their turn, for so it goes in this world, but the massacre fulfilled the supreme law, and this only gives cause for rejoicing [!]" (*Njegoš* 348). In the folk poem from which Njegoš took his subject, Bishop Danilo is not, interestingly enough, portrayed as at all irresolute; right at the beginning he gives the straightforward order, "Let us slaughter Turks in Montenegro" and when the job is done he shouts for joy, "Dear God, thank you for everything,/ I have yearned for this feast for a long time!" (Koljević 167). In any case, Tim Judah notes that if this glorification of massacre in the mouth of an abbot in a poem penned by a bishop should seem "incongruous", we should not forget "the context in which Njegoš wrote ... Outside his monastery window were arrayed the impaled heads of slain Turks" (64). Judah is alluding to the story of a visit to Bishop Petar Petrović Njegoš by an English officer named Gardner Wilkinson published in *Blackwood's Magazine* for January 1845; when Wilkinson, aghast at the impaled heads and welter of skulls, remonstrated with the bishop, the latter explained that if the Montenegrins ceased to pay the Turks in their own coin, the Turks might interpret this as weakness and invade. The egregious Rebecca West, who regales us with this story, adds her own addendum: "He might also have pointed out that the Montenegrins were constantly obliged to cut off the heads of their fellow-countrymen who were wounded on the field of battle lest the Turks should find them alive and torture and mutilate them; and that they could hardly be blamed if they did to the Turks what the Turks had often forced them to do to their own kind" (1047). Thus does West see a gruesomely logical circle complete itself.

At any rate, Djilas's own summing up of the message of Njegoš's verse-drama is as unambiguous as that of Njegoš's Abbot Stephen: "The struggle in the *Mountain Wreath* is resolved in the end—the good triumphs, being the essence, if not the very aim, of life and of the world" (*Njegoš* 359). He goes on to speak of how "this poem of limpid and boundless mountain beauties" sings of the past "as though it were still alive," that, indeed, *The Mountain Wreath* "is a link between past and present, directed toward the future"—"For art is action" (ibid., 361, 340).

This ominous implication has more than fulfilled itself. We can begin with Gravilo Princeps, a young Bosnian Serb with but a high school education, who nonetheless was one of those who knew *The Mountain Wreath* by heart, and was filled with the spirit of Miloš Obilić, the assassin of Sultan Murad at the ancient battle of Kosovo, whom the Christoslavic heroes of *The Mountain Wreath* held up as their great prototype in the war against Islam. A member of the militant Serb nationalist group known as *Narodna Odbrana* (Union or Death), dedicated to the unification of all "Serbdom," brooding over the 1878 annexation of Bosnia by the Austro-Hungarian Empire, Gavrilo proved himself one of those who make happen those things "men thought could never be," by assassinating Archduke Ferdinand in Sarajevo on June 28, 1914. It was no accident that the assassination was carried out on June 28, or Vidovdan (St. Vitus Day), the anniversary of the Battle of Kosovo (see Dedijer, chapter XI).

But this singular act, overwhelming as its consequences may have been, does not begin to take the measure of the impact of *The Mountain Wreath* on cultural and political history. Commentary on the poem, even in academic sources, has been almost entirely in a nationalistic vein and silent about the implications of ethnocide, as is evident in the work of Emmert (*Serbian Golgotha*) and Dragnich and Todorovich (*Saga of Kosovo*), and the essays from the Stanford symposium collected in *Kosovo / Legacy of a Medieval Battle*, edited by Vucinich and Emmert. It is only the "ethnic cleansing" campaign of the Bosnian war that has begun to prompt a revised moral critique of the poem and the tradition it represents. As Tim Judah has recently put it, "There was another side to *The Mountain Wreath* far more sinister than its praise of tyrannicide. With its call for the extermination of those Montenegrins who had converted to Islam, the poem was also a paean to ethnic cleansing" (65). To be blunter yet, I would suggest that we can view the poem as a virtual *blueprint* for the campaign of "ethnic cleansing" waged in Bosnia from 1992 through 1995, culminating in the mass exterminations carried out in the UN-proclaimed "safe area" of Srebrenica in July 1995 as the hapless leaders of the United Nations and NATO went into denial and looked the other way. Srebrenica represented perhaps the single worst war crime perpetrated in Europe since World War II, but it took David Rohde's series of articles in the *Christian Science Monitor* in August 1995 to force the world to acknowledge it, just as Roy Gutman's articles for *Newsday* had forced a reluctant Western world to acknowledge the reality of the death camp at Omarska and the use of mass rape as a weapon in the Serb campaign of "ethnic cleansing" in Bosnia in 1992 (see Honig and Both, Gutman, Allen).

And now how chilling in retrospect are those seemingly dispassionate analyses, such as Milovan Djilas's, that view the massacres of *The Mountain Wreath* not as definitive acts, but symbols of an "inevitable" historical, even cosmic, process (*Njegoš* 310, 315, 320). Viewed from what Djilas calls "a dogmatically humanistic standpoint, the massacre seems identical with the St. Bartholomew's Day massacre of the Huguenots—the extermination of human beings because they are of another religion. Yet nothing," he continues, "could be further from the truth." This extermination of Islamicized kinsmen is, instead, Djilas argues, a "necessity" of "spiritual survival," and "by its inevitability it became the most sacred obligation" (ibid., 317); driven "to fulfill a higher, absolute necessity involving his brethren turned Turk. ... 'One must plunge into the river of blood' ... For if absolute law makes evil and misfortune inevitable, then the struggle against them is also inevitable" (ibid., 342-343, 345). The genocidal events in Bosnia from 1992-1995 (as Simon Wiesenthal has said, and as Elie Wiesel told President Clinton at the dedication of the Holocaust Memorial Museum in Washington, this was genocide, "absolutely") have now definitively demonstrated the consequences of such cosmic allegorizing of ethnic politics. Translator James Wiles said more than he realized in his introduction to *The Mountain Wreath* when he noted somewhat casually that "It is one of the remarkable things about Yugoslav legend that so much of it has come true" ("Tale" 37). Indeed it has, and the international tribunal for crimes against humanity is currently attempting to deal with the consequences.

In light of these horrific events in Bosnia, the role of epic heroic literature in inculcating values of "ethnic cleansing" is far from negligible. Literature teachers are fond of citing the adage that, while it may be hard to get the meanings out of poems, people all over the world are dying for lack of what's in them. But how much more hermeneutically painful it is when promoters of culture have to acknowledge a situation where people are dying, in part, *because of* poetry. If not precisely part of the "core curriculum" of Serb education, *The Mountain Wreath* was, as already noted, "widely known by heart by the illiterate population of Montenegro and naively taken to justify the eradication of the Islamicized population of Montenegro by their Christian brothers, appropriately enough, on a Christmas Eve at the end of the seventeenth century. This reading was fully endorsed by patriotic scholarly opinion" (Koljević 166). And now we have seen the reprise of that process in relation to the killing fields of Bosnia. In a general way, to be sure, we have long been aware of "patriotic gore" as a literary project, of what Wilfried Owen in "Dulce et decorum est" identified as the purveying with "high zest" the lies of patriotic self-sacrifice. Nonetheless, it must still have come as something of a shock to most viewers of the Paul Pawlikowski documentary "Serbian epics" (broadcast on BBC2's "Bookmark," December 16, 1992) to see Radovan Karadžić, the Bosnian Serb leader and now indicted war criminal, playing a gusla and singing a favourite epic poem in the home of his distinguished forebear and folklorist Vuk Karadžić. "Even more stunning," Tim Judah comments, "were the soldier gusla players Pawlikowski found who were singing for a new generation of Serbian warriors."

> Not only did they sing the old songs: 'Oh, beautiful Turkish daughter/ Our monks will soon baptize you,' but they also composed new ones to suit the situation: 'Sarajevo in the valley/ The Serbs have encircled you.' As Karadžić prepared to depart for Geneva for peace talks, one gusla singer compared him to Karadjordje, who had led the first uprising against the Turks in 1804:
>
> > Hey, Radovan, you man of steel!
> > The greatest leader since Karadjordje!
> > Defend our freedom and our faith,
> > On the shores of Lake Geneva.   (Judah 43)

Thus, it is important not to isolate *The Mountain Wreath* as a singular anomaly, but rather to recognize it as a kind of culmination of an age-old epic tradition which had flourished primarily as an oral bardic tradition, especially in the rugged and isolated Dinaric highlands of Montenegro, Herzegovina and the Krajina ever since the Ottoman Turks established their presence and much of their culture in the towns and fertile valleys of the Balkan lands. These were the bardic poems that Vuk Karadžić spent his life collecting and publishing, and which exerted such a powerful influence on Njegoš in his *Mountain Wreath*. It was the tradition that Milman Parry, along with Albert Lord and their collabora-tors, recorded and documented in their monumental project, *Serbo-Croatian Heroic Songs* (the remarkable works Parry collected from individual bards included one by Avdo Mededović, recorded in 1935, amounting to 13,326 verses, "making it by far the lengthiest single text of oral poetry that has come to us from any European tradition since Homer" [Bynum ix])

Amongst the vast corpus of Serbo-Croatian oral epic poetry, the overwhelmingly most important for *The Mountain Wreath* and for contemporary Balkan politics are the poems of the Kosovo Cycle. These are the poems, each recorded in many individual variants, that celebrate the events surrounding the Battle of Kosovo on June 28, 1389, which Serb mythologised history records as the decisive defeat of the Orthodox Christian Serbs by the overwhelming forces of the Ottoman Turks under Sultan Murad, ushering in almost five hundred years of Turkish occupation and Islamicization. The battle is traditionally viewed by Serb writers as not only the national catastrophe that threatened to abort forever the political independence of the medieval Serb kingdom, the very survival of what had been a flourishing Orthodox Serb medieval culture, but as a great turning-point in European and indeed world history (greater even than the more familiar Fall of Constantinople in 1453), one which gave Islam and the Ottoman Turks hegemony over South-Eastern Europe until the nineteenth century. Modern documentary historians, including Serb historians, question most of the mythologising of the battle—it is not even clear, for instance, whether the battle was a clear-cut Turkish victory: both the Sultan and the Serb Prince Lazar lost their lives, and Lazar's ally, the Bosnian King Turtko, originally reported the battle as a Christian victory.

But, in any case, within a hundred years of Kosovo, the Balkans were under Turkish occupation, including, of course, Kosovo itself, the heartland of old Serbia, with its finest Orthodox monuments, and the bards of the Dinaric highlands, especially in the inaccessible fastnesses of Montenegro, largely left alone by the Turkish authorities, had begun to weave their tales of Kosovo into the Serb national epic. And a distinctive national epic it was, celebrating at its centre a catastrophic defeat; as Tihomir Djordjević, formerly professor of Ethnography at the University of Belgrade, once put it in a tribute to the national tradition, "There is no other epic which even distantly resembles that of Kosovo. Neither is there any other instance of States, not involved in a national downfall, adopting this downfall as their own, and celebrating it," as have Slavs all over the world (Djordjević 32). The reason, as Djordjević and others give in their celebrations of what has variously been called the Kosovo spirit, the Kosovo commitment, and even the Kosovo religion, is that this was not only an occasion of epic heroism against overwhelming odds, not only a tragic defeat of the small Christian nation abandoned to the Saracens by its more powerful European neighbours, not only a Serbian crucifixion and a Serbian Golgotha, but a glorious martyrdom which signifies not defeat but resurrection and spiritual conquest (see Emmert, Dragnich and Todorovich, and the essays collected in the anthologies *Kosovo/Legacy of a Battle*, edited by Vucinich and Emmert; and *Kosovo 1389-1989*, a special issue of the *Serbian Literary Quarterly*). This theme is especially richly developed by Orthodox Church commentators—indeed, it is the leitmotiv of the whole monograph on *The Serbian Folk Epic: Its Theology and Anthropology* by the Rev. Kristivoj Kotur, as it is of the lavish commemorative volume on *Kosovo* sponsored and published by The Kosovo Charity Fund '92 of the Serbian Orthodox Diocese of Western America.

The theme of national martyrdom is indeed deeply embedded in the traditional Kosovo epic poems, including the keystone poem of the whole cycle, "The Downfall of the Kingdom of Serbia". In this poem, Prince Lazar is given a message from the Blessed Mother herself, inviting him to make a choice on the eve of the battle: to make immediate preparations for an attack at dawn and certain victory over the Turks, or to first build a tent-like church of silk and velvet, to offer communion to his troops and then to perish utterly but win the heavenly kingdom: "And Lazarus chose heaven, not the earth" (*Battle of Kosovo* 31). This becomes the option of the heavenly kingdom, the martyr's wreath, which Bishop Atanasije Jevtić celebrates in his essay on the ethnic of Kosovo, "The Heavenly Kingdom in Serbia's Historic Destiny" (Jevtić 63-65), as does Dimitrije Bogdanović in "The Battle of Kosovo in the History and Consciousness of the Serbian Nation" (Bogdanović 17-20). It is also the topic of Zoran Mišić's essay "What is the Kosovo Commitment?":

> The Kosovo commitment is the commitment of those who rather choose 'death through a heroic deed, than a life with shame'. ... The epic of Kosovo is founded not only on the conqueror's pride, but on the pride of those who defeat the conqueror with a spiritual weapon. ... The Kosovo commitment is the highest ethical principle which, handed down to us from the Greeks, has become our historical experience. But also concisely expressed in it is that ancient law of the abolition of opposites, which has been manifest in this world from the days of Heraclitus to our own. The heavenly kingdom which Lazar chose, is that supreme point of the spirit where ... all contradictions are resolved, ... where dream and reality wed. (Mišić 168)

This, of course, is the same vein of allegorical interpretation we have already noticed with reference to Djilas's commentary on *The Mountain Wreath*, and indeed it is a characteristic theme of Eastern Orthodox ascetic spirituality from the early Greek Fathers to their unlikely bedfellow, Nikos Kazantzakis.

Many other characters and incidents in the Kosovo Cycle of poems contributed, of course, to the Kosovo complex. Foremost among them was assuredly the figure of Miloš Obilić, the assassin of Sultan Murad and the prime example of self-sacrificing heroism in the cycle; he was the great prototype of tyrannicide that was such an inspiration to Gavrilo Princeps and his circle. Miloš is the hero of the poem "Supper in Krushevats," which describes the ceremonial meal on the eve of battle at which Prince Lazar toasts his warriors; but Lazar's toast to Miloš is painfully ambiguous: "Hail, Cousin, friend of mine and traitor! / first of all my friend—but finally my betrayer. / Tomorrow you'll betray me on the field of Kosovo." But Miloš has "sworn to die for you at Kosovo," and the next day he proves this by sacrificing his own life to assassinate the Sultan in his tent (*Battle of Kosovo* 33-35). The real betrayer is another noble, Vuk Branković, whose withdrawal of forces at a crucial moment causes Lazar's defeat. From other poems we learn that Lazar is captured and beheaded before the eyes of the dying Sultan, completing the tragic blood-ending. Many commentators have made explicit the obvious analogy between Lazar's supper and the Last Supper. The Kosovo legend is a "nationalized Christ-epic," as Rev. Krstivoj Kotur points out, "For what is the supper on the day before St. Vitus' Day—the eve of Vidovdan, other than the Last Supper, and who is Vuk Brankovich but Judas; who is Lazarus but Christ, Milosh but Peter, the mother of Jugovich but the Mother of God, and the Maid of Kosovo but Mary Magdalene, and finally the discovery of Lazarus' head but the experience upon Mt. Tabor?" (Kotur 149). Nor is this purely a matter of literary symbolism, as Lazar is a canonized saint of the Serbian Orthodox Church and his relics a much-visited, though much-relocated, shrine whose travels mirror the Serbian diaspora through the ages (see Dragnich and Todorovich, "The Saga of Kosovo," in *Kosovo* 33).

The iconography of the Kosovo Cycle has been enshrined in a host of Serbo-Croatian literary and artistic works, from medieval icons of St. Lazar, to 19th-century romantic paintings of the Prince Lazar's Supper, Miloš Obilić, and the Maid of Kosovo (see Emmert; Ljubica Popovich; and the commemorative album *Kosovo*). A monumental project never completed, though important individual components exist—rather like Michelangelo's tomb for Pope Julius—was the Temple of Kosovo by the Croatian Ivan Meštrović, Yugoslavia's foremost sculpture. Meštrović also designed a medallion "To the Avengers of Kosovo, 1912-1913," in celebration of Serbia's regaining of the province of Kosovo in the Second Balkan War.

As the rest of the world, which has generally ignored Balkan politics, when it could, as an uninterpretable morass, now knows, the matter of Kosovo was hardly settled in 1913. The problem, from the Serb point of view, is that the population of Kosovo has increasingly, since the Serb exodus of 1690 (prompted by Turkish retaliation), become Albanian Muslim. Tito's solution was to grant Kosovo the status of, first, Autonomous Region, and then, Autonomous Republic, though technically still within Serbia. But after Tito's death and with the looming disintegration of Yugoslavia, what Serb nationalists called the "Albanian problem" began to come to a boil. Ethnic Albanians claimed discrimination against them in a region within which they were a vast majority, and Serbs countered with accusations that their own monuments, culture and history were under systematic assault in Albanian-dominated Kosovo. Upon his election as President of Serbia, Slobodan Milošević began to carry out the promises he first made to a massive Serb rally on the Field of Kosovo on June 28, 1989, the 600th anniversary of the battle, including the abrogation of Kosovo's autonomous status. While the West's attention gradually came to focus on Serb aggression in Bosnia, it is clear that for Serb nationalist intelligentsia, the main order of business was really the reclamation of Kosovo for Serbdom (see the special issue of the *Serbian Literary Quarterly* for 1989, *Kosovo 1389-1989*, and the commemorative album, *Kosovo*, published by the Serbian Orthodox Diocese of Western America).

This long-term cultural program dedicated to the Kosovo Complex, this steady diet of national and cultural martyrdom and self-sacrifice, always misunderstood and even despised by the outside world, has assuredly had its impact on Balkan affairs. Here is how poet and critic Milan Komnenić summed up the Serbian situation in an essay titled "The Kosovo Cataclysm" for that special Kosovo issue of the *Serbian Literary Quarterly*:

HUNDREDS OF YEARS OF SERBIAN SOLITUDE

Suffering has been uninterrupted, migrations have been frequent, flight has been inevitable since the sixteenth century when the Serbian land in Kosovo and Metohija was first plundered until this day. The migrations of 1690 and 1737 had almost the same impact on the fate of the Serbian people as the Battle of Kosovo in 1389.

Hundreds of years of Serbian solitude! A distant outpost of European culture, the Serbian people were left to contend with barbarianism. They plunged the cross of their doom into the bloody wasteland, but they also proved to have faith in higher justice. Thus, they have expressed their historical attitude, which we justifiably call a commitment to Kosovo. And this commitment, in totality, will last into the afterlife. (Komnenić 67)

The unkindest cut of all, now, as Zoran Mišić argues in a companion essay in that same volume, is that this very "Kosovo Commitment," the mere mention of Meštrović's Vidovdan Temple, of the Maid of Kosovo, or the hero Miloš, even the name Kosovo itself, all bring charges from the rest of the world of "obsolete nationalism ... if not something even worse" (Mišić 165), so that our past has become "our shame." Now Serbs, as Mišić sees it, must defensively insist that "looting and massacring are not our only vocation, that blood feuding is not our only spiritual nourishment, that we are not only the homeland of 'cruelty and legendary misery', as foreigners write about us"; now, he urges his fellow Serbs, it is necessary to insist that "those are lying who say to us" that it is "inborn in us to die in battle, to avenge, to be exterminated by the Turks, and in turn to exterminate converts to Islam" (Ibid., 166, 167).

That defensive cri de cœur was published in 1989. Since then we have been witness to the campaign of "ethnic cleansing" in Bosnia from Omarska in 1992 to Srebrenica in 1995. Is the "Kosovo Commitment" to blame? Is The Mountain Wreath? No one could say such a simplistic thing. But neither do the cosmic allegorizations of extermination campaigns, no matter how ingenious, dispel the consequences of a steady diet of anti-Muslim hate literature. Much recent critical attention has been devoted to Daniel Goldhagen's attempt to explain Hitler's "willing executioners". We are also faced today with trying to comprehend Milošević's—and Karadžić's—willing executioners. Because the journalistic cliché of "ancient ethnic hatreds," like the fiction of "three warring factions," as more thoughtful and informed commentators have been systematically pointing out, is simply an evasion of critical thinking about Bosnia. What the media consistently avoided reporting was that the so-called "Muslim faction" under siege in Sarajevo was, right until the end of the siege, a multi-cultural government, and society, of Muslims, Orthodox Christians (labelled "Bosnian Serbs"), Catholics (labelled "Bosnian Croats"), as well as Jews, Gypsies, and others. Somehow lost in the reporting, and even more in the Vance/Owen diplomacy, was the fact that most, not some, but most, marriages in Sarajevo were interfaith, that Sarajevo represented one of the most "multi-cultural" metropolises in Europe, and that what was true in Sarajevo was true but to a lesser extent in other major urban centres of Bosnia, such as Banja Luka, Mostar, Goražde, Tuzla and, yes, Srebrenica. These were cities that were not, Ivo Andrić's *Bridge over the Drina* to the contrary, sites of constant "ethnic conflict" and "ancient ethnic hatreds".

On the other hand, despite the well-documented role of the army of ex-Yugoslavia, essentially under Serbian control, and of Milošević's Greater Serbia nationalism imported across the Bosnia/Serb border, there is no point in denying the role of Bosnians—Orthodox "Serb," Catholic "Croat," and Bosnian Muslim alike, but not in equal measure, to be sure—in the ethnic cleansing campaigns carried out by, or at least acquiesced in by, former neighbours (for a dramatic instance, see the video, "We Are All Neighbours—Bosnia" in the *Disappearing World* series). What turned these former neighbours, whatever their degree of distance or closeness, into "willing executioners"? The steady diet of "Kosovo Commitment" surely had a role to play—but how much?

One factor, which has been discussed by only a few commentators, and to which we should have recourse but warily, is the pattern that the Bosnian "war" most commonly resolved itself into a siege of cities and towns, including the notorious UNPROFOR (Un-Protection Force) "safe havens." It is the cities and towns of Bosnia that had something of a multicultural heritage, whereas the isolated mountainous hinterlands tended to be less "cosmopolitan," more committed to "ethnically pure," patriarchal family/clan structures. This is the famous "Dinaric syndrome" originally formulated by Yugoslavian ethnographer Cvijić, and subsequently by the Croatian sociologist Tomašić (see Cvijić; Tomašić; Denitch; and Meštrović). This was the portrait of a patriarchal personality type, bred in the Dinaric highlands in isolation from the cosmopolitan influences of the cities and towns; this was the world of mostly Christian poor herders and peasants; a world of unrelenting resistance to Turkish hegemony and landlord-ism and to Slavic Islamicizing; it was the breeding ground of the Kosovo oral epic tradition; and it was that world that formed the character of Petar Petrović Njegoš and *The Mountain Wreath*. With all the just grievances of the rural poor against the economic and social control of the cities down through the centuries, we still need to ask whether what the world witnessed in Bosnia was not, in part, the same kind of war of an "ethnically pure" folk culture against a relatively cosmopolitan, and therefore "decadent" urban culture that we witnessed fifty years earlier with the rise of Fascism in Bavaria and Austria.

George L. Scheper
Baltimore

Bibliography

Allen, Beverly. 1996. *Rape Warfare / the Hidden Genocide in Bosnia-Herzegovina and Croatia*. University of Minnesota Press.

An Anthology of Medieval Serbian Literature in English. 1978. Edited by Mateja Matejić and Dragan Milivojević. Columbus: Slavica Pub.

Andrić, Ivo. 1977. *The Bridge on the Drina* [1945]. Trans. Lovett Edwards. Chicago: University of Chicago Press.

————. 1990. *The Development of Spiritual Life in Bosnia under the Influence of Turkish Rule* [1924]. Ed. & Trans. Želimir Juričić & John Loud. Durham: Duke University Press.

The Battle of Kosovo. 1987. Translated from the Serbian by Jahn Matthias and Vladeta Vučković. Preface by Charles Simić. Athens, Ohio: Swallow Press / Ohio University Press.

Bogdanović, Dimitrije. 1989. "The Battle of Kosovo in the History and Consciousness of the Serbian Nation." Trans. Radmilja Nastić. *Kosovo 1389-1989.* 17-20.

Bogert, Ralph. 1991. "Paradigm of Victory or Defeat? The Kosovo Myth vs. the Kosovo Covenant in Fiction." *Kosovo/Legacy.* 173-188.

Bringa, Tone. 1995. *Being Muslim the Bosnian Way / Identity and Community in a Central Bosnian Village*. Princeton University Press.

Brkić, Jovan. 1961. *Moral Concepts in Traditional Serbian Epic Poetry.* The Hague: Mouton.

Bynum, David E. 1980. "Prolegomena." *Serbo-Croatian Heroic Songs Collected by Milman Parry.* Publications of the Milman Parry Collection. General Editor Albert B. Lord. Texts and Translation Series. Vol. 6. Advo Medjedović: Ženidba Vlahinjić Alije. Edited with Prolegomena and Notes by David E. Bynum. Cambridge: Harvard University Press. ix-il.

Cvijić, Jovan. 1918. *La Péninsule balkanique: Géographie humanine*. Paris.

————. 1930. "Studies in Jugoslav Psychology." Trans. Fanny Foster. *The Slavonic Review* IX.26 (December 1930), 375-390.

Cushman, Thomas & Stjepan G. Meštrović. 1996. *This Time We Knew/ Western Responses to Genocide in Bosnia*. New York University Press.

Dedijer, Vladimir. 1966. *The Road to Sarajevo*. New York: Simon and Schuster.

Denitch, Bogdan. 1994. *Ethnic Nationalism / The Tragic Death of Yugoslavia*. Minneapolis: University of Minnesota Press.

Djilas, Milovan. 1952. *Njegoš: Poet Prince Bishop*. Intro. and Trans. Michael B. Petrovich. Preface by William Jovanovich. New York: Harcourt, Brace & World.

————. 1958. *Land Without Justice*. Introduction and notes by William Jovanovich. New York: Harcourt, Brace & World. Rpt. 1965.

Djordjević, Tihomir. 1989. "Kosovo, 1389." *Kosovo 1389-1989.* 31-37.

Dragnich, Alex N. (Ed.) 1994. *Serbia's Historical Heritage*. Boulder: East European Monographs, No. CCCXLVII. Distributed by the Columbia University Press.

Dragnich, Alex and Slavko Todorovich. 1984. *The Saga of Kosovo / Focus on Serbian-Albanian Relations*. East European Monographs. Columbia University Press.

————. 1992. "The Saga of Kosovo." *Kosovo,* compiled by Dorich. 23-33.

Emmert, Thomas A. 1990. *Serbian Golgotha / Kosovo, 1389.* East European Monographs. Columbia University Press.

Gorup, Radmila. 1991. "Kosovo and Epic Poetry." *Kosovo / Legacy.* 109-121.

Gutman, Roy. 1993. *A Witness to Genocide*. New York: Macmillan.

Honig, Jan Willem & Norbert Both. 1996. *Srebrenica / Record of a War Crime*. Harmondsworth: Penguin.

Jevtić, Right Rev. Bishop Atanasije. 1992. "The Heavenly Kingdom in Serbia's Historic Destiny." *Kosovo,* compiled by Dorich. 63-69.

Judah, Tim. 1997. *The Serbs / History, Myths & the Destruction of Yugoslavia.* Yale University Press.

Koljević, Svetozar. 1989. "Folk Tradition in Serbo-Croatian Literary Culture." *Tradition and Modern Society / A Symposium at the Royal Academy of Letters, History and Antiquities, Stockholm, November 26-29, 1987.* Ed. Sven Gustavsson. Stockholm: Almqvist & Wiskell International. 163-177.

—————. 1991. "The Battle of Kosovo in its Epic Mosaic." *Kosovo / Legacy.* 123-139.

Komnenić, Milan. 1989. "The Kosovo Cataclysm." Trans. Laura J. Silber and Nina Vlahović. *Kosovo 1389-1989.* 67-76.

Kosovo 1389-1989. Serbian Literary Quarterly. 1989, 1-3. Special Edition on the Occasion of 600 Years since the Battle of Kosovo. Editor-in-Chief Alek Vukadinović. Trans. Vidosava Janković, et al. Beograd: The Association of Serbian Writers.

Kosovo. 1992. Compiled and produced by William Dorich. Ed. Basil W.R. Jenkins. Alhambra, California: The Kosovo Charity Fund '92 / Serbian Orthodox Diocese of Western America.

Kosovo / Legacy of a Medieval Battle. 1991. Ed. Wayne Vucinich and Thomas A. Emmert. Minnesota Mediterranean and East European Monographs, vol. 1. Minneapolis: University of Minnesota.

Kotur, Rev. Dr. Krstivoj. 1977. *The Serbian Folk Epic: Its Theology and Anthropology.* New York: Philosophical Library.

Meštrović, Stjepan G. 1993. *Habits of the Balkan Heart / Social Character and the Fall of Communism.* College Station, Texas: A&M Press.

Meštrović, Stjepan G. 1996. *Genocide After Emotion / The Postemotional Balkan War.* New York: Routledge.

Mihailovich, Vasa D. 1986. "Introduction." *The Mountain Wreath.* By P.P. Njegos. Trans. & ed. Vasa D. Mihailovich. Irvine, California: Charles Schlacks, Jr., vii-xvii.

—————. 1991. "The Tradition of Kosovo in Serbian Literature." *Kosovo / Legacy.* 141-158.

Mišić, Zoran. 1989. "What Is the Kosovo Commitment?" Trans. Radmilja Nastic. *Kosovo 1389-1989.* 165-170.

Njegoš, Petar Petrovich. 1986. *The Mountain Wreath [Gorsk vijenac].* Trans. & ed. Vasa D. Mihailovich. Irvine, California: Charles Schlacks, Jr.

Njegoš, Petar Petrovich. 1970. *The Mountain Wreath of P.P. Nyegosh (Petar II) Prince-Bishop of Montenegro 1830-1851.* Trans. James W. Wiles. Intro. Vladeta Popović [orig. pub. 1930 by Allen & Unwin, London]. Reprint. Westport, Connecticut: Greenwood Press.

Popović, Vladeta. 1970. "Introduction. Njegoš, *The Mountain Wreath,* trans. Wiles. 21-27.

Popovich, Ljubica. 1991. "The Battle of Kosovo (1389) and Battle Themes in Serbian Art." *Kosovo / Legacy.* 227-307.

Sells, Michael. 1996. *The Bridge Betrayed / Religion and Genocide in Bosnia.* Berkeley: University of California Press.

Stiglmayer, Alexandra (ed.). 1994. *Mass Rape / The War Against Women in Bosnia-Herzegovina.* Translations by Marion Faber. University of Nebraska Press.

Tomašić, Dinko. 1946. "The Structure of Balkan Society." *American Journal of Sociology* 53 (1946): 367-375.

Tomašić, Dinko. 1948. *Personality and Culture in Eastern European Politics.* New York: George Stewart.

"We Are All Neighbors (Bosnia)." 1993. *Disappearing World: War Trilogy.* VHS. Granada Television, distributed by Films Incorporated Video. ·

West, Rebecca. 1940. *Black Lamb and Grey Falcon / A Journey through Yugoslavia.* New York: Viking. One volume edition 1943.

Why Bosnia? / Writings on the Balkan War. 1993. Ed. Rabia Ali and Lawrence Lifschultz. Stony Creek, Connecticut: The Pamphleteer's Press.

Wiles, James W. 1970. "A Tale To Be Chanted and Told." Njegoš, *The Mountain Wreath,* trans. Wiles 29-40.

—————. 1970. "Translator's Introduction." Njegoš, *The Mountain Wreath,* trans. Wiles 49-57.

—————. 1970. "Scope and Setting of the Poem." Njegoš, *The Mountain Wreath,* trans. Wiles 61.

Yugoslavia the Former and Future / Reflections by Scholars from the Region. 1995. Ed. Payam Akhavan & Robert Howse. Washington: The Brookings Institution.

Zorić, Pavle. 1989. "The Ever-Present Kosovo." *Kosovo 1389-1989.* 79-80.

Literature as Cultural Memory

Unfinished History: the French Revolution as Subtext in Hölderlin's *Tod des Empedokles*

Hölderlin's drama *Der Tod des Empedokles* is one of the most fascinating and one of the most puzzling literary works of its time. Written in 1798-1800 in three fragmentary versions, the text shows an exceptional force and beauty of language, yet it fails as a tragedy, because it lacks in dramatic tension. The work displays a strong concern with the social and political problems of its time, yet it ultimately celebrates pantheism and myth. The writing of the drama is accompanied by extensive reflections on the function and structure of tragedy in the modern age, yet as the manuscripts of these reflective essays grow in size, Hölderlin's textual production dwindles.

Hölderlin planned his drama in 1797 when he was a private tutor in the family of a rich banker in Frankfort. He fell in love with the mother of his pupils, Susette Gontard. The affection was mutual, the affair was discovered, and when Hölderlin was thrown out of the house, he found shelter with his friend Isaak von Sinclair in the nearby town of Homburg. During this stay at Homburg, the *Empedokles* manuscript was written. The first (incomplete) version, containing roughly 2000 verses, was drafted in 1798, the second version, a fragment of about 700 verses, was written in 1799, and in the winter of 1799/1800 a third version was produced, a fragment of only 500 verses. Prior to this last stage, Hölderlin had written the essays "Über das Tragische" and "Grund zum Empedokles", which attest to his intense manner of reflecting on the problems of writing a tragedy after the demise of classical poetics. However, the abstract constructions of these essays hardly proved fruitful for Hölderlin's work on the text. They even seemed to hamper the author in his undertaking: shortly afterwards he abandoned his work altogether.

There seems to be another reason for giving up the project: Hölderlin's strange choice of plot. It is doubtful whether the tale about the pre-socratic philosopher Empedocles, who—according to tradition—had ended his life by leaping into the crater of Mount Etna, was the appropriate dramatic subject for the representation of late eighteenth-century conflicts. Hölderlin showed a lifelong fascination with Empedocles, his teachings and his life. Empedocles (483/482 to ca. 420 BC) was the first of the Greek philosophers who had taught that there were four elements in nature; he called earth, water, fire, and air "the roots of all things." To Empedocles, the four elements were spiritual-material phenomena with divine qualities, while their relationships were determined by "friendship" and "strife", "love" and "hate" (Böhme/Böhme 1996: 93-101). In the classical text on Empedocles, written by Diogenes Laertius, he is described as a "freedom-loving man, averse to all forms of rulership, who, as a consequence, declined the honour of being made king" (Prignitz 1985: 9).

In Empedocles, the philosopher, Hölderlin saw a man akin to himself, the modern poet. Hölderlin was intrigued by Empedocles's solitude, by his isolation from the crowd—while, at the same time, this crowd was in need of his word and guidance. Hölderlin was fascinated by the sheer otherness of this Greek philosopher who, it was said, had been raised by nature rather than by human beings.

In the first version of Hölderlin's drama, Empedokles is depicted as a man who lives in intimacy with nature, as a friend and beloved of the gods, and as a political reformer in the city-state of Agrigentum. Yet his old intimacy with the gods has already been lost when the action of the drama begins. Empedokles had placed himself too close to the divine powers, he had tried to rule nature, and his hubris had caused the old relationship to disappear, leaving him empty, without his former strength. Having thus lost part of himself, Empedokles is also no longer capable of guiding the people that once venerated him.

The priest of the city, Hermokrates, takes advantage of this moment of crisis: "for the gods have taken the power from him." This priest, who is a representative of the old order, of ritual and orthodoxy, seeks to keep the populace dependent and irresolute. He succeeds in stirring up hateful feelings and when he banishes Empedokles, the people sever all ties with the philosopher.

Later, however, the people change their mind. When they start missing the presence and inspiration of Empedokles, they free themselves from the influence of Hermokrates and search for Empedokles on the slopes of Mount Etna where the philosopher has fled, accompanied by a disciple. There they implore him to return and even to become their king. Rejecting their plea, Empedokles says the famous words: "Dies ist die Zeit der Könige nicht mehr" ("this is not the time of kings anymore"; Hölderlin 1994: 337).

Empedokles adds a long speech which, in a sense, constitutes his spiritual testament (he has already decided that he will die on Mount Etna).

> Nicht ratlos stehen laß' ich euch
> Ihr Lieben! aber fürchtet nichts! Es scheun
> Die Erdenkinder meist das Neu und Fremde,
> Daheim in sich zu bleiben strebet nur
> 1490   Der Pflanze Leben und das frohe Tier.
> Beschränkt im Eigentume sorgen sie
> Wie sie bestehn, und weiter reicht ihr Sinn
> Im Leben nicht. Doch müssen sie zuletzt
> Die Ängstigen heraus, und sterbend kehrt
> Ins Element ein jedes, daß es da
> Zu neuer Jugend, wie im Bade, sich
> Erfrische. Menschen ist die große
> Lust Gegeben, daß sie selber sich verjüngen.
> Und aus dem reinigenden Tode, den
> 1500   Sie selber sich zu rechter Zeit gewählt,
> Erstehn, wie aus dem Styx Achill, die Völker.
> O gebt euch der Natur, eh sie euch nimmt! —
> Ihr dürstet längst nach Ungewöhnlichem,
> Und wie aus krankem Körper sehnt der Geist
> Von Agrigent sich aus dem alten Gleise.
> So wagts! was ihr geerbt, was ihr erworben,
> Was euch der Väter Mund erzählt, gelehrt,
> Gesetz und Brauch, der alten Götter Namen,
> Vergeßt es kühn, und hebt, wie Neugeborne,
> 1510   Die Augen auf zur göttlichen Natur,

Wenn dann der Geist sich an des Himmels Licht
Entzündet, süßer Lebensothem euch
Den Busen, wie zum erstenmale tränkt,
Und goldner Früchte voll die Wälder rauschen
Und Quellen aus dem Fels, wenn euch das Leben
Der Welt ergreift, ihr Friedensgeist, und euchs
Wie heilger Wiegensang die Seele stillet,
Dann aus der Wonne schöner Dämmerung
Der Erde Grün von neuem euch erglänzt
1520   Und Berg und Meer und Wolken und Gestirn,
Die edeln Kräfte, Heldenbrüdern gleich,
Vor euer Auge kommen, daß die Brust
Wie Waffenträgern euch nach Taten klopft,
Und eigner schöner Welt, dann reicht die Hände
Euch wieder, gebt das Wort und teilt das Gut,
O dann ihr Lieben — teilet Tat und Ruhm,
Wie treue Dioskuren; jeder sei,
Wie alle, — wie auf schlanken Säulen, ruh
Auf richtigen Ordnungen das neue Leben
1530   Und euern Bund befest'ge das Gesetz.
Dann o ihr Genien der wandelnden
Natur! dann ladet euch, ihr heitern,
Die ihr aus Tiefen und aus Höhn die Freude nimmt
Und sie wie Müh und Glück und Sonnenschein und Regen
Den engbeschränkten Sterblichen ans Herz
Aus ferner fremder Welt herbei bringt,
Das freie Volk zu seinen Festen ein,
Gastfreundlich! fromm! denn liebend gibt
Der Sterbliche vom Besten, schließt und engt
Den Busen ihm die Knechtschaft nicht —
(Hölderlin 1994: 340-341)

In his speech Empedokles envisages a time of palingenesis, of rejuvenation, for the people of Agrigentum, during which the "Nation" will "forget law and custom". Instead, there will be another medium of orientation, "Nature" itself. The experience of nature with all of its wonders will bring back the fullness of sensory perception and human emotion, capacities which until now have been curtailed.

Such new experiences will lead to new forms of communal life. What Empedokles is projecting here bears a strong resemblance to the tenets of the French Revolution. For instance, the phrases "reicht die Hände euch" ("takes each other's hands"), "jeder sei wie alle" ("each one be as all"), and "das freie Volk" ("the free people") point to *fraternité, égalité*, and *liberté*. A "new covenant" ("ein neuer Bund") will bring new laws, whereupon the "old Saturnian days" will return, full of spontaneous festivals (Hölderlin 1994: 343).

That such phrases can be viewed as references to the French Revolution is supported by the fact that the author had had a keen interest in the political developments in France after 1789 (borne out by his letters). He enthusiastically greeted the first phase of the Revolution. During the Reign of Terror, however, Hölderlin got disillusioned, as so many other European intellectuals of his time. Yet he remained a republican in his views ("Republikaner [...] im Geist und in der Wahrheit," said his friend Böhlendorff of him; Beck 1975: 74). This is borne out by the fact that Höderlin's enthusiasm returned when, in 1796, the troops of the French Republic conquered part of Southern Germany. Hölderlin's home state Wurttemberg was under siege. The collapse of the old order seemed imminent: the absolute princedoms of Southern Germany would soon disappear. This was also the fervent hope of Hölderlin's friend Sinclair, who became an emissary to the Congress of Rastatt in November of 1798. Hölderlin accompanied Isaak von Sinclair, expecting reform and even radical political change from this French-German congress. Indeed, for a time it seemed likely that new constitutions would be drawn up for the Southern states of Germany. Disappointment followed: the French Government, the Directoire, showed little interest in German political reform. It concentrated on military gains alone, leaving the German democrats in the lurch.

Viewed against this historical and biographical background, it seems almost irrefutable that the speech of Empedokles contains direct references to the revolutionary developments of the 1790s (this is the view put forward by Prignitz [1985], Mögel [1994] and others). There is a problem, however, with this straightforward form of interpretation. Hölderlin, in a number of passages of his drama, stresses the preconditions for political renewal: the spiritual rejuvenation has to come first. At the centre of this spiritual renewal is the regained experience of nature. This will be the necessary training ground of the collective soul.

Also, by looking more closely at some formulations, one can detect that Hölderlin's text, although it underwrites some of the main principles of the French Revolution, does not really endorse its practices. There are frequent negative allusions to new forms of communal life that are based on reason alone. A political change that is not more than the result of secularization and enlightenment leads to selfishness and constant scheming ("berechnend" is a key word). Viewed from this angle, the rituals of the French Revolution are largely decorative, even where they celebrate nature. They do not reach deep down to the level of a renewed harmony with the cosmic forces, the program put forward by Hölderlin's Empedokles.

At the centre of the revolution envisaged in Hölderlin's drama is the mythical moment, the moment when the Pre-Christian gods will return, when the human and the divine spheres will not be separated anymore. Only after this mythical union has been achieved, will communal harmony follow. Hölderlin's Empedokles does not aim at practices which have already seen the light of history, but at a form of life which is still to come. The task will be to surpass the French Revolution.

Looking at the first version of the drama as a whole, there remains a difficulty. Within the utopian context that I just referred to, it is hard to see what kind of function Empedokles's suicide can have. The last speech of Empedokles and his suicide are hardly connected at all (Heise 1988: 336). Empedokles chooses death in the volcano in order to be close to nature again, more exactly: to disappear into the elements. Immediately after Empedokles has decided on this course of action, his self-assuredness returns: he feels again that he is the beloved of nature. This means that his death is nothing but the salvation of his own spiritual being — which, of course, has little to do with the collective renewal that his speech envisaged. The people of Agrigentum must change their own reality, while Empedokles withdraws.

It seems that this unsolved problem was part of the reason why Hölderlin abandoned the first manuscript and started rewriting the drama in 1799. However, there is little in the manuscript of the second version that significantly differs from the first version; therefore one can only guess as to the exact plans of this stage.

Things are different with the third version of the drama. Although the fragment is short, the overall design is clear again, because we know the author's intentions from a written plan. The textual changes, which are considerable, follow this plan closely. The reason for Empedokles's suicide in this version is sacrificial rather than self-centred: Empedokles offers himself to a power which he calls the "master of time"; he wants to absolve the community from disharmony and division ("Entzweiung"). Empedokles's sublime action becomes the inspirational symbol: all individuation stops here; the being that dissented from the whole of nature sacrifices itself.

Thereby the third version moves away from any overt references to political revolution. Empedokles's sacrificial death, with its strong religious overtones, primarily aims at a communion with fellow-man. To what extent this union can be transformed into a republican community, remains an open question. This corresponds to the fact that the third version begins with scenes on Mount Etna. Right from the beginning, Empedokles is removed from the world of everyday activity. His destiny unfolds in a landscape of death.

The conception of time has changed as well. The movement of history is not seen as progression anymore, but as regression and degradation. All that remains is a pessimistic outlook that conceives of history as the eternal return of the past: "Es kehret alles wieder" (Hölderlin 1994: 401). In other words, the modern political meaning of the term 'revolution' (the equivalent of 'bouleversement', 'Umwälzung') has given way to the older understanding of the word, derived from astronomy: 'revolution' as 'revolutio', which designates the revolving movement, the unfailing return of the same. Only through the sacrificial union, through the mythical leap, can one escape from this fatal movement.

Part of the scenario of degradation is the anarchic way of life of the people of Agrigentum. The city is in turmoil, the actions of its inhabitants are driven by egotism and petty concerns. Terms as "Gärung" ("fermentation"), "brodeln" ("to bubble"), and "Unruhe" ("unrest") characterize the situation. Such words have a special ring in the 1790s: they belong to the vocabulary of critical observers of the French Revolution (see Von der Thüsen 1996). Indeed, Hölderlin himself had used these and comparable terms in his rejection of the Reign of Terror.

Fermentation, the bubbling mass, the threat of eruption: these historical metaphors belong to the semantic field of the active volcano. The use of such terms in the *Empedokles* drama is most astonishing because the volcano here appears in a negative connotative field, while Mount Etna, with its active crater, has positive associations only. Its lava is seen as a consuming fire of purity and sacredness ("heilge Flammen," "furchtbare Flamme, du Seele des Lebendigen," "Feuerkelch, mit Geist gefüllt"). To be sure, the power of Mount Etna is described as terrible, too, but it is important to note that its sublimity does not derive from its dark, wild, and amorphous qualities, but from the purifying nature of its fire.

Thus, Mount Etna is reduced to *one* of its elements, fire. It is not seen, as one would expect, as the opaque mixture of earth and fire (alluded to in many late eighteenth-century texts). Indeed, *"Father* Etna," as the mountain is called by Empedokles, belongs to a different realm of the imagination than *"Mother* Earth". "Father Etna" ("Vater Ätna") is closer to divine ether ("Vater Äther"), than to the productive, motherly element. By planning to throw himself into the crater of Mount Etna, Empedokles knows that the body will leave no trace. It will become fuel for the elements themselves. To Empedokles, this is victory over decay; it contains the promise of complete transformation in death.

By thus dividing the volcano into a pure and sublime force on the one hand and a magmatic and chaotic power on the other, Hölderlin's imagery reproduces the thematic discrepancy that encumbered his project from the outset. Just as the negative volcano metaphors reserved for the anarchic crowd have nothing in common with the positive visions as a force of transcendence, the sublime death of Empedokles remains isolated from the realm of historical action. In the end, the mythic union between Empedokles and the people remains a mere postulate.

When, in 1800, Hölderlin abandoned his drama project, he turned to poetry again. In his later hymns the mythical element figured prominently. Hölderlin's later poems, however, kept the mythical within the confines of the poetic. Here, the mythical was reduced to a *form of the imagination*, the only way it could survive in an age after the demise of all mythologies.

Joachim von der Thüsen
Utrecht

Joachim von der Thüsen

Bibliography

Beck, Adolf. 1975. *Hölderlin: Chronik seines Lebens*. Frankfurt/Main: Insel.

Binder, Wolfgang. 1983. "Aether und Abgrund in Hölderlins Dichtung." *"Frankfurt aber ist der Nabel dieser Erde": Das Schicksal einer Generation der Goethezeit*. Ed. Christoph Jamme. Stuttgart: Metzler. 349-369.

Böhme, Gernot, and Hartmut Böhme. 1996. *Feuer, Wasser, Erde, Luft: Eine Kulturgeschichte der Elemente*. Munich: Beck.

Cornelissen, Maria. 1966. "Die Manes-Szene in Hölderlins Trauerspiel *Der Tod des Empedokles*." *Hölderlin-Jahrbuch* 14: 97-109.

Heise, Wolfgang. 1988. *Hölderlin: Schönheit und Geschichte*. Berlin: Aufbau.

Hölderlin, Friedrich. 1994. *Hyperion, Empedokles, Aufsätze und Übertragungen*. Kritische und kommentierte Edition. Ed. Jochen Schmidt. Frankfurt/Main: Deutscher Klassiker Verlag.

Mögel, Ernst. 1994. *Natur als Revolution: Hölderlins Empedokles-Tragödie*. Stuttgart: Metzler.

Prignitz, Christoph. 1985. *Hölderlins 'Empedokles': Die Vision einer erneuerten Gesellschaft und ihre zeitgeschichtlichen Hintergründe*. Hamburg: Buske.

Von der Thüsen, Joachim. 1996. "'Die Lava der Revolution fließt majestätisch': Vulkanische Metaphorik zur Zeit der Französischen Revolution." *Francia: Forschungen zur westeuropäischen Geschichte*. 23/2: 113-143.